T0337398

The Great Upheaval

At the turn of the 21st century, Asia pulled one billion people out of poverty in one generation, a meteoric rise suddenly stalled by the COVID-19 pandemic. This volume examines the strengths of the Asian-Pacific response to the pandemic and weaknesses that the region must re-engineer to rebound.

The 18 authors included in this volume reimagine social and economic pathways to inform policymakers, development practitioners and other readers about opportunities to revamp production modes and networks to rekindle sustainable growth. They call for bolstering investments in universal public health, education and social protection to strengthen human capabilities and recommend marshalling a suite of global public goods to fortify societies for new digital and climactic realities.

Home to three-fifths of the world's population, the Asia-Pacific Region already accounts for close to half of all global output. By 2050 – after a detour of two centuries and a few pandemics – Asia-Pacific can again become a centrifugal economic and social force. This volume sets out options for policymakers to consider as we head into a new Asia-Pacific Century, one where economic strength will be necessary but insufficient by itself, as inclusion, resilience and sustainability – once seen as moral choices – become imperatives for the planet's future.

Swarnim Waglé is the chief economic advisor at the UNDP Regional Bureau for Asia and the Pacific in New York. Waglé also chairs the Institute for Integrated Development Studies, a South Asian think-tank. Previously, he served as a member and vice-chair of the National Planning Commission of Nepal (for three intermittent years between 2014 and 2018) and as a senior economist at the World Bank in Washington, DC, and UNDP in Hanoi, Colombo and New York.

Kanni Wignaraja is the United Nations assistant secretary-general and director of the UNDP Regional Bureau for Asia and the Pacific. Previously the director of the United Nations Development Operations Coordination Office, Wignaraja has worked for the UN for over 25 years in the United States and the Asia-Pacific and Africa Regions, including as UN Resident Coordinator and UNDP Resident Representative in Zambia. Wignaraja has published articles on human rights, development policy, leadership and sustainability.

The Great Upheaval

Resetting Development Policy and Institutions for
the Decade of Action in Asia and the Pacific

Edited by
Swarnim Waglé
Kanni Wignaraja

CAMBRIDGE
UNIVERSITY PRESS

University Printing House, Cambridge CB2 8BS, United Kingdom

One Liberty Plaza, 20th Floor, New York, NY 10006, USA

477 Williamstown Road, Port Melbourne, vic 3207, Australia

314 to 321, 3rd Floor, Plot No.3, Splendor Forum, Jasola District Centre, New Delhi 110025, India

103 Penang Road, #05–06/07, Visioncrest Commercial, Singapore 238467

Cambridge University Press is part of the University of Cambridge.

It furthers the University's mission by disseminating knowledge in the pursuit of education, learning and research at the highest international levels of excellence.

www.cambridge.org
Information on this title: www.cambridge.org/9781009224321

First published 2022

Printed in India by Thomson Press India Ltd.

A catalogue record for this publication is available from the British Library

ISBN 978-1-009-22432-1 Hardback

Contents

Figures

Tables

Boxes

Appendices

Abbreviations

APR	Asia and Pacific Region
ASEAN	Association of Southeast Asian Nations
CO_2	carbon dioxide
CFR	case fatality rate
C	Celsius
COVID-19	coronavirus disease-2019
COVAX	COVID-19 Vaccines Global Access
EUR	Euro (currency)
GAVI	Gavi, the Vaccine Alliance
GPG	global public good
GVC	global value chain
GDP	gross domestic product
GNI	gross national income
G20	Group of 20
HDI	Human Development Index
IDR	Indonesian rupiah (currency)
ILO	International Labour Organization
km	kilometre
Lao PDR	Lao People's Democratic Republic
LDCs	least developed countries
LMICs	low- and middle-income countries
MERS	Middle East Respiratory Syndrome
mRNA	messenger ribonucleic acid
MPI	Multidimensional Poverty Index
NPI	non-pharmaceutical intervention
ODA	Official Development Assistance
OECD	Organisation for Economic Co-operation and Development
p.c.	per capita

RCEP	Regional Comprehensive Economic Partnership
RMB	renminbi (currency)
SARS-CoV-2	severe acute respiratory syndrome coronavirus 2
SMEs	small and medium-sized enterprises
SAARC	South Asian Association for Regional Cooperation
SAR	Special Administrative Region
SEA	South East Asia
SDG	Sustainable Development Goal
UK	United Kingdom
UN	United Nations
UNCTAD	United Nations Conference on Aid and Development
UNDP	United Nations Development Programme
UNESCO	United Nations Educational, Scientific and Cultural Organization
UNFCCC	United Nations Framework Convention on Climate Change
UNICEF	United Nations International Children's Emergency Fund
US	United States
US$	United States dollar (currency)
WHO	World Health Organization
WTO	World Trade Organization
$	United States dollar

Foreword

Being ready for the future requires unleashing our creativity, questioning our long-held assumptions, changing our behaviour and exercising adaptive governance to better use scarce resources. Above all, it requires greater investment in human development and institutional capabilities to confront the immense challenges of the 21st century – from climate change and growing inequalities to the digital transformation and rapid urbanization. While there is uncertainty whether and when the COVID-19 pandemic will become endemic, what is certain is that the pandemic has already changed our lives and livelihoods forever. This has profound implications for the way we will go on to organize and govern our societies. Multilateralism, the primary means to successfully tackle old and new development risks, is under strain in a world that is increasingly interdependent on the one hand, but torn by many nations' tendencies to look inward. Yet the ground-breaking 2015 Paris Climate Accords and 2021 United Nations Climate Summit, COP26, point to an ever-increasing public and political appetite to realize a greener, net-zero-emissions future.

Countries in the Asia-Pacific Region perch on the frontlines of the climate crisis, given their densely populated coastal areas and inadequate institutional readiness. The effects of climate change will increasingly affect their high dependency on natural resources and agriculture for income and food. Therefore, moving Asian and other economies towards net-zero emissions to arrest climate disruption is a top priority. However, such a move will not happen automatically. An inclusive green recovery from COVID-19 and a just energy transition calls for political will, new systems and smart policies. In particular, countries must put a price on carbon, phase out fossil fuel subsidies and incentivize green infrastructure investments. Countries will also need to find new ways to raise funding to finance achievement of the United Nations Sustainable Development Goals (SDGs) – the world's internationally agreed plan to tackle challenges that range from eradicating poverty and inequality to protecting and restoring our natural world. Remarkably, allocating just 1 per cent of the total assets held by commercial banks, institutional investors and asset managers towards the SDGs could fill the annual financing gap. Other innovative finance mechanisms, such as debt-for-nature and debt-for-climate swaps, also hold enormous potential to catalyse much-needed financing for development.

The COVID-19 pandemic has also highlighted how digital connectivity is fast becoming *the* global metric of inclusion, even as 2.9 billion people remain unconnected. Renewed efforts are needed to extend access to affordable broadband, the nervous system of today's digital economy. A worthwhile investment of US$428 billion could achieve universal broadband connectivity by 2030. It would allow thousands of small and medium-sized enterprises to do business online for the first time, generating new, sustainable jobs and livelihoods. In the pandemic's wake, we must build on the momentum it generated to ensure that digital finance applications bolster vital social protection programmes, especially for the half of the global population that lacks healthcare and social security. More affordable broadband and social-protection coverage will help mitigate poverty and better prepare countries for the next crisis.

Over 200 years ago, nine out of ten people lived in extreme poverty. By 2019, even though the global population had risen by 6.5 billion, only one in ten people lived in extreme poverty. Much of this success took place in Asia and the Pacific Region. While the COVID-19 pandemic has set back progress in poverty reduction, it has highlighted the way forward. Once again, the Asia-Pacific Region can take a leading role in driving human development by forging a bold new pathway towards a net-zero future. Informed by fresh wounds from the pandemic and the stubborn challenges that preceded it, *The Great Upheaval* aims to help inform the ambitious policy choices that countries now need to make at this pivotal moment for people and the planet.

Achim Steiner
UNDP Administrator

Acknowledgements

It takes a village. Gathering contributions for this volume from dozens of scholars and collaborators around the world at a time of restricted travel in the middle of a pandemic was no easy feat. We are, therefore, profoundly grateful to all our collaborators, especially the contributing authors who graciously engaged with us throughout the laborious production schedule.

Suzan Nolan and Leila Whittemore were rigorous and professional in patiently managing a demanding editorial process. We are grateful to Anwesha Rana and her team at Cambridge University Press for a rewarding collaboration.

Our colleagues at the United Nations Development Programme (UNDP) helped refine the chapters in their various incarnations. We greatly appreciate Achim Steiner writing the foreword to this volume. Balazs Horvath and Bishwa Nath Tiwari, together with two anonymous peer reviewers assigned by Cambridge University Press, examined the chapters with diligence and provided thoughtful suggestions. Alessandra Bassi, Uyanga Gankhuyag, Aarathi Krishnan, Mizuho Okimoto-Kaewtathip, Renata Rubian, Stanislav Saling, Elena Tischenko and Claire Van der Vaeren provided helpful inputs and comments throughout the process.

Diana Gao ably administrated everything logistical, along with Annaliza del Rosario and Besian Xhezo. We thank the UNDP Regional Bureau for Asia and the Pacific (RBAP) senior management team and our New York colleagues for their advice and encouraging nudges.

Throughout 2021, we organized several high-level policy dialogues; insights gained from the events infuse these pages. For their enthusiastic participation in these policy events, we thank our Eminent Advisory Council members, professors Kaushik Basu, Mariana Mazzucato, Branko Milanovich, Rohini Pande and Danny Quah; and the permanent representatives to the United Nations from Asia-Pacific countries. We also acknowledge the input and guidance received from all resident representatives, deputy resident representatives, and senior staff of UNDP country offices across Asia and the Pacific and the Bangkok Regional Hub.

Peter Ørntoft, an excellent graphics designer, created each figure with great skill. Hari Marasini designed the cover with flair. Ragini Upadhyaya kindly allowed us to use her original painting to depict the pandemic with a masked man and woman, appropriately sanitized and distanced.

Swarnim Waglé
Kanni Wignaraja

Introduction

Swarnim Waglé and Kanni Wignaraja

The years 2020 and 2021 gave us a glimpse of the universe of complex development policy issues we will likely deal with in this century – issues unprecedented in scale and unpredictability. Let us begin with three vignettes that have profound implications for the themes covered in this volume.

First, the year 2020 marked a momentous tipping point from a planetary perspective. For the first time in the 4.5-billion-year history of the Earth, the weight of human-made materials will likely exceed that of all life on the planet. Artificial materials, such as metals, concrete, bricks and plastic now outweigh the biomass of all living plants and animals (Elhacham et al., 2020). Specifically, this is a once-in-an-epoch event where the anthropogenic artificial mass will exceed the trillion tons (1.1 teraton) of living biomass. The United Nations Development Programme's (UNDP) 2020 *Human Development Report* explains the costs of such effects and details the enormous pressure we have placed on our fragile planet (UNDP, 2020). We may indeed be exiting the Holocene lasting the past 12,000 years, and entering the Anthropocene, a proposed geologic epoch in which humans have become the dominant force shaping the Earth (not the other way round).

Second, partly as a result of human squeezing and straining of local ecosystems, livestock and wildlife, an unfamiliar cellular microbe triggered the COVID-19 pandemic. Over five million people have died and the global economy lost at least US$10 trillion in unrealized output in 2020 alone (*The Economist*, 2021). Further economic damage and collateral social and health costs will continue to accumulate, as will the pandemic's impact on stretched state capacities and governance.

Third, the year 2020 marks a decisive shift in global geopolitics. The 'Rebalance' has accelerated, with countries of the Asia-Pacific now accounting for close to half of world output (a phenomenon last seen before the Industrial Revolution). In this regard, many economic historians see the past two centuries as a 'detour' for Asia, but a major difference exists between the pre-industrial era of Asian dominance and the present (Maddison, 2007; UNDP, 2013). Throughout human history until the 19th century, the average annual economic growth rate, rounded down to one decimal place, stood at zero. It took centuries for average incomes to double and for the quality of life to noticeably improve across generations. Because of the Industrial Revolution, it became conceivable by the early 20th century that living standards would increase by 50 to 75 per cent within a single human lifespan. The more recent Green Revolution of the 1950s and 1960s extended progress for large parts of the Asia-Pacific population, heavily dependent on the agricultural sector, by increasing yields and addressing food scarcity. At the economic growth rates seen in Asia over the past few decades, living standards for its growing population do not simply double in a single human life span, but rise 100-fold, or 10,000 per cent.

With this rapid economic rise comes growing prestige, power, voice and influence in the region, and therefore new possibilities for accelerating human progress. These three vignettes imply that we must leap into new ways of living, working and cooperating, within the Asia-Pacific Region and well beyond. Governments' roles remain central, together with a renewed role for other actors and institutions. Mechanisms of scalable action need undergirding with robust norms and incentives to become effective. To echo Jean Monnet, "nothing is possible without humans. Nothing is sustainable without institutions".

With greater voice will come a responsibility to contribute to universal solutions. While a more multipolar world will probably check the excesses of a mono- or duo-polar world, it also brings a risk of inaction and indecisiveness, if multiple actors squabble to serve only their national interests. As seen in the growing challenges of climate change, some of the larger Asia-Pacific economies have voluntarily reconsidered the principle of 'common but differentiated responsibilities' (CBDR); meanwhile, decades-long measures and definitions of 'developing' call for refreshing, as reality shows the lack of equality within the Global South. The growing economic powerhouses and large carbon emitters, both North and South, will have to step up to carry larger responsibility for regional and global actions.

This backdrop informs the ethos of the chapters contained in this policy compendium. It documents lessons that can underpin current policy dialogues and outreach to governments, thinktanks, social movements and the private sector on development priorities leading to 2030. The 13 chapters address three major themes: policy shifts accelerated by the pandemic, including climate change, sovereign finance, digitalization, global value chains and productivity growth; measures and aspirations for improved human conditions, such as equality of opportunities, multi-dimensional poverty, human security and vaccine equity; and new modes of state capacity and international governance, including global public goods, regional cooperation and lessons from pandemic governance. A summary follows of each chapter's essential insights.

Manuel Montes and Arnico Panday take on two distinct, and relatively less-explored, facets of the climate emergency. Montes reviews how the upside of Asia's rise, or 're-emergence,' has spawned an accelerating pattern of environmental costs, many induced by enlarged manufacturing activities, increased incomes that have, in turn, expanded consumption baskets, and urbanization. If climate change charts a path of technological, social and economic development, the question becomes one not of reducing *costs* but instead accelerating *investment* in pursuit of development ambitions. Montes examines how the Asia-Pacific Region might reorient investment and its financing as forms of climate action, focusing on economic restructuring, a strengthened care economy and technological development as key problems. He warns that the hazardous features of the international financial system, without the ability to secure long-term financing, may frustrate actions against climate change.

Panday presents the Himalayas (The Third Pole) as Exhibit A of climate change. Even with the increase in global average temperature capped at 1.5°C above pre-industrial levels, glaciers in the region will lose one third of their ice volume by the year 2100. The region contains the world's third largest storage of frozen water: Its glaciers feed into ten major river systems affecting agriculture, drinking water and hydroelectricity production. Food grown in these river basins reaches three billion people. The melting of the Third Pole, however, does not take place in isolation. It is closely connected to the same human activities and drivers that also pollute the region's air, driving global climate change and raising sea levels. To move to net zero emissions of greenhouse gases, we must shift away from fossil fuel use in energy, transport and other sectors, while changing diets and agricultural practices. The countries of the region also need to reduce emissions of black carbon and other short-lived air pollutants that have a climate impact. Distilling the latest science, Panday shows that addressing many of the same combustion sources provides climate, air quality and health co-benefits.

The pandemic highlighted the urgency of efforts to close the digital divide. It showed that we have not aimed high enough. Basic connectivity targets simply lead to greater inequalities in basic and enhanced capabilities. In his chapter on accelerating digital connectivity, Paul Garnett argues that new goals should reflect where technology is going, not where it is today or where it was a decade ago. Regulatory, marketplace and technological hurdles impede current efforts to achieve universal affordable broadband access across the Asia-Pacific Region. Technological options exist to deliver cost-effective, affordable connectivity to underserved communities. Garnett provides a comprehensive overview of different approaches that both the private and public sectors could adopt for financing the extension of affordable broadband access.

Global value chains (GVCs) drew massive policy attention during the pandemic. As industrialized economies moved away from domestic supply chains, the GVCs failed to rise to the unprecedented demands of the early days of the COVID-19 pandemic. The chapter by Ben Shepherd discusses how trade policies dictate GVC development and why the GVC paradigm of the future must become more resilient to shocks. He cautions that the pandemic experience was unusual because of the strong correlation among country-level shocks across all regions. Under normal conditions, the ability to diversify risk by relying on multiple suppliers in multiple countries becomes an advantage of the GVC system. While a much stronger case exists for using public sector resources to maintain inventories of critical equipment in circumstances where the private sector cannot do so optimally, that would involve forward-looking purchase arrangements between governments and GVCs.

As developing countries come out of the pandemic, and in view of the unfolding climate and inequality crises, Palma and Pincus argue that development approaches need to turn away from orthodox economic policies whose potential to drive growth has been exhausted. Their chapter presents compelling evidence of a premature slow-down in productivity growth across the emerging countries of Southeast Asia, comparing them to stagnant middle-income Latin American countries. Palma and Pincus recommend that countries revive productivity growth, decrease income inequality and mitigate climate damage by adding value to exports: processing raw commodities domestically, strengthening backward and forward linkages, and enhancing the sophistication of assembly operations in manufacturing.

The second cluster of chapters look at the human development impacts and implications at this present juncture. John Roemer and Avidit Acharya make a renewed case for equalizing opportunities (not outcomes) as a measure of development. They postulate three categories of inputs that determine 'fairness.' The first set of factors are the individual's *choices*, which includes the effort she puts in, the decision of which sector to work in, and so on. The second set includes *circumstances*: all individual-specific factors relevant for success but not chosen, such as ethnicity, gender and socioeconomic status. Roemer and Acharya argue that individuals should be held accountable for their choices, but not their circumstances. Public policy, therefore, should blunt the effect of circumstances, while amplifying the relative importance choices have in an individual's success. When individuals consider fairness, they think not just about entitlements but responsibilities. They argue that the reason, or source, of inequality matters. With equalized opportunities, how well individuals do in achieving shared objectives does not depend at all on their circumstances. If opportunities remain unequal, then public policy must seek to equalize them by neutralizing the effects of the circumstances. This intervention moves the collective towards a fairer society.

The chapter by Sabina Alkire and Alexandra Fortacz presents policy insights from an international measure of acute poverty, one covering simultaneous deprivations in ten indicators related to health, education and living standards. Their chapter examines how the Multidimensional Poverty Index (MPI) helps identify the most vulnerable people, reveal poverty patterns within countries and over time, and enable policymakers to target resources effectively. The use of new metrics to design integrated policies, and to manage and measure change, is still in its initial phase in the Asia-Pacific Region. However, both the global MPI and national-level MPIs have permitted more granular analyses of poverty that dovetail with national efforts to achieve the United Nations' Sustainable Development Goals (SDGs). Alkire and Fortacz urge countries in the region to change what they measure in order to innovate quickly and skilfully, in turn helping end abject conditions while empowering impoverished persons and communities as agents and leaders.

In his chapter, A. K. Shiva Kumar revisits the idea of human security to note that the COVID-19 pandemic has exposed the fragility of development achievements accrued over decades. He positions the debate on the provisioning of basic social services by arguing that no country has managed to provide universal healthcare or universal schooling without the dominant policy presence and investment of the public sector. Differentiated strategies under the umbrella of universal coverage could ensure that the most disadvantaged groups also gain access to basic social services and social protection benefits. Many schisms in society have roots in misconceptions and entrenched belief systems that obstruct the building of social cohesion and solidarity behind common purpose. He urges policymakers to seek active citizen engagement on the sustainable development agenda. Governments can incentivize change in norms and behaviour, promote agency through participatory approaches and introduce laws that encourage desirable innovation. Kumar emphasizes an all-of-society approach because high incomes alone cannot guarantee human security. In fact, countries do not have to become rich before reducing vulnerabilities and promoting human dignity.

The chapter on vaccine access and equity by Partha Mukhopadhyay anticipates policy challenges for the future even with mass vaccination against COVID-19 underway (unevenly) across the world (at the time of this volume's completion). Will getting through this first global vaccination campaign suffice to check the pandemic, or will it need repeating year after year? Would we have the resources and the delivery capacity to do so? As long as substantial numbers remain unvaccinated, a reservoir will remain for the virus to recoup and to develop variants that could overcome immunity from existing vaccinations. Experts warn that severe acute respiratory syndrome coronavirus 2 (SARS-CoV-2 causes COVID-19) may likely, or very likely, become endemic. No disease in the history of humankind with a strong zoonotic component – in origin or transmission – has ever disappeared completely. If SARS-CoV-2 does indeed become endemic, will the same degree of global cooperation displayed in manufacturing the vaccine apply to administering it to holdout populations? The precautionary principle requires us to consider this question about the future, to examine how we can build on our successes in order to prevent or address future SARS-CoV or other pandemics.

The final chapters focus on state capacity, regional and global governance, and lessons for development policy and institutions. Inge Kaul revisits the agenda of global public goods (GPGs) in the current context. Communicable diseases, climate change and financial stability to cybersecurity, safe use of new technologies, including artificial intelligence, nuclear non-proliferation and cross-border terrorism – all require a renewed international cooperation. The under-provisioning of GPGs raises questions about basic adequacies in the present system of multilateral cooperation. Kaul calls for a reinvigorated universal multilateralism made 'fit for purpose,' replacing power politics with a primary operating principle of mutual compatibility between international cooperation and sovereignty. She proposes recognizing GPGs as a new type of policy challenge and ending their conflation with development assistance; adopting a mission-oriented approach to resolving GPG-related challenges; and promoting autochthonous organizations from all regions in the system of global governance as meso-level intermediaries. Does this represent a case of idealism trumping reality? Kaul suggests that the post-pandemic impetus must witness a massive rethinking, propelled by an apparent broad-based and strong ambition 'to do better' among policymakers and the global public alike.

Khalil Hamdani's chapter on regionalism reminds us of its use as an effective vehicle in past crises, from the Chiang Mai currency swap initiative that eased balance-of-payments difficulties in the 1997 Asian financial crisis, to a global framework for risk reduction that addresses national-level vulnerabilities to natural disasters. In the post-COVID-19 era, regional cooperation that 'builds forward better' should help economies safely reopen to one another, restoring travel, trade and supply-chains; it should revive domestic economies through cross-border connectivity and access to regional finance and investment. Hamdani reminds us that effective regionalism has assisted the least developed and developing landlocked and island economies in finding opportunities to advance sustainability, address climate change and devise new forms of multi-country cooperation to reduce vulnerabilities. How much this will work to build resilience to future shocks remains to be seen. Hamdani suggests a delineation of regional public goods, involving coordination and collaboration on regulatory standards in multiple areas, such as public health, trade, finance and technology.

Sakiko Fukuda-Parr focuses on diverse national responses to highlight the wide-ranging impacts of COVID-19 on implicit and explicit social contracts, rights and freedoms, and divergent conceptions of individual and collective welfare. She also signals the power asymmetries that played out based on resource ownership. She argues that most Asian-Pacific countries fought the pandemic quite successfully without the abundance of technological assets and financial resources found in Europe and North America, stressing the critical role played by their capacity strengths in governmental and societal institutions. She calls for the redoubling of efforts aimed at redressing the underfunding of public health infrastructure and the under-provisioning of global public goods, and shines a light on the harsh neglect of low-wage workers in the global economy. Like Kumar, Fukuda-Parr highlights the nuanced distinction between institutional capacities and capabilities.

In the final chapter on lessons emerging from the worldwide experience of fighting COVID-19, Sanjay Reddy offers major takeaways for rejuvenating development policy and institutions. The shockingly diverse pandemic-induced economic and health outcomes that we see today, even for countries at comparable levels of income, suggest a fundamental distinction between state 'capacity' and 'capability'. Using the unforeseen ill-timed release of the 2019 Johns Hopkins rankings on global health security, Reddy argues that countries that had the best capacity still proved unable to deploy this capacity into capabilities, the latter having to do with the ability to apply capacities in a given context to achieve a desired outcome. Reddy also argues that adaptive and integrated policymaking narrows the trade-off between efficiency and resilience. Policymaking constantly informed by feedback loops, self-learning, humility and transparency probably saved lives. Countries with these successes in pandemic policy also exhibited greater public trust in scientific expertise and in state authority, data and information.

According to the World Bank, at least $800 billion globally was invested in 1,400 social protection measures in the first nine months of 2020, but cash transfer programmes lasted just 3.3 months on average, and average spending per capita in low-income countries was only $6 (Gentilini et al., 2020). This supports Reddy's inference that a standing architecture for social safety nets provides a more secure buffer for vulnerable people than ad-hoc measures, and that traditional fiscal constraints need not limit social choices. This set of chapters uses different arguments and illustrations to come to a shared conclusion – that in an interconnected world, it will take more regional and international cooperation, not less: Cooperation with mutually assured benefits will prove indispensable to achieving the Sustainable Development Goals.

In September 2019, the UN Secretary-General called on all sectors of society to mobilize for a decade of action (2020–2030) on three levels: *global action* to secure greater leadership, more resources and smarter solutions for the Sustainable Development Goals; *local action* embedding needed transitions in the policies, budgets, institutions and regulatory frameworks of governments, cities and local authorities; and *people action*, including by youth, civil society, the media, the private sector, unions, academia and other stakeholders, to generate an unstoppable movement pushing for the required transformations (United Nations, 2021). Even before COVID-19 upended the world, this decade has been called "the most consequential in human history". We now have the means – capital, technology, policies and the scientific knowledge – to choose a path of reconstruction and regeneration, in contrast to the constraints faced by earlier generations (Carrington, 2020).

We hope this policy compendium provides a glimpse into a range of issues that have a significant call on the policy choices and directions for sustainable development in the Asia-Pacific Region. Many of these issues animate policy debates currently underway; they imply that national-, regional- and global-level policy influencers must set more ambitious targets and act on bolder recommendations, if this vast and dynamic region is to play its part in ensurlng a safer and more sustainable world.

REFERENCES

Carrington, D. 2020. 'Christiana Figueres on the Climate Emergency: "This Is the Decade and We Are the Generation"'. *The Guardian*, 15 February. theguardian.com/ environment/2020/feb/15/christiana-figueres-climate-emergency-this-is-the-decade-the-future-we-choose.

Elhacham, E., Ben-Uri, L. and Grozovski, J. 2020. 'Global Human-Made Mass Exceeds All Living Biomass'. *Nature* 588, 442–444.

Gentilini, U., Almenfi, M. and Dale, P. 2020. *Social Protection and Jobs Responses to COVID-19: A Real-Time Review of Country Measures*. Washington, DC: The World Bank.

Maddison, A. 2007. *Contours of the World Economy 1-2030 AD: Essays in Macro-economic History*. Oxford: Oxford University Press.

The Economist. 2021. 'What Is the Economic Cost of Covid-19?' 7 January.

United Nations (UN). 2021. 'Decade of Action: Ten Years to Transform Our World'. United Nations, New York. un.org/sustainabledevelopment/decade-of-action/.

United Nations Development Programme (UNDP). 2013. *Human Development Report 2013: The Rise of the South: Human Progress in a Diverse World*. New York: United Nations Development Programme.

———. 2020. *Human Development Report 2020: The Next Frontier – Human Development and the Anthropocene*. New York: United Nations Development Programme. hdr.undp.org/sites/default/files/hdr2020.pdf.

1 | Aligning Sovereign Debt Financing with Climate Action in the Asia-Pacific Region

Manuel F. Montes

All my life, though some have changed,
Some forever, not for better.
— *In My Life* by John Lennon and Paul McCartney (1965)

INTRODUCTION

A 2011 study projected that if the Asia-Pacific Region (APR) continues its upward trajectory, by 2050 it could account for more than half of global gross domestic product (GDP), trade and investment (ADB 2011). One could see this as a kind of 'Great Re-emergence', since the territories in the APR had accounted for this same proportion of the global economy before industrial development began in the West. Whole swaths of the APR have undergone permanent change, accompanied by corresponding disruptions and widespread adjustments in social and political arrangements.

These permanent transformations have been enabled by decades of vigorous economic growth, and these growth trends have, themselves, spawned an accelerating pattern of environmental costs, many induced by enlarged manufacturing activities, increased incomes that have in turn spurred expanded consumption baskets, and urbanization. Global climate change, interacting with the APR's achieved economic successes, threatens to increase the steepness of the climb towards development. Without the necessary course corrections in its current growth path, which has relied heavily on installing the fossil-based technology of the West's industrial dominance, development in the APR may stall sometime in this century.

This chapter argues that acting now, both as individual nations and on a regional basis, can both avert this stall and mitigate the human and economic costs of the action itself. In fact, if climate change marks out a path of technological, social and economic development, the question becomes one not of reducing costs but instead of accelerating investment in pursuit of development ambitions (UN, 2011, 2015; Stern, 2015).

The ongoing COVID-19 pandemic offers a window into the developmental and climate action issues facing countries in the APR. First, the pandemic highlights the heightened degree of interdependence among economies in the APR arising from commerce, travel, financial flows and shared geography. With its network of global value chains, the APR has more intense economic integration than other regions of the world (Baldwin, 2016). With increasing urbanization and the region's dependence on ports for trade and on food production from coastal and river-basin areas, climate change presents a clear threat to the economic model. How can societies reorient their investment decisions (and mobilize the necessary finances) to sustain growth and the degree of interdependence among the APR's nations? Second, the pandemic reveals that economies in the APR depend upon their social provisioning and care sectors, the capabilities of which may either hinder or stimulate their development successes. Will societies in the APR summon the social and political resolve to steadily upgrade these sectors in tandem with their economic growth to keep their populations safe and thriving in a climate-warming world? Third, the pandemic exposes the human limits of technological capabilities needed to respond to natural events. Will capabilities in the APR advance rapidly enough in all societies to access, adapt and innovate with the technologies required for climate change?

This chapter examines how the APR might reorient investment and its financing as forms of climate action, focusing on economic restructuring, a strengthened care economy and technological development as key problems. It warns that the hazardous features of the international financial system may frustrate the climate actions needed to keep the APR on its development trajectory. It also notes that these hazards would pose problems even in a non-warming climate and demonstrate the need for thoroughgoing reforms in global finance. The first section surveys the climate challenges confronting the APR and their corresponding economic costs. The second section examines the limitations of the current financial system in generating the kind of finance required for climate action. The third section offers recommendations for further unpacking the question of climate-action investment and financing in the APR.

CLIMATE CHALLENGES IN THE ASIA-PACIFIC REGION

Asian-Pacific countries find themselves confronting escalating development costs because of three forces: natural disasters; domestic pressures, such as those arising from public health concerns and the need to reverse environmental degradation; and the combination of national requirements and international obligations, such as commitments in the United Nations Framework Convention on Climate Change (UNFCCC), to reduce their greenhouse-gas emissions. Global climate change trajectories dominate the first and third cost sources; thus, the countries in the APR do not fully control the costs confronting them. The second source arises from rapid economic growth and human habitation expansion interacting with a natural environment not given enough time to regenerate itself. All of these costs would hinder the APR's current development models unless they evolve rapidly enough to undertake the appropriate physical investments.

Could the APR simply continue current development paths without the extensive and expensive alternative investments? Recent events suggest that the answer is 'No', and that the business-as-usual option may be no more feasible than desirable. Most climate assessments issue a warning, exhorting governments and societies to do more and sooner to keep warming to well below 2 degrees Celsius at most. This section assumes probable delays in the emergence of an effective global response. Policy actions should reflect an extrapolation from the most recent costs and allow for their acceleration in the near term, although the scale of future acceleration remains uncertain.

Escalating human and physical impacts

First of all, based on the recent record, Asia-Pacific nations cannot evade the human and physical impacts of globally driven climate change. With its diverse geography, including the Tibetan plateau, the APR has witnessed a variety of both long-term trends (also called 'slow onset' events) and extreme weather events, with climate change driving the duration and frequency of both.

One emblematic case of an ongoing climate change trend is the melting of the Himalayan glaciers. In 2017, around 1.9 billion people lived in the ten river basins with headwaters located in the Hindu Kush region, including 240 million people in the region itself (Wester et al., 2019). These populations face the prospect of widespread livelihood dislocation, vulnerability to flooding events and increasing outmigration pressures.

In the past two decades, the APR has suffered more from extreme weather events than other world regions. Between 2000 and 2018, 82 per cent of natural disasters in Asia came from extreme weather events (ADB, 2019). In the same period, developing countries in Asia accounted for 84 per cent of the 206 million people affected by disasters on the average each year. At an estimated annual average of almost 38,000 fatalities in the same period, the APR accounted for 55 per cent of the 60,000 global disaster fatalities (ADB, 2019). As elsewhere in the world, the poor, the rural, the marginalized and the isolated absorb most of the costs of these disasters. Isolated Pacific Island nations, with limited economic diversification, are particularly vulnerable to extreme weather events.

Under the current global climate trajectory, countries in the APR must find a way to absorb these kinds of costs, even once an effective global regime begins to deflect the path of emissions and warming. Most countries will experience an increasing number of warm days and decreasing number of cold days. Water demand will also increase, exacerbated by poor water management policies.

In the case of the second cost source – reversing environmental degradation – the more rapidly growing economies in the APR have already absorbed significant costs in terms of human health and economic production. For example, in China, smog-inducing ozone and fine particles cause an estimated 1.1 million premature deaths annually, while destroying 20 million tons of rice, wheat, maize and soybeans (Gu et al., 2018). Despite the locally generated character of pollution and its principally domestic impact, domestic efforts to mitigate pollution nevertheless would also advance global objectives to reduce greenhouse emissions.

Economic impacts already borne

Second, the economic impacts of climate-related events indicate that the affected countries already bear the costs and will continue to do so regardless of policy. While responses cannot produce instantaneous results, in the long run, countries would benefit from investments that reduce these cumulative costs.

In the 11 years between 1989 and 2018, countries in the APR absorbed US$687.6 billion in physical damage from weather-related[1] causes, affecting 5.2 billion people (ADB, 2020). In 2014, India bore $16 billion in physical damage from flooding in September. In 2017, floods in June and July and a storm in July caused $6 billion and $3.5 billion, respectively, in physical damages in China (ADB, 2020).

A widely cited 2015 model covering most[2] countries estimated 13.6 per cent to be the average (among countries) of the amount taken off per capita GDP production capacity by mid-century (defined as the span of years 2040–2059) by climate change (Burke, Hsiang and Miguel, 2015). These estimates are considered on the high side because of an assumption that gives cumulative negative impacts for higher temperatures (Aufhammer, 2019). This estimate of climate impacts suggests that the average country could afford to invest 13.6 of their per capita output over the 44 years between 2015 and 2059 – much less than one per cent per capita annually – to evade or mitigate its harmful impacts on production capacity.

However, assessing the affordability of climate investments requires at least four caveats. First, climate investments and related spending, compared to other investments, tend to require high upfront costs, with a declining cost or positive benefits afterward. Second, climate costs entail cumulative processes, as implied in the cost methodology cited above, although early action to obtain financing for upfront costs can arrest the pattern. Third, national climate efforts must contend with the fact that the action, inaction, or inadequate action of other nations determines the scale of national action. If, for example, certain countries maintain higher fossil-fuel subsidies over an extended period, then the costs become shared among other countries. This underlines the indispensability of international cooperation and the essential practice of common but differentiated responsibilities in climate action

(Montes and Williams, 2017). The mitigation efforts of large countries in the APR – China, India, Indonesia, Japan and the Republic of Korea – have profound global impact. Regional authorities must actively engage in global climate rule making and evolution. These large countries can also contribute immensely as global innovators in technological development and the economic and social aspects of climate action. Fourth, countries experience a widely unequal distribution of negative impacts on production capacity. Projections for mid-century give impacts from climate change alone on per capita GDP a range from -40 per cent (Pakistan) to +88 per cent (Mongolia) (Aufhammer, 2019). This wide range of impacts will require major efforts in multilateral cooperation and sharing in investment resources, despite the earlier observation that the investment requirement would be about one per cent of per capita GDP for the average country.

Table 1.1 provides a window into the variety of climate change impacts among the countries in the APR. The data in Table 1.1 affirm the starting point of the International Finance Corporation (IFC) (2020) analysis that identifies South Asia as home to three of the five countries most vulnerable to climate change. For Bangladesh, India, Nepal and Pakistan, the loss in GDP per capita by mid-century may exceed 30 per cent. The maritime-exposed countries of Southeast Asia also risk losses of the same order. China's estimated loss is below 10 per cent.

Table 1.1   Range of climate change impacts on Asia-Pacific country GDP, 2040–2059

Country	Change in per capita G DP
Afghanistan	−4.78
Armenia	19.28
Australia	−12.60
Azerbaijan	−2.53
Bangladesh	−36.49
Brunei Darussalam	−34.16
Bhutan	−1.17
Cambodia	−38.94
People's Republic of China	−7.51
Fiji	−23.63
Georgia	5.52
Indonesia	−31.44
India	−38.78
Japan	−5.97

(Continued)

Table 1.1   *(Continued)*

Country	Change in per capita G DP
Kazakhstan	32.17
Korea, Republic of	3.09
Kyrgyz Republic	29.53
Lao People's Democratic Republic	−32.21
Malaysia	−33.53
Mongolia	87.81
Nepal	−31.08
New Zealand	−0.41
Papua New Guinea	−24.30
Pakistan	−39.54
Philippines	−30.61
Samoa	−27.87
Solomon Islands	−39.54
Tajikistan	−31.35
Thailand	−37.81
Turkmenistan	−14.10
Uzbekistan	−8.45
Vanuatu	−26.14
Viet Nam	−33.60

Sources: Auffhammer (2019); Burke, Hsiang and Miguel (2015).

We must recognize that the countries facing the global climate threat are at different stages of development; not all have shared the rate of success in recent decades that has given the APR its reputation for economic growth.

Five developing economies, two already industrialized, and five fast-growing middle-income converging economies – India, Indonesia, Japan, Malaysia, People's Republic of China, Republic of Korea and Thailand – have led the others in an economic model that relied on linkages to export markets beyond the APR. Climate change imperils the sustainability of such production chains. For example, catastrophic flooding in Thailand in 2011 severely disrupted production activities far beyond its borders (Haraguchi and Lall, 2015). Therefore, these leading countries have important roles in global value chains that require safeguarding against climate change.

The APR also has important commodity exporters, many among the less-diversified (least-developed[3]) countries (LDCs). These countries have not been immune to extreme weather events, such as the devastating 2019 floods in Myanmar. They share an important characteristic in their vulnerability to external financing difficulties; Lao PDR, in fact, appears as a country facing high probability of debt distress in the International Monetary Fund's (IMF) annual debt sustainability framework for 2019 (World Bank and IMF, 2019).

All APR countries will be compelled by their circumstances, national and international requirements, and their development ambitions to undertake all three of the standard categories of climate action: loss-and-damage, adaptation, and mitigation.

Loss-and-damage applies to the negative effects of climate variability and climate change that overwhelm people's capacities to cope or adapt.[4] National governments already bear the costs of damage arising from extreme weather events. Investments in insurance[5] pools, at the national and international level, could mitigate the sudden call on public resources in such contingencies (Warner et al., 2012a). A significant proportion of the losses from climate events fall upon the populations directly affected; risk-sharing mechanisms with unaffected populations will fall far short of requirements in such cases (Warner et al., 2012b). Through regulatory policies, private insurance could also play an important part in risk-sharing. The ADB (2020) estimate of weather-related damage costing $687.60 billion indicates an annual requirement of about $63 billion, which could be pooled across the region. Such a pool will not have to disburse this amount every year and could require more in specific years; different countries would also draw upon it at different times.

Adaptation actions to climate-proof infrastructure, telecommunications, transportation, farms, manufacturing operations, offices and residences represent an important portion of the climate investment requirements. Questions about investment financing immediately arise in adaptation because it entails installation or erection of new facilities that produce returns over the life of the investment. Financing to pay for the immediate costs of installations is required at the start and must be paid back over the life of new facilities. Estimates from a recent IFC study (2020) on climate investment opportunities in South Asia illustrate the following adaptation-associated[6] sectors and the corresponding estimates of investment potential[7] for the period 2018 to 2030: green buildings $1.53 trillion, transport infrastructure $0.3 trillion, municipal solid waste $0.02 trillion, climate smart urban water $0.1 trillion and climate smart agriculture $0.2 trillion. These by no means exhaust the list of adaptation requirements; it only names those that might offer private investors reasonable returns. Such returns would be possible once inadequate facilities are remedied through investment and the resulting savings get redirected to investors from the present publicly borne costs.

For mitigation, investment requirements are strongly shaped, in part, by international commitments – the Nationally Determined Contributions (NDCs) of countries under the Paris Agreement. Investment requirements are even more strongly shaped by the most significant of these costs: human health and premature deaths in urban areas. The national studies for China have consistently shown that the costs of pollution exceed the costs of investments to avoid harmful effects. For example, air pollution in China costs an estimated 6.5 per cent of GDP per annum (Crane and Mao, 2015).

Financing needs for international commitments on mitigation

Countries in all the major Asia-Pacific subregions have made time-bound commitments to reduce greenhouse gas (GHG) emissions under the Paris Agreement. International journals are rife with analyses of these NDCs; a recent study of South Asian NDCs raises doubts about how strongly these plans have elicited stakeholder support (Haque et al., 2019). The APR has an extraordinarily strong climate mitigation potential, not only given the low level of clean energy sources currently installed, but also in terms of sources of wind and insolation[8] power (Climate Analytics, 2019). For any country, meeting their NDC commitment raises the question of financing the investment and installing the supporting regulatory and market frameworks for transitioning to clean energy generation and transport.

Presuming an extension of their high-growth record, Southeast Asian countries have committed to ambitious mitigation targets in the future under their NDCs. NDC plans involve transitions to cleaner sources of primary and indirect energy, including increased dependence on gas and biofuel. One should note that the increased biofuels may create a potential impact on food security, especially if climate change impairs agricultural productivity. The commitments also propose significant conversions in the transport sector, including public transport. Among Southeast Asian countries, the Philippines offer the most ambitious emission cuts, which include a 50 per cent reduction in CO_2 emissions below 1990 level. The implied target of per capita CO_2 emissions below 1 ton would be one of the lowest in the world (Fulton et al., 2017). Fulton et al. (2017) underscore that Southeast Asian NDC commitments are highly contingent on flows of external finance. This amounts to 70 per cent in the Philippines, 41 per cent in Indonesia, 45 per cent in Malaysia and 25 per cent in both Thailand and Viet Nam.

LIMITATIONS AND VULNERABILITIES IN THE INTERNATIONAL FINANCIAL SYSTEM

The cost of finance for the most credit-worthy borrowers has remained near zero since the onset of the 2008 subprime financial crisis. Logically, this situation presents an exceptional opportunity for governments and private investors to mobilize finance for climate investment. In this section, we seek to explain a crucial part of the anomalous situation, one that has seen enormous growth in financial investment, as opposed to investment in the physical, long-term requirements for climate action.

Addressing the inadequacies of finance in this area will prove critical to the APR's development prospects and climate action success.

One should also recognize that the financial system itself has responded to an economic environment where the price of carbon is 'too low' from fuel subsidies along with other policies that, in effect, do not internalize the cost of air pollution (Coady et al., 2019; IEA, 2020). The cost of borrowing has stood at historically low levels due to the quantitative easing policies chosen by advanced economies (the European Union, Japan and the United States) to forestall a financial markets collapse following the 2007-2008 financial crisis. This strategy reduced the cost of borrowing to near zero and provided abundant global liquidity in exchange for unprecedented expansions of central-bank balance sheets.

Many central banks in industrialized countries reverted to quantitative easing policies with the onset of the COVID-19 crisis in February 2020. As in the previous episode, global liquidity has expanded enormously. In this instance, the US Federal Reserve System has engaged in generous purchases of high-risk ('junk') private bonds. The resulting liquidity in private companies may either go to purchases of equipment or increased hiring (the Federal Reserve's preferred channel), or to investments in other financial assets.

As of December 2020, the main debt propellants for developing countries are the fiscal demands arising from responses to the COVID-19 pandemic. Developing country debt balances have dramatically worsened because of the pandemic, coming on the heels of already proliferating debt difficulties in 2019. The pandemic has thrown a harsh light on the limitations and vulnerabilities of the international development financing system.

Not fit for purpose

Structurally, the international financial system mobilizes too little financing for physical investments required for the 'dirty' business-as-usual (BAU) economy. Thus, it is also unable to finance investment in newer, more technologically appropriate 'green' activities in production and consumption. Climate action also requires securing long-term financing. For the global community to have any chance of mobilizing adequate financing for climate action, thoroughgoing changes in the international financial system will be required (UNEP 2015). Asian-Pacific developing countries, most with open capital accounts, must manage their macroeconomies to fend off surges of inflows to avoid unwanted exchange rate appreciation and avoid sudden capital outflows in the short-term (Montes, 2013b). The great bulk of investment by private actors lies in other financial assets, with an eye to capital gains within a short period of time. In the starkest terms, UNEP (2015) characterized the system as 'not fit-for-purpose' and the "stability and effectiveness of key parts of the financial system, for example, remain at risk from short-termism and excessive leverage".

The dominance of capital-gains-seeking investments follows from reforms in regulations (such as the 1980s reforms that weakened prohibitions against corporations[9] buying back their own shares) and in accounting and tax treatments (such as lowering tax rates on capital gains). The structure of international finance caters to profitability through elevated financial returns without necessarily stimulating real (physical) investment. With market outcomes dominated by short-term considerations, climate-vulnerable countries and sectors will be unable to finance investments (Mackenzie, 2021).

Under a capital-gains dynamic, profit from portfolio investments arises from changes in the price of a financial asset between the time of its purchase and the time of resale. This means that profits are also available on a portfolio position, called a 'short', based on a contract to sell an asset at a future date, after the asset price has fallen. Investors do not have to make a judgement about whether a project will succeed in the long run; they can make money on positions that an asset price will fall. For example, a position based on the judgement that a project will fail, or a particular country's exchange rate will fall, can become enormously profitable within a short time frame. Shorts exacerbate the short-term bias of financial markets. In contrast, the returns on physical investments are only recovered in the long term, in fractional annual amounts.

International finance's differentiated welcome mat

Economists have scrambled to explain why US interest rates and inflation expectations have remained low despite the massive injections of liquidity since 2008. These liquidity injections have spilled over internationally, leading to debt increases in developing countries. This unexpected pattern arises from the relentless trend in growing income and wealth inequality (both internally and internationally); if this explanation is correct, it makes the question of mobilizing climate finance even more complex.

Persistent trends in income and wealth inequality feed accumulations of financial asset pools in advanced economies that, in turn, generate a strong demand for so-called safe assets,[10] defined as assets that keep their face value in the event of a systemic crisis. The supply of safe assets falls short of the demand, and fuels short-term placements in developing countries impelled by the 'hunt for yield'. This mechanism, as explained in Caballero and Farhi (2017), creates a self-feeding 'safety trap'. In advanced economies, the flagging capabilities of labour to secure its share of social output and the low consumption demand from the top 20 per cent have slain the inflation dragon and pinned down interest rates to around zero (Mian et al., 2020). Labour's flagging capacity to protect its share of value added had been greatly abetted by the collapse of the Soviet Union and China's entry into world markets; both greatly augmented the global labour force and drove the consequent reduction in consumer goods prices as mobile capital moved production to lower-wage areas (Goodhart and Pradhan, 2020).

Weak macroeconomic demand sustained by inequality ensconces a trend towards lower secular growth and lower fixed capital investment in advanced countries. Because the safe-asset trap arises from income inequality (or wealth inequality), and because reversing income inequality cannot happen instantaneously, the differences in financing costs between advanced and developing countries can hold sway for quite some time. Among countries, a stark gap has arisen in the cost of accessing funds from the same international pools. While borrowing rates remain near zero in advanced economies, developing countries borrow at rates of about 5 per cent and higher.[11]

Global governance mechanisms lack a process for sovereign debt resolution: a non-arbitrary (rule-based), comprehensive, predictable and equitable method. International creditor committees currently manage such matters with little or no oversight – notably the Paris Club, properly called a club with the cachet of exclusivity, and one that violates common notions of good governance. In debt restructuring episodes, the debtor country barely sees[12] the so-called bailout resources, which pass through the debtor to the creditor claimants in exchange for an increased level of indebtedness. Moreover, with the default risk transferred away from creditors by the debt regime, restructuring has triggered the vigorous restart of lending to debt-distressed countries, as we see in the enthusiastic private resumption of lending to Latin American countries.

The outbreak of developing country debt difficulties triggered by the pandemic has exacerbated could provide another opportunity for the establishment of an effective sovereign debt regime. In 2001, the IMF spurred a substantial but failed attempt to establish a sovereign debt restructuring mechanism (SDRM), while, in 2014 and 2015, Bolivia and Argentina led a United Nations centred initiative with the support of the Group of 77 and China (El-Erian, 2021; Montes, 2016). Neither produced lasting results.

The analysis presented here assumes that the international financial system will remain substantially unchanged for at least a decade. During this decade, climate action cannot be set aside. The economies in the APR as a whole form one of two regions in the world that are net savers, excluding North America and Europe; the other region is the Middle East. Authorities in the APR need to acknowledge that, while these sets of countries have privileged access to international finance, they remain rule-takers, not rule-makers, in international finance.

Similarly, in international financial matters, economies in the APR function as price-takers rather than price-setters, and do not host the dominant managers of the supply of international finance. It would be prudent for the authorities in the APR to participate in and support developing country efforts intended to reform the hazard-laden international debt system, if only to protect their own development and climate action space. Authorities should not miss the opportunity – should it arise – to actively participate in a fundamental reform of the global sovereign debt regime.

As internationally oriented economies, logic dictates that these nations stand on the side of eliminating inefficiencies and inequities in the international financial system.

Financing climate action in an unfavourable financial setting

There is little controversy over the lead role that states must play in climate action. Production and service activities almost everywhere depend on fossil-fuel technology. All investments and actions require the introduction of infrastructure and activities not yet in wide commercial usage. This section will focus on the matter of financing climate action. There is an urgent necessity to ramp-up public revenue performance within the ongoing global tax reform effort (Montes, Uribe and Danish, 2018). For climate mitigation action, Asian-Pacific countries seeking to introduce domestic[13] carbon surcharges to lessen public deficits and reliance on foreign funding will require the sacrifice of part their international competitiveness in exports and in attracting foreign investment. A threat looms in recent European Community discussions about carbon border adjustment measures (CBAM);[14] such measures could have implications for the APR's trade-based growth model, given its dependence on internationally dispersed production processes. Standard economic theory posits that such policies could tilt the terms of trade in favour of developed countries as a whole.

International public resources offer a second source of climate-action financing. Asian-Pacific countries have strong access to international finance institutions (IFIs). The emergence of new IFIs – notably the Asian Infrastructure Investment Bank (AIIB) and the New Development Bank, both under the leadership of China – has expanded the opportunities for the APR.

The third source is private financing from large international pools that are hypothetically available for climate finance. In the pursuit of effective climate action, with private financing mainly available as the short-term placements depicted earlier, governments may increasingly need to fully finance investments from tax revenues, or else compel the private sector to redirect the resources it now principally keeps in liquid financial assets towards physical investments for climate action. To compete with the private-profit bias towards quick asset-price gains, the public sector must also set priorities in extensive regulatory and standard setting actions congruent with climate priorities. These will not reduce the cost of climate action but can mobilize private investment; based on the record, public subsidies would also be required to prod private-sector behaviour towards new arrangements.

A direct route would introduce strong regulations designed to trigger private actions; such regulations would be strengthened by enforcing them via private insurance markets. For example, governments could upgrade building codes to limit new construction permits to climate-resilient facilities. These types of policies do not, however, reduce the costs of climate investments. The introduction of environmental, social and governance (ESG) standards into the activities of private companies resident in Asian-Pacific countries can, of course, reduce the attractiveness of host countries.

Climate-motivated regulations, including ESG standards, aim to compel economic actors to internalize the prospective costs of climate change.[15] These standards would apply both to public and private actors. Volz et al. (2020), for example, suggest that the countries most vulnerable to climate-change damage have paid 275 basis points more on the average on their sovereign debt. The finding derives from research measuring the implicit relationship between observed climate change costs and the sovereign risk premia. The result does not mean that finance providers have incorporated these costs directly in setting their risk premia (see the next section for a discussion on this). Credit rating agencies, for example, have not incorporated these considerations in assigning bond ratings, although this practice has changed for large, internationally active companies.

These kinds of results bolster the argument that governments should invest and introduce regulations to reduce climate costs and strengthen environmental risk management, aiming to trigger market-driven adjustments. They have also been used to suggest that credit rating agencies should begin to incorporate climate considerations in their evaluations. However, credit agencies will only gradually apply these criteria to corporate bond ratings because of the lack of agreed standards on methodology (see next section).

This brings us to the concept of 'stranded assets,' those that suffer from unanticipated or premature write-downs, devaluations, or conversion to liabilities (Caldecott, Howarth and McSharry, 2013). Collapses in the value of assets apply to all kinds of physical facilities, including farmland, manufacturing plants and power generation, and strike at the heart of the capital-gains dynamic of international financial markets – but not all at once. An effective response to such vulnerability would introduce regulations that force assets to be priced to fully reflect their climate vulnerabilities.

On 2 November 2021, during the 26th UN Climate Change Conference of the Parties (COP26), former Bank of England Governor Mark Carney, who originally warned of the systemic dangers of stranded assets (Carney, 2015), announced the formation of the Glasgow Financial Alliance for Net Zero (GFANZ), with $130 trillion in private capital committed (GFANZ, 2021). We take the view, in line with UNEP (2015), that such an operation has the potential to wreak enormous damage on developing countries, similar to crises seen in the aftermath of petrodollar recycling in the 1970s, if global regulatory frameworks and private incentives are not comprehensively recast.

ESG standards and finance

ESG measurement methodologies involve reforms accounting standards in the first instance, augmented by other metrics to ensure that financial actors appropriately consider the climate impacts of their actions. A burgeoning global civil society movement that aims to require IFIs – all owned by state parties – to halt all financing for all fossil-fuel energy projects is a regulatory version of this kind of consideration.

In the private sector, as reflected in the start-ups of numerous international task forces, intense interest has developed in finance, and most especially in the matters of ESG standards and climate-contingent debt instrument designs. These activities react to a mounting interest on the part of investors and willing-to-lend savers in increasing their exposure to climate change-related financing. Government climate action must emphasize the introduction of mandatory annual financial disclosures on climate risks for large enterprises.

A truly valuable development would be genuine behavioural change on the part of private companies (financial and non-financial), one that fully incorporates climate costs in their operations and in their investment decisions. Incorporating climate costs in operations will reduce accounting profits in the same instance that it can create reserves that could feed into climate-insurance pools.

RECOMMENDATIONS

In arranging their financing for climate action, APR economies must operate within the international financial environment. Countries will have to raise climate finance in competition with external opportunities offering short-term returns. This section examines the various options countries could consider.

Domestic fiscal and monetary actions

Prioritizing domestic action appears prudent in the uncertain and volatile international development climate. A first and necessary step in this direction is for Asian-Pacific countries to incorporate their climate change objectives and actions into their development planning and implementation. The all-inclusive SDG framework poses a challenge for each Asia-Pacific society in aligning its social progress, industrialization and poverty eradication ambitions with the framework's urgent call to combat climate change and its impacts.

Rethinking capital account openness

After decades of applauding capital-account openness on the part of development analysts and IFI staff, the IMF and analysts have begun to reconsider these kinds of policies (Kose and Prasad, 2020). Most countries in the APR have liberalized their capital accounts, even after the Asian financial crisis (Montes, 2013b). In contrast, China has applied a policy of phased opening, even after its currency qualified to become one of five in the IMF's special drawing rights (SDR) pool. In an article entitled 'Neoliberalism: Oversold?' Ostry, Louganis and Furceri (2016) find the recurrence of balance-of-payments crises as a pattern that has reversed growth and worsened inequality. The authors cite Ghosh, Ostry and Qureshi (2016) on the dangers of capital surges through open capital accounts as a predicate for many of these crises. The IMF has already gone on record as supporting macroprudential controls during balance-of-payments crises.[16]

For expanding climate finance, capital controls offer a key advantage: a borrowing rate for physical projects that does not compete with short-term external financial returns. China supplies one example of a country that has made good use of its gradual capital account opening. China's controls help its state banks provide low-interest-rate loans to businesses. Capital controls also help China limit volatility that could otherwise impair the soundness of its commercial banks – especially given the country's weak regulatory institutions – and induce price volatility in its real estate market, the main investment opportunity for Chinese households (Shaw and Eidelman, 2011).

The Republic of Korea also has a well-known record of extensive capital controls during its period of rapid growth within its state-led development strategy (Noland, 2007). Park (2011) characterizes the shift in the view towards capital controls as one from cardinal sin to policy agenda, based on Korea's experience with financial crises from 1997 to 2011. The 2010 Seoul G20 summit, over which the Republic of Korea presided, discussed policies to reduce balance-of-payments imbalances, including capital control policies (Park, 2011).

One should recognize caveats concerning the perils of reintroducing capital controls in countries that already have open capital accounts. For these countries, whether they would have benefited on a net basis or not, private portfolio inflows and outflows remain critical for balance-of-payments health. Any reintroduction of controls should take place in a phased manner that gives external portfolio investors time to understand their purpose, to avoid drastic reversals in portfolio positions that would themselves trigger a crisis.

In the APR, private financial flows have earned a hair-trigger reputation – one susceptible to 'herd behaviour' as seen in the Asian financial crisis (Montes, 1998). For example, at the beginning of COVID-19 pandemic, to provide fiscal space for eligible low-income[17] economies (such as Myanmar), the Group of 20 (G20) introduced a Debt Service Suspension Initiative (DSSI)[18] that suspended developing countries' debt service payments to G20 bilateral lenders effective May 2020 (Reuters, 2020). As of early November 2021, only 46 of the 73 eligible countries have applied for the suspension, owing to their authorities' fears of a credit rating downgrade (Kaiser and Kopper, 2020). The interpretation that debt-service suspension reduces the credit standing of an economy conflicts with a view that having greater fiscal resources improves it. To manage the introduction of capital controls, Asian-Pacific countries should seriously consider negotiating a set of mutually acceptable standards on these kinds of policies.

Reforming regulatory approaches to elicit climate finance

As discussed earlier, some of the needed financing can flow through regulatory changes. Well-known actions of this kind include feed-in tariff regimes or the upgrading of construction and building standards and codes, enforced by insurers. Authorities can withdraw incentives and subsidies for 'dirty' economic activities at a rate that avoids employment dislocation. Mandatory disclosure and reporting requirements for enterprises can elicit private actions that draw on financing flows from ESG-inspired funding pools.

Strengthening national tax systems

Actions that strengthen national tax systems and make them more progressive will build a longer-term underpinning for APR development financing. Such actions can include increasing taxes on monopoly-position rents. Countries could initiate these even while the pandemic continues. Developing countries in the APR would do well to expand their participation in growing efforts to change international standards of allocating taxing rights among tax jurisdictions. Unfortunately, predominant standards backed by developed countries through the Organisation for Economic Cooperation and Development (OECD) facilitate the transfer of profits out of the territory where they originate, disadvantaging developing countries that host foreign investment (Montes, Uribe and Danish, 2018). Because it was launched on the mandate that the OECD project on Base Erosion and Profit Shifting (BEPS) would sidestep issues involving the allocation of taxing rights between source and resident countries, the outcomes of the project did not address the channels through which profit transfer facilitation takes place in developing countries, such as in mining subsidiaries and payments for technical services among related companies (Montes, Uribe and Danish, 2018). The *Wall Street Journal* (2021) characterized the resulting October 2021 G20 agreement on OECD-designed tax reforms as "G-20 Backs Tax Overhaul That Makes Rich Countries Big Winners."

Asian-Pacific countries must oppose trade regimes that create a permanent hole in their public finances, such as making permanent the tariff moratorium on digitalizable goods trade under the World Trade Organization (Kelsey et al., 2020).

Governments will need to direct new and additional public resources towards climate and development action consistent with efforts to achieve the SDGs – and not towards external debt service.

Tapping external sources of finance

The modalities, the volume, and the possibility of external financing for climate action have garnered the greatest policy and diplomatic attention; the discussion of the previous section must serve as a corrective and a caution. Given the potentially enormous resources required for climate action, Asian-Pacific countries must take care not to walk into the trap of external indebtedness from climate action financing. Here we shall review various actions for accessing external finance and examine their implications for national indebtedness and development space.

Borrowing from international sources

Sovereign borrowing from international sources has evolved in a variety of ways. The number of funds has proliferated, driven by donor interest and the variety[19] of needs with perceived climate-related purposes. For example, dedicated funds now exist for adaptation, but these remain of a much smaller size than the variety of mitigation funds set up by donor countries. Each of these funds has its own modality of access, but all share the feature of lending based on intended projects (or programmes) for repayment. The Green Climate Fund, the financial agency under the UNFCCC, has the distinction of having a board providing equal representation among industrialized and developing countries.

This section will not evaluate these funds from the point of view of APR climate funding. Mariama Williams (2019) provides a useful summary and state of play of these funds. Instead, this section will focus on new developments in borrowing for climate financing. Many of the caveats identified in this section would also apply to other funds with a longer record.

Green bonds and SDG bonds

In keeping with the overall growth of debt finance globally, green bonds have recently shown robust growth. While no single standard exists for what constitutes a green bond, the equity fund Blackrock (2020) reports an estimated $700 billion of green bonds outstanding – less than 1 per cent of the size of the global bond market (about $128.3 trillion). Nevertheless, these kinds of bonds have attracted much attention, and the largest equity and hedge fund companies' home pages trumpet their interest in financing climate sustainability. In the APR, China is one of the large issuers globally; other countries have done issues on a much smaller scale, including Indonesia, the Philippines, Singapore and Thailand, even though the attractiveness of green bonds suffers in comparison with standard bonds given their higher costs to the issuer (O'Donnellan, 2019).

The SDG bond has emerged as a new and significant type, with its first example in an offering that UNDP (2020) helped to facilitate in September 2020, generating substantial interest. Because a key feature of the first SDG bond involves domestic economic reforms, questions that bedevilled the conditional lending that IFIs undertook as part of the structural adjustment effort in the 1980s and 1990s resurface. In those years, indebtedness in exchange for economic reforms did facilitate a faster rate of access to foreign exchange but did not necessarily bring about the necessary increase in output and domestic incomes required to service external debt. In the case of structural adjustment loans, trade liberalization was supposed to bolster exports performance (for example), but such increases did not materialize in a timely manner, and the loans instead resulted in higher external debt[20] when imports increased much faster.

In the case of climate finance, the main issue – paralleling the one that authorities should have paid attention to in the case of structural adjustment – concerns timing: the point when shadow prices from environmental considerations will generate actual user payments and additional tax revenues, making it possible to service the green or the SDG bonds. How much longer will fossil-fuel prices remain low in actually existing markets? These considerations also argue for giving more attention to adaptation and loss-and-damage projects, which may generate user fees or savings in terms of avoided damage from climate disasters.

International private debt markets also still bear the same pitfalls as in the past, though now with a greater variety of lenders and investors. The main drawback is the debtor-bearing-all default-risk feature, as in other external funding instruments. In an important sense, and even as green bonds have already become more expensive to the issuer, these debt instruments are mispriced, in that they do not reflect the possibility of restructuring and debt service delays if the underlying assumptions prove overly optimistic.

Asian-Pacific countries must consider restricting external borrowing for climate finance to those portions of a project or programme that genuinely require hard currency: for instance, features requiring imports. Relying on green bonds or SDG bonds to fund chronic trade deficits that externally obtained resources will not directly alleviate could eventually prove inimical to climate action.

Debt restructuring for climate finance

Since the developing country debt crises of the 1980s, various mechanisms have been proposed that might generate climate finance.

Debt-for-nature swaps

The periodic onset of developing country debt crisis has elicited debt-for-nature swap proposals; a few of these have been tried, with mixed results (Fresnillo, 2020; Kessel, 2006). While debt swaps for environment projects could serve as part of the climate finance toolkit of those Asian-Pacific countries in need of debt restructuring, they call for very judicious use to avoid the pitfalls of previous projects.

Almost all debt-restructuring operations have involved the swapping of one bond for another – a debt-for-debt swap, with the new debt extinguishing a portion of previous debt service obligations but with an upgraded seniority status. Debt-for-nature swaps apply to specific loans and projects, instead of involving an overall (national) debt workout; in this lies the basis of many of their difficulties. These kinds of swaps came from suggestions made by the international environmental movement. Their pitfalls and vulnerabilities have generated a longstanding literature arising from public priority distortions. Solving the debt-servicing problems of a particular loan or project raises the priority of that project in the universe of domestic economic priorities. In many cases, these kinds of swaps create privileged claims for certain policies and for specific sectors in the domestic economy whose agendas coincide with the interests of the foreign financing party, but not necessarily with domestic priorities. Indebted countries should only consider such swaps if they are willing to reorder domestic priorities in their favour.

Swaps raise the issue of the role of policy conditionality. These debt manoeuvres have often required the mediation of international financial institutions whose policy preferences may clash with those of distressed sovereign states. There are cases where these swap projects have ridden roughshod over the rights of indigenous groups, as have other foreign-funded projects, especially since national governments may pay little attention to these local issues, such as the need for a livelihood (Bryant and Bailey, 1997).

Because of their complex payment schedules, there could be cases where a straight write down of the face value of the debtor country's external liability could free more resources for climate action than a debt-for-nature swap. Swaps can also create claims on future public current expenditures if they trigger yet-unbudgeted operating and enforcement activities.

Voluntary debt buybacks

Developing country debt crises create opportunities for voluntary debt buybacks. Savings from debt buybacks can go towards financing climate action, as recently proposed by Stiglitz and Rashid (2020). A voluntary debt buyback takes advantage of the discount on the face value of sovereign debt paper. Stiglitz and Rashid (2020) propose a Bretton Woods-mediated process. The IMF can play a central role by purchasing developing country bonds at the discount, perhaps funded through its New Agreements to Borrow facility or donations of SDRs. Such an approach to a debt crisis offers the advantage of avoiding the austerity measures often required for countries in distress to maintain debt service.

Stiglitz and Rashid (2020: 19) further propose an alternative conditionality – that debtors "agree to spend the savings on creating and promoting global public goods", in which they include public health expenditures and climate change mitigation and adaptation (but not loss-and-damage). They argue that this will enhance donor buy-in and inhibit creditors whose bonds do not receive buyback from resorting to litigation. Nothing would prevent developing countries from buying their own bonds using the resources they have on hand, for example using some of their international reserves, especially with steep discounts available. This will create climate finance space in the future at the cost of drawing down current reserves.

Unlike a new-issue SDR, voluntary debt buybacks do not create additional fiscal space instantaneously. They have usually appeared in debt restructuring processes involving conflicts with private creditors or with credit-rating agencies. These agencies have the power to determine the market basis of such actions – that is, whether they are truly voluntary or the equivalent of a default that could affect the indebted country's credit standing. Even with the bespoke participation of a market-maker, such as the IMF, credit rating agencies could very well classify a buyback as a loan restructuring, effectively a default, just as in the case of the Brady bond swaps in the late 1980s (Federal Reserve System, 2011). Furthermore, in previous experiences (most recently for Greece), news of the possibility of a generous buyback shrank the discount and thus the level of debt reduction achieved, although that did not prevent large hedge funds from making enormous asset gains from the transaction by buying early at the lower price (Thomas, 2012).

Special drawing rights-facilitated climate finance

SDRs are international reserve assets of the 189 member states of the IMF. SDRs are not issued by the IMF staff but by IMF-member countries, as provisions to increase their supply of bank reserves useful for international transactions. Countries can use SDRs to meet external financing needs, help ward off financial crises and balance-of-payments crises, and maintain the confidence of financial markets.

New issues of SDRs

SDRs are a liability of the IMF, which is a cooperative, rather than the debt of any single country. The IMF pays interest on SDRs based on the weighted average of the short-term rates of the five currencies in the SDR basket (US dollar, Euro, Japanese yen, pound sterling, Chinese renminbi). Developing countries pay much higher interest rates on their external borrowings. Newly issued SDRs thus provide developing countries access to the holiest of holies, usually only reserved to the world's largest economies – expansion of their fiscal space using international resources at the lowest interest rates possible.

The standard method of SDR allocation follows existing quotas, which means that countries with more votes in the IMF get considerably more resources. Industrialized countries, with their greater weight of IMF votes, will receive an overwhelming proportion of a standard SDR distribution (Mnuchin, 2020). However, large SDR distributions may have considerable scope without risking global inflation, as suggested in a study commissioned by the IMF that finds the probability of SDRs igniting global inflation highly unlikely, with other factors serving as more important determinants (Cooper, 2011). Larger SDR distributions can augment the reserves of the smaller countries, which can convert these new reserves to hard currency for financing climate action, without taking on more debt.

Another possibility is the use of SDRs as asset backing for the issuance of international bonds to finance climate action, as explored in Bredenkamp and Patillo (2010). IMF member states could authorize issuance of new SDRs for this purpose. Countries that do not need their SDRs could donate their balances as equity to the fund. Such a fund would borrow on international capital markets and on-lend the resources for climate projects.

A third possibility would be to issue SDRs independent of the IMF quota allocation, as proposed by the Group of 77 (G77) and China at the United Nations 'Conference on the World Financial and Economic Crisis and Its Impact on Development' (24–30 June 2009, New York). Both this kind of action, and one for a new SDR issuance beyond the current capital corpus of the IMF, will require US Congressional approval. However, the executive branch of the United States can vote for an amount equal to the IMF's capital (around SDR 500) and only requires notification of Congress.

As an example, in response to the COVID-19 pandemic, an overwhelming majority of IMF members supported a call for a new issuance of SDRs in 2020. With its 16.5 per cent voting weight in the IMF, and seigniorage advantages in the global payments system, the United States has an essential role in situations when SDRs are urgently needed. Under its new administration, the United States joined other IMF members so that on 23 August 2021, a new general allocation of SDR 500 billion (about $650 billion) became effective (IMF, 2021). This sets a precedent for further new allocations.

SDR facilities to bolster climate financing could increase soon

At the COP26 in November 2021, Barbados Prime Minister Mia Mottley called for another new, annual SDR issuance of $500 billion for 20 years to be applied to climate finance (Worley, 2021). New SDR issuances can support climate finance in two ways – first on a country-by-country basis, second as backing to raise international finance. The first option would provide hard currency resources for Asian-Pacific countries without creating new debt. The second one would create a pool of funds that provide a lending facility.

Should the prime minister's proposal find concurrence, it could finance a significant proportion of the commitment made by developed countries in 2010 under the UNFCC (United Nations, 2011a) to provide $100 billion annually in climate finance beginning in 2020, a deadline they missed.

The most climate-secure path to turn this proposal into a reality would start with a decision of the country-Parties in the UNFCCC. That would be followed by the IMF board of governors enacting the annual SDR distribution to its members (who are the same country-Parties), because new SDR distributions require an 85 per cent majority of weighted IMF-member votes in order to be accepted. Once again, the United States, which controls 16.5 per cent of the weighted votes, must be part of this UNFCCC and IMF decision.

Such an SDR distribution, when distributed in the standard way according to quotas of member states, would be deposited as additional balances in IMF members' international reserves. When distributed according to existing quotas, the group of developing countries would receive 39.5 per cent of the issuance. Because the resources originate with the UNFCCC, the developing countries would be morally bound to apply them to climate action.

Developed countries would be similarly bound to apply their share of the new resources to financing climate action in developing countries. The developed countries could either donate these resources directly to an IMF-managed trust fund or they could make grants directly to developing countries, using facilities mediated by the IMF. The advantage of direct grants is that they do not require conditionality and do not increase developing-country debt.

POLITICAL ECONOMY CONSIDERATIONS

This analysis rests on the premise that the structural features of the international financial system severely hamper climate finance options. Developing economies in the APR must contend with high financing costs for their physical climate investments because they must compete with the higher returns available to their private investors. The remedies proposed in this chapter, beyond a proliferation of genuinely national climate action plans, call for greater regulation of international capital flows, strengthened tax systems and support from authorities in the APR for reformed sovereign-debt processes and increased use of SDRs. As an analysis addressed to the APR, these proposals carry important political economy considerations.

While the APR is not a dominant venue of financial centres, a few of its countries have sought to expand their reach and ascendancy in these markets. These countries would tend towards scepticism and hostility to greater national interventions regarding capital flows, in taxation and sovereign-debt resolution reforms. This chapter argues that the proposed remedies would not only be appropriate for financing climate action; they would also prove necessary for the long-term sustainability and efficiency of international financial markets.

The differences among sovereign states in the APR also arise from dissimilar notions about what constitutes efficiency in international markets, or about the most effective strategies for development. Even with these differences, more detailed research can inform progress towards action – for example, on the borrowing rate needed to finance physical investments that reduce the cost of extreme weather damage. From this basis, the APR may to consider how to facilitate finance for such requirements.

Most probably, authorities in the APR will wade into financing climate action within the existing financial system. In 2021, interest rates have begun to rise in response to indicators of a solid economic recovery in the United States; this will raise external funding costs in developing countries (Adrian, 2021). Higher external funding costs will increase the probability of debt restructuring events in developing countries, a trend which had already begun in 2020 (Munevar, 2021). There is a non-zero probability of a global financial crisis beginning in 2022 if real economic recovery in industrialized countries proves unexpectedly strong. Authorities in the APR should move quickly towards a more proactive stance in addressing the sufficiency of climate finance and placing their financial sectors on a surer footing.

ACKNOWLEDGEMENTS

Comments and suggestions on earlier drafts from Kanni Wignaraja, Balazs Horvath and Swarnim Waglé are gratefully acknowledged.

NOTES

1.   Excluding earthquakes, landslides and dry-mass earth movements.
2.   Countries not included did not have enough of the data needed to apply the methodology.
3.   These countries also fall into Poverty Reduction and Growth Trust fund (PRGT) eligible grouping of the IMF.
4.   The UNFCC has not agreed on an official definition and this formulation is from Warner et al. (2012). For more information, see Durand and Huq (2013).
5.   Financing innovations through options pricing or contingent bonds to cover exposure to catastrophic natural event remain in an 'experimental' stage.
6.   In the IFC (2020) list, it is difficult to differentiate mitigation from adaptation investments, but the analysis here treats headings with greater adaptation content as adaptation projects.
7.   The countries included in the estimates were Bangladesh, Bhutan, India, Maldives, Nepal and Sri Lanka.
8.   Exposure to the sun's rays.
9.   This rule, instituted in the 1930s to obviate stock market speculation in company shares, was weakened in the United States' Reagan administration to encourage savings and financial investment. Along with the Friedmanesque (1970) admonition that the sole social responsibility of private companies is to increase profits, and the tying of management compensation to the company's share price, the rule change fostered management obsession with manoeuvres, such as stock buybacks and mergers and acquisitions involving substantial job cuts. As a result, companies have redirected profits towards supporting share prices without increasing physical capital investments by the enterprise (Lazonick, 2014).
10. For more information, see Caballero, Farhi and Gourinchas (2008).
11. Interest rates on sovereign bonds fluctuate according to global market conditions and increase on countries with lower credit ratings. For rates during a period of abundant liquidity and low interest rates, see Presbiteroa et al. (2016). Interest for

most developing country sovereign borrowing has increased with the pandemic (Chilkoti, 2020).

12. Greece as an international debtor is a recent example. See, among many other narratives, Nelson, Belkin and Jackson (2017) in which the persistent debt resolution issue always revolved around whether Greece would be able to meet the next payment owed to external creditors.

13. 'Domestic' is important here to preclude violating national treatment obligations in the World Trade Organization (WTO) and other trade obligations.

14. For more information, see European Commission (2020). This discussion will only intensify in the coming years.

15. For a contrary view – that markets augmented by freedom to contract already take care of externalities arising from corporate activities – see Fama (2020).

16. Note that capital controls should remain available even in normal times, in order to reinstate monetary and fiscal policy tools that industrialized country authorities have increasingly made available (Montes, 2013b). See also Shaw and Eidelman's (2011) elaboration.

17. Eligibility included the least-developed countries and those participating in the PRGT or Poverty Reduction and Growth Trust (PRGT), a concessional lending vehicle of the International Monetary Fund.

18. In November 2020, the G20 began replacing the DSSI with the Common Framework for Debt Treatments Beyond the DSSI, applicable to the countries qualifying for DSSI but now recognizing the need for debt restructurings (euphemistically termed 'debt treatments') to address solvency issues whilst DSSI only dealt with liquidity shortfalls (Ministry of the Economy and Finance, 2020).

19. For a listing of the existing funds, see Henrich Böll Stiftung and ODI (2020).

20. See, for example, Kızılgöl and ipek (2014) for Turkey and Zafar and Butt (2008) for Pakistan.

REFERENCES

Adrian, T. 2021. 'An Asynchronous and Divergent Recovery May Put Financial Stability at Risk'. IMF Blog, 6 April. blogs.imf.org/2021/04/06/an-asynchronous-and-divergent-recovery-may-put-financial-stability-at-risk/.

Asian Development Bank (ADB). 2011. *Asia 2050: Realizing the Asian Century*. Manila: Asian Development Bank.

———. 2017. *A Region at Risk: The Human Dimensions of Climate Change in Asia and the Pacific*. Manila: Asian Development Bank.

———. 2019. *Asian Development Outlook 2019: Strengthening Disaster Resilience*. Manila: Asian Development Bank.

———. 2020. 'Climate Change and Disasters in Asia and the Pacific'. Manila: Asian Development Bank. adb.org/news/infographics/climate-change-and-disasters-asia-and-pacific.

Auffhammer, M. 2019. 'The (Economic) Impacts of Climate Change: Some Implications for Asian Economies'. ADBI working paper, 1051, Asian Development Bank Institute, Tokyo. adb.org/sites/default/files/publication/543321/adbi-wp1051.pdf.

Baldwin, R. 2016. *The Great Convergence Information Technology and the New Globalization.* Cambridge MA: Harvard University Press.

Bryant, R. and Bailey, S. 1997. *Third World Political Ecology: An Introduction.* London: Routledge.

Bredenkamp, H. and Pattillo, C. 2010. *Financing the Response to Climate Change.* Washington, DC: International Monetary Fund.

Burke, M., Hsiang, S. M. and Miguel, E. 2015. 'Global Non-Linear Effect of Temperature on Economic'. *Nature* 527, 235–239.

Caballero, R. J. and Farhi, E. 2017. 'The Safety Trap'. Cambridge, MA: National Bureau of Economic Research. nber.org/papers/w19927.

Caballero, R. J., Farhi, E. and Gourinchas, P.-O. 2008. 'An Equilibrium Model of "Global Imbalances" and Low Interest Rates'. *American Economic Review* 98(1), 358–393.

Caldecott, B., Howarth, N. and McSharry, P. 2013. *Stranded Assets in Agriculture: Protecting Value from Environment-Related Risks.* Oxford: Smith School of Enterprise and the Environment, University of Oxford. smithschool.ox.ac.uk/publications/reports/stranded-assets-agriculture-report-final.pdf.

Carney, M. 2015. 'Breaking the Tragedy of the Horizon – Climate Change and Financial Stability'. Bank of England, 29 September. bankofengland.co.uk/-/media/boe/files/speech/2015/breaking-the-tragedy-of-the-horizon-climate-change-and-financial-stability.pdf.

Chilkoti, A. 2020. 'Investors Buy Up Debt from Stronger Developing Countries'. *Wall Street Journal*, 26 August.

Climate Analytics. 2019. *Decarbonising South and South East Asia: Shifting Energy Supply in South Asia and South East Asia to Non-fossil Fuel-based Energy Systems in Line with the Paris Agreement Long-term Temperature Goal and Achievement of Sustainable Development Goals.* Berlin: Climate Analytics. climateanalytics.org/media/decarbonisingasia2019-fullreport-climateanalytics.pdf.

Coady, D., Parry, I., Le, N.-P. and Shang, B. 2019. *Global Fossil Fuel Subsidies Remain Large: An Update Based on Country-Level Estimates.* Washington, DC: International Monetary Fund.

Crane, K. and Mao, Z. 2015. *Costs of Selected Policies to Address Air Pollution in China.* Santa Monica, CA: RAND Corporation. rand.org/content/dam/rand/pubs/research_reports/RR800/RR861/RAND_RR861.pdf.

Durand, A. and Huq, S. 2013. 'A Simple Guide to the Warsaw International Mechanism on Loss and Damage'. United Nations Framework Convention on Climate Change, New York. unfccc.int/sites/default/files/resource/Online_Guide_feb_2020.pdf.

El-Erian, M. 2021. 'Private Lenders to Emerging Markets Face Threat Pressure Is Increasing on Creditors to Help Avoid Debt Traps'. *Financial Times*, 13 April. ft.com/content/00c824c5-3962-44da-8ac6-4efe1d0fd586.

European Commission. 2020. 'Commission Launches Public Consultations on Energy Taxation and a Carbon Border Adjustment Mechanism'. European Commission, Brussels. ec.europa.eu/taxation_customs/news/commission-launches-public-consultations-energy-taxation-and-carbon-border-adjustment-mechanism_en.

Fama, E. F. 2020. 'Market Forces Already Address ESG Issues and the Issues Raised by Stakeholder Capitalism'. In L. Zingales, J. Kasperkevic and A. Schechter, eds., *Milton*

Friedman 50 Years Later. Chicago, IL: ProMarket, 59–64. promarket.org/wp-content/uploads/2020/11/Milton-Friedman-50-years-later-ebook.pdf.

Federal Reserve System. 2011. 'Brady Bonds and Other Emerging-Markets Bonds Section 4255'. In *Trading and Capital-Markets Activities Manual*. Washington, DC: Board of Governors of the Federal Reserve System.

Fresnillo, I. 2020. 'A Tale of Two Emergencies: The Interplay of Sovereign Debt and Climate Crises in the Global South'. European Network on Debt and Development, Brussels. https://d3n8a8pro7vhmx.cloudfront.net/eurodad/pages/1945/attachments/original/1610462143/debt-and-climate-briefing-final.pdf.

Friedman, M. 1970. 'The Social Responsibility of Business Is to Increase Its Profits'. *New York Times Magazine*, 13 September. umich.edu/~thecore/doc/Friedman.pdf.

Fulton, L., Mejia, A., Arioli, M., Dematera, K. and Lah, O. 2017. 'Climate Change Mitigation Pathways for Southeast Asia: CO_2 Emissions Reduction Policies for the Energy and Transport Sectors'. *Sustainability* 9(1160).

Gaspar, V., Amaglobeli, D., Garcia-Escribano, M., Prady, D. and Soto, M. 2019. *Fiscal Policy and Development: Human, Social, and Physical Investment for the SDGs*. Washington, DC: International Monetary Fund.

Ghosh, A. R., Ostry, J. D. and Qureshi, M. S. 2016. 'When Do Capital Inflow Surges End in Tears?' *American Economic Review* 106(5), 581–585.

Glasgow Financial Alliance for Net Zero (GFANZ). 2021. 'Amount of Finance Committed to Achieving 1.5°C Now at Scale Needed to Deliver the Transition'. GFANZ Secretariat, New York. gfanzero.com/press/amount-of-finance-committed-to-achieving-1-5c-now-at-scale-needed-to-deliver-the-transition/.

Goodhart, C. and Pradhan, M. 2020. *The Great Demographic Reversal: Ageing Societies, Waning Inequality, and an Inflation Revival*. London: Palgrave Macmillan.

Griffith-Jones, S. and Ocampo, J. A. 2018. *The Future of National Development Banks*. Oxford: Oxford University Press.

Gu, Y., Wong, T. W., Law, C. K., Dong, G. H., Ho, K. F., Yang, Y. and Yim, S. H. L. 2018. 'Impacts of Sectoral Emissions in China and the Implications: Air Quality, Public Health, Crop Production, and Economic Costs'. *Environmental Research Letters* 13(8). doi.org/10.1088/1748-9326/aad138.

Haraguchi, M. and Lall, U. 2015. 'Flood Risks and Impacts: A Case Study of Thailand's Floods in 2011 and Research Questions for Supply Chain Decision'. *International Journal of Disaster Risk Reduction* 14(3), 256–272.

Haque, A. K. E., Lohano, H. D., Mukhopadhyay, P., Nepal, M., Shafeeqa, F., Vidanage, S. P. 2019. 'NDC Pledges of South Asia: Are the Stakeholders Onboard?' *Climatic Change* 155, 237–244.

Henrich Böll Stiftung and Overseas Development Institute (ODI). 2020. 'Climate Funds Update, The Funds'. Overseas Development Institute, London. climatefundsupdate.org/the-funds/.

Horn, S., Reinhart, C. and Trebesch, C. 2020. 'China's Overseas Lending'. Kiel working paper 2132, Kiel Institute for the World Economy, Kiel.

International Energy Agency (IEA). 2020. 'Value of Fossil Fuel Consumption Subsidies, 2010-2020'. International Energy Agency, Paris. iea.org/data-and-statistics/charts/value-of-fossil-fuel-consumption-subsidies-2010-2020.

International Finance Corporation (IFC). 2020. *Climate Investment Opportunities in South Asia*. Washington, DC: The World Bank Group.

International Monetary Fund (IMF). 2021. 'IMF Managing Director Announces the US$650 billion SDR Allocation Comes into Effect'. International Monetary Fund, Washington, DC. imf.org/en/News/Articles/2021/08/23/pr21248-imf-managing-director-announces-the-us-650-billion-sdr-allocation-comes-into-effect.

Kaiser, J. and Kopper, E. 2020. 'Debt Relief? Thanks, but No Thanks'. *IPS Journal* (28 September). ips-journal.eu/topics/foreign-and-security-policy/debt-relief-thanks-but-no-thanks-4671/.

Kelsey, J., Bush, J., Montes, M. and Ndubai, J. 2020. *How 'Digital Trade' Rules Would Impede Taxation of the Digitalised Economy in the Global South*. Penang: Third World Network. twn.my/title2/latestwto/general/News/Digital%20Tax.pdf.

Kessel, A. 2006. *Debt-for-Nature Swaps: A Critical Approach*. Saint Paul, MN: Macalester University. macalester.edu/geography/wp-content/uploads/sites/18/2012/03/kessel.pdf.

Kızılgöl, Ö. A. and Pike, E. 2014. 'An Empirical Evaluation of the Relationship between Trade Openness and External Debt: Turkish Case'. *International Econometric Review* 6(1), 42–58.

Kose, M. A. and Prasad, E. 2020. *Capital Accounts: Liberalize or Not?* Washington, DC: International Monetary Fund.

Lazonick, W. 2014. 'Profits without Prosperity'. *Harvard Business Review*, September. hbr.org/2014/09/profits-without-prosperity.

Mackenzie, K. 2021. 'Uneven Channels'. *Phenomenal World*, 30 October. phenomenalworld.org/analysis/cop26-finance-climate-governance/.

Mian, A. R., Straub, L. and Sufi, A. 2020. 'Indebted Demand'. National Bureau of Economic Research, Cambridge, MA. nber.org/papers/w26940.

Ministry of the Economy and Finance. 2020. 'The Common Framework for Debt Treatment beyond the DSSI'. Government of Italy, Rome. mef.gov.it/en/G20-Italy/common-framework.html.

Mnuchin, S. T. 2020. 'U.S. Treasury Secretary Steven T. Mnuchin's Joint IMFC and Development Committee Statement, 982'. United States Treasury, Washington, DC. home.treasury.gov/news/press-releases/sm982.

Montes, M. F. 1998. *The Currency Crisis in Southeast Asia*, Updated Edition. Singapore: Institute of Southeast Asian Studies.

———. 2013a. *Climate Change Financing Requirements of Developing Countries*. Geneva: South Centre.

———. 2013b. 'Capital Controls, Investment Chapters, and Asian Development Objectives'. In *Capital Account Regulations and the Trading System: A Compatibility Review*. Boston, MA: Frederick S. Pardee Center for International Futures, 91–100. networkideas.org/wp-content/uploads/2016/08/CAR_Trading_System.pdf.

———. 2016. *UN-Prinzipien für den fairen Umgang mit überschuldeten Staaten* (UN Adopts Nine Basic Principles on Sovereign Debt Restructuring). In M. Haasler, J.Hollenhorst, J. Kaiser. M. Liebal, K. Rehbein and K. Schilde, eds., *2016 Schuldenreport Debt 20*. Dusseldorf: Entwicklung braucht Entschuldung, 32–34. erlassjahr.de/wordpress/wp-content/uploads/2016/03/Schuldenreport-2016.pdf.

————. 2017a. 'Indonesia's 1997–1998 Economic Crisis: A Teachable Case Wasted'. In J. P. Bohoslavsky and K. Raffer, eds., *Sovereign Debt Crises*. Cambridge: Cambridge University Press, 123–142.

————. 2017. 'Public–Private Partnerships as the Answer . . . What Was the Question?' Inter Press Service, 26 September. ipsnews.net/2017/09/public-private-partnerships-answer-question/.

Montes, M. F. and Williams, M. 2017. 'Common but Differentiated Responsibilities: Which Way Forward?' *Development* 59(1), 114–120.

Montes, M. F., Uribe, D. and Danish. 2018. 'Stemming "Commercial" Illicit Financial Flows and Developing Country Innovations in the Global Tax Reform Agenda'. South Centre, Geneva. https://www.southcentre.int/research-paper-87-november-2018/.

Munevar, D. 2021. 'A Debt Pandemic Is Engulfing the Global South'. *IPS Journal Europe* (15 April). ips-journal.eu/topics/economy-and-ecology/a-debt-pandemic-is-engulfing-the-global-south-5114/.

Nelson, R. M., Belkin, P. and Jackson, J. K. 2017. 'The Greek Debt Crisis: Overview and Implications for the United States'. In *CRS Report Prepared for Members and Committees of Congress*. Washington, DC: Congressional Research Service.

Noland, M. 2007. 'South Korea's Experience with International Capital Flows'. In S. Edwards, ed., *Capital Controls and Capital Flows in Emerging Economies: Policies, Practices and Consequences*. Chicago: University of Chicago. nber.org/books/edwa06-1.

O'Donnellan, R. 2019. 'Green Bonds Are Growing Fast – But There Are Challenges'. *Intuition*, 21 October. intuition.com/green-bonds-are-growing-fast-but-there-are-challenges/.

Ostry, J. D., Ghosh, A. R., Habermeier, K., Laeven, L., Chamon, M., Qureshi, M. S. and Kokenyne, A. 2011. *Managing Capital Inflows: What Tools to Use?* Washington, DC: International Monetary Fund.

Ostry, J. D., Loungani, P. and Furceri, D. 2016. 'Neoliberalism: Oversold?' *IMF Finance and Development*. https://www.imf.org/external/pubs/ft/fandd/2016/06/pdf/ostry.pdf.

Park, J. 2011. 'From "Cardinal Sin" to Policy Agenda? The Role of Capital Controls in Emerging Market Economies: A Study of the Korean Case, 1997–2011'. *Emerging Voices* 22, 7–20. keia.org/sites/default/files/publications/emergingvoices_final_junepark.pdf.

Presbiteroa, A. F., Ghurab, D., Adedejib, O. S. and Njeb, L. 2016. 'Sovereign Bonds in Developing Countries: Drivers of Issuance and Spreads'. *Review of Development Finance* 6(2016), 1–15.

Reuters. 2020. 'Factbox: How the G20's Debt Service Suspension Initiative Works'. 15 October. reuters.com/article/us-imf-worldbank-emerging-debtrelief-fac/factbox-how-the-g20s-debt-service-suspension-initiative-works-idUSKBN27021V.

Shaw, W. and Eidelman, V. 2011. 'Why Are Capital Controls So Popular?' In U. Dadush and V. Eidelman, eds., *Currency Wars*. Washington, DC: Carnegie Endowment for International Peace, 33–38.

Stern, N. 2006. *The Economics of Climate Change: The Stern Review*. Cambridge: Cambridge University Press.

————. 2015. 'Economic Development, Climate and Values: Making Policy'. *Proceedings of the Royal Society* 282(20150820). dx.doi.org/10.1098/rspb.2015.0820.

Thomas, L. Jr. 2012. 'Buying Back Greek Debt Rewarded Hedge Funds'. *New York Times*, 23 December. nytimes.com/2012/12/24/business/global/greek-bond-buyback-may-have-been-cheaper-under-collective-action-clause.html

United Nations (UN). 2011a. *World Economic and Social Survey 2011: The Great Green Technological Transformation*. New York: United Nations.

———. 2011b. 'Cancun Accord. Decision 1/CP.16. UN Framework Convention on Climate Change (UNFCCC), 11 March'. United Nations, New York. unfccc.int/sites/default/files/resource/docs/2010/cop16/eng/07a01.p.

———. 2015. 'Transforming Our World: The 2030 Agenda for Sustainable Development'. United Nations, New York. https://documents-dds-ny.un.org/doc/UNDOC/GEN/N15/291/89/PDF/N1529189.pdf.

———. 2020. *Inter-agency Task Force on Financing for Development, Financing for Sustainable Development Report 2019*. New York: United Nations. developmentfinance.un.org/fsdr2020.

United Nations Development Programme (UNDP). 2020. 'Historic $890 Million Sustainable Development Goals Bond Issued by Mexico'. United Nations Development Programme, New York. undp.org/content/undp/en/home/news-centre/news/2020/Historic_890_million_SDG_Bond_issued_by_Mexico.html.

Volz, U., Beirne, J., Preudhomme, N. A., Fenton, A., Mazzacurati, E., Renzhi, N. and Stampe, J. 2020. *Climate Change and Sovereign Risk*. London: University of London. doi.org/10.25501/SOAS.00033524.

Wall Street Journal. 2021. 'G-20 Backs Tax Overhaul That Makes Rich Countries Big Winners'. 30 October. wsj.com/articles/g-20-to-back-tax-overhaul-that-makes-rich-countries-big-winners-11635586202.

Warner, K., Kreft, S., Zissener, M., Höppe, P., Bals, C., Loster, T., Linnerooth-Bayer, J., Tschudi, S., Fursenko, E., Haas, A., Young, S., Kovacs, P., Dlugolecki, A. and Oxley, A. 2012a. *Insurance Solutions in the Context of Climate Change-Related Loss and Damage*. Munich: Munich Climate Insurance Initiative.

Warner, K., van der Geest, K. and Kreft, S. 2012b. *Evidence from the Frontlines of Climate Change: Loss and Damage to Communities Despite Coping and Adaptation*. New York: United Nations University Institute for Environment and Human Security. collections.unu.edu/eserv/UNU:1847/pdf10584.pdf.

Weng, E. 2020. 'How Green Is Your Bond?' BlackRock, New York. blackrock.com/us/individual/insights/how-green-is-your-bond.

Wester, P., Mishra, A., Mukherji, A. and Shrestha, A. B., eds. 2019. *The Hindu Kush Himalaya Assessment: Mountains, Climate Change, Sustainability and People*. Cham: Springer Nature. springer.com/gp/book/9783319922874.

Williams, M. 2019. *The State of Play of Climate Finance: UNFCCC Funds and the $100 Billion Question*. Geneva: South Centre.

World Bank. 2015. 'From Billions to Trillions: MDB Contributions to Financing for Development.' The World Bank Group, Washington, DC. worldbank.org/mdgs/documents/FfD-MDB-Contributions-July-13-2015.pdf.

World Bank and International Monetary Fund (IMF). 2019. 'Lao People's Democratic Republic: Joint World Bank–IMF Debt Sustainability Analysis'. The World Bank Group, Washington, DC. openknowledge.worldbank.org/handle/10986/32557.

Worley, W. (2021). 'COP 26 World Leaders Summit: 5 Takeaways for the Development Sector'. *Devex*, 1 November. devex.com/news/cop-26-world-leaders-summit-5-takeaways-for-the-development-sector-101972.

Zafar, S. and Butt, M. S. 2008. 'Impact of Trade Liberalization on External Debt Burden: Econometric Evidence from Pakistan'. Munich Personal RePEc Archive, 9548. mpra. ub.uni-muenchen.de/9548/.

2 | Melting Glaciers, Threatened Livelihoods

Confronting Climate Change to Save the Third Pole

Arnico K. Panday

INTRODUCTION

Earth's third largest storage of frozen water after Antarctica and the Arctic[1] lies in the high mountains of Asia. This has prompted the region's nickname: the Third Pole.[2] Centred on the Tibetan Plateau, this region contains every peak on Earth taller than 7,000 metres. The Himalayan arc flanks the region's south, starting from northern Myanmar in the east, spanning several thousand kilometres (km) to the southern edge of the Tibetan Plateau, the northern edge of northeast India, and across Bhutan, Sikkim, Nepal and the western Himalayan states of India. Separated from the Western Himalaya by the arid Ladakh Valley, the Karakoram range extends north-westwards, connecting to the Hindu Kush Mountains on the Afghanistan–Pakistan border. Together these ranges form the Hindu Kush Karakoram Himalaya (HKH). The Hengduan and Quilian Mountains sit at the eastern side of the Tibetan Plateau, with the Kunlun on the northwest and north. The Pamir Mountains extend north from the Hindu Kush, shared by Afghanistan, China, Kyrgyzstan and Tajikistan. Further north are the Tien Shan Mountains, shared by China, Kazakhstan and Kyrgyzstan, and extending eastwards around the northern edge of the arid Tarim Basin. Figure 2.1 shows a map of High Mountain Asia and its sub-regions.

High Mountain Asia's frozen water, its cryosphere, is stored in several different forms, including in snowfields, glaciers, permafrost and seasonal ice on lakes and rivers. In 2015, glaciers covered almost 100,000 square km^3 of High Mountain Asia, containing 3,000-4,700 cubic km of ice (Bolch et al., 2019), with just under half in the Himalaya and Karakoram (Nie et al., 2021). During winters, large parts of High Mountain Asia experience snowfall, while many lakes and high altitude stretches of rivers freeze. When glaciers retreat, vacated depressions often fill with water, forming glacial lakes. The exact number of glacial lakes is not firmly established, and

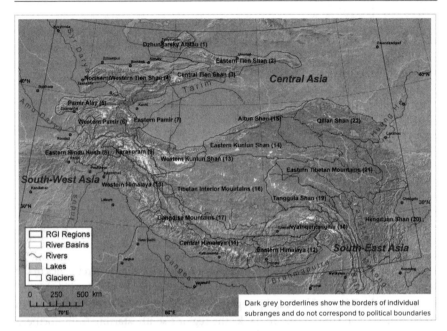

Figure 2.1   The individual mountain ranges of High Mountain Asia
Source: Wester et al. (2019).

varies in time; estimates range from 4,260 to 8,200 for the HKH region, including 1,466 to 2,323 lakes in Nepal alone (Bolch et al., 2019).

Sometimes called the Water Tower of Asia (Immerzeel et al., 2010), or of the World (Xu et al., 2008), the Third Pole cryosphere plays a critical role in regulating the water supply over a large region. Glaciers and snowmelt supply key sources of dry-season water in the 10 major river systems that originate in the HKH (Scott et al., 2019): the Amu Darya, Brahmaputra, Ganges, Indus, Irrawaddy, Mekong, Salween, Tarim, Yangtse and Yellow (Sharma et al., 2019).

Cryospheric storage and dry-season release of water provide vital support for agriculture, hydroelectricity and drinking water (Nie et al., 2021). Over 240 million people live in the region's mountains; 1.7 billion live in the river basins downstream, while food grown in these river basins reaches 3 billion people (Sharma et al., 2019). Anthropogenic climate change has caused much of the Third Pole cryosphere to melt rapidly, with potentially far-reaching consequences. With a few exceptions, the area and the volume of glaciers has steadily decreased throughout the region. While the melting cryosphere of High Mountain Asia has far-reaching downstream impacts, this takes place in the context of larger changes. The melting is driven by broader anthropogenic modifications of the atmosphere, and accompanied by broader impacts of these modifications. The Third Pole lies downwind from some of the most heavily polluted places on Earth. Air pollutants do not only threaten health, agriculture and the global climate, but they also contribute directly to changing precipitation and melting of the cryosphere. The monsoon system itself is also sensitive to climate change and air pollution.

The same solutions that will clean up the region's air and dampen other aspects of climate change will also protect High Mountain Asia's cryosphere and prevent the disasters that are a direct result of its melting. Such solutions require coordinated actions from local to global levels (Box 2.1). Protecting the cryosphere of High Mountain Asia, and addressing interrelated issues needs a broadening of attention beyond climate adaptation to ambitious mitigation.

Box 2.1   Summary of problems and solutions

Current global emission trends are disastrous for High Mountain Asia, and would result in a loss of two-thirds of all glacier mass by the end of the century, accompanied by a range of other interconnected problems. The Paris Agreement's target of stabilizing global average temperatures at less than 2°C above pre-industrial is insufficient to protect the snow and ice of High Mountain Asia. In fact, even stabilizing the global average temperature at 1.5°C will be too warm, as that will still cause a warming of 1.8 to 2.2°C in High Mountain Asia, resulting in a loss of a third of the region's glacier mass by the end of the century. Investment in adaptation to the changing water availability due to Third Pole melting, and to broader impacts of climate change, will do much to protect the most vulnerable people and nations, but adaptation alone is insufficient. The melting of glaciers and snowfield of High Mountain Asia is driven by the global increase in greenhouse gases as well as by black carbon and other pollutants of regional origin. The same phenomena also drive the region's air pollution problem and changes in the monsoon. The shrinking of the glaciers and its impacts are not an isolated disaster, but a symptom and a symbol of a broader problem with how humans treat the atmosphere. To save High Mountain Asia's glaciers, clean up the region's air, protect the monsoon system and address climate change on a global level, the world's economy urgently needs to draw down greenhouse gases. It needs to stop using fossil fuels and also reduce emissions of black carbon and other short-lived climate pollutants. This calls not only for clean transport and power generation, but also for shifting billions of people to clean cooking and heating, bringing about major changes in agricultural practices and diets, and massively reducing open fires. It also requires a rethinking of urban spaces and promoting sustainable walkable cities. The United Nations Development Programme (UNDP) itself can play a major role, setting an example at its offices, educating politicians and voters about responsible leadership, and obtaining pledges from big technology firms. Protection of High Mountain Asia's snow and ice can become a unifying and politically neutral goal around which to build international cooperation and collaboration during the challenging decade ahead.

The Narrow Story: A Melting Third Pole and Its Impacts

This section summarizes current scientific knowledge on past, present and future changes in the Third Pole's cryosphere, and on the downstream impacts of these changes.

Observations and forecasts of the Third Pole cryosphere

Atmospheric temperatures around the globe have increased rapidly in recent decades and are projected to continue rising. A 140-year-old ice core record from a central Tibetan glacier shows several colder and warmer periods, with the strongest warming starting in the 1990s (Yang et al., 2008). Air temperature records from the Tibetan Plateau show significant warming beginning already in the 1950s (Liu and Chen, 2000), when global average temperatures remained relatively flat due to atmospheric dimming by heavy pollution in industrialized nations (Wild et al., 2007). Over the past two decades, temperature increases in High Mountain Asia have become more pronounced: Across the region, average temperatures increased by around 0.104°C per decade between 2001 and 2014 (Krishnan et al., 2019). By current projections, temperatures will continue to increase till mid-century, regardless of the climate scenario (Hock et al., 2019).

Model simulations predict that even if global average temperatures stabilize at 1.5°C above pre-industrial levels, at least 1.8°C of warming in the Himalaya and 2.2°C in the Karakoram will still occur (Krishnan et al., 2019). Temperatures in High Mountain Asia are rising faster than almost anywhere else on the globe except in the Arctic and Antarctic. Elevation-dependent warming (EDW) has been observed across the Tibetan Plateau and the HKH, whereby the higher you go, the more rapid the increase in temperature.[4]

Theory says that rising temperatures affect the cryosphere in several ways. First, a larger fraction of precipitation falls as rain rather than snow, at a higher altitude. Rain falling onto snow or ice surfaces causes rapid melting. With increasing average temperatures, the snow line[5] moves up, leaving progressively smaller snow 'islands' around the peaks. Finally, snowmelt already occurs earlier in the spring (Barnett et al., 2005).

The region's extreme geographic diversity means that cryosphere impacts vary significantly, with some places becoming more vulnerable than others. While the Himalaya receive four fifths of their snowfall during the summer monsoon, the Karakoram receive two thirds of their snowfall in winter as a result of westerly disturbances. The upper Indus Basin generally has more snow at lower elevations than the Himalaya (Bolch et al., 2019) and the glaciers in the Karakoram stretch down to lower elevations than in the Himalaya (Nie et al., 2021). Himalayan glaciers appear more sensitive to temperature increases because summer snowfall is more likely to turn into rain than winter snowfall (Bolch et al., 2012).

With the exception of parts of the Karakoram, eastern Pamir and western Kunlun, High Mountain Asia has experienced widespread decreases in both the area and volume of glaciers in the past three decades (Bolch et al., 2012; Nie et al., 2021). Glaciers in the Himalaya have been retreating since the mid-19th Century, although from the 1920s to the 1940s many remained stable. Glacial retreat accelerated in the 1990s (Bolch et al., 2012). Figure 2.2 represents the observed changes in glacier mass in different sub-regions pre- and post-2000, illustrating both the results and the limited availability of data.

The glaciers of the Karakoram also receded from the 1920s and early 1990s, just like glaciers elsewhere in the world, but since the mid-1990s a number of large glaciers have surged forward (Hewitt, 2005). Individual glaciers in the Karakoram sometimes rapidly surge forward and retreat again (Bolch et al., 2019). The Karakoram region has experienced an increase in precipitation and a small decrease in summer temperatures (Hewitt, 2005), which may explain the surge in glaciers. However, the western disturbances that bring snowfall to the Karakoram have shown increasing variability (Krishnan et al., 2019). Other mountain ranges in High Mountain Asia, including the Hengduan, the Qilian, the Tien Shan, as well as the

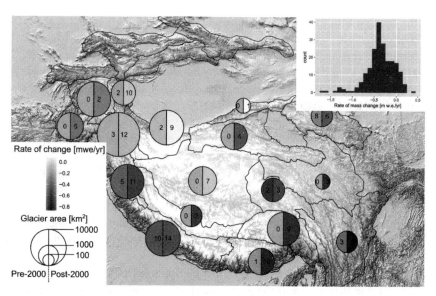

Figure 2.2   Changes in glacier mass in different subregions
Source: Wester et al. (2019).
Note: The circle size represents the glaciated area; the colour denotes the rate of change in metre water equivalent (MWE) per year pre-2000 and post-2000. Numbers inside the circles denote the number of studies available pre- and post-2000 for that region.

rest of the Pamir and Kunlun, have all seen reductions in both glacier mass and glacier area since around 1970 (Bolch et al., 2019).

Models forecast a loss of two-thirds of the HKH's glacial mass if current anthropogenic emissions trends continue (Bolch et al., 2019).[6] This model scenario (IPCC RCP8.5) assumes that economies will keep growing without significant greening. All modelled scenarios, regardless of emission assumptions, project continued loss of glacier mass in the near-term. All also project accelerated deglaciation in the Karakoram (Bolch et al., 2019). By mid-century, model results diverge on the rate of melting, depending on which IPCC emissions scenario for greenhouse gases they assume. In the IPCC RCP8.5 scenario, the extended region will lose two thirds of its glacial mass, with the eastern Himalaya seeing a near total loss of its glaciers (Bolch et al., 2019). While hope remains that mitigation can achieve the Paris Agreement target of not exceeding a temperature increase of 2°C, the IPCC special report on the impacts of global warming of 1.5°C makes clear the enormous difference in impacts between global temperatures stabilized at 1.5°C versus 2°C above pre-industrial levels (IPCC, 2018). This has inspired the global discourse to shift towards the aspiration of a 1.5°C world. But even this may not suffice for High Mountain Asia; *The Hindu Kush Himalaya Assessment*[7] points out that even if global average temperatures stabilize at 1.5°C above pre-industrial levels, High Mountain Asia would still likely lose one third of its glacier mass by the end of the century, with the Himalaya losing half of its glacier mass (Bolch et al., 2019; Wester et al., 2019).[8] Stabilizing temperatures at 1.5 °C above preindustrial is itself becoming increasingly unlikely as deep cuts to CO2 emissions are postponed (IPCC, 2021). In fact, even if countries were to fully honour all the commitments made as of the Summer of 2021, global average temperatures would still reach 2.7 °C above preindustrial levels by year 2100 (UNEP, 2021).

Glaciers are not the only shrinking part of the cryosphere. Seasonal snow cover has also decreased. While snow cover has strong interannual variability, it has clearly decreased at lower elevations, where precipitation has switched from snow to rain (Hock et al., 2019). The snow line – the altitude above which snow persists year-round – has gradually shifted to higher altitudes, leaving smaller areas snow-covered. Shrinkage of snow-covered areas and snow volume will likely continue in the coming decades in response to warming, with the snow line continuing to climb to higher elevations (Bolch et al., 2019). Figure 2.3 shows the loss of both glacier and snow cover on a prominent Himalayan peak.

A decrease in snow cover causes further climate impacts. The amount of snow on the Tibetan Plateau affects the plateau's reflectivity, and thus its surface heating and the strength of the low pressure that forms over the plateau. This has a strong impact on atmospheric circulation and on the Asian monsoon (Bolch et al., 2019).[9] Reduction in snow cover also creates a local feedback: When snow disappears from a small patch to reveal darker rock underneath, the surface albedo (reflectivity)

Figure 2.3   Mt Machhapuchhare in the Annapurna Himalaya in 1973 (a), 2011 (b), and 2021 (c, d)
Source: Photos by (a) Fritz Berger; (b) Arnico Panday; (c) and (d) Ananya Panday.
Note: In (c) massive high altitude forest fires obscured the views of the peak on 31 December 2020, while (d) shows the peak the next morning on 1 January 2021. Note that the glacier seen in the mountain's lap in 1973 has already been lost for more than a decade.

decreases and the dark rock absorbs more sunlight. This warms up the air above the dark rock, which comes into contact with nearby snow, melting it even faster.

The region's permafrost has also decreased, although fewer studies have documented this. Large portions of the Tibetan Plateau and high-altitude sections of the region's mountains have soil-water in frozen rather than liquid form. Below a certain depth, this remains frozen all year around, but near the surface, in places where summer temperatures rise above freezing, the uppermost soil layers thaw seasonally. Rising temperatures will likely thaw these soils to greater depths (Bolch et al., 2019).[10] In places with infrastructure built on top of permafrost, such as the highways and railroads on the Tibetan Plateau, thawing of soils can create undulations and other damage. Melting permafrost on steep slopes can trigger landslides and rockfalls (Hock et al., 2019); if these fall onto glacial lakes they can create waves that breach the moraines holding back the lakes (Bolch et al., 2019).

As glaciers have receded across the region, the number of glacial lakes has grown. Glacial lakes can grow rapidly, often held back by unstable moraine dams. When a moraine dam fails, a catastrophic glacial lake outburst flood (GLOF) drains the entire lake down the valley. 65 GLOFs have been recorded in the Himalaya since 1930 (Nie et al., 2021). GLOFs have destroyed roads, trails, houses, fields, hydropower plants and lives, as happened during the Dig Tsho GLOF in Nepal in 1985 (Hock et al., 2019).[11] Some glacial lakes in the region have grown rapidly, causing alarm (Fujita et al., 2009). While no consensus has yet arisen about whether data show an increasing occurrence of GLOF events in recent decades, there is consensus that the growth in number and size of glacial lakes increases the risks for the future (Nie et al., 2021). Twenty-one dangerous lakes have been identified in Nepal and 52 in India (Bolch et al., 2019). Emergency action averted a potential GLOF from Tso Rolpa Lake in Nepal in 2000, by constructing a siphon and an open channel that allowed a reduction in the lake's water level (Pokharel, n.d.).

The Third Pole is not unique. In mountainous regions around the world, the cryosphere is melting. Observations confirm alarming and ongoing decreases in the cryosphere from the Antarctic through the Andes, the Caucasus, the East African Highlands, the European Alps, New Zealand Alps, the Rockies and Scandinavian and north Asian mountains (Hock et al., 2019). The melting rates in High Mountain Asia are higher than the global average, but not overwhelmingly so. The difference from other mountainous regions is that the Third Pole contains a larger volume of frozen water, and the changes here affect a far larger number of people.

Downstream and human impacts of a melting Third Pole

A warming Third Pole, with a retreating cryosphere, affects water availability in the rivers downstream. Already by 2005, the HKH and its downstream river basins had caught attention as the global region where retreating glaciers would most critically affect water supply in the coming decades (Barnett et al., 2005). While changes in annual precipitation affect the annual total amount of water available in a basin, temperature change affects the fraction stored in frozen form rather than running off, and thus impacts the timing of water availability (Barnett et al., 2005). In basins with a cryosphere fed by winter snow, warming temperatures lead to the spring peak flow shifting to earlier in the season (Bolch et al., 2012).

The level of dependence on the cryosphere depends on the river basin. Rivers can have four potential sources of water: snow melt, glacier melt, rainfall and groundwater. Their proportional contributions vary at each point along a river, as well as in time (Shrestha et al., 2015). In the mountainous upper reaches of river basins, a large fraction of the water in streams and rivers might originate from the melting snow and glaciers. This fraction shrinks as one travels down the length of a river and more rain-fed tributaries join it (Bolch et al., 2012). The dependence on the cryosphere varies among river basins; for example, while only 9 per cent of the water reaching the delta of the Ganges originates in glaciers and snow, the Indus flows through a much more arid region, collecting far fewer rainfed tributaries: 78 per cent of the water at the mouth of the Indus originates in the cryosphere, including 46 per cent from snow and 32 per cent from glaciers (Immerzeel et al., 2010; Scott et al., 2019). In fact, the Indus Basin is the second most water-stressed basin in the world (Shrestha et al., 2015).

Climate changes and retreating glaciers affect water availability in several ways. As a glacier recedes and thus reduces its store of frozen water, it sends more water into the river downstream earlier in the spring. However, as the glacier shrinks further, there comes a point when that process slows down and less water becomes available (Hock et al., 2019). While glacial water has already declined in some areas in the world with small cryospheres, the contribution of the Himalayan cryosphere to rivers will likely peak in the 2040s (Hock et al., 2019). The seasonality of cryospheric impacts on river water also varies: Monsoon-fed tributaries of the Ganges and Brahmaputra will continue to experience their peak flows during the summer, regardless of whether they receive less water from shrinking glaciers in the spring. In contrast, warmer winter temperatures and less snow in the Karakoram will have a bigger impact on the Indus River's peak flow in the spring (Bolch et al., 2012). As the amount of water storage in the cryosphere shrinks, river basins become more dependent upon highly variable monsoon rainfall (Nie et al., 2021).

The changing water availability due to a shrinking cryosphere has wide-ranging impacts on economies and livelihoods. In the Himalaya, decreasing water availability in the dry spring months will increasingly affect hydropower production during what has already become the most challenging season (Scott et al., 2019). In fact, across the region, 15 per cent to 40 per cent of hydropower production depends on glacial meltwater during the dry season (Nie et al., 2021). While few studies have examined the economic impacts of this dependence in High Mountain Asia, a study in Peru found losses of US$5 million per year from the reduction of water to the operator of the Cañón del Pato hydropower plant, resulting in a loss of $20 million per year for the broader economy (Hock et al., 2019). In addition to changing water availability, glacier retreat and moraine erosion change the silt load in rivers, potentially filling reservoirs faster (Hock et al., 2019). High altitude rainfall events in Nepal in June 2021 demonstrated the potential for rapid erosion of soils that previously only experienced snowfall, and resulted in downstream siltation.

Changing water availability in rivers due to a shrinking cryosphere affects agriculture in certain regions. Scientists have projected reduced productivity in irrigated agriculture in the Indus basin, as well as in some other high mountain areas (Hock et al., 2019). Parts of northern Pakistan and Ladakh have irrigation systems that depend solely on glaciers and snowmelt (Scott et al., 2019). For high mountain pastures and farms, less winter snow cover means less soil moisture (Hock et al., 2019). Rainfed terraced farms on hill slopes are less affected by changes in the cryosphere, but fields in the valley bottoms might see impacts if their irrigation depends on large snow-fed rivers. In India and Pakistan, more than 100 million farmers depend upon on irrigation water coming directly from the Indus and Ganges Rivers rather than from their tributaries (Hock et al., 2019).[12] In many places, glacial meltwater provides critical protection during droughts, when other water sources fail; this has proven particularly important in the Indus and Tarim Basins (Nie et al., 2021).

A shrinking cryosphere affects availability of drinking water, not just in villages immediately below glaciers, but also in certain far-away cities. Sporadic reports of decreased access to drinking water have come out of Nepali villages that rely directly on glacier-fed streams (Hock et al., 2019). Andean cities, meanwhile, have received significant attention that may prove relevant; for example, during droughts, 80 per cent of La Paz's water supply comes from glacial runoff. Kathmandu in Nepal, a Himalayan metropolis with more than 4 million inhabitants, inaugurated in April 2021 a half-billion-dollar solution to solve its shortage of rainfed water: A tunnel to import water from the snow-fed Melamchi River that would increase its future dependence on a shrinking cryosphere (Mandal, 2021). Catastrophic debris flows in June and July 2021 buried the project's inlet under 14 metres of rubble, and the tunnel's future is now uncertain.

A melting cryosphere also affects biodiversity and tourism. As temperatures increase, lowland species shift their ranges uphill, while upland species become confined to a smaller and more fragmented range in shrinking 'islands' around the peaks (Hock et al., 2019). Tourism will also see impacts, not just in the closure of the small number of ski resorts in the region (in Kashmir, Kyrgyzstan and Tajikistan), but also because many other tourism products in the region, including trekking, depend on selling vistas of snow-covered mountains, such as those in Figure 2.3.

While no evidence has appeared of increased frequency of GLOF occurrences in recent years, rapidly retreating glaciers will allow the growth of many new potentially dangerous glacial lakes in the coming decades, including lakes that do not yet exist (Hock et al., 2019). With the building of more dams, diversions, hydropower plants, bridges, roads and valley-bottom settlements, there is a high likelihood of increased damage and casualties from GLOF events.

Response one: Improved adaptation and disaster resilience

As we discussed earlier, even in the best-case scenarios, High Mountain Asia will lose a substantial part of its cryosphere in the next decades and thus a substantial part of its water storage abilities, resulting in increased water stress in high mountain areas, along with impacts on agriculture, hydropower and drinking water in cryosphere-dependent river basins. The risk of GLOFs will persist and perhaps increase in the coming decades. At the same time, a changing climate will cause more extreme events in the monsoon, resulting in additional floods and landslides. Consequences of cryospheric melting will become part of a larger picture of how a changing atmosphere and climate will negatively impact people's wellbeing.[13] We have no choice but to adapt to the changing world to protect the lives and livelihoods of the vulnerable.

Policies and actions must address the needs of key stakeholders affected by water stress, whether caused directly by a shrinking cryosphere, or by changing precipitation patterns. These include mountain farmers: water scarcity can seriously impact smallholder subsistence farmers, and it has links to the depletion of local water sources, deforestation, increased demand from growing populations, increased competition for access, and problems with affordability, as well as water quality (Shivakoti et al., 2014). People in High Mountain Asia have responded to increasing water stresses in several ways. Some have switched to crops that need less water; some have adopted new irrigation technologies – for example, an engineer in Ladakh, Sonam Wangchuk invented 'ice stupas' to store water in frozen artificial glaciers (Hock et al., 2019). Farmers will need support to design and invest in locally appropriate water storage solutions, or to shift to agricultural practices that consume less water.

Hydropower producers will need to adapt. A shrinking cryosphere will affect the availability of water in rivers, in some cases shifting and increasing early spring run-off, and in other cases reducing dry-season water availability. The amount of silt in the rivers will also change. While existing hydropower plants may have fewer available solutions and more difficulty recouping investments, designs of new hydropower plants and grids will need to take into account the changing climate and water availability.

Infrastructure design will need to accommodate larger floods. Designs of hydropower projects, roads and bridges will also need to take into account the existence of current or potential future glacial lakes upstream, and the potential size of a GLOF. Even on slopes and valleys not at risk for GLOFs, more extreme rainfall will require larger storm drains and more attention to slope stability. All of this calls for surveys, calculations and additional engineering capacity. While in some cases, siphoning off glacial lakes can mitigate the risk of GLOFs, it will not be possible to avoid disasters altogether.

Disasters caused directly by cryospheric change will comprise a small fraction of the disasters occurring in the region, but all need better preparedness. High Mountain Asia faces disasters of many kinds, from low-frequency earthquakes to high-frequency landslides, floods and storms (Vaidya et al., 2019). Most floods occur during the monsoon season and have no direct connection to the cryosphere. While dozens of GLOFs have been recorded, some with heavy losses of lives and infrastructure, their overall impacts amount to a small fraction of those created annually through monsoon-induced floods and landslides (Bolch et al., 2019; Vaidya et al., 2019). Cryosphere-induced disasters need the same sort of preparation as others: early warning systems, infrastructure designed to withstand low-probability-high-loss events, emergency services trained and on stand-by, as well as institutional mechanisms in place to support victims in rebuilding their lives. The latter has special importance in mountain areas, which have a higher incidence of poverty than the plains (Wester et al., 2019). In many places, vulnerability to other impacts of climate change (precipitation, temperature and their impacts on livelihoods) will exceed those triggered by cryospheric changes.

One key priority is the protection of the most vulnerable. Climate change exposure is one of several vulnerabilities in the mountains; adaptive capacity depends on many non-climatic factors, including poverty, but also policies, institutions and processes (Gioli et al., 2019). Societies and individuals in the mountains have considerable practice in adapting to variability, and farmers appear to have already begun changing their practices. However, concern remains that they will have limited ability to tackle the newly emerging 'surprise' challenges associated with accelerating climate change (Mishra et al., 2019).

Improving adaptation requires data and information, capacity-building and early warning systems, as well as better designed infrastructure. This calls for sufficient funding and large-scale coordination. Countries in the region have begun to follow their National Adaptation Plans via policies and budgeting that focus on current and immediate threats (Mishra et al., 2019). They still require longer-term thinking, including investments in redundancy in infrastructure networks.[14] Many impacts of the cryosphere and climate change extend across national borders. While the International Centre for Integrated Mountain Development (ICIMOD), an intergovernmental learning and knowledge-sharing centre for the HKH region, has piloted a small number of cross-border flood early warning systems, no formal agreement or mechanism for regional collaboration on climate change adaptation exists today for the broader High Mountain Asia region (Prabhakar et al., 2018). These structures urgently need creation, alongside increased investment and cross-border collaborations on data collection and monitoring (Nie et al., 2021).

The Broader Story with the Same Drivers: Air Pollution, Monsoon Change and the Global Climate

The melting of High Mountain Asia's cryosphere, its downstream impacts, and needs for adaptation are only part of the bigger story. In this section, we examine the main drivers of the melting Third Pole and their broader impacts, including increases in atmospheric concentrations of long-lived greenhouse gases and short-lived climate pollutants, due to human activities.

The drivers of atmospheric change: Greenhouse gases and short-lived climate pollutants

The global increase in both long-lived greenhouse gases and short-lived climate pollutants drives the melting of the cryosphere. Globally, the biggest driver of warming is carbon dioxide (CO_2). Since the mid-1800s, atmospheric CO_2 levels have increased by almost 50 per cent due to two human activities: the burning of fossil fuels, which transfers to the atmosphere carbon that was stored underground for millions of years; and large-scale deforestation, which transfers to the atmosphere carbon that was stored in the biosphere (Hawken, 2017). With an atmospheric lifetime of 100+ years, CO_2 is well-mixed[15] around the globe. Its impacts thus do not depend on its source or source region and will also persist even after emissions reduction. Along with other greenhouse gases (methane, nitrous oxide, ozone, sulphur hexafluoride and various hydrofluorocarbons [HFCs]), CO_2 warms the atmosphere by absorbing outgoing infrared radiation, and radiating some of that back to the surface.[16]

Globally, the second biggest contributor to warming is black carbon (BC), which is emitted into the atmosphere during incomplete combustion in the form of fine charred particles (Bond et al., 2013). BC warms the atmosphere by absorbing incoming sunlight. When present in elevated atmospheric layers, it warms them, reducing the sunlight reaching the land surface (Ramanathan and Carmichael, 2008; Tripathi et al., 2007). This can cause local dimming of up to 10 to 20 Watts per square metre (Streets et al., 2006; UNEP/WMO, 2011). BC has an atmospheric lifetime of days to weeks; much of it thus remains concentrated in a handful of heavily polluted regions. High Mountain Asia is near three of the world's five regions with the heaviest BC loads: East Asia, South Asia (particularly the Indo-Gangetic Plains) and Southeast Asia (Gertler et al., 2016). Modelling studies have shown that much of the BC reaching the high mountains has an anthropogenic origin (Alvarado, 2018). Along with the greenhouse gases methane, ozone and HFCs, BC is classified as a short-lived-climate pollutant (SLCP). Because of SLPCs' short atmospheric lifetimes, their mitigation yields rapid climate results, while also giving other co-benefits (UNEP, 2011). In fact, mitigating SLCPs globally will provide a one-time reduction in warming of up to 0.5°C (IPCC, 2018; Shindell et al., 2017).

Along with wind-blown dust, BC also helps melt the cryosphere in a second way: when BC deposits onto white snow or ice surfaces,[17] it darkens those surfaces, increasing the absorption of sunlight and accelerating melting (Gertler et al., 2016; Yasunari et al., 2010).[18] Although less dark than black carbon, desert dust can play a similar role. Snow darkening by wind-blown dust particles from the Thar Desert has been observed high in the Himalaya (Gautam et al., 2009; Saikawa et al., 2019), while dust from the Taklimakan Desert in the Tarim Basin reaches the Kunlun Mountains and the northern Tibetan Plateau (Xia et al., 2008). Figure 2.4(a) shows an elevated atmospheric layer of particles in the Himalaya, while Figure 2.4(b) shows darkened slopes explicable only by the deposit of dark particles. Bare surfaces left behind by retreating glaciers provide additional sources of dust that may blow onto what remains of the glaciers, accelerating their melting (Hock et al., 2019).

The Indo-Gangetic Plains (IGP) are one of the biggest sources of particles reaching High Mountain Asia (Kang et al., 2019; Saikawa et al., 2019). With a population of close to 800 million, these fertile plains contain many of the world's most polluted cities as well as heavily polluted rural areas (Saikawa et al., 2019; Chen et al., 2020; Rupakheti et al., 2017; Wan et al., 2017). Figure 2.5 shows a satellite image of a typical winter day, with the ground of the IGP barely visible through the haze.

Figure 2.4 Haze layer reaching high altitudes in the Annapurna Himalaya (a), Snow darkening by deposited particles distinctly visible in the Kanchenjunga Himalaya (below the dashed line drawn onto the photo) (b)
Source: Photos by Arnico Panday.

Figure 2.5 Gray haze covering the Indo-Gangetic Plains on 4 December 2020
Source: NASA (2020).

The atmosphere above the IGP has warmed at a rate of 0.25°C per decade, while the surface has dimmed and cooled (UNEP, 2019). On Yala Glacier in Langtang, Nepal, 56 per cent of BC was identified as fossil-fuel in origin – much of it from the plains of Nepal and India, but with occasional increased atmospheric BC concentrations from nearby forest fires (Gul et al., 2021).

Although the Himalaya are the tallest mountain range in the world, they are within reach for pollutants from the IGP, and they also do not block the transport of pollutants over to the Tibetan Plateau. High levels of black carbon have been recorded at 5 km altitude in the Nepal Himalaya, in the Karakoram and on the Tibetan Plateau (Gul et al., 2021; Marinoni et al., 2010; Rai et al., 2019; Chen et al., 2019; Cong et al., 2009; Saikawa et al., 2019). Pollutants from the IGP reach the Tibetan Plateau along several pathways. They can cross through deep valleys such as the Arun and the Kali Gandaki or at high altitude during favourable weather conditions (Brun et al., 2011; Dhungel et al., 2018; Kang et al., 2019; Lüthi et al., 2014; Xia et al., 2011). Figure 2.6 illustrates some of the processes responsible for the transport of pollutants from the IGP to the high Himalaya and on to the Tibetan Plateau. From 1996 to 2010, the BC on the Tibetan Plateau from outside sources increased by 41 per cent (UNEP, 2019). Figure 2.7 illustrates the complex interplay between processes that lead to the melting of the cryosphere, along with its direct and associated impacts.

Industries, vehicles, household energy and agriculture all contribute to increased emissions of carbon dioxide, short-lived climate pollutants (SLCPs) and other air pollutants. Increased atmospheric concentrations of carbon dioxide and SLCPs contribute to increases in the regional temperature. When warmer air touches frozen surfaces, this accelerates their melting. Additional melting occurs when black carbon particles as well as windblow dust settle on snow and ice surfaces, darkening them,

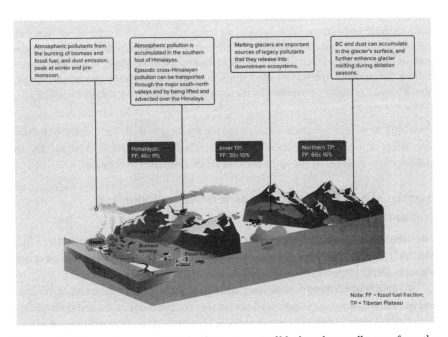

Figure 2.6 Processes responsible for the transport of black carbon pollutants from the Indo-Gangetic Plains across the Himalaya to the Tibetan Plateau, along with impacts
Source: Kang et al. (2019).

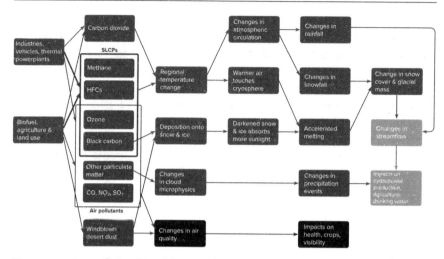

Figure 2.7   Interrelationship of drivers of cryospheric melting with other processes and impacts

Source: Author.

Note: Industries, vehicles, household energy and agriculture all contribute to increased emissions of carbon dioxide, short-lived climate pollutants (SLCPs) and other air pollutants. Increased atmospheric concentrations of carbon dioxide and SLCPs contribute to increases in the regional temperature. When warmer air touches frozen surfaces, this accelerates their melting. Additional melting occurs when black carbon particles as well as wind-blown dust settle on snow and ice surfaces, darkening them, absorbing more sunlight, and accelerating the melting. Temperature changes also affect atmospheric circulation, which affects precipitation. Meanwhile, air pollutants co-emitted by the same sources affect air quality and health.

absorbing more sunlight, and accelerating the melting as well. Temperature changes also affect atmospheric circulation, which affects precipitation. Meanwhile, air pollutants co-emitted by the same sources affect air quality and health.

Associated impacts of the same drivers: Air pollution and monsoon changes

The combustion sources responsible for the BC emissions that reach the High Mountain Asia cryosphere, as well as for the region's CO2 emissions, also have other, arguably larger impacts on human health and wellbeing.

Widespread cooking and heating with solid fuels, poorly maintained vehicles and industries, as well as widespread open fires produce some of the worst air quality in the world in the regions upwind of High Mountain Asia. In South Asia, outdoor fires plus cooking with biomass may contribute more than half of atmospheric BC (Gustafsson et al., 2009). Fifty out of 51 cities around the HKH in the World Health Organization (WHO) database have annual average levels of fine particulate matter

(PM2.5) exceeding WHO guidelines. Among these cities, a dozen exceeds WHO standards for annual average concentrations more than tenfold, including New Delhi (Figure 2.8a) (Saikawa et al., 2019). These levels have immense health impacts in cities, especially for the most exposed populations, such as street vendors, traffic police and others who spend considerable time on the street (Gurung and Bell, 2012; Shakya et al., 2017). In fact, the highest average levels of PM2.5 exposure in the Asia-Pacific Region are in Bangladesh, Bhutan, China, India, Myanmar, Nepal and Pakistan (UNEP, 2019).

Poor air quality is not limited to large cities. Observations in rural Uttar Pradesh, Chitwan and Lumbini have found pollution levels comparable to those in very polluted cities, indicating that hundreds of millions of people on the IGP face exposure to very unhealthy air (Praveen et al., 2012; Mehra et al., 2018; Rupakheti et al., 2018; Rupakheti et al., 2017; Wan et al., 2017). During the dry season, emissions from millions of local pollution sources across the IGP merge into a thick haze layer that can last for months and extend up into the mountains (Figure 2.5 and Figure 2.8b and c). This has consequences for local climate and visibility (Dey and Girolamo, 2010; Gautam et al., 2010; Di Girolamo et al., 2004; Praveen et al., 2012; Saikawa et al., 2019).

Figure 2.8   Haze obscuring aerial view of New Delhi during November 2014 (a), view of Kathmandu on a clear day 28 February 2013 (b), same view two days later, on 2 March 2013, with regional haze present (c)
Source: Photos by Arnico Panday.

The reduced sunlight and poor air quality have also led to significant impacts on agricultural productivity (Auffhammer et al., 2006; UNEP, 2019).

One particular concern arises from the high level of indoor air pollution to which women and children are exposed in households using solid fuels for cooking and heating. Indoor combustion of solid fuels is also a very large source of outdoor pollution. 1.9 billion people in Asia and the Pacific use solid fuels for cooking and heating (UNEP/WMO, 2011). Figure 2.9 shows the death rate due to air pollution in countries of Asia-Pacific. Almost two thirds of the 7 million annual premature deaths attributed to indoor and outdoor air pollution globally take place in Asia, mostly in the countries surrounding High Mountain Asia (UNEP, 2019).

Air pollution in the region has started to alter the region's meteorology, affecting monsoon precipitation. Airborne particulates change rainclouds by

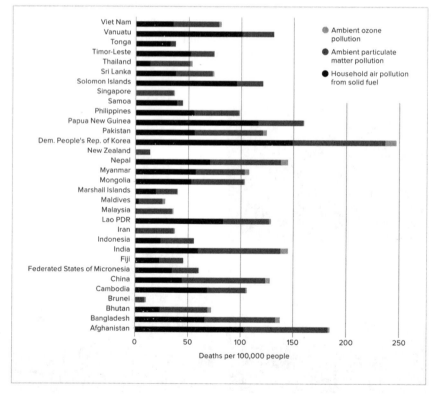

Figure 2.9 Annual deaths per 100,000 people due to household and outdoor air pollution, 2016

Source: UNEP (2019).

Note: Household air pollution due to cooking and heating with solid fuels; ambient (outdoor) pollution due to particulates and ozone gas.

affecting the number and size distribution of cloud droplets, which can delay and then intensify a rain event.[19] In recent years, scientists have found direct ties between heavy precipitation events and air pollution impacts on cloud properties (Cho et al., 2016; Choudhury et al., 2020). Meanwhile, light-absorbing particles also change atmospheric heating patterns, affecting the timing and location of where convective clouds form (Gautam et al., 2010; Lau and Kim, 2006; Lau et al., 2006). Despite the complicated interaction of these processes,[20] increasing evidence suggests that air pollution is responsible for a weakening of the South Asian summer monsoon (UNEP, 2019). Since the 1950s, rainfall patterns in India have shown a reduction in the number of rainy days, in rainfall early and late in the season, and in the number of days with low and moderate rainfall, but an increase in the frequency and magnitude of extreme rainfall events (UNEP/WMO, 2011).

Global climate change is also likely significantly altering monsoon precipitation, causing large shifts in the timing and location of rainfall, causing major impacts on agriculture (Krishnan et al., 2019). The impacts of global CO2 emissions thus have acutely felt effects in this region. Nepal, for example, expects to see fewer rainy days, but more days with extreme precipitation in the future (MoFE, 2019). Changing monsoon patterns mean that agriculture and drinking water supply in some places will suffer as a result of water shortages, while other places will suffer from too much water bringing floods and landslides. Just four large flood events in rivers downstream from High Mountain Asia between 2000 and 2013 together killed more than 10,000 people and displaced 50 million (Prabhakar et al., 2018). While precipitation forecasts are more uncertain than temperature forecasts, total summer precipitation will likely increase in the Ganges, upper Salween and upper Mekong Basins, but not in the Indus and Brahmaputra Basins; total winter precipitation on the other hand, will likely increase in the upper Salween and upper Mekong Basins (Shrestha et al., 2015).

The regional climate is changing in other ways too. During the past two decades, the IGP have seen an increase in persistent winter fog events tied to increased air pollution and changing agricultural practices (Saikawa et al., 2019; Syed et al., 2012). Stretching over hundreds of kilometres and lasting for weeks, these fog events affect the daily lives of hundreds of millions of people, with a particularly large impact on the lives and livelihoods of the poorest as well as on air, rail and road transport (Ganguly et al., 2006; Gautam et al., 2007; Saikawa et al., 2019; Syed et al., 2012; UNEP, 2019). Recent projections expect increasingly severe summer heat waves in the IGP, again with impacts on the health and well-being of hundreds of millions of people (Krishnan et al., 2019; Prabhakar et al., 2018).

While the melting Third Pole is very visible, with large downstream consequences, the impacts of other anthropogenic changes to the atmosphere might arguably lead to even more widespread human suffering. The same set of human activities, causing emissions of specific gases and particulates drive both the

melting of the Third Pole and these other changes. A recent report by the World
Bank (Mani, 2021) says "managing BC emissions in South Asia has the potential
not only to achieve global and regional climate benefits, but also to offer other
valuable advantages for the region. For example, cleaner cooking and fuel burning,
in addition to reducing BC deposits on glaciers, would improve local air quality;
[and] help achieve long-term energy security." The interconnected problems and
solutions call for coordinated policies, incentives and actions for effective mitigation
(UNEP, 2019). The Third Pole's loss of snow and ice is not just a symptom of larger
problems, but can also serve as a unifying symbol to address them.

Response two: Mitigation, with co-benefits

Figure 2.7 illustrates the inter-connections between processes that change the Third
Pole cryosphere and processes that drive air pollution and monsoon changes. The
individual problems cannot be addressed in isolation; they all require changes in the
drivers on the left side of the figure.

Required changes

While some amount of climate change, and some loss of High Mountain Asia's
cryosphere, is unavoidable and needs adapting to, keeping these changes within limits
is critically important. The Paris Agreement focuses on keeping global temperature
increase 'well below' 2°C while making an effort to keep it below 1.5°C. The special
report on the impacts of global warming of 1.5°C by the IPCC (2018), however,
emphasizes the huge difference in climate impacts between a world with temperature
stabilized at 1.5 versus 2.0°C above pre-industrial levels. This has driven the global
discourse towards stabilizing the climate at 1.5°C by achieving net zero CO_2 emissions
in the coming decades. This would entail investment in a wide variety of solutions,
some currently cost-effective, some less, in sectors ranging from buildings and cities,
to energy, food, land use, materials and transport (Hawken, 2017). One important
priority is ending fossil fuel subsidies; according to an International Monetary Fund
estimate, in 2015 the fossil fuel industry received $5.3 trillion in direct and indirect
subsidies, equivalent to 6.5 per cent of global GDP (Hawken, 2017).

The protection of the snowfields and glaciers of High Mountain Asia, along
with the region's air quality and monsoon system, requires concerted global action
well beyond the Paris Agreement in order to stabilize Earth's climate at a lower
temperature. This requires going far beyond gradually phasing out CO_2 emissions,
and making a concerted effort to reach a peak as soon as possible and then draw
down[21] atmospheric CO_2 concentrations. Since impacts of CO_2 emissions do not
depend on the source, and emissions take place across many different sources and
sectors, one should start with feasible sources that provide the biggest potential for
quick and easy reductions. Project Drawdown, a California-based organization,

has worked with hundreds of experts to quantify the impacts and costs of the most promising such solutions (Hawken, 2017). The top ten include removing HFCs from refrigeration, investing in wind and solar power, reducing food waste and switching away from meat, letting trees grow on pastures, and reducing population growth through education of girls and improved access to family planning.

Due to CO_2's long lifetime, it will take far too long to stabilize global temperatures through CO_2 mitigation alone. This is where mitigating short-lived climate pollutants comes in. By scaling up existing technologies, (UNEP/WMO, 2011), reduction of SLCPs can provide a 0.5°C of avoided warming while achieving significant societal co-benefits (Shindell et al., 2017; UNEP, 2011). In fact, as illustrated in Figure 2.10, without reducing SLCPs it will be almost impossible to contain global temperatures within 1.5°C by the year 2100 (IPCC, 2018). Mitigating SLCPs alone also makes no sense, since warming driven by CO_2 would continue and at some point overwhelm the one time temperature reduction of 0.5°C from SLCP mitigation (Shindell et al., 2017). Effective mitigation will require a set of integrated solutions based on an analysis of all the impacts.

The interrelated nature of many of the problems and solutions makes it easy to address multiple issues in an integrated way through politically expedient framing. For example, the assessment report *Air Pollution in Asia and the Pacific: Science-Based Solutions*, published jointly by Climate and Clean Air Coalition (CCAC), United

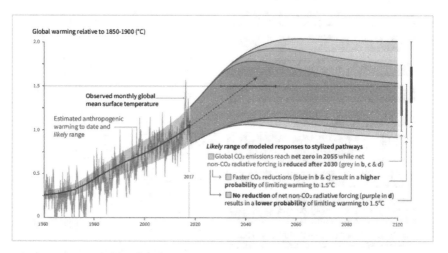

Figure 2.10 Probable global average temperature pathways under three different scenarios

Source: IPCC (2018).

Note: Ignoring non-CO_2 radiative forcing by short-lived climate pollutants (SLCPs) makes it difficult to stabilize temperature at 1.5 degree. SLCP mitigation and fast CO_2 mitigation are both needed.

Nations Environment Programme (UNEP) and Asia Pacific Clean Air Partnership (2019),[22] rested on the premise that the most effective way to motivate climate change mitigation in Asia would focus on reducing the region's fine particulate pollution – a widely agreed problem – which would also yield a positive impact on climate. Through a sophisticated modelling approach, the assessment identifies the 25 most promising measures that, if implemented in Asia and the Pacific, would both significantly clean up the region's air pollution, and achieve 0.3°C of avoided global warming by mid-century (Box 2.2).

The 25 most important measures to clean up Asia-Pacific's air quality fall into three categories. The first category is called 'Regional Application of Conventional Measures'. These comprise measures that normally form centrepieces in air quality

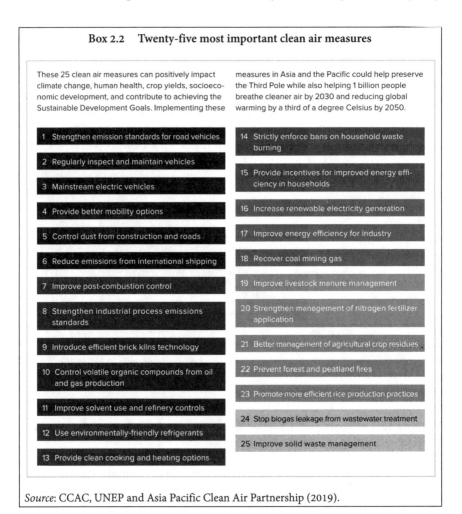

Box 2.2   Twenty-five most important clean air measures

These 25 clean air measures can positively impact climate change, human health, crop yields, socioeconomic development, and contribute to achieving the Sustainable Development Goals. Implementing these measures in Asia and the Pacific could help preserve the Third Pole while also helping 1 billion people breathe cleaner air by 2030 and reducing global warming by a third of a degree Celsius by 2050.

1   Strengthen emission standards for road vehicles

2   Regularly inspect and maintain vehicles

3   Mainstream electric vehicles

4   Provide better mobility options

5   Control dust from construction and roads

6   Reduce emissions from international shipping

7   Improve post-combustion control

8   Strengthen industrial process emissions standards

9   Introduce efficient brick kilns technology

10 Control volatile organic compounds from oil and gas production

11 Improve solvent use and refinery controls

12 Use environmentally-friendly refrigerants

13 Provide clean cooking and heating options

14 Strictly enforce bans on household waste burning

15 Provide incentives for improved energy efficiency in households

16 Increase renewable electricity generation

17 Improve energy efficiency for industry

18 Recover coal mining gas

19 Improve livestock manure management

20 Strengthen management of nitrogen fertilizer application

21 Better management of agricultural crop residues

22 Prevent forest and peatland fires

23 Promote more efficient rice production practices

24 Stop biogas leakage from wastewater treatment

25 Improve solid waste management

Source: CCAC, UNEP and Asia Pacific Clean Air Partnership (2019).

management, but have not seen broad deployment around the region. They include industrial emission control through end-of-pipe devices and emissions standards; emission standards for vehicles, along with vehicular inspection and maintenance; and dust control on construction sites and roads. The second category of measures, 'Next-stage Air Quality Measures' remain uncommon in Asia and the Pacific. These include banning open burning of agricultural crop residue and residential waste, preventing forest and peatland fires, livestock manure management (to reduce methane emissions), better management of fertilizer application, improved brick kilns, reducing emissions from international shipping, and reducing leaks and emissions from refineries and paint production. The third category consists of measures that contribute to economic and human development priority goals through air quality benefits. The first of these involves switching households away from solid fuels, to cook and heat with electricity or gas. In fact, one study identified switching to clean cooking as the most important measure to reduce black carbon reaching the cryosphere (World Bank, 2013). Other solutions include shifting electricity production from thermal to solar, wind and hydropower; giving households incentives for more energy-efficient appliances and for installing rooftop solar panels; introducing energy efficiency standards for industries; promoting electric vehicles; improving public transport; improving solid waste management; several measures to reduce methane emissions including intermittent aeration of rice fields, two-stage water treatment and biogas recovery, pre-mining recovery of coal mine gas, stopping routine flaring and reducing leaks in oil and gas production; as well as full compliance with the Kigali Amendment to replace HFCs in refrigeration. A number of these measures are identical to ones listed by Project Drawdown to reduce CO_2 globally, underscoring the interconnectedness of the problems and solutions.

Figure 2.11 illustrates the impact of implementing these 25 measures on levels of PM2.5 exposure. While implementation of current legislation already ensures that the number exposed to high levels of air pollution will not grow by 2030, implementation of the 25 measures will greatly decrease the exposure levels faced by these four billion people. Figure 2.12 illustrates this data in a different form, looking at the impact of the measures on average PM2.5 exposure faced by residents of Asia. The implementation of conventional, next-stage and development-priority measures will bring the average annual PM2.5 to within 20 micrograms per cubic metre – just double the WHO guideline!

The countries of Asia and the Pacific span the ranks from among the smallest to the largest. Global CO_2 emissions are dominated by China, the United States, the European Union and India; significant emission reduction in those countries will make a big difference globally, while the current net-zero conditions in Bhutan have virtually no impact on the global environment. Smaller countries, states and cities, however, have the opportunity to become more ambitious more quickly than larger countries, demonstrating proofs-of-concept before their wider introduction in larger countries. A case in point: the work carried out by the team that focused on

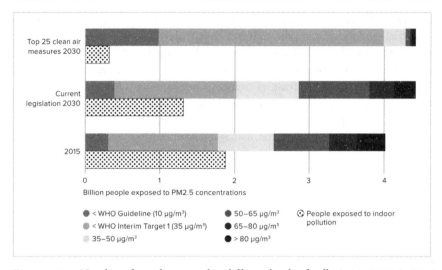

Figure 2.11   Number of people exposed to different levels of pollution in 2015, in 2030 under current legislation, and if the 25 measures are implemented
Source: UNEP (2019).

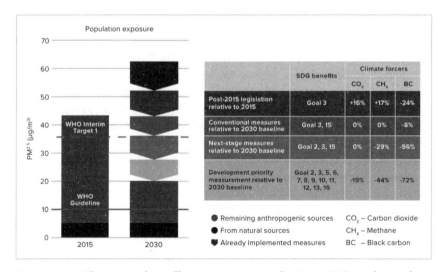

Figure 2.12   Clean-air policy effects on emission reductions, SDGs and cumulative CO2 in Asia and the Pacific, 2015 versus 2030 (population-weighted PM2.5)
Source: UNEP (2019).

the 100 or so brick kilns in the Kathmandu Valley, Nepal, after the 2015 earthquake. They introduced design changes that improved combustion and thermal efficiency, resulting in significant reductions in air pollution along with savings for the kiln owners (Nepal et al., 2019). The improved kilns attracted visitors from the region, leading to policy changes that required the clean-up of 20,000 kilns in Punjab Province, Pakistan, and catalysed the formation of the South Asian Pacific Federation of Brick Kiln Associations. To give another example, small countries with a high proportion of clean hydropower, such as Bhutan and Nepal, should find it easier to switch to all-electric vehicle fleets than some of the larger countries.

Necessary actions

Achieving effective and lasting actions that limit the damage caused by climate change in High Mountain Asia requires attention to several priorities:

(1) While the broader picture of interrelated processes has started to emerge, specific decisions require new data and more research. The region is one of the most complex in the world, and only detailed environmental monitoring and research will detect vulnerabilities and future challenges. This requires allocation of sufficient funds to environmental monitoring and research.

(2) Many countries of the region have notoriously low levels of communication between academics and decision-makers. These countries should develop platforms that allow effective communication of physical as well as social science results relevant to policymaking, along with questions from policymakers that require academic input.

(3) As the complex interplay between human activities, drivers of environmental change, and impacts cross a variety of sectors, governments will need to strengthen cross-sectoral institutions that can reach across typically siloed ministry structures.

(4) Issues and problems cross borders, both between subnational jurisdictions and between countries. This calls for developing effective communication platforms to ensure cross-border sharing of data, information, knowledge and experiences.

(5) Multinational and intergovernmental institutions and fora need strengthening, along with a mandate to develop regional frameworks and targets, agreed upon by the region's governments, to protect the Third Pole. This can become a unifying goal that takes attention away from smaller contentions in the region such as border disputes.

(6) Globally, the loss of snow and ice from High Mountain Asia's peaks needs to be seen not as a distant problem, but as a symbol and a symptom of a global system imbalance that calls for urgent action.

UNDP's status and presence in the countries throughout the region give it an opportunity to engage with actors at different levels and to shape the discourse over the coming decade. Keeping the Third Pole snow and ice covered, the skies blue, the lungs healthy and rainfall regular, requires taking responsibility at all levels, from individuals to firms, local and national governments and global organizations. This is a message that UNDP can emphasize.

Regardless of their socioeconomic status, individuals have a responsibility to inform themselves and to make appropriate consumer choices. This includes, for example, giving priority to buying clean cookstoves over flashy gadgets and adjusting to a more plant-based diet. Wealthier individuals have the responsibility to choose sustainable ways to travel, to limit fossil-fuel-powered road and air travel, to reduce the use of plastics, to change their diet, and to pay attention to the source of their material purchases. Local and municipal governments have a responsibility to discourage harmful activities within their jurisdictions and to build healthy sustainable cities. They will need to provide disincentives for burning crop residue and garbage, and create walkable cities with convenient public transport. They may also be able to restrict entry of vehicles and materials that do not meet certain standards. National governments have the responsibility to adopt taxes and rules that promote clean transport and energy, that promote investments by firms in appropriate areas. They also have the responsibility to treat climate change as the emergency that it is, and to allocate sufficient resources for both adaptation and mitigation.

Regional and global organizations, from the HKH-based ICIMOD, to the Climate and Clean Air Coalition (CCAC), as well as various UN bodies need to use the weight of international mandate to push for cross-border coordination, cooperation and sharing. At times, they may need to grow louder about calling their member countries to action. UNDP itself can play an important role both globally and within member countries. First, it can set an example through its country offices, replacing its vehicle fleets with only electric vehicles and powering its offices through renewable energy. Second, it can launch an educational campaign on what responsible leadership means for the next decade, providing guidelines to politicians but also raising the expectations of voters. Finally, it can seek to enter into partnerships with big technology firms, getting them to pledge to use only renewable energy at their server farms and to use their platforms to educate the public and to provide complete lifecycle analyses and environmental impact information for all of the products they sell. In concluding its review of a broad range of challenges facing High Mountain Asia, *The Hindu Kush Himalaya Assessment* notes that, while significant knowledge gaps remain about the region, "we know enough to take action" (Wester et al., 2019). As we look at the decade ahead, it will be critical for individuals, governments, businesses and organizations to give priority to stabilizing the global climate, thereby also protecting the Third Pole and the lives and livelihoods of the people living downstream from it.

NOTES

1. Including Greenland.

2. While the origin of the term 'Third Pole' is unclear, it obviously relates to the vast amounts of snow and ice that characterize the other two polar regions. The author himself does not like the term 'Third Pole', because a pole is the point of intersection between a planet and its rotational axis, which only exists at the North Pole and the South Pole, whereas the glaciated high mountains of Asia span across several thousand kilometres and do not sit anywhere near the axis of rotation. The IPCC Special Report on the Ocean and Cryosphere in a Changing Climate uses the term 'High Mountain Asia' for the same region. This chapter will use the terms 'Third Pole' and 'High Mountain Asia' interchangeably. Incidentally, these same mountains also appear in the cryosphere chapter of *The Hindu Kush Himalaya Assessment* by Bolch et al. (2019), itself based on the classification in the Randolph Glacier Inventory (see glims.org/ RGI/index.html) and are consistent with the region considered by the Third Pole Environment programme based in Beijing (see tpe.ac.cn/webindex/).

3. Estimates of glacier area in the High Mountain Asia range from between 76,580 square km and 81,140 square km (Bolch et al., 2019) to 97,605 square km (Hock et al., 2019).

4. While data collection at high altitudes is sparse, it has firmly established EDW in the region. A variety of researchers have hypothesized mechanisms to explain EDW (Krishnan et al., 2019; Pepin et al., 2015). These mechanisms include: (1) The albedo effect, whereby a rising snow line and tree line decrease the surface reflectivity (compared to snow covered and bare surfaces), leading to absorption of more sunlight, greater heating of the surface and warming of the air. (2) An increase in elevation of the cloud condensation level (and thus an increase in the temperature at which cloud formation releases heat). (3) An increase in water vapor, thus increasing its greenhouse effect. (4) Elevated pollution layers that absorb sunlight (Bolch et al., 2019; Pepin et al., 2015).

5. The snow line is the altitude above which snow can persist year-round.

6. This assumes IPCC scenario RCP8.5.

7. Arnico Panday was a coordinating lead author of this assessment. *The Hindu Kush Himalaya Assessment*, edited by Wester et al. (2019), has been published under the terms of the Creative Commons Attribution 4.0 International License (creativecommons. org/licenses/by/4.0/), which permits use, sharing, adaptation, distribution and reproduction in any medium or format, as long as you give appropriate credit to the original author(s) and the source, provide a link to the Creative Commons licence and indicate if changes were made.

8. There is some uncertainty in these projections: IPCC attaches medium confidence to the prediction of magnitude and timing of glacier losses in future climate scenarios, but, as pointed out earlier, a 1.5°C increase in global average temperature would result in higher temperatures in High Mountain Asia (Hock et al., 2019).

9. Teleconnections like this are common: The 2010 floods in Pakistan were connected to a heatwave in Russia, while the monsoon is also connected to Atlantic Multidecadal Oscillation (Lau and Kim, 2012; Wang et al., 2009).

10. Mountain permafrost contains less soil carbon than Arctic permafrost, so its melting might have less feedback on climate than the melting of the Arctic Tundra, which would release large amounts of methane into the atmosphere (Hock et al., 2019).

11. Note that the Kedarnath disaster in India that killed several thousand in 2013 resulted from a landslide damming a stream, creating a lake that then burst out, and not from a GLOF as occasionally reported (Shrestha et al., 2015); see downtoearth.org.in/news/what-really-happened-in-uttarakhand-41550.

12. Note that many residents in the Ganges Basin depend on pumping ground water, with an estimated 20 million pumps (Scott et al., 2019).

13. For example, many springs in the HKH foothills have dried up for reasons unconnected to the cryosphere (Scott et al., 2019).

14. For example, to make sure that access remains possible even if a bridge or a stretch of road is damaged.

15. When a gas is 'well-mixed' its concentration varies very little over long distances.

16. This is similar to the way glass panes on a greenhouse keep the interior warmer or the way a blanket keeps a person warm at night.

17. Absorption of sunlight by dark particles plays a bigger role in melting snowfields and white glaciers than it does in melting Himalayan glaciers covered by debris (Bolch et al., 2019).

18. Each particle of black carbon plays a similar role to that seen when the sun shines onto a leaf that has fallen onto the snow: while the snow around it reflects most of the sunlight, the darker leaf or the darker particle absorbs the sunlight, heats up, and melts the snow underneath, sinking into the snow.

19. By providing a larger number of surfaces onto which water droplets condense, pollution initially spreads the available water in a cloud among a larger number of smaller droplets too small to rain out, thereby delaying rainfall. However, as the cloud collects more water and the larger number of droplets grows big enough to rain out, the delayed rainfall will become much heavier (Rosenfeld et al., 2008).

20. And they take place at scales ranging from individual cloud droplets to entire mountain ranges.

21. *Project Drawdown* by Hawken (2017) looks for solutions beyond reducing emissions to finding ways to reduce atmospheric CO2 concentrations.

22. Arnico Panday was a lead author on this report.

REFERENCES

Alvarado, M. J., Winijkul, E., Adams-Selin, R., Hunt, E. Brodowski, C., Lonsdale, C. R., et al. 2018. 'Sources of Black Carbon Deposition to the Himalayan Glaciers in Current and Future Climates'. *Journal of Geophysical Research: Atmospheres* 123, 7482–7505. doi.org/10.1020/2018JD029049.

Auffhammer, M., Ramanathan, V. and Vincent, J. R. 2006. 'Integrated Model Shows That Atmospheric Brown Clouds and Greenhouse Gases Have Reduced Rice Harvests in India'. *Proceedings of the National Academy of Sciences*103(52), 19668–19672. doi.org/10.1073/pnas.0609584104.

Barnett, T. P., Adam, J. C. and Lettenmeier, D. P. 2005. 'Potential Impacts of a Warming Climate on Water Availability in Snow-Dominated Regions'. *Nature* 438, 303–309.

Bolch, T., Kulkarni, A., Kääb, A., Huggel, C., Paul, F. and Cogley, J. G. 2012. 'The State and Fate of Himalayan Glaciers'. *Science* 336(6079), 310–314. doi.org/10.1126/science.1215828.

Bolch, T., Shea, J. M., Liu, S., Azam, F. M., Gao, Y. and Gruber, S. 2019. 'Status and Change of the Cryosphere in the Extended Hindu Kush Himalaya Region'. In P. Wester, A. Mishra, A. Mukherji and A. B. Shrestha, eds., *The Hindu Kush Himalaya Assessment*. New York: Springer International Publishing, 209–255. doi.org/10.1007/978-3-319-92288-1_7.

Bond, T. C., Doherty, S. J., Fahey, D. W., Forster, P. M., Berntsen, T. and Deangelo, B. J. 2013. 'Bounding the Role of Black Carbon in the Climate System: A Scientific Assessment'. *Journal of Geophysical Research Atmospheres* 118(11), 5380–5552. doi.org/10.1002/jgrd.50171.

Brun, J., Shrestha, P. and Barros, A. P. 2011. 'Mapping Aerosol Intrusion in Himalayan Valleys Using the Moderate Resolution Imaging Spectroradiometer (MODIS) and Cloud-Aerosol Lidar and Infrared Pathfinder Satellite Observation (CALIPSO)'. *Atmospheric Environment* 45(35), 6382–6392. doi.org/10.1016/j.atmosenv.2011.08.026.

Chen, P., Kang, S., Li, C., Zhang, Q., Guo, J. and Tripathee, L. 2019. Carbonaceous Aerosol Characteristics on the Third Pole: A Primary Study Based on the Atmospheric Pollution and Cryospheric Change (APCC) Network'. *Environmental Pollution* 253, 49–60. doi.org/10.1016/j.envpol.2019.06.112.

Chen, P., Kang, S., Tripathee, L., Panday, A. K., Rupakheti, M. and Rupakheti, D. 2020. 'Severe Air Pollution and Characteristics of Light-Absorbing Particles in a Typical Rural Area of the Indo-Gangetic Plain'. *Environmental Science and Pollution Research* 27(10), 10617–10628. doi.org/10.1007/s11356-020-07618-6.

Cho, C., Li, R., Wang, S. Y., Yoon, J. H. and Gillies, R. R. 2016. 'Anthropogenic Footprint of Climate Change in the June 2013 Northern India Flood'. *Climate Dynamics* 46(3–4), 797–805. doi.org/10.1007/s00382-015-2613-2.

Choudhury, G., Tyagi, B., Vissa, N. K., Singh, J., Sarangi, C., Tripathi, S. N. and Tesche, M. 2020. 'Aerosol-enhanced High Precipitation Events near the Himalayan Foothills'. *Atmospheric Chemistry and Physics* 20(23), 15389–15399. doi.org/10.5194/acp-20-15389-2020.

Climate and Clean Air Coalition (CCAC), United Nations Environment Programme (UNEP) and Asia Pacific Clean Air Partnership. 2019. *Air Pollution in Asia and the Pacific: Science-based Solutions*. Nairobi: United Nations Environment Programme. ccacoalition.org/en/file/6836/download.

Cong, Z., Kang, S., Smirnov, A. and Holben, B. 2009. 'Aerosol Optical Properties at Nam Co, a Remote Site in Central Tibetan Plateau'. *Atmospheric Research* 92(1), 42–48.

Dey, S. and Girolamo, L. D. 2010. 'A Climatology of Aerosol Optical and Microphysical Properties over the Indian Subcontinent from 9 Years (2000–2008) of Multiangle Imaging Spectroradiometer (MSIR) Data'. *Journal of Geophysical Research* 115(D15). doi.org/10.1029/2009JD013395.

Dhungel, S., Kathayat, B., Mahata, K. and Panday, A. 2018. 'Transport of Regional Pollutants through a Remote Trans-Himalayan Valley in Nepal'. *Atmospheric Chemistry and Physics* 18(2), 1203–1216. doi.org/10.5194/acp-18-1203-2018.

Di Girolamo, L., Bond, T. C., Bramer, D., Diner, D. J., Fettinger, F. and Kahn, R. A. 2004. 'Analysis of Multi-angle Imaging Spectro Radiometer (MISR) Aerosol Optical Depths over Greater India during Winter 2001–2004'. *Geophysical Research Letters* 31(23). doi:10.1029/2004GL021273.

Fujita, K., Sakai, A., Nuimura, T., Yamaguchi, S. and Sharma, R. R. 2009. 'Recent Changes in Imja Glacial Lake and Its Damming Moraine in the Nepal Himalaya Revealed by In Situ Surveys and Multi-temporal ASTER Imagery'. *Environmental Research Letters* 4(4). doi.org/1088/1748-9326/4/4/045205.

Ganguly, D., Jayaraman, A., Rajesh, T. A. and Gadhavi, H. 2006. 'Wintertime Aerosol Properties During Foggy and Nonfoggy Days over Urban Center Delhi and Their Implications for Shortwave Radiative Forcing'. *Journal of Geophysical Research* 111(D15). doi.org/10.1029/2005JD007029.

Gautam, R., Hsu, N. C., Kafatos, M. and Tsay, S.-C. 2007. 'Influences of Winter Haze on Fog/ Low Cloud over the Indo-Gangetic Plains'. *Journal of Geophysical Research* 112(D5). doi.org/10.1029/2005JD007036.

Gautam, R., Hsu, N. C. and Lau, K.-M. 2010. 'Premonsoon Aerosol Characterization and Radiative Effects over the Indo-Gangetic Plains: Implications for Regional Climate Warming'. *Journal of Geophysical Research* 115(D17208). doi.org/10.1029/ 2010JD013819.

Gautam, R., Liu, Z., Singh, R. P. and Hsu, N. C. 2009. 'Two Contrasting Dust Dominant Periods over India Observed from MODIS and CALIPSO Data'. *Geophysical Research Letters* 36(L06813). doi.org/10.1029/2008GL036967.

Gertler, C. G., Puppala, S. P., Panday, A., Stumm, D. and Shea, J. 2016. 'Black Carbon and the Himalayan Cryosphere: A Review'. *Atmospheric Environment* 125(B), 404–417. doi. org/10.1016/j.atmosenv.2015.08.078.

Gioli, G., Thapa, G., Khan, F., Dasgupta, P., Nathan, D. and Chhetri, N. 2019. 'Understanding and Tackling Poverty and Vulnerability in Mountain Livelihoods in the Hindu Kush Himalaya'. In P. Wester, A. Mishra, A. Mukherji and A. B. Shrestha, eds., *The Hindu Kush Himalaya Assessment*. New York: Springer International Publishing, 421–455. doi.org/10.1007/978-3-319-92288-1_12.

Gul, C., Kang, P. S. M. S., Praveen Kumar Singh, Wu, X., He, C. and Kumar, R. 2021. 'Black Carbon Concentration in the Central Himalayas: Impact on Glacier Melt and Potential Source Contribution'. *Environmental Pollution* 273(116544). doi.org/10.1016/j. envpol.2021.116544.

Gul, C., Praveen Puppala, S., Kang, S., Adhikary, B., Zhang, Y. and Ali, S. 2018. 'Concentrations and Source Regions of Light-Absorbing Particles in Snow/Ice in Northern Pakistan and Their Impact on Snow Albedo'. *Atmospheric Chemistry and Physics* 18(7). doi. org/10.5194/acp-18-4981-2018.

Gurung, A. and Bell, M. 2012. 'Exposure to Airborne Particulate Matter in Kathmandu Valley, Nepal'. *Journal of Exposure Science and Environmental Epidemiology* 22, 235–242. doi.org/10.1038/jes.2012.14.

Gustafsson, Ö., Kruså, M., Zencak, Z., Sheesley, R. J., Granat, L. and Engström, E. 2009. 'Brown Clouds over South Asia: Biomass or Fossil Fuel Combustion'. *Science* 323, 495–498.

Hawken, P. 2017. *Drawdown: The Most Comprehensive Plan Ever Proposed to Reverse Global Warming*. New York: Penguin Books.

Hewitt, K. 2005. 'The Karakoram Anomaly? Glacier Expansion and the "Elevation Effect," Karakoram Himalaya'. *Mountain Research and Development* 25(4), 332–340.

Hock, R., Rasul, G., Adler, C., Cáceres, B., Gruber, S. and Hirabayashi, Y. 2019. 'High Mountain Areas. IPCC Special Report on the Ocean and Cryosphere in a Changing Climate'. In H.-O. Pörtner, D. C. Roberts, V. Masson-Delmotte, P. Zhai, M. Tignor, E. Poloczanska, K. Mintenbeck, A. Alegría, M. Nicolai, A. Okem, J. Petzold, B. Rama and N. M. Weyer, eds., *IPCC Special Report on the Ocean and Cryosphere in a Changing Climate*. Geneva: Intergovernmental Panel on Climate Change.

Immerzeel, W. W., Van Beek, L. P. H. and Bierkens, M. F. P. 2010. 'Climate Change Will Affect the Asian Water Towers'. *Science* 328(5984), 1382–1385. doi.org/10.1126/science.1183188.

Intergovernmental Panel on Climate Change (IPCC). 2018. *An IPCC Special Report on the Impacts of Global Warming of 1.5°C*. Geneva: Intergovernmental Panel on Climate Change.

————. 2021. 'IPCC, 2021: Summary for Policymakers'. In V. Masson-Delmotte, P. Zhai, A. Pirani, S. L. Connors, C. Péan, S. Berger, N. Caud, Y. Chen, L. Goldfarb, M. I. Gomis, M. Huang, K. Leitzell, E. Lonnoy, J.B.R. Matthews, T. K. Maycock, T. Waterfield, O. Yelekçi, R. Yu and B. Zhou, eds., *Climate Change 2021: The Physical Science Basis. Contribution of Working Group I to the Sixth Assessment Report of the Intergovernmental Panel on Climate Change*. Cambridge: Cambridge University Press, SPM1-41.

Kang, S., Zhang, Q., Qian, Y., Ji, Z., Li, C. and Cong, Z. 2019. 'Linking Atmospheric Pollution to Cryospheric Change in the Third Pole Region: Current Progress and Future Prospects'. *National Science Review* 6(4), 796–809. doi.org/10.1093/nsr/nwz031.

Krishnan, R., Shrestha, A. B., Ren, G., Rajbhandari, R., Saeed, S. and Sanjay, J. 2019. 'Unravelling Climate Change in the Hindu Kush Himalaya: Rapid Warming in the Mountains and Increasing Extremes'. In P. Wester, A. Mishra, A. Mukherji and A. B. Shrestha, eds., *The Hindu Kush Himalaya Assessment*. New York: Springer International Publishing, 57–97. doi.org/10.1007/978-3-319-92288-1_3.

Lau, K.-M. and Kim, K.-M. 2006. 'Observational Relationships between Aerosol and Asian Monsoon Rainfall, and Circulation'. *Geophysical Research Letters* 33(L21810). doi.org/10.1029/2006GL027546.

Lau, K. M., Kim, M. K. and Kim, K. M. 2006. 'Asian Summer Monsoon Anomalies Induced by Aerosol Direct Forcing: The Role of the Tibetan Plateau'. *Climate Dynamics* 26, 855–864. link.springer.com/article/10.1007/s00382-006-0114-z.

Lau, W. K. M. and Kim, K. M. 2012. 'The 2010 Pakistan Flood and Russian Heat Wave: Teleconnection of Hydrometeorological Extremes'. *Journal of Hydrometeorology* 13(1). doi.org/10.1175/JHM-D-11-016.1.

Liu, X. and Chen, B. 2000. 'Climatic Warming in the Tibetan Plateau during Recent Decades'. *International Journal of Climatology* 20(14), 1729–1742.

Lüthi, Z. L., Škerlak, B., Kim, S.-W., Lauer, A., Mues, A., Rupakheti, M. and Kang, S. 2014. 'Atmospheric Brown Clouds Reach the Tibetan Plateau by Crossing the Himalayas'. *Atmospheric Chemistry and Physics Discussions* 14(20). doi.org/10.5194/acpd-14-28105-2014.

Mandal, C.K. 2021. 'Water from Melamchi Finally Arrives in Kathmandu'. *Kathmandu Post*, 7 March. tkpo.st/3efHWj3.

Mani, M. 2021. *Glaciers of the Himalayas: Climate Change, Black Carbon, and Regional Resilience*. South Asia Development Forum. Washington, DC: The World Bank Group. openknowledge.worldbank.org/handle/10986/35600.

Marinoni, A., Cristofanelli, P., Laj, P., Duchi, R., Calzolari, F. and Deceseri, S. 2010. 'Aerosol Mass and Black Carbon Concentrations, a Two-Year Record at NCO-P (5079m, Southern Himalayas)'. *Atmospheric Chemistry and Physics* 10, 8551–8562.

Maskey, R., Khanal, S., Kayastha, R., Bhochhibhoya, S., Aryal, N., Manandhar, A. and Ghimire, P. 2013. 'Water and Energy Security Mountainous Region of Nepal: Lesson from Dig-Tsho, Tsho-Rolpa and Imja Glacial Lakes'. Paper presented at International DAAD Alumni Expert Seminar 'Science meets Economy Water and Waste Water Management', 9-16 October, Mumbai, India.

Mehra, M., Panday, A., Praveen, P. S., Adhikary, B., Pokhrel, C. and Ram, K. 2018. *Influence of Open Fires on Air Quality over Chitwan, Nepal*. Kathmandu: Science and Policy Dialogue Workshop.

Ministry of Forests and Environment (MoFE) Nepal. 2019. *Climate Change Scenarios for Nepal for National Adaptation Plan (NAP)*. Kathmandu: Ministry of Forests and Environment.

Mishra, A., Appadurai, A. N., Choudhury, D., Regmi, B. R., Kelkar, U., and Alam, M. 2019. 'Adaptation to Climate Change in the Hindu Kush Himalaya: Stronger Action Urgently Needed'. In P. Wester, A. Mishra, A. Mukherji and A. B. Shrestha, eds., *The Hindu Kush Himalaya Assessment*. New York: Springer International Publishing, 457–490. doi.org/10.1007/978-3-319-92288-1_13.

National Aeronautics and Space Administration (NASA). 2020. 'NASA Worldview'. National Aeronautics and Space Administration, Washington, DC. worldview.earthdata.nasa.gov/.

Nepal, S., Mahapatra, P. S., Adhikari, S., Shrestha, S., Sharma, P. and Shrestha, K. L. 2019. 'A Comparative Study of Stack Emissions from Straight-Line and Zigzag Brick Kilns in Nepal'. *Atmosphere* 10(3). doi.org/10.3390/atmos10030107.

Nie, Y., Pritchard, H. D., Liu, Q., Hennig, T., Wang, W., Wang, X., Liu, S., Nepal, S., Samyn, D., Hewitt, K. and Chen, X. 2021. 'Glacial Change and Hydrological Implications in the Himalaya and Karakoram'. *Nature Reviews* 2, 91–106. doi.org/10.1038/s43017-020-00124-w.

Pepin, N., Bradley, H. F., Baraer, M., Caceres, E. B., Forsythe, N. and Fowler, H. 2015. 'Elevation-Dependent Warming in Mountain Regions of the World'. *Nature Climate Change* 5, 424–430.

Pokharel, L. N. No date. 'Countermeasures at the Tsho Rolpa Glacier Lake'. Asian Disaster Reduction Center, Kobe. adrc.asia/management/NPL/TSHO_ROLPA_GLACIER_LAKE.html.

Prabhakar, S. V. R. K., Shivakoti, B. R., Scheyvens, H. and Corral, A. 2018. *Transboundary Impacts of Climate Change in Asia: Making a Case for Regional Adaptation Planning and Cooperation*. Hayama: Institute for Global Environmental Strategies. iges.or.jp/en/pub/transboundary-impacts-climate-change-asia/en.

Praveen, P. S., Ahmed, T., Kar, A., Rehman, I. H. and Ramanathan, V. 2012. 'Link between Local Scale BC Emissions in the Indo-Gangetic Plains and Large Scale Atmospheric Solar Absorption'. *Atmospheric Chemistry and Physics* 12(2), 1173–1187.

Rai, M., Mahapatra, P. S., Gul, C., Kayastha, R. B., Panday, A. K. and Puppala, S. P. 2019. 'Aerosol Radiative Forcing Estimation over a Remote High-Altitude Location (~4900 masl) near Yala Glacier, Nepal'. *Aerosol and Air Quality Research* 19(8). doi. org/10.4209/aaqr.2018.09.0342.

Ramanathan, V. and Carmichael, G. 2008. 'Global and Regional Climate Changes due to Black Carbon'. *Nature Geoscience* 1, 221–227.

Rosenfeld, D., Lohmann, U., Raga, G. B., O'Dowd, C. D., Kulmala, M. and Fuzzi, S. No date. 'Flood or Drought: How Do Aerosols Affect Precipitation?' *Science* 321, 1309–1313.

Rupakheti, D., Adhikary, B., Praveen, P. S., Rupakheti, M., Kang, S., Mahata, K. S., et al. 2017. 'Pre-Monsoon Air Quality over Lumbini, a World Heritage Site along the Himalayan Foothills'. *Atmospheric Chemistry and Physics* 17. doi.org/10.5194/acp-17-11041-2017.

Rupakheti, D., Kang, S., Cong, Z., Rupakheti, M., Tripathee, L., Panday, A. K. and Holben, B. 2018. 'Study of Aerosol Optical Properties over Two Sites in the Foothills of the Central Himalayas'. *International Archives of the Photogrammetry, Remote Sensing and Spatial Information Sciences* 42(3). doi.org/10.5194/isprs-archives-XLII-3-1493-2018.

Saikawa, E., Panday, A., Kang, S., Gautam, R., Zusman, E. and Cong, Z. 2019. 'Air Pollution in the Hindu Kush Himalaya'. In P. Wester, A. Mishra, A. Mukherji and A. B. Shrestha, eds., *The Hindu Kush Himalaya Assessment*. New York: Springer International Publishing, 339–387. doi.org/10.1007/978-3-319-92288-1_10.

Scott, C. A., Zhang, F., Mukherji, A., Immerzeel, W., Mustafa, D. and Bharati, L. 2019. 'Water in the Hindu Kush Himalaya'. In P. Wester, A. Mishra, A. Mukherji and A. B. Shrestha, eds., *The Hindu Kush Himalaya Assessment*. New York: Springer International Publishing, 257–299. doi.org/10.1007/978-3-319-92288-1_8.

Shakya, K. M., Rupakheti, M., Shahi, A., Maskey, R., Pradhan, B. and Panday, A. 2017. 'Near-Road Sampling of PM2. 5, BC, and Fine-Particle Chemical Components in Kathmandu Valley, Nepal'. *Atmospheric Chemistry and Physics* 17(10). doi.org/10.5194/acp-17-6503-2017.

Sharma, E., Molden, D., Rahman, A., Khatiwada, Y. R., Zhang, L. and Singh, S. P. 2019. 'Introduction to the Hindu Kush Himalaya Assessment'. In P. Wester, A. Mishra, A. Mukherji and A. B. Shrestha, eds., *The Hindu Kush Himalaya Assessment*. New York: Springer International Publishing, 1–16. doi.org/10.1007/978-3-319-92288-1_1.

Shindell, D., Borgford-Parnell, N., Brauer, M., Haines, A., Kuylenstierna, J. C. I. and Leonard, S. A. 2017. 'A Climate Policy Pathway for Near- and Long-Term Benefits'. *Science* 356(6337), 493–494. doi.org/10.1126/science.aak9521.

Shivakoti, B. R., Lopez-Casero, F., Kataoka, Y. and Shrestha, S. 2014. *Climate Change, Changing Rainfall and Increasing Water Scarcity: An Integrated Approach for Planning Adaptation and Building Resilience of Smallholder Subsistence Livelihoods in Nepal*. Kanagawa: Institute for Global Environmental Strategies. jstor.org/stable/resrep00885.1?seq=1#metadata_info_tab_contents.

Shrestha, A., Agrawal, N., Alfthan, B., Bajracharya, S., Maréchal, J. and van Oort, B. 2015. *The Himalayan Climate and Water Atlas: Impact of Climate Change on Water Resources in Five of Asia's Major River Basins*. Lalitpur: The International Centre for Integrated Mountain Development, Arendal: GRID-Arendal and Oslo: CICERO Center for International Climate Research.

Streets, D. G., Wu, Y. and Chin, M. 2006. 'Two-Decadal Aerosol Trends as a Likely Explanation of the Global Dimming/Brightening Transition'. *Geophysical Research Letters* 33(L15806). doi.org/10.1029/2006GL026471.

Syed, F. S., Kornich, H. and Tjernstrom, M. 2012. 'On the Fog Variability over South Asia'. *Climate Dynamics* 39, 2993–3005.

Tripathi, S. N., Srivastava, A. K., Dey, S., Satheesh, S. K. and Krishnamoorthy, K. 2007. 'The Vertical Profile of Atmospheric Heating Rate of Black Carbon Aerosols at Kanpur in Northern India'. *Atmospheric Environment* 41(32), 6909–6915.

United Nations Environment Programme (UNEP). 2011. *Near-Term Climate Protection and Clean Air Benefits: Actions for Controlling Short-Lived Climate Forcers*. Nairobi: Climate and Clean Air Coalition. ccacoalition.org/en/resources/near-term-climate-protection-and-clean-air-benefits-actions-controlling-short-lived.

———. 2019. *Air Pollution in Asia and the Pacific: Science-Based Solutions: Full Report*. Nairobi: United Nations Environment Programme.

———. 2021. *Emissions Gap Report 2021: The Heat Is On – A World of Climate Promises Not Yet Delivered*. Nairobi: United Nations Environment Programme.

United Nations Environment Programme (UNEP) and World Meteorological Organization (WMO). 2011. *Integrated Assessment of Black Carbon and Tropospheric Ozone*. New York: United Nations Environment Programme.

Vaidya, R. A., Shrestha, M. S., Nasab, N., Gurung, D. R., Kozo, N., Pradhan, N. S. and Wasson, R. J. 2019. 'Disaster Risk Reduction and Building Resilience in the Hindu Kush Himalaya'. In P. Wester, A. Mishra, A. Mukherji and A. B. Shrestha, eds., *The Hindu Kush Himalaya Assessment*. New York: Springer International Publishing, 389–419. doi.org/10.1007/978-3-319-92288-1_11.

Wan, X., Kang, S., Li, Q., Rupakheti, D., Zhang, Q. and Guo, J. 2017. 'Organic Molecular Tracers in the Atmospheric Aerosols from Lumbini, Nepal, in the Northern Indo-Gangetic Plain: Influence of Biomass Burning'. *Atmospheric Chemistry and Physics* 17(14). doi.org/10.5194/acp-17-8867-2017.

Wang, Y., Li, S. and Luo, D. 2009. 'Seasonal Response of Asian Monsoonal Climate to the Atlantic Multidecadal Oscillation'. *Journal of Geophysical Research* 114(D02112). doi.org/10.1029/2008JD010929.

Wester, P., Mishra, A., Mukherji, A. and Shrestha, A. B., eds. 2019. *The Hindu Kush Himalaya Assessment: Mountains, Climate Change, Sustainability and People*. Cham: Springer Nature. springer.com/gp/book/9783319922874.

Wild, M., Ohmura, A. and Makowski, K. 2007. 'Impact of Global Dimming and Brightening Global Warming'. *Geophysical Research Letters* 34(L04702). doi.org/10.1029/2006GL028031.

World Bank. 2013. *On Thin Ice: How Cutting Pollution Can Slow Warming and Save Lives*. Washington, DC: The World Bank Group.

Xia, X., Wang, P., Wang, Y., Li, Z., Xin, J., Liu, J. and Chen, H. 2008. 'Aerosol Optical Depth over the Tibetan Plateau and Its Relation to Aerosols over the Taklimakan Desert'. *Geophysical Research Letters*, 35(L16804). doi.org/10.1029/2008GL034981.

Xia, X., Zong, X., Cong, Z., Chen, H., Kang, S. and Wang, P. 2011. 'Baseline Continental Aerosol over The Central Tibetan Plateau and a Case Study of Aerosol Transport from South Asia'. *Atmospheric Environment* 45(39). doi.org/10.1016/j.atmosenv.2011.07.067.

Xu, X., Lu, C., Shi, X. and Gao, S. 2008. 'World Water Tower: An Atmospheric Perspective'. *Geophysical Research Letters* 35(L20815). doi.org/10.1029/2008GL035867.

Yang, B., Tang, L., Bräuning, A., Davis, M. E., Shao, J. and Jingjing, L. 2008. 'Summer Temperature Reconstruction on the Central Tibetan Plateau during 1860–2002 Derived from Annually Resolved Ice Core Pollen'. *Journal of Geophysical Research* 113(D24102). doi.org/10.1029/2007JD010142.

Yasunari, T. J., Bonasoni, P., Laj, P., Fujita, K., Vuillermoz, E. and Marinoni, A. 2010. 'Estimated Impact of Black Carbon Deposition during Pre-Monsoon Season from Nepal Climate Observatory: Pyramid Data and Snow Albedo Changes over Himalayan Glaciers'. *Atmospheric Chemistry and Physics* 10(14), 6603–6615. doi.org/10.5194/acp-10-6603-2010.

3 | Accelerating Universal Digital Connectivity

Paul Garnett

INTRODUCTION

Even with all the progress made over the last few decades, the United Nations Development Programme (UNDP) has reported that widespread disparities remain in human development and continue to widen across many dimensions and regions (UNDP, 2019).[1] The digital divide, or lack of universal affordable digital connectivity, is one manifestation of this trend. As depicted in Figure 3.1, gains have occurred in basic capabilities (UNDP, 2019). As with other measures of human development,

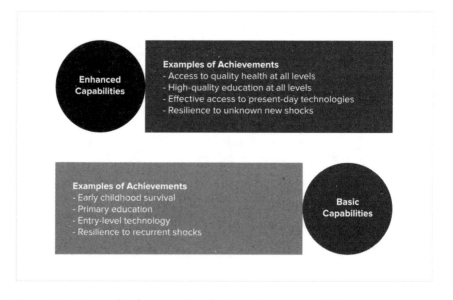

Figure 3.1 Human development, from basic to enhanced capabilities
Source: UNDP (2019).

those at the bottom have made advances in the basics of Internet access, such as basic mobile connectivity and limited Wi-Fi kiosk access. However, divergence appears in enhanced capabilities, including unlimited data consumption on high-speed mobile and fixed connections at home and access to cloud-based productivity tools. Gaps in enhanced capabilities exceed those in the basic ones, and gaps have continued to rise.

With rapid progress in technologies, digital inequality runs the risk of widening at an accelerating pace over time. This undermines the achievement of fundamental freedoms to make life choices. As with income inequality and other indicators of human development, reversing trends towards digital inequality calls for urgent steps in the near future. The foundational role of connectivity in human development has found wider recognition in recent years (UNDP, 2019; Broadband Commission, 2020a). Universal connectivity now appears as a fundamental element of an inclusive and sustainable world – for improving the quality of education and health care, standards of living, personal safety, freedom of choice and overall life satisfaction. One cannot achieve the United Nations (UN) Sustainable Development Goals (SDGs) without universal affordable broadband availability. The global COVID-19 pandemic has only amplified the importance of connectivity for social and economic inclusion, including access to education, healthcare, remote work and political participation. COVID-19's impact on childhood education has proven particularly acute.

With its tremendous economic and cultural diversity, the Asia and the Pacific Region (APR) very much exemplifies what we see globally on broadband availability and adoption. The data show that the APR has made significant progress over the last decade increasing the availability and affordability of Internet connectivity, but more than half of people in the APR remain offline, and fixed and mobile broadband remains unaffordable in most APR countries. The data also show that digital inequality disproportionately impacts the following groups in the APR: low-income populations residing in the least developed countries (LDCs); those located in rural areas, in small island developing nations and in landlocked developing countries; those lacking literacy and digital skills; and those from traditionally disenfranchised groups, such as women and girls, persons with disabilities and ethnic minorities. The Broadband Commission for Sustainable Development (Broadband Commission), a joint initiative by the International Telecommunication Union (ITU) and the United Nations Educational, Scientific and Cultural Organization (UNESCO) to promote universal broadband Internet access, has observed that digital inequality persists around the world even in countries with high-speed connectivity infrastructure (Broadband Commission, 2020b).

Global efforts to close the digital divide have not aimed high enough. Basic connectivity targets will simply lead to greater inequalities in basic and enhanced capabilities in the future. New goals should reflect where technology is going, not where it is today (or, worse yet, where it was 10–20 years ago). Achieving aggressive digital inclusion targets will need a coordinated and concerted effort, one that incorporates proven, as well as new, technological, financial, and regulatory approaches.

Currently, regulatory, marketplace and technological hurdles impede efforts to achieve universal affordable broadband access across the APR. These include regulatory uncertainty and fragmentation, lack of access to financing, uneven availability of infrastructure and technologies, lack of service affordability and consumability, uneven digital skills attainment (and literacy), and unequal relevance and accessibility of online content.

Fortunately, governments and network operators have a growing menu of technology options available to them for delivering cost-effective, affordable connectivity to underserved and unserved communities. Funding for digital infrastructure primarily comes from three sources – the private sector, governments, and international financial institutions (IFIs) (in the case of emerging markets); but providers will need to consider innovative financing mechanisms in order to spur market entry, expansion, and technology and business-model innovation.

In this chapter, we discuss efforts across the APR to accelerate universal digital connectivity.[2] In the first section, we provide an overview of the state of global broadband access and UN and ITU goals and efforts to achieve global universal digital connectivity and discuss the implications of the COVID-19 pandemic for global efforts to expand Internet connectivity. In the second section, we provide an overview and analysis of digital connectivity across the APR. In the third section, we discuss marketplace, technological, and regulatory hurdles that impede efforts to achieve universal and affordable broadband across the region. In the fourth section, we provide an overview of different approaches both the private and public sectors have taken and could adopt for financing the extension of affordable broadband access. In the fifth section, we assess various technology options available to governments and network operators looking to extend affordable broadband access to underserved and unserved communities. Finally, in the sixth section, we give an overview of successful policy approaches that Asian-Pacific and other governments have taken to help close digital divides in their countries.

Overview

According to the latest ITU data, global Internet user penetration is currently at 51 per cent, or about 4 billion people online, meaning that about 3.7 billion people around the world still do not have access to the Internet (ITU, 2020a). Global Internet user penetration is 44 per cent in developing countries, but only 19 per cent in LDCs. According to the ITU, the proportion of all women using the Internet globally is 48 per cent, against 55 per cent of all men (ITU, 2020a). More men than women use the Internet in every region of the world except the Americas, which has near-equality (ITU, 2020a).

Lack of Internet access also stymies the potential of children and young people. According to a new report commissioned by United Nations International Children's Emergency Fund (UNICEF) and the ITU Development Sector, 2.2 billion, or 67 per cent of children and young people aged 25 years or under, lack Internet access at home (UNICEF and ITU, 2020). In East Asia and the Pacific, 46 per cent of children and young people aged 25 years or under (369 million) lack home Internet access. In South Asia that number is 86 per cent (768 million young people) (UNICEF and ITU, 2020). Stark differences appear between rich and poor countries, with 94 per cent of children and young people in low-income countries lacking Internet access compared to 13 per cent in high-income countries.

In 2016, the United Nations General Assembly passed a resolution stressing the importance of "applying a comprehensive human rights-based approach in providing and in expanding access to Internet", requesting "all States to make efforts to bridge the many forms of digital divides" (UNDP, 2019: 233). This expansion must be consistent with general human rights principles: "The same rights that people have offline must also be protected online, in particular freedom of expression" (UNDP, 2019: 233).

UN Secretary-General António Guterres's Roadmap for Digital Cooperation represents a call to connect, respect, and protect the online world. It includes concrete actions in the following areas: achieving universal connectivity by 2030 – everyone should have safe and affordable access to the Internet; ensuring digital inclusion for all, including the most vulnerable – under-served groups need equal access to digital tools to accelerate development; and strengthening digital capacity – fostering skills development and training around the world (UN Secretary-General, 2020; UN, 2019).

The Broadband Commission for Sustainable Development,[3] established in 2010 by the ITU and UNESCO, aims to boost the importance of broadband on the international policy agenda and expand broadband access in every country, thus accelerating progress towards national and international development targets (Broadband Commission, 2020a). The Broadband Commission has established seven Advocacy Targets seeking to expand broadband infrastructure and Internet access and use by populations around the world:

- Advocacy Target 1 (policy): By 2025, all countries should have a funded national broadband plan or strategy, or include broadband in their universal access and services (UAS) definition.
- Advocacy Target 2 (affordability): By 2025, developing countries should make entry-level broadband services affordable, at less than 2 per cent of monthly per capita gross national income (GNI).

- Advocacy Target 3 (connectivity): By 2025, broadband-Internet user penetration should reach 75 per cent of the world's population overall, including 65 per cent in developing countries, and 35 per cent in LDCs.
- Advocacy Target 4 (skills): By 2025, 60 per cent of youth and adults should have achieved at least a minimum level of proficiency in sustainable digital skills.
- Advocacy Target 5 (digital finance): By 2025, 40 per cent of the world's population should be using digital financial services.
- Advocacy Target 6 (SMEs connectivity): By 2025, lack of Internet connectedness among micro-, small- and medium-sized enterprises (SMEs) should be reduced by 50 per cent, by sector.
- Advocacy Target 7 (gender equality): By 2025, gender equality should be achieved across all targets (Broadband Commission, 2020b).

The Broadband Commission has observed, "achieving affordable universal connectivity is essential for achieving the 17 Sustainable Development Goals (SDGs) and making good on our pledge to Leave No-one Behind" (Broadband Commission, 2020a: 20). According to the Broadband Commission, 4 of the 17 SDGs include targets related to information and communications technologies (ICT), and at least 38 other targets rely on universal and affordable access to ICT and broadband to reach SDG achievement (Broadband Commission, 2020b: 4).

THE IMPACT OF COVID-19

As noted earlier, the global COVID-19 pandemic has amplified the importance of connectivity for social and economic inclusion. According to the Broadband Commission, "the pandemic and its socio-economic impacts have underscored the urgency of concrete, coordinated actions across all sectors and geographies. With less than ten years remaining until 2030, now is the time to establish digital connectivity as the foundational pillar for our shared Global Goals" (Broadband Commission, 2020a: 2).

While the impact of the COVID-19 pandemic has manifested in numerous settings implicating connectivity to the Internet, its impact on childhood education appears particularly acute. Based on an August 2020 UN policy brief, school closures and learning disruptions resulting from the COVID-19 pandemic have impacted 94 per cent of the world's student population; in low- and lower-middle-income countries, up to 99 per cent of the student population has been affected (UN, 2020). This amounts to nearly 1.6 billion learners in more than 190 countries and on all continents, producing the largest disruption of education systems in history (UN, 2020: 2, 5). According to the UNDP, as a result of school closures and the lack of affordable broadband, 60 per cent of children are simply not receiving an education, leading to global education levels not seen since the 1980s (UNDP, 2020a, 2020b).

Some 23.8 million children and youth (from pre-primary to tertiary schools) may drop out or not have access to school in the coming year because of the pandemic's economic impact (UN, 2020: 10).

According to a recent UNDP report, "[t]he closure of schools can widen the digital gender divide due to unequal access to the Internet and technologies" (Rivera et al.: 8). As discussed later, there is a persistent gender gap in Internet utilization, with women and girls less likely than men and boys to own Internet-enabled devices and connect to the Internet, especially in South Asia. If women and girls are less likely than men and boys to access the Internet at home and therefore have less access to online educational content, then a school closure is likely to more acutely and detrimentally impact girls than boys.

The broader social and economic impacts of the COVID-19 pandemic appear equally startling. The World Bank has projected that – for the first time in 20 years – an additional 150 million people could sink into extreme poverty in 2021 as a result of the pandemic (World Bank, 2020; UNDP, 2020c). Another study, by the Pardee Center for International Futures at the University of Denver, finds that COVID-19 could drive the number of people living in extreme poverty to over 1 billion by 2030, with a quarter of a billion as a direct result of the pandemic (UNDP, 2020c). Because of COVID-19 pandemic's triple hit to health, education, and income, the UNDP has forecast an overall decline in the global Human Development Index for the first time since 1990 (UNDP, 2020a). These factors surely will place a drag on efforts to close the digital divide.

In its most recent *State of Broadband* report, the Broadband Commission has conceded that, at current rates of growth, it will probably not achieve its 2025 connectivity goals (Broadband Commission, 2020b: 21). Forecasts based on current growth projections suggest that global Internet adoption by 2025 may only reach 70 per cent, five percentage points below the 2025 Advocacy Target (Broadband Commission, 202b: 21). For LDCs, the 2025 forecast level only comes to 31 per cent, four points below the Advocacy Target (Broadband Commission, 202b: 21). Changing this trajectory will require a coordinated and concerted effort, one involving increased vigour and incorporating new technologies, business models and regulatory approaches.

THE STATUS OF DIGITAL CONNECTIVITY IN THE ASIA-PACIFIC REGION

The following is an overview of the current status of digital connectivity across the 38 countries of the APR. The region has seen significant progress; indeed, many of its countries are global leaders in digital connectivity. At the same time, more than half of people in the APR remain offline, with significant and persistent rural and gender divides in access, while affordability remains a challenge in less-developed and insular countries across the region.

Global Internet user penetration currently runs 51 per cent, or about 4 billion people online (ITU, 2020a). In the APR, penetration currently runs 45 per cent, or about 2 billion people online (ITU, 2020a; ITU, 2020b). As a reference point, in 2005, the APR had an Internet user penetration rate of 9.5 per cent, or about 355 million people online.

At the country level, Internet user penetration varies widely across the APR. This is consistent with patterns seen globally. Internet user penetration is over 80 per cent in countries and territories such as Australia, Brunei, Hong Kong SAR (China), Japan, Republic of Korea, Macao SAR (China), Malaysia, New Zealand and Singapore. By contrast, in populous and less-developed countries, such as Bangladesh, India and Pakistan, user penetration only reaches 20 per cent (ITU, 2020c).

A significant gender gap persists in Internet utilization as well. The proportion of all women using the Internet in the APR runs at 41 per cent, against 48 per cent of all men (versus 48 per cent and 55 per cent globally, as noted earlier), and – cause for even greater concern – the gap appears to be growing (ITU, 2020a, 2020b: 3–4). The gender gap in Internet use also correlates with one in mobile device ownership, globally and in the APR (ITU, 2020a: 6). At the same time, the mobile gender gap varies widely across Asia (GSMA, 2020). South Asia has the largest mobile gender gap of any region worldwide – a 23 per cent gender gap in mobile-device ownership and a 51 per cent gender gap in mobile-Internet use – while the most digitally mature low- and middle-income countries (LMICs) in East Asia and the Pacific have more equal levels of mobile ownership and use (GSMA, 2020).

Most of the world's population accesses the Internet through mobile networks. While 97 per cent of the global population and 95.4 per cent of the APR population live within reach of mobile network coverage, only 51 per cent globally and 45 per cent in the APR are online (ITU, 2020a: 8).[4] This indicates that Internet access alone is not sufficient to induce online activity. As discussed later, the quality (throughput and reliability) and cost of Internet access (including data consumption limits), as well as the cost of devices, availability of relevant content, digital skills and other factors, impact whether and how people access the Internet.

The Broadband Commission's second 2025 target would make entry-level mobile and fixed broadband services affordable in developing countries, at less than 2 per cent of monthly per capita GNI. For mobile broadband, the Commission defines entry-level service as providing at least 1.5 gigabytes (GB) of monthly data consumption on at least a 3G mobile network connection; for fixed broadband, this would mean at least 5GB of monthly data consumption on a connection providing at least 256 kilobits (kbits)/second (ITU, 2020a: 5). On these measures, the APR as a whole has made significant progress over the last decade or so and now fares well compared to other regions.

Figure 3.2 shows how the cost of fixed broadband in the APR has declined from 26.76 per cent of per capita GNI in 2008 to 5.1 per cent of per capita GNI in 2019 (ITU, 2021a). Figure 3.3 shows how the cost of data-only mobile broadband in the APR has declined from 7.92 per cent of per capita GNI in 2013 to 2.36 per cent of per capita GNI in 2019 – approaching the Broadband Commission's target. However, the rate of decline in the per cent of monthly per capita GNI for both fixed and mobile broadband has slowed in the last few years, indicating a need for further interventions to achieve the Broadband Commission's goals.

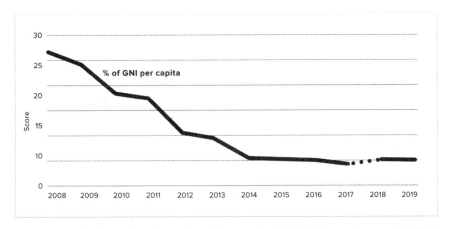

Figure 3.2 Decline in fixed-broadband data cost in Asia-Pacific, 2008–2019 (% GNI)
Source: ITU (2021a).

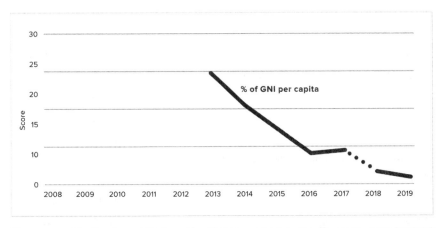

Figure 3.3 Decline in mobile-broadband data cost in Asia-Pacific, 2008–2019 (% GNI)
Source: ITU (2021a)

Table 3.1 shows that fixed broadband expenditure in the APR amounts to 5.1 per cent of per capita GNI, compared to 8.73 per cent globally (ITU, 2021b). Likewise, mobile-data-only packages amount to 2.36 per cent of per capita GNI, compared to 3.18 per cent globally. Pricing for mobile voice and short-message service (SMS) and voice, SMS and data in the APR also compares favourably with the rest of the world (ITU, 2021b).

At the same time, the APR is perhaps the most economically and socially diverse region on the planet, a fact reflected in widely varying digital service affordability across APR member states. While the price of fixed broadband is affordable in several countries (primarily developed economies) in the APR, it remains unaffordable in several markets (Table 3.2). Those countries with the highest percentage of per capita

Table 3.1 Comparison of fixed, mobile and voice telecommunications cost in Asia-Pacific versus World average (% GNI)

	World	Asia-Pacific
Fixed-broadband basket (5GB)		
% of GNI p.c.	8.73	5.1
US$	26.66	21.55
PPP$	42.44	33.85
Mobile-cellular basket low usage (70 min + 20 SMS)		
% of GNI p.c.	2.9	1.95
US$	11.8	9.38
PPP$	18.67	13.53
Low usage voice and data basket (70 min + 20 SMS + 500 MB)		
% of GNI p.c.	5.73	4.59
US$	15.07	13.46
PPP$	23.86	19.98
Data-only mobile broadband basket (1.5 GB)		
% of GNI p.c.	3.18	2.36
US$	13.22	9.88
PPP$	19.93	14.82
High usage voice and data basket (140 min + 70 SMS + 1.5GB)		
% of GNI p.c.	10.3	6.54
US$	25.27	22.02
PPP$	37.76	31.34

Source: ITU (2021b).

Table 3.2 Fixed-broadband tends to be the least affordable in the least-developed Asian-Pacific countries and territories (% GNI)

Global Rank	Economy	% of GNI p.c.	US$	PPP$	Tax rate included (%)
1	Macao SAR (China)	0.12	7.8	9.72	0
3	Hong Kong SAR (China)	0.51	21.43	26.23	0
4	China	0.57	4.53	7.87	0
8	Brunei	0.72	18.53	33.02	0
9	Iran	0.73	3.33	10.64	9
12	Singapore	0.76	36.99	44.01	7
26	Sri Lanka	0.98	3.32	10.12	19
28	Japan	1.02	35.21	35.81	8
36	Australia	1.18	52.3	45.51	10
37	Republic of Korea	1.23	31.48	36.02	10
41	New Zealand	1.32	44.97	40.49	15
67	Tonga	2.15	7.71	10.07	15
68	Mongolia	2.16	6.43	17.72	10
70	Nepal	2.3	1.84	5.38	13
72	Malaysia	2.38	20.75	50.4	6
80	Bangladesh	2.83	4.13	10.15	15
81	Bhutan	2.84	7.3	21.96	5
85	India	3.06	5.16	17.08	18
88	Maldives	3.11	24.11	31.68	6
94	Thailand	3.6	19.84	51.41	7
95	Viet Nam	3.65	7.3	17.77	10
99	Fiji	3.83	18.68	29.53	9
102	Philippines	4.16	13.27	34.23	12
118	Micronesia	6.7	20	20.47	0
131	Indonesia	8.69	27.81	78	10
133	Lao PDR	8.85	18.14	48.25	10
134	Samoa	8.86	30.92	42.48	15
137	Cambodia	10.43	12	29.36	10
138	Pakistan	10.6	13.95	50.69	0

(Continued)

Table 3.2 *(Continued)*

Global Rank	Economy	% of GNI p.c.	US$	PPP$	Tax rate included (%)
140	Marshall Islands	12.65	49.95	N/A	0
141	Myanmar	12.81	13.99	55.01	5
143	Afghanistan	15.13	6.94	23.61	0
152	Vanuatu	22.31	55.21	51.82	15
159	Papua New Guinea	30.67	64.65	78.52	10
161	Timor-Leste	32.31	49	76.22	5

Source: ITU (2021c).

GNI in the APR tend to be low-income states, landlocked developing countries, and small island developing states (ITU, 2021c).

In terms of entry-level fixed-broadband service, nine countries in the APR meet the Broadband Commission's 2 per cent threshold for 5GB of data: Australia, Brunei, China (including Hong Kong SAR and Macao SAR), Iran, Japan, New Zealand, Republic of Korea, Singapore and Sri Lanka. None of the APR LDCs, landlocked developing countries, or small island developing states meet the 2 per cent threshold for fixed-broadband services.

Table 3.3 shows that, while the price of mobile-data-only packages in the APR is generally affordable in the developed economies, it remains unaffordable in one low-income state and the majority of landlocked developing countries and small island developing states (ITU, 2021c).

Additionally, a major urban–rural divide exists in the APR: 70 per cent of urban households access the Internet, but only 37 per cent of rural households do so (ITU, 2020d). In East Asia and the Pacific, the percentage of children and young people aged 25 years or less with Internet access at home is 72 per cent in urban areas, but only 53 per cent in rural areas. In South Asia, the percentage of children and young people aged 25 years or less with Internet access at home is 22 per cent in urban areas, but only 9 per cent in rural areas (UNICEF and ITU, 2020, p.8).

Overall, this review of data shows that while the APR has made significant progress over the last decade with regard to digital services, more than half of people in the region remain offline; access divides persist between urban and rural areas, with women and girls less likely to be online than men and boys. Fixed and mobile broadband remains unaffordable in most APR countries. The COVID-19 pandemic both exacerbates these divides and increases the urgency of taking action to address them.

Table 3.3   Mobile-broadband data tends to be the least affordable in the least developed Asian-Pacific countries and territories (% GNI)

Global Rank	Economy	% of GNI p.c.	US$	PPP$	Tax rate included (%)
2	Macao SAR (China)	0.19	12.14	15.12	0
6	Hong Kong SAR (China)	0.29	12.25	14.99	0
7	Singapore	0.3	14.83	17.64	7
16	New Zealand	0.39	13.15	11.84	15
19	Republic of Korea	0.44	11.24	12.86	10
21	Australia	0.49	21.67	18.85	10
25	Brunei	0.57	14.83	26.42	0
29	Sri Lanka	0.63	2.15	6.56	19
35	Iran	0.75	3.4	10.86	9
36	Indonesia	0.75	2.39	6.66	10
37	Pakistan	0.75	0.99	3.58	0
49	India	0.85	1.43	4.75	18
50	Malaysia	0.85	7.43	18.05	0
56	China	0.96	7.56	13.11	0
57	Myanmar	0.96	1.05	4.12	5
61	Japan	0.99	34.23	34.82	8
66	Viet Nam	1.11	2.21	5.39	10
68	Bhutan	1.13	2.91	8.76	5
79	Thailand	1.44	7.91	20.51	7
82	Tonga	1.5	5.37	7	15
87	Cambodia	1.74	2	4.89	10
89	Philippines	1.78	5.68	14.64	12
91	Bangladesh	1.88	2.74	6.73	21
96	Maldives	2.04	15.84	20.82	6
103	Mongolia	2.24	6.67	18.39	10
106	Nauru	2.47	23.16	N/A	15
110	Fiji	2.74	13.39	21.17	9
111	Nepal	2.75	2.2	6.46	26

(Continued)

Table 3.3   *(Continued)*

Global Rank	Economy	% of GNI p.c.	US$	PPP$	Tax rate included (%)
119	Lao PDR	3.16	6.48	17.23	10
127	Vanuatu	3.67	9.08	8.52	15
137	Samoa	4.43	15.46	21.24	15
145	Timor-Leste	5.27	8	12.44	5
150	Kiribati	5.71	14.94	N/A	0
162	Afghanistan	9.08	4.16	14.17	0
165	Micronesia	10.06	30	30.7	0
167	Papua New Guinea	10.41	21.96	26.67	10
171	Solomon Islands	16.6	27.66	28.52	10

Source: ITU (2021c).

HURDLES TO ATTAINING GREATER CONNECTIVITY

The following section identifies regulatory, marketplace and technological hurdles that impede efforts to achieve universal affordable broadband access across the APR. Figure 3.4 represents the range of issues one needs to address in extending broadband and digital services to unserved and underserved communities.

Legal and regulatory issues can offer both inducements and impediments to investment in broadband service deployment. With the right regulatory environment in place, a government can attract investment needed to extend broadband into underserved and unserved communities. Good regulations can literally change the cost-economics of broadband deployments, allowing unprofitable investments to become profitable.[5] On the other hand, the absence of a regulatory framework can discourage investment. In addition, the lack of harmonized regulations (that is, fragmentation) across a region can discourage investment, especially in small markets, such as small island developing states, which might not attract investment

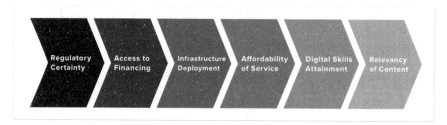

Figure 3.4   Range of issues for the extension of broadband and digital services
Source: Author.

on their own. Moreover, regulatory uncertainty (or a constantly changing regulatory environment) creates risk and can also discourage investment.

Telecommunications is a capital-intensive industry requiring large-scale multi-year investments prior to delivering services. It is also a scale industry: The incremental costs of delivering bandwidth to customers decline as networks grow larger and serve more customers. This creates high barriers to entry for prospective market participants and holds especially true for first- and middle-mile infrastructure, as well as for mobile wireless and fibre-based fixed last-mile infrastructure. This also holds for satellite communications. Some forms of fixed-wireless infrastructure have lower upfront capital requirements and, therefore, lower barriers to market entry.

Access to financing poses one of the greatest challenges facing companies looking to deploy digital services in emerging markets. In the next section, we discuss costs and financing options for achieving universal broadband.

According to the GSM Association for the mobile industry, 3.3 billion people live in areas covered by mobile broadband networks but do not use mobile Internet – a usage gap more than four times greater than the coverage gap (GSMA, 2019). In low- and middle-income countries, in addition to unaffordability and low digital literacy and skills discussed earlier, a perceived lack of relevance and safety and security concerns pose the next most important barriers to mobile Internet use from a consumer point of view (GSMA, 2019). Addressing these barriers will prove critical in further reducing the usage gap and driving digital inclusion (GSMA, 2019). These same issues hinder adoption of fixed broadband services.

If we intend to achieve universal broadband, we will need to make it affordable for more of the world's population. One important piece to the affordability puzzle is selling broadband access in a way that allows for different types of customers. A post-paid monthly subscription (often with annual or multi-year commitments) is common in developed markets; it also serves higher-income consumers, businesses and government customers in emerging ones. By contrast, the prepaid or pay-as-you-go model offers Internet access to low-income consumers in developed markets and to most customers in emerging ones. These latter customers often purchase their Internet access in small increments, measured in 10s of megabytes (MBs) of data consumption, in the same way that they purchase other goods and services. In many markets, such customers are unbanked: Fully "two billion adults are still without access to a bank account, but some 1.6 billion people in this group have access to a mobile phone, presenting the opportunity to explore strategies that leverage the widespread use of mobile phones to offer financial inclusion options" (Broadband Commission, 2020b: 28). As discussed earlier, the Broadband Commission's Advocacy Target 5 calls for at least 40 per cent of the world's population to use digital financial services by 2025. Even as more of the world's population gains access to such services, Internet service providers need to have payment infrastructure in place that can accommodate both post-paid monthly subscription customers and prepaid pay-as-you-go customers.

However, even with access to affordable services, many people in the APR still do not use them: a lack of literacy and digital skills and the lack of relevant content ranked higher than affordability for low- and middle-income-country consumers surveyed in South Asia and East Asia (GSMA, 2019: 33). Digital skills – in essence, understanding how to use technology – are critical for fully benefiting from digital services. The Broadband Commission's Advocacy Target 4 calls for 60 per cent of youth and adults to achieve at least a minimum level of proficiency in sustainable digital skills by 2025 (GSMA, 2019). For mobile Internet use, literacy and skills remain the most significant self-reported barrier across the world, accounting for 37 per cent of responses in South Asia and 35 per cent in East Asia. For example, in Bangladesh's recent National ICT Household Survey 2018–2019, the number one reason for non-connectivity is '[c]annot use Internet' (GSMA, 2019: 35). Governments should prioritize digital-skills programmes for school children and young people, as well as adults of all ages and for other groups with low adoption rates (Broadband Commission, 2020b).[6]

Finally, and crucially, consumers should have access to content relevant to them and in their first language. Consumers who are not online report a lack of both as barriers and disincentives (GSMA, 2019). As Internet content becomes more relevant, consumers should prove more willing and able to make productive use of their Internet access. While the English language continues to dominate the Internet, numerous efforts are underway to encourage the development of relevant content in more local languages (W3Techs, 2021).[7]

Costs and Financing Options for Universal Connectivity

This section provides an overview of different approaches open to both the private and public sectors in financing affordable broadband access in underserved communities. Funding for universal service connectivity comes from three primary sources: the private sector; governments; and international financial institutions in the case of emerging markets (Broadband Commission, 2019).

Network operators and service providers will probably play a critical role as key investors in broadband networks through continued and increased levels of commitment to expand network coverage beyond urban population centres – essentially deploying funding from existing operations gained through cost reductions and by raising capital from commercial banks and private investors. Other options include the network as a service, in which infrastructure and equipment vendors share investment risk with service providers (for example, through revenue sharing). In addition, network operators focusing on underserved and unserved communities could benefit from the emergence of environmental, social and governance (ESG) investing, in which investors target investments and accept lower returns in exchange for socially beneficial outcomes (Garnett, 2020; Digital Ubiquity Capital, 2021). The Broadband Commission has observed that achieving commercially sustainable investment will require innovations that lower the capital expenditure and operating expense of towers and infrastructure overall, while enhancing demands for mobile and fixed broadband services and corresponding market growth (Broadband Commission, 2019: 110; ITU, 2021e).

Some areas will not have scope for profitable deployment of networks and services, and therefore the market alone will not support investment needed for universal broadband. In such cases, governments must take an increasing role as 'investors' in broadband infrastructure in order to ensure that countries can achieve their national development agendas. Governments have adopted various approaches to funding these plans: dedicated funds, universal service funds (overseen by the national regulator and in some cases independently administered), direct government subsidies and grants, government equity and loans, public-private partnerships and investment tax zones.[8] It is critical that governments not only invest their resources effectively but also, as discussed later, that they develop policy and regulatory environments that will incentivize and promote investments and market growth.

Multilateral development banks, such as the World Bank, and regional development banks, such as the Asian Development Bank, have supplied funding for infrastructure and projects in general, alongside other donors (Broadband Commission, 2019: 110). These organizations may lend at preferential rates for long-term projects in some cases, focusing their resources on projects with high economic development impact (Broadband Commission, 2014). They can also provide equally critical research, consulting and other resources, usually through non-refundable grants, as well as expertise and knowledge – very useful, for example, in a public–private partnership process. The ITU also has a key role in coordinating technical, economic and regulatory matters relating to ensuring universal, affordable and good-quality broadband connectivity.

Options in technology and infrastructure

There are various technology options available to governments and network operators looking to extend affordable broadband access to underserved and unserved communities, including traditional fibre, coaxial cable and copper infrastructure, various fixed and mobile terrestrial wireless solutions, geo-stationary and low-earth-orbit satellites, and other emerging and experimental technologies. Governments and network operators have a growing menu of options available to them for cost-effective delivery of affordable connectivity.

The broadband network value chain (or building blocks) for developing universal, affordable and high-quality broadband Internet access comprises four broad segments: first mile, middle mile, last mile and invisible mile (Broadband Commission, 2019). Delivery of fixed or mobile Internet access requires connecting all parts of the value chain, along with supporting infrastructure, such as data centres and a reliable electricity supply, and devices used to access the Internet.

The first mile is where the Internet enters a country (Broadband Commission, 2019). The network components include international access infrastructure, such as submarine cables, landing stations, satellite dishes, cross-border microwave and fibre links, domain name registration and so on. Countries need connections to undersea cables or via cross-border terrestrial links, particularly for landlocked countries. Many countries in the APR have access to submarine cable systems, either directly through local landing points or through terrestrial connections (ITU, 2020d). However, some small island developing states in the APR, such as Nauru, Kiribati and Tuvalu, lack access to submarine cable systems and therefore must rely on satellite connectivity in the first mile (ITU, 2020d).

The middle mile is where the Internet passes through a country (Broadband Commission, 2019). The network components here are the national backbone and intercity networks, including the fibre optic cables or copper wires, microwave, satellite links, Internet exchange points (IXPs), local hosting of content, and so on. Once connected to high-speed Internet at the border, countries in the APR require fibre backbones to carry Internet traffic from the border to urban and rural centres; they also require backhaul or metro networks to extend further. Satellite transmission remains important in the APR small island developing states and other rural or remote locations that lack access to terrestrial first- or middle-mile networks. In addition, while most APR countries have IXPs, with the exception of Vanuatu most of the small island developing states do not, nor do Bangladesh, Lao PDR, Mongolia, Papua New Guinea, Timor-Leste and Sri Lanka (Internet Exchange Map, 2021). These countries have their domestic Internet traffic exchanged through points outside their borders, usually through satellite or fibre across international hubs, to reach their destinations.

The last mile is where the Internet reaches the end-user (Broadband Commission, 2019). Once high-speed Internet arrives at a population centre, via the first and middle miles, network operators provide mobile or fixed Internet access services to consumers, businesses and governments. Network components include central office exchanges, the local loop -- historically composed of copper cables, but now increasingly replaced with fibre for last-mile connections in urban or suburban areas – and wireless masts for mobile and fixed wireless connectivity, as well as satellite connections in remote locations that do not permit an economic deployment of terrestrial networks (ITU, 2020e). New developments have also enabled network operators to cost-effectively deploy high-speed last-mile networks to locations outside of population centres. For example, new high-capacity terrestrial fixed-wireless access solutions have become viable in more places, and pilot projects have begun to test other innovative solutions such as drones or balloons. Additionally, new Low Earth Orbit satellite solutions promise to deliver lower latency and higher throughput Internet connections to locations around the world (Broadband Commission, 2017).

The invisible mile consists of the hidden elements vital to ensuring the integrity of the value chain (Broadband Commission, 2019). These include unseen network components, such as the radio spectrum, network databases (for example, for numbering), cybersecurity, and so on, but can also include potential bottlenecks, such as market concentration, multi-layered taxation of activities, lack of access to rights-of-way and inefficient regulations including transborder regulatory issues.

Access to reliable electricity also poses a major constraint to the expansion of digital infrastructure in some parts of the APR. Bangladesh, Democratic People's Republic of Korea, India, Myanmar and Pakistan are among the 20 countries in the world with the greatest electricity access deficits (IEA et al., 2019). Digital access requires electricity for a range of activities, from charging devices to powering networks. Even in some grid-connected areas, electricity-service quality is often low, with frequent and sometimes long-lasting outages.

In addition, some countries have difficulty sustaining electricity costs, adding to the cost of broadband access. Moreover, the same urban–rural and gender divides that plague Internet usage also impact electricity usage (IEA et al., 2019). Fortunately, increasing investment in rural electricity mini-grids and off-grid solar has started to offer more cost-effective solutions than grid extensions to remote and rural areas (IEA et al., 2019).

POLICY APPROACHES AND SUGGESTIONS

This section provides an overview of policy approaches that Asian-Pacific and other governments have adopted to help close the digital divides in their countries through a review of competition, spectrum, universal services, and other policies; also included are brief suggestions for further steps that policymakers and regulators could take to improve their chances of success.

A well-designed broadband plan can offer an important blueprint for addressing digital inequality. The Broadband Commission's Advocacy Target 1 aims for all countries to have a funded national broadband plan or strategy, or to include broadband in their universal access and service (UAS) definition, by 2025. In 2012, the ITU Telecommunication Development Sector developed best practices for national broadband plans, digital agendas and digital strategies (ITU, 2012).[9] Today, 174 countries worldwide have a national broadband plan, with several countries currently in the process of adopting one (Broadband Commission, 2020b). Broadband plans can also be developed at the regional level. For example, the countries of the Association of Southeast Asian Nations (ASEAN) adopted an ASEAN ICT Masterplan in 2015 (AIM, 2015) and subsequently updated that plan in 2020 to focus more on consumer choice, quality and price (ASEAN, 2020). That plan seeks to move beyond focusing only on connectivity to identifying and supporting isolated or underserved communities, and increasing the demand, usage, affordability and connectivity of broadband services across ASEAN member states (ASEAN, 2020).

While some countries have developed new or updated national broadband plans, many countries have shifted their focus to other matters, such as upgrading their universal access and service definitions or terms of service, or developing broader digital transformation strategies and plans, with connectivity as a core component, among other major issues (Broadband Commission, 2020b). In addition, governments and regulators need to monitor and evaluate the current state of national plan implementation (Broadband Commission, 2020b). In some cases, even after publishing and endorsing a national plan, government transitions and competing priorities lead to situations that interrupt or impede effective national plans, calling for revised targets in order to maintain progress on broadband adoption (Broadband Commission, 2020b).

The Alliance for Affordable Internet Access (A4AI) notes that in 2020, Malaysia stands out with one of the highest three scores for national broadband planning. Malaysia earned this distinction due to the quality of its national broadband plan targets and the widespread impact of these targets. Malaysia set targets, led the sector and left evidence of impact in its wake. An array of supply- and demand-side regulatory interventions helped achieve the plan's broadband availability and adoption targets. As a result, Malaysia now enjoys widespread affordable access to the Internet (Alliance for Affordable Internet, 2020).

Regardless of where a country stands in its development process, it should have a plan in place to address digital inequality. While a variety of efforts have tried to develop best practices for national broadband plans, each country will design its own plan based on its unique needs. We would highlight five key elements of national broadband plans: data collection and broadband definitions, competition policies, spectrum policies, universal service goals and policies, and measures to address adoption gaps. Prerequisites for good policymakers include a stable, transparent, impartial – and ideally independent – regulator, one not subject to undue influence by market actors (Broadband Commission, 2014).

One cannot solve a problem that one does not understand. This holds for the digital divide as well. Regulators should be collecting high-quality, finely grained data that track mobile and fixed broadband availability and adoption at all available speeds across residential, business and government customers. Additionally, regulators should track data on adoption according to income, gender and identification with marginalized groups. Regulators should also garner data from network operators at least yearly and make it publicly available. Data collection should also aim for as finely grained a geographic basis as possible.[10]

The definition of broadband is a key consideration that will impact a variety of policy interventions meant to eliminate digital inequality. The definition of broadband changes over time to reflect advances in technology, market offerings, and consumer demand. Broadband definitions vary widely across the APR and necessarily require some balancing of the realistic and the desired. If governments adopt an antiquated broadband definition and update it too infrequently, they risk further increasing the digital divide.

To the extent that a national regulator wants to promote competition, it will need to establish competition rules. Effective competition needs effective protection, particularly at the early stages of market opening (Broadband Commission, 2014). An investor seeking entry into a given market will look for competition rules that offer protection from anti-competitive behaviour by a dominant incumbent or a collusive group. Effective competition requires two main elements: clear rules and effective enforcement by the appropriate authorities. Anti-competitive practices subject to proscription – either by general competition, if it exists, or by telecommunication legislation – usually include predatory pricing, undue price discrimination, excessive pricing, margin squeeze, refusal to supply, or other strategies to foreclose the market (Broadband Commission, 2014).

As discussed previously, most of the world's population accesses the Internet on a mobile or fixed wireless connection. For this reason, spectrum policy, or the way in which regulators manage their national radio frequencies, will play a critical role in achieving universal connectivity goals. Smart spectrum policy can literally change the cost-economics of deploying wireless networks[11] – expanding access in underserved and to unserved communities, increasing competition, and reducing costs for consumers. To support network operator deployments, regulators should make spectrum available across a range of low-band, mid-band, and high-band frequencies. They should also allocate sufficient spectrum on an exclusive-use basis for mobile operator networks. Spectrum should also be made available on a non-exclusive unlicensed or license-exempt basis for Wi-Fi, Bluetooth, and a variety of other technologies used for providing fixed-wireless last-mile access. These fixed wireless technologies include those that can operate on low-band (for example, TV white spaces[12]), mid-band (for example, 5GHz bands), and high-band spectrum (for example, millimetre wave bands). The emergence of various types of spectrum-sharing technologies have enabled something called dynamic spectrum access, giving regulators tools to allow wireless networks operators access to new spectrum bands without displacing governmental or other users. In addition, regulators need to consider licensing for space-based satellite communications and experimental high-altitude platforms.

Universal service programmes also have a role in the regulator's toolkit, especially in instances when the market alone cannot be relied upon to deliver affordable mobile or fixed broadband to an underserved or unserved community. The ITU estimates that delivering high-quality mobile broadband to the remaining global unconnected will require US$428 billion in additional investment over ten years (ITU, 2020f). It recently published a comprehensive report on financing universal access to digital technologies and services, which could serve as a guide for governments as they consider the development of universal service programmes (ITU, 2021d). To know when to intervene in the marketplace, regulators should establish clear and transparent universal access goals and policies. For example, the Broadband Commission's Advocacy Target 3 states that, by 2025, broadband-Internet user penetration should reach 75 per cent of the world's population, 65 per cent in developing countries and 35 per cent in LDCs. This would typically require universal service programmes focused on both broadband availability and adoption for the general population and for specified groups. For example, programmes could ensure every child has access to broadband Internet or help close the gender gap (ASEAN, 2020; Worldwide Web Foundation, 2018). Universal-service programme design should adhere to certain principles, including maintaining technology and competitive neutrality, rewarding efficiency and speed of deployment, minimizing market distortions and holding fund recipients accountable for achieving quantifiable targets.

CONCLUSION

This chapter has provided an overview of efforts across the APR to accelerate universal digital connectivity. A consistent theme is the persistence of digital inequality that impacts people across the entire region. The COVID-19 pandemic has shined a bright light on these inequalities and increased the urgency of addressing them. With rapid progress in technologies, digital inequality runs the risk of widening at an accelerating pace over time. Addressing digital inequality, therefore, should be at the top of any government's agenda. This inequality disproportionately impacts people in several classes: residents of low-income and least-developed countries; those located in rural areas, in small island developing nations, and in landlocked developing countries; those lacking literacy and digital skills; and those from traditionally disenfranchised groups, such as women and girls, persons with disabilities, and ethnic minorities.

These digital divides will pose challenges central to development and economic policy as well as the SDGs. We have examined some of the policy decisions that governments will need to make and ways that the private sector and the international community may contribute to digital expansion. Ultimately, universal connectivity will prove a matter of more than simply creating access; it also will entail creating relevant and accessible content, making intensive efforts to expand digital literacy, and ensuring that connectivity and other digital solutions are affordable for all.

Notes

1. According to the UNDP, income inequality is on the rise — the richest 10 per cent have up to 40 per cent of global income whereas the poorest 10 per cent earn only between 2 to 7 per cent. Income inequality has increased nearly everywhere in recent decades, but at different speeds. And if one takes population growth into account, inequality in developing countries has increased by 11 per cent (UNDP, 2021)

2. In this chapter, the Asia-Pacific Region (APR) is comprised of 38 countries: Afghanistan, Australia, Bangladesh, Bhutan, Brunei, Cambodia, People's Republic of China (including Hong Kong SAR, Taiwan [Province of China], and Macao SAR), Democratic People's Republic of Korea, Fiji, India, Indonesia, Iran, Japan, Kiribati, Lao People's Democratic Republic (PDR), Malaysia, Mongolia, Myanmar, Maldives, Marshall Islands, Federated States of Micronesia, Nauru, Nepal, New Zealand, Papua New Guinea, Pakistan, Philippines, Republic of Korea, Samoa, Singapore, Sri Lanka, Solomon Islands, Thailand, Timor-Leste, Tonga, Tuvalu, Vanuatu, and Viet Nam. The 11 least developed countries (LDCs) in the APR are Afghanistan, Bangladesh, Bhutan, Cambodia, Kiribati, Lao PDR, Myanmar, Nepal Solomon Islands, Timor-Leste and Tuvalu. The 12 small island developing states in the APR are Fiji, Kiribati, Maldives, Marshall Islands, Federated States of Micronesia, Nauru, Papua New Guinea, Samoa, Solomon Islands, Tonga, Tuvalu, and Vanuatu. The 8 low-income countries (LICs) in the APR are the Democratic People's Republic of Korea, India, Indonesia, Mongolia, Pakistan, the Philippines, Sri Lanka and Viet Nam. The 10 remaining countries in the APR are Australia, Brunei, China, Iran, Japan, Malaysia, New Zealand, Singapore, Republic of Korea, and Thailand. The five landlocked developing countries in the APR are Afghanistan, Bhutan, Lao PDR, Mongolia, and Nepal.

3. In September 2015, the Sustainable Development Goals (SDGs) replaced the Millennium Development Goals (MDGs) as the international policy framework for socioeconomic development and poverty reduction.

4. Industry data shows that 81.8 per cent of the world's population and 91.5 per cent of the APR population is covered by a 4G LTE network, capable of providing mobile broadband connectivity (ITU, 2020a).

5. An example of this might be infrastructure-sharing regulations that enable network operators to share the costs of fibre and tower deployments, instead of each network operator having to deploy its own infrastructure.

6. Numerous mobile and fixed network operators, as well as trade associations, such as the GSMA (with its Connected Society Programme) have implemented programmes meant to address the skills gap (GSMA, 2021). Additionally, several major technology companies, such as Microsoft and Amazon, have launched digital skilling programs (Microsoft, 2020; Amazon, 2020, 2021).

7. For example, the Internet Society works with governments, local entrepreneurs and civil society on efforts to develop Internet content in local languages (Internet Society, 2016). In addition, technology companies have various efforts underway to enable consumers to translate content into their first language, including tools such as Google Translate, Bing Translator and Microsoft Translator (Microsoft, 2021).

8. According to the Broadband Commission Working Group on Financing and Investment, sovereign wealth funds (SWFs) are another possible source of financing

for telecommunication infrastructure projects. SWFs are investment funds owned by the governments of sovereign states and funded mainly by foreign exchange and reserve assets (Broadband Commission, 2014).

9. Data unavailable for Democratic People's Republic of Korea, Marshall Islands and Tuvalu.

10. The Broadband Commission noted, "Some of the data available for measuring progress against the targets is more robust for developed countries and remains a challenge for some developing countries. There may be other methodologies to collect similar, or proxy, datasets, and/or consider reporting on a semi-annual basis rather than annual. As such, further discussion on these challenges, possibilities and trade-offs is required" (Broadband Commission, 2020b: 39).

11. By opening up more large swaths of spectrum across complementary the low-, mid- and high-band spectrum, a regulator will enable a wireless network operator to optimize the placement of towers and other network infrastructure and thereby enable the network operator to serve more customers in more places at lower costs.

12. The TV white spaces are frequencies that have not been assigned or are otherwise not being used by broadcasters and other licensees in the VHF and UHF broadcast bands.

REFERENCES

Alliance for Affordable Internet. 2020. *The Affordability Report 2020*. Washington, DC: World Wide Web Foundation. https://1e8q3q16vyc81g8l3h3md6q5f5e-wpengine. netdna-ssl.com/wp-content/uploads/2020/12/Affordability-Report-2020.pdf.

Amazon. 2020. 'Amazon's Upskilling 2025 Program'. Amazon.com, Inc., Seattle, WA. aboutamazon.com/news/workplace/upskilling-2025.

———. 2021. 'Amazon's Future Engineer Program'. Amazon.com, Inc., Seattle, WA. aboutamazon.com/impact/community/stem-education.

Association of Southeast Asian Nations. 2020. *ASEAN ICT Master Plan*. Jakarta: The ASEAN Secretariat. asean.org/storage/images/2015/November/ICT/15b%20--%20AIM%20 2020_Publication_Final.pdf.

Broadband Commission for Digital Development. 2014. *Creating a Favourable Environment for Attracting Finance and Investment in Broadband Infrastructure*. Geneva: International Telecommunication Union and United Nations Educational, Scientific and Cultural Organization. broadbandcommission.org/Documents/reports/WG-Fin-Invest-2014.pdf.

———. 2017. *Working Group on Technologies in Space and the Upper-Atmosphere Identifying the Potential of New Communications Technologies for Sustainable Development*. Geneva: International Telecommunication Union and United Nations Educational, Scientific and Cultural Organization. broadbandcommission.org/ Documents/publications/WG-Technologies-in-Space-Report2017.pdf.

———. 2019. *Connecting Africa through Broadband: A Strategy for Doubling Connectivity by 2021 and Reaching Universal Access by 2030*. Geneva: International Telecommunication Union and United Nations Educational, Scientific and Cultural Organization. broadbandcommission.org/Documents/workinggroups/DigitalMoonshotforAfrica_ Report.pdf.

————. 2020a. 'Global Goal of Universal Connectivity: Manifesto'. International Telecommunication Union and United Nations Educational, Scientific and Cultural Organization, Geneva. broadbandcommission.org/Manifesto_Universal_Connectivity/Pages/default.aspx.

————. 2020b. *The State of Broadband: Tackling Digital Inequalities, A Decade for Action.* Geneva: International Telecommunication Union and United Nations Educational, Scientific and Cultural Organization. itu.int/dms_pub/itu-s/opb/pol/S-POL-BROADBAND.21-2020-PDF-E.pdf.

Digital Ubiquity Capital. 2021. 'Connectivity Capital'. Digital Ubiquity Capital, Ontario. digitalubiquitycapital.com/.

Garnett, P. 2020. 'It's Time for Wall Street to Get Serious about Closing the Global Broadband Gap'. *Medium*, 23 November. pgarnett.medium.com/its-time-for-wall-street-to-get-serious-about-closing-the-global-broadband-gap-70e83af0fdd3.

GSM Association (GSMA). 2019. *Connected Society: State of Mobile Internet Connectivity 2019.* London: GSM Association. gsma.com/mobilefordevelopment/.

————. 2020. *Mobile Gender Gap Report.* London: GSM Association. gsma.com/r/gender-gap/.

————. 2021. 'Mobile For Development'. GSM Association, London. gsma.com/mobilefordevelopment/connected-society/.

International Energy Agency (IEA), International Renewable Energy Agency, United Nations Statistics Division, World Bank and World Health Organization. 2019. *Tracking SDG 7: The Energy Progress Report 2019.* Washington, DC: The World Bank Group. https://trackingsdg7.esmap.org/data/files/download-documents/2019-Tracking SDG7-Full Report.pdf.

International Telecommunications Union (ITU). 2012. *Trends in Telecommunication Reform 2012: Smart Regulation for a Broadband World.* Geneva: International Telecommunication Union. itu.int/dms_pub/itu-d/opb/pref/D-PREF-TTR.13-2012-SUM-PDF-E.pdf.

————. 2020a. *Measuring Digital Development, Facts and Figures 2020.* Geneva: International Telecommunication Union. itu.int/en/ITU-D/Statistics/Documents/facts/FactsFigures2020.pdf.

————. 2020b. *End-19 Estimates for Key ICT Indicators.* Geneva: International Telecommunication Union. itu.int/en/ITU-D/Statistics/Documents/statistics/2019/ITU_Key_2005-2019_ICT_data_with%20LDCs_28Oct2019_Final.xls.

————. 2020c. *Country ICT Data: Core Indicators on Access to and Use of ICT by Households and Individuals.* Geneva: International Telecommunication Union. itu.int/en/ITU-D/Statistics/Documents/statistics/2020/CoreHouseholdIndicators%20(20-08-20).xlsx.

————. 2020d. 'ITU Interactive Terrestrial Transmission/ESCAP Asia-Pacific Information Superhighway Maps'. International Telecommunication Union, Geneva. itu.int/itu-d/tnd-map-public/.

————. 2020e. *The Last-Mile Internet Connectivity Solutions Guide: Sustainable Connectivity Options for Unconnected Sites.* Geneva: International Telecommunication Union. https://assets.foleon.com/eu-west-2/uploads-7e3kk3/16601/the_last-mile_Internet_connectivity_solutions_guide.3b7086016604.pdf.

———. 2020f. *Connecting Humanity: Assessing Investment Needs of Connecting Humanity to the Internet by 2030*. Geneva: International Telecommunication Union. itu.int/ myitu/-/media/Publications/2020-Publications/Connecting-Humanity.pdf.

———. 2021a. 'ICT Price Basket Time Series'. International Telecommunication Union, Geneva. itu.int/net4/itu-d/ipb/#ipbtimeseries-tab.

———. 2021b. 'ITU ICT Price Basket Comparisons'. International Telecommunication Union, Geneva. itu.int/net4/itu-d/ipb/#ipbcomparison-tab.

———. 2021c. 'ITU ICT Price Basket Rankings'. International Telecommunication Union, Geneva. itu.int/net4/itu-d/ipb/#ipbrank-tab.

———. 2021d. *Financing Universal Access to Digital Technologies and Services*. Geneva: International Telecommunication Union. itu.int/en/myitu/Publications/ 2021/09/28/11/09/Financing-universal-access-to-digital-technologies-and-services.

———. 2021e. *Telecommunications Industry in the Post-COVID-19 World: Report of the 7th Economic Experts Roundtable*. Geneva, International Telecommunication Union. itu.int/en/myitu/Publications/2021/05/11/08/10/The-telecommunication-industry-in-the-post-COVID-19-world.

Internet Exchange Map. 2021. 'Internet Exchange Map'. Washington, DC: TeleGeography, Inc. Internetexchangemap.com/

Internet Society. 2016. 'Local Content in Local Languages Matters'. Internet Society, Reston, VA. .Internetsociety.org/blog/2016/08/local-content-in-local-languages-matters/.

Microsoft. 2020. 'Microsoft's Program to Bring more Digital Skills to 25 Million People Worldwide by the End of the Year 2020'. Microsoft Corporation, Redmond, WA. blogs. microsoft.com/blog/2020/06/30/microsoft-launches-initiative-to-help-25-million-people-worldwide-acquire-the-digital-skills-needed-in-a-covid-19-economy/.

———. 2021. 'Local Language Program Bridges Languages, Cultures and Technology'. Microsoft Corporation, Redmond, WA. news.microsoft.com/2012/02/21/microsofts-local-language-program-bridges-languages-cultures-and-technology/.

Rivera, C., Hsu, Y.-C., Pavez Esbry, F. and Dugarova, E. No date. *Gender Inequality and the COVID-19 Crisis: A Human Development Perspective*. New York: United Nations Development Programme. hdr.undp.org/sites/default/files/covid-19_and_human_ development_-_gender_dashboards_final.pdf.

United Nations (UN). 2019. *The Age of Digital Interdependence: Report of the UN Secretary General's High-level Panel on Digital Cooperation*. New York: United Nations. digitalcooperation.org/wp-content/uploads/2019/06/DigitalCooperation-report-web-FINAL-1.pdf.

———. 2020. 'Policy Brief: Education During COVID-19 and Beyond'. United Nations, New York. reliefweb.int/report/world/policy-brief-education-during-covid-19-and-beyond-august-2020.

United Nations Children's Fund (UNICEF) and International Telecommunications Union (ITU). 2020. 'How Many Children and Young People have Internet Access at Home? Estimating Digital Connectivity during the COVID-19 Pandemic'. United Nations Children's Fund, New York. data.unicef.org/wp-content/uploads/2020/11/Children-and-young-people-digital-connectivity-covid19_English.pdf.

———. 2013. *Humanity Divided: Confronting Inequality in Developing Countries*. New York: United Nations Development Programme. undp.org/content/dam/undp/

library/Poverty%20Reduction/Inclusive%20development/Humanity%20Divided/ HumanityDivided_Full-Report.pdf.

———. 2019. *Human Development Report 2019: Beyond Income, Beyond Averages, Beyond Today – Inequalities in Human Development in the 21st Century*. New York: United Nations Development Programme. hdr.undp.org/sites/default/files/hdr2019.pdf.

———. 2020a. 'COVID-19: Human Development on Course to Decline This Year for the First Time since 1990'. New York: United Nations Development Programme. undp. org/content/undp/en/home/presscenter/pressreleases/2020/COVID19_Human_ development_on_course_to_decline_for_the_first_time_since_1990.html.

———. 2020b. *2020 Human Development Perspectives, COVID-19 and Human Development: Assessing the Crisis, Envisioning the Recovery*. New York: United Nations Development Programme. hdr.undp.org/sites/default/files/covid-19_and_human_ development_0.pdf.

———. 2020c. 'Impact of COVID-19 on the Sustainable Development Goals'. United Nations Development Programme, New York. sdgintegration.undp.org/accelerating-development-progressduring-covid-19.

———. 2021. 'Goal 10: Reduced Inequalities'. United Nations Development Programme, New York. undp.org/content/undp/en/home/sustainable-development-goals/goal-10-reduced-inequalities.html.

United Nations Secretary-General. 2020. *Roadmap for Digital Cooperation*. New York: United Nations. un.org/en/content/digital-cooperation-roadmap/.

Web Technology Surveys (W3Techs). 2021. 'Usage Statistics and Market Share of Content Languages for Websites'. Web Technology Surveys, Johannesburg. w3techs.com/ technologies/overview/content_language.

World Bank. 2020. 'COVID-19 to Add as Many as 150 Million Extreme Poor by 2021'. The World Bank Group, Washington, DC. worldbank.org/en/news/press-release/2020/10/07/covid-19-to-add-as-many-as-150-million-extreme-poor-by-2021.

Worldwide Web Foundation. 2018. 'Universal Service and Access Funds: An Untapped Resource to Close the Gender Digital Divide'. Worldwide Web Foundation, Washington, DC. webfoundation.org/docs/2018/03/Using-USAFs-to-Close-the-Gender-Digital-Divide-in-Africa.pdf.

4 The Post-COVID-19 Future for Global Value Chains

Ben Shepherd

INTRODUCTION

There are two 'unbundlings' that have taken place in the modern economy (Baldwin, 2011). The first is the geographical separation of production and consumption, visible in the growth of world trade post-1945: consumers became increasingly less reliant on national sources of supply, while producers became increasingly less reliant on national markets for their output. More recently, the production process itself has undergone a similar disintegration. For much of the 20th century, goods were largely produced in one place using domestic supply chains (even if shipped somewhere else for final consumption), but the latter part of the 20th century and the first decades of the 21st have seen an important shift towards the internationalization of production. From domestic supply chains, we have increasingly moved towards global value chains (GVCs), which divide production into distinct units, split across locations according to narrow patterns of comparative advantage. Indeed the 'chain' terminology is something of a misnomer: GVCs, in fact, operate more like networks, in the sense that they are complex and nonlinear, rather than linear chains.

Conceptually, a value chain "describes the full range of activities that firms and workers do to bring a product/good or service from its conception to its end use and beyond. This includes activities such as design, production, marketing, distribution, and support to the final consumer" (Frederick, 2016). A GVC, therefore, arises when actors carry out these activities in different countries, rather than within the confines of a single country. As the International Trade Center (2017) points out, many GVCs are regional rather than global in scope, as they focus on firms within a single geographical region covering more than one country. True GVCs are most frequently the domain of very large firms that have the resources to research and coordinate suppliers from all over the globe, but the analysis of GVCs and regional value chains (RVCs) is conceptually very similar, so we combine them into a single analysis here, only drawing a distinction when it has analytical salience.

From an analytical standpoint, the rise of GVCs favours a number of shifts in emphasis in thinking about trade and investment relationships (Cattaneo et al., 2013). On the one hand, spreading production activities across numerous countries tends to make countries somewhat less relevant as units of analysis, and firms somewhat more relevant. Of course, both remain relevant in an overall sense, but the change in relative emphasis is significant. Similarly, trade policy usually focuses on industries or sectors as economic aggregates, but GVCs make the paradigm of trading in tasks more relevant (Grossman and Rossi-Hansberg, 2008); the definition of activities becomes finer and incorporates services as goods. Finally, government policies remain important determinants of the location of economic activity, but the role of GVC lead firms means that private standards assume greater relative importance than in the past.

As Baldwin (2011) points out, the rise of GVCs has provided developing countries with a new lens through which to view outward-oriented growth. Industrializing countries in the 1970s and 1980s focused on developing full domestic supply chains in key industries, namely final-goods producers supported by ecosystems of input suppliers. Baldwin presents the Republic of Korea as the paradigmatic case. The focus in the 2000s shifted towards joining existing value chains, rather than developing new ones from the ground up. Over time, countries shifted into higher value-added activities. Baldwin (2011) notes that China's use of its external sector to support rapid growth has had some elements of this approach, as has Viet Nam. In the GVC development model, specialization by comparative advantage takes place at the level of narrowly defined tasks rather than sectors. Similarly, trade in intermediate goods and services takes on increased importance. GVCs operate as finely optimized complex systems, with inventories reduced to low levels in order to reduce carrying costs, and reliance placed on sophisticated and efficient transport and logistics systems.

While the policy world has seen extensive discussions of GVCs over recent years, the COVID-19 pandemic has lent new salience to this process. On the one hand, the years since the 2008 global financial crisis have generally seen slower growth of world trade and GVCs than in the preceding decade or so. But, at the same time, political pressures in some leading economies have suggested that internationalized production may be seen as less desirable from the perspective of the domestic economy and society than was the case in the recent past. This questioning is reinforced by difficulties observed in some supply chains in the early days of the COVID-19 pandemic, when initial shortfalls for products, such as personal protective equipment and hand sanitizer, may have posed risks for public health. Stating these issues by no means prejudges our response to them, but their prominence in public discussions increases the importance of bringing facts, data and analysis into the discussion, with the aim of reaching a robust and nuanced understanding of the issues.

Against this background, this chapter seeks to provide further evidence about the economic and social implications of GVCs. In addition, it will chart out some forces that may influence GVCs' future development. It explicitly adopts the point of view of developing countries, by which we mean low- and middle-income countries as determined by World Bank data.[1]

The chapter proceeds as follows. The next section discusses the measurement of GVC activity and provides some basic information on the nature and extent of GVC integration around the world. We then discuss economic and social impacts of GVCs in more detail. We follow with a focus on trade policy, in particular the question of the extent to which recent moves by some large economies can disrupt GVC development elsewhere. We then turn to the future, by addressing a selection of major issues that will influence GVC development over the medium term. The final section concludes by addressing key findings and policy implications.

GLOBAL VALUE CHAINS: A DESCRIPTION OF THE CURRENT STATE OF PLAY

Standard trade data do not give much help in identifying or measuring GVC trade.[2] The reason is that they measure trade on a gross-shipments basis; for example, the recorded value of a mobile phone imported into Japan from China is the full shipped price of the mobile phone. However, if the mobile phone was produced in a GVC, as is typically the case, then it embodies inputs from all around the world: the screen comes from one country, the processor from another, design services from another still, and pre-loaded apps from yet another. Measuring GVC trade would ideally identify all of these instances of value addition separately, so that the number of exports recorded from China to Japan corresponds to the value added by Chinese firms. Meanwhile, one would also 'unbundle' the single transaction to show movements of value added from all of the input-supplying countries to Japan, as well. Finally, an ideal measure would account for the fact that some inputs move across borders multiple times during production, and net such inputs out from the count, something standard trade data do not do. For an individual product, one could conceivably identify the different sources of value added by tracing them through inter-firm linkages in the supply chain,[3] but systematic application of the approach calls for more sophisticated methods.

With this in mind, economists have developed a number of approaches for measuring trade in value-added terms, in essence an attempt to reframe the available data so as to focus on movements of value added rather than the simple gross value movements captured by standard sources. The operations involved are complex, involving a marriage of standard trade data and input–output tables. Given that reporting lags for detailed national accounts – used to construct input–output tables – trade in value-added data typically only become available with a delay of some years from the relevant date. Still, they have already offered important insights into GVC growth and development since research in this area started in earnest in the early 2010s.

The literature discloses two key summary measures of GVC integration that come from trade in value-added data. Backward participation captures the proportion of a country's gross exports accounted for by value added sourced elsewhere; that is, it summarizes the extent to which a country's gross exports embody inputs, both goods and services, sourced from abroad. Forward participation is the mirror image: the proportion of a country's gross exports used by other countries in order to produce their own exports; that is, the extent to which a country's gross exports are embodied in those of other countries. While there are numerous methodologies available to measure these linkages, all with subtle differences, one example suffices to provide a general impression of GVC spread and development. We use the methodology from Borin and Mancini (2019), as it appears in World Bank (2020). Results are based on the Eora global input–output table, which currently extends to 2015 only, due to the reporting lag referred to earlier.

Figure 4.1 provides a first cut of these data, focusing on differences across exporting regions. Experience varies considerably from one region to another, as evidenced, for instance, by different balances of backward and forward linkages in gross exports. The general finding, however, is the same: by 2015, GVC trade, by which we mean the total proportion of backward and forward linkages in gross exports, comprised at least one third of the total in all world regions, and as much as 50 per cent or more in some cases. Between 2000 and 2015, the proportion of GVC trade in total exports grew in all regions except Latin America and the Caribbean and North America. The two Asian regions, East Asia and the Pacific and South Asia, both saw increases in the proportion of GVC trade in total exports, particularly in South Asia. Within Asia, nonetheless, GVC trade takes place primarily in East Asia and the Pacific; South Asia sees a more limited amount of this type of interaction, in keeping with the much lower level of regional integration. Moreover, the time period in Figure 4.1 masks two distinct evolutions: more rapid increase generally took place prior to 2009 rather than following it, in line with a general slowdown of global trade growth post-global financial crisis.

An important point to keep in mind is that, while GVC analysis first arose in the context of manufacturing sectors, such as electronics and motor vehicles, the phenomenon itself is ubiquitous across sectors, including primary industries and services. While intensities differ, GVCs have the scope to operate in most parts of the economy, in particular with the rise of digital technologies and more liberal policies that make services more tradable than in the past. Figure 4.2 provides some evidence to support this point, namely backward and forward linkages for each of the 26 sectors in the Eora database (for the most recent year of available data, namely 2015). It clearly shows that GVC trade is significant in all sectors, even some services typically not provided commercially (where trade values are very low, the data appear in proportional terms, which masks this fact). While manufacturing sectors certainly see the highest proportions of GVC trade, the

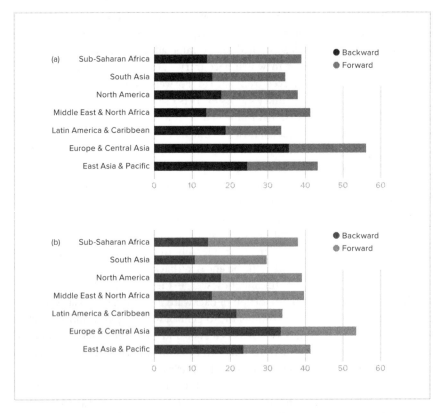

Figure 4.1 GVC trade by exporting region, per cent of gross exports, 2000 (a) and 2015 (b)
Source: Borin and Mancini (2019).

model is also important in agriculture and mining among primary sectors, and in services sectors, such as wholesale trade, financial or business services, and telecommunications.

Asia has considerable experience in GVCs in a range of sectors. Standout examples include transport equipment, electronics, and textiles and apparel. Specialization varies from country to country, but in a global context, Asian countries have enjoyed notable success in these sectors. From a future standpoint, evolutions in consumer preferences towards environmentally focused goods, such as electric vehicles or green energy products like solar cells, mean that existing value chains may need to retool to produce distinct, but related, goods. Given the continent's history in the sectors in question, it would appear relatively well-positioned to take advantage of new opportunities in these areas.

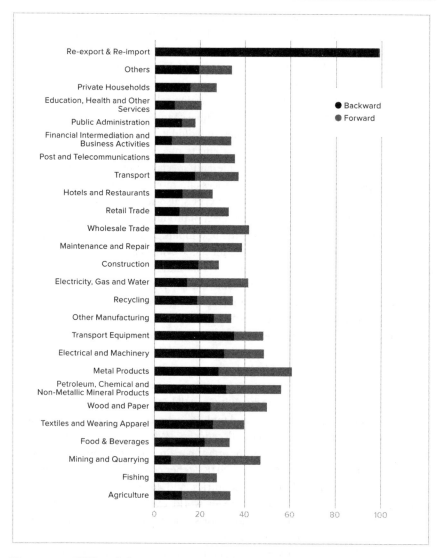

Figure 4.2   GVC trade by sector, per cent of gross exports, 2015
Source: Borin and Mancini (2019).

ECONOMIC AND SOCIAL IMPACTS OF GVCS: WHAT DOES THE EVIDENCE SAY?

Having established that the GVC model plays an important part in global trade in most regions and sectors, attention now turns to the economic and social consequences of that model. At the outset, it is important to be clear about how to assess this question. The counterfactual benchmark is vital: Namely, what would the economic and social consequences be of restricting GVC trade relative to its actual observed levels? Stating the question in this way makes clear that it is not enough to highlight a particular negative consequence of GVC participation and to assume that restricting GVC development would eliminate that consequence; it could just as easily make it worse. So, the analytical question relates to the way in which the evidence shapes up as to the impact of a marginal change in GVC integration: Would it improve economic and social outcomes, or would it worsen them?

From an economic perspective, the effects of GVCs are best understood as a particular case of the gains from trade and specialization. All of the standard arguments apply: trade results in lower prices and more variety for consumers, and larger markets for producers. But because GVCs also result in substantial changes to input sourcing, they also offer the prospect of productivity gains at the firm level, stemming from their ability to source the best inputs available globally. Despite the difficulty of teasing out causal effects, the anecdotal evidence tells us that productivity grew faster during 2000 to 2017 than between 1980 and 2000 in most low- and middle-income countries. Breaking down the same data by region shows that all countries in South Asia and 86 per cent of countries in East Asia and the Pacific likewise saw stronger productivity growth between 2000 and 2017 than between 1980 and 2000, within the limits of the available data by country. So, the spread of GVCs at least coincides with a pick-up in productivity growth in the developing world, and the available evidence looking at GVC linkages specifically, such as Alfaro-Urena et al. (2020) on Costa Rica, shows that the link is indeed causal.

This increase in the rate of productivity growth has translated into a substantially changing world economy, with low- and middle-income countries now occupying a greater share of world exports than two decades ago. While the rise of large countries like China and India has played an important part in this development, it has had a much wider reach: Between 2000 and 2018, 56 per cent of low-income countries, 51 per cent of lower-middle-income countries, and 46 per cent of upper-middle-income countries increased their share in world exports – meaning that their exports grew at a faster rate than world exports as a whole, and this during a period of unusually rapid global trade integration.

A large literature using micro-data has arisen showing that firms that engage with the international economy, including through GVC linkages, tend to be larger and more productive than firms that focus on the domestic market only, and that they also pay higher wages to their workers than domestically focused firms (for example, Brambilla et al., 2017). Recent literature also shows that internationally engaged firms in developing countries tend to employ more women than firms that focus on the domestic market only (for example, Shepherd, 2018; Rocha and Winkler, 2019). Results like these suggest that international engagement can have benefits for workers through increased employment rates and higher wages, which, in turn, can translate into gains in human wellbeing and enhanced capability.

How does this technical literature sit with other work that emphasizes the sometimes-poor working conditions in some GVC sectors, such as apparel? Saxena (2020) brings together a collection of contributions looking at GVC governance in light of the Rana Plaza disaster in Bangladesh, while Blattman and Dercon (2017) use an experimental approach to highlight the limited benefits of factory work in Ethiopia relative to other opportunities, such as self-employment. From a social perspective, civil society should concern itself about ensuring safe and sanitary working conditions in firms of all types, including those linked to GVCs. But there is no evidence suggesting that internationally engaged firms perform systematically worse on this metric than do firms that serve the domestic market only. From a causal perspective, the culprit is more likely to be lax standards or lack of enforcement, rather than internationally linked status. Indeed, international linkages could conceivably prove an advantage, to the extent that lead firms have the ability to propagate superior standards throughout their supply chains and take steps to monitor compliance (for example, UNCTAD, 2012). International initiatives to improve such standards, boost compliance capabilities, and monitor performance offer key steps in supporting better working conditions in low- and middle-income countries around the world, including in Asia. Historically, low- and middle-income countries have generally sought to avoid linkages between trade and labour standards in forums, such as the World Trade Organization (WTO), and this stance has caused friction with high-income countries. The development of private-sector standards and the availability of financial and human resources to support compliance have improved prospects relative to the pre-GVC era and with arguably less risk of countries becoming locked out of international trade as a result of labour issues. Clearly, finance for firm upgrading in developing countries remains a key priority in this area.

This analysis shows the importance of keeping counterfactuals in mind when assessing the development impacts of international engagement, including through GVCs: the appropriate yardstick is whether a marginal decrease in international engagement or, equivalently, an increased focus on the domestic market would promote human development through higher wages or better working conditions. No empirical evidence exists for such a link, with the policy literature sometimes distracted by comparisons between desired working conditions and those observed, rather than those observed and those potentially observable with a change in the variable of interest.

An additional set of considerations relates to the distributional impacts of trade opening. But these issues are again not specific to GVCs but, rather, a particular manifestation of standard trade economics. Trade economists have long accepted that a marginal increase in openness benefits some people in the domestic economy but harms others, for instance through unemployment or lower incomes, based on the distribution of comparative advantage by sector (for example, Stolper and Samuelson, 1941). However, the size of the gains from opening is large enough to fully compensate those who lose. Although the point is well-established, it is rarely put into practice. Adjustment assistance for displaced workers remains woefully inadequate, even in many high-income countries. In low- and middle-income countries, this inadequacy signals broader difficulties in creating effective social safety nets. The answer, however, is not to restrict trade but instead to work on the institutional and political economy issues that have made it difficult to protect people properly from the negative consequences of either economic policy changes or, more broadly, the vicissitudes of life. As economies continue to become more reliant on trade linkages, including through GVCs, the point becomes increasingly salient and urgent (Hoekman and Shepherd, 2020). From a human development perspective, distributional issues play a key role, as they do from a political economy standpoint. But policymakers need to be careful to avoid kneejerk responses that do not pay sufficient attention to the underlying economic mechanisms. Focusing on developing general redistribution policies as well as social safety nets is both more efficient and effective in the medium to long term in promoting human development objectives than is restricting trade and investment flows.

Trade Policy, Resilience, and GVCs: How Fragile and What Solutions?

Indeed, concerns over distribution have partly driven recent changes in trade policy in the United States, which has imposed duties unilaterally against China. A fair reading of the literature on the 'China shock,' namely the huge increase in imports from China in the 2000s, would be that adjustment costs proved higher than had generally been believed, and that unemployment of displaced workers has lasted longer than expected (Autor et al., 2016); but at the same time, increased demand for United States' exports, particularly in services, created more jobs than those lost in manufacturing (Feenstra and Sasahara, 2018). Nonetheless, a part of public opinion in the United States has focused on trade as the vector not only of manufacturing job losses, but also of rising inequality. All of this led to the imposition of unilateral tariffs against China under the Trump administration. The disconnect between expert analysis and a section of public opinion in the United States and other countries highlights the way in which international economic linkages intersect with broader geopolitical questions, which are outside the scope of this chapter.

An additional issue that has arisen during the COVID-19 pandemic relates to the fragility of GVCs themselves. Anecdotally, important goods underwent shortages in the early days of the pandemic, with standout examples in personal protective equipment and hand sanitizer (APIC, 2020). To some extent, restrictive trade policies amplified the shock, as producing countries restricted exports (Park, 2020). Given this context, concerns over ensuring supply continuity of critical goods have transformed into a discussion about the merits of 're-shoring,' or the shortening of GVCs to emphasize a greater amount of local content.

These interlinked dynamics give rise to two important empirical questions, which, as yet, have no conclusive answers in the literature. First, how easily can the spread of GVCs be undone through the imposition of unilateral trade policies, such as tariffs? And second, how desirable is it—from a supply-chain resilience point of view – to use such measures to bring about a substantial re-shoring of some activities currently undertaken through GVCs?

A global trade model with GVCs can provide an answer to the first question. The unilateral tariffs, to which China responded in kind, are very high relative to baseline levels, up to 25 per cent ad valorem in some cases. The trade policy shock is therefore very large. However, while there is some unravelling of GVC linkages, there is by no means a wholesale disintegration of the model, at least in terms of the proportion of gross exports accounted for by GVC trade. While GVC trade shrinks substantially in absolute terms, so, too, do other kinds of trade, so that the change in terms of proportions appears much smaller. We estimate that the tariff shock represents between three- and five-years' worth of undoing GVC growth at the previous trend rate in the affected countries. The effect is far from negligible, but, given the very large shock involved, the analysis shows that in the absence of policies designed specifically to disrupt production sharing – for instance, by targeting foreign input use rather than trade in general – it is extremely costly to radically alter the prevalence of GVC trade.

The flipside of this analysis uses the same trade model to examine the impacts of two mega-regional trade agreements on GVC trade, the Regional Comprehensive Economic Partnership (RCEP) and the Comprehensive and Progressive Trans-Pacific Partnership (CPTPP), both of which involve a number of economies in Asia. Lowering trade barriers through these agreements has significant potential to boost GVC trade. For CPTPP countries, the agreement produces the equivalent of 12 years of additional GVC integration, based on the rate observed between 2000 and 2018. For RCEP, the figure is around five years. Importantly, GVC integration increases with countries outside the agreements as well. From this perspective, continued efforts to move forward on regional integration seem likely to support, rather than disrupt, existing GVC structures.

From the perspective of re-shoring, OECD (2020) uses their own global trade model to look at the impacts of shifting to more domestically focused supply chains. They find that, far from decreasing volatility, this, in fact, increases it. The result should not be surprising given that most economic shocks are not perfectly correlated across countries, so diversifying suppliers allows countries to effectively diversify risk. Having a purely domestic supply chain means that, if a shock hits the local economy, it has no shock absorber, and this results in increased volatility.

Despite these results, the issue of supply chain resilience remains an important one, in particular when GVCs produce public health or safety necessities. Indeed, there is evidence that the private sector has already taken steps to improve resilience in light of the vulnerabilities exposed by the COVID-19 pandemic. But these efforts focus on diversification, supplier redundancy, and technology, rather than large scale re-shoring (McKinsey Global Institute, 2020). While the issue may call for policy intervention at some point, the case for a broad-based policy response appears weak as long as the private sector has undertaken steps that may go at least some way towards remedying the problem. In time, there may be a case for greater regulation of some GVCs on the grounds of ensuring public health, but such needs will require case-by-case assessment rather than general approaches. In any case, any intervention will need to balance the efficiency advantages of GVC production against other social objectives.

Experience with past shocks offers a useful guide to potential redesign of GVCs in the immediate future, without wholesale changes to the business model. The floods in Thailand in 2011 led to a global shortage of some electronics components, particularly hard drives. However, technological change combined with private-sector reassessment of risk has led to an effective diversification of suppliers, with countries specialized in alternative technologies, such as solid-state, drives effectively assuming part of the global market (Reuters, 2016). Despite the strategic importance of the sector and the size of the shock, public policy changes in importing markets ultimately did not become necessary to deal with the aftermath of the 2011 floods.

FUTURE ISSUES: SERVICES, DIGITALIZATION AND AUTOMATION

Hoekman and Shepherd (2020) argue that the world economy has seen a rise in the proportion of services as a component of overall economic activity, at the same time that services have, through technological and regulatory change, become more tradable. WTO law recognizes four modes of trading services: a lawyer in Buenos Aires can advise a client in Seoul by email; the client can travel from Seoul to Buenos Aires, then return home; the Argentinean law firm can establish a subsidiary in the Republic of Korea and use it to sell services to the client; and, finally, the lawyer can travel temporarily from Buenos Aires to Seoul. These four modes of supply for internationally traded services are difficult to measure, even 25 years after their inclusion in the WTO legal framework. They do not fit easily with standard approaches to tracking trade data.

Statisticians at the WTO have developed an experimental dataset that uses advanced techniques and the available data to provide a first, approximate picture of trade in services by mode of supply. Figure 4.3 shows that services trade has grown steadily over recent years, with mode 3 (entry through a foreign subsidiary) the dominant one. Both points are important, the first because world trade growth overall has been relatively muted since 2009, the second because discussions on the tradability of services often ignore this mode of supply. Under the WTO's four modes of supply, there is no longer any such thing as a 'non-tradable' service; high costs or other impediments may make such trade rarer, but the structure in principle allows for the trading of all service activities. Figure 4.3 shows that this kind of trade is robust and quite comparable in importance to the global economy to total merchandise trade. Moreover, we showed earlier that a substantial proportion of this trade takes place through GVC structures, now an important fixture in many services sectors.

The rise of the services economy has caused concern among some economists and policymakers, who emphasize the special role manufacturing has played in successful development stories (for example, Rodrik, 2015). They argue that manufacturing has three characteristics that make it particularly desirable from a

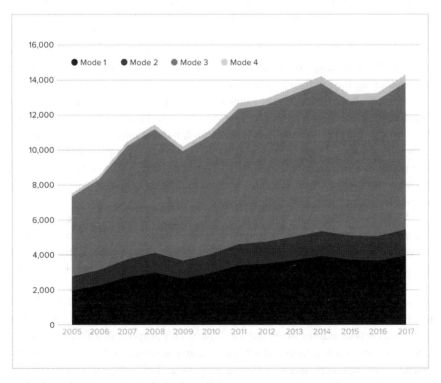

Figure 4.3   Total world exports of services by mode of supply, 2005–2017 (US$ billion)
Source: WTO TISMOS database (2021).

development point of view: it generates positive spillovers; it supports productivity growth through competitive pressures coming from world markets, since manufactured goods are easily tradable; and it creates large numbers of jobs for workers with limited education. Such an argument implicitly assumes that services do not possess these characteristics.

But as Helble and Shepherd (2019) point out, services in fact constitute a very large economic aggregate with a huge amount of heterogeneity across subsectors. When examined in detail, the data do not always support the contention that manufacturing has the three characteristics listed above while commercial services do not. With increasing trade in services, as shown earlier, competitive pressures that can promote productivity upgrading have correspondingly intensified. While measurement remains challenging, there is evidence that some services sectors have seen rapid rates of productivity growth, on par with some manufacturing sectors, and, in particular, that the two sectors have closely linked productivity rates due to the increasingly strong input–output relationship between them (Hoekman and Shepherd, 2015). Indeed, Shepherd (2019) shows that productivity growth in services served as an important, but under-recognized, aspect of the development of 'Factory Asia' in the 1990s and 2000s; revealed productivity growth rates in the rapidly industrializing Asian countries proved only slightly below those seen in their booming manufacturing sectors. In addition, Winkler (2019) shows that service firms can generate positive spillovers at the local level in much the same way as occurs in manufacturing, though firm characteristics appear as an important mediating factor.

There are important points of similarity in the modern world economy between manufactured goods and commercial services. Where the distinction appears most problematic is in terms of the third point above, namely jobs. Anecdotally, jobs in high-productivity services sectors tend to require a relatively high level of education. The premature deindustrialization thesis therefore carries most weight regarding the large number of jobs needed in low- and middle-income countries – jobs that the service sector must create going forward.

Many forces underpin this increased importance of services. One deals with preferences: as incomes rise, consumer spending tends to shift towards services. However, technological change is also an important part of the equation. Recent decades have seen manufacturing firms using more and more services inputs, sourced both commercially in the market and internally through employment of service-performing workers. Surveys by Low and Pasadilla (2016) indicate that in the Asia-Pacific Region, manufacturing firms could, on average, see around half of their total costs accounted for by services inputs. This proportion will likely increase given the trend towards more automation in manufacturing, with its accompanying demand for engineers and technicians. The same holds true for digitalization, where one can understand the transformation of physical goods into disembodied information as a shift from goods to services.

While these kinds of technological changes have real potential to bring about changes in global trade, they have important implications from an empirical perspective. On the one hand, there is evidence that automation can pose genuine problems on the score of employment, although it may benefit some workers as well (Acemoglu and Restrepo, 2019). Yet, anecdotally, countries with higher levels of automation than the United States, such as Japan, continue to perform strongly when it comes to employment.

From a trade perspective, a key issue relates to the interplay between these new technologies and comparative advantage. Industrializing countries have traditionally used their low labour costs to compete effectively in world markets. The GVC model too depends to some extent on this initial entry point. But does that comparative advantage disappear with large-scale automation? Freund et al. (2019) examine whether or not this has happened with the rise of 3D printing in the market for hearing aids. While this development could have led to a re-shoring of production from Mexico and other countries, the data suggest that it has had less empirical importance in general; indeed, exports of physical hearing aids from other countries may even have increased. So, this one piece of evidence suggests that in some circumstances, technological change that appears to undercut a labour-cost advantage may not lead to decreased trade and GVC integration.

We offer another example that gives reason for scepticism: case of e-books: This technological change should have allowed countries to abandon trade in physical books in favour of trade in data files only. Again, the data do not support this contention. There is little evidence that increased uptake of e-books caused a decrease in trade in physical books.

Of course, low- and middle-income countries will not automatically and necessarily benefit from these technological changes. There is good reason for concern about exclusion and marginalization, but, for the moment, the data do not suggest those effects are widespread. More broadly, these changes make clear that low- and middle-income countries need to continue investing in their own technological capacity, as well as in their human capital. Doing so will not only avoid potential dislocation should the analysis here prove unduly optimistic, but will also position them to move up into higher value-added activities within existing GVCs. Indeed, these priorities align with the need to create jobs in services sectors, which typically require higher levels of qualification, at least in comparable internationally integrated sectors. Continued investment in both basic and further education will play a vital role in strong employment performance, which, in turn, helps reduce poverty.

CONCLUSIONS AND POLICY RECOMMENDATIONS

By 2021, GVCs have become a well-established feature of the global economic landscape. The COVID-19 pandemic initially placed them under stress, but they have also provided part of the response, from producing and distributing large quantities of personal protective equipment, to developing and distributing vaccines. There is thus no simple answer about the impact of the pandemic on GVCs, but it seems premature to diagnose a wholesale failure of the system, or to forecast a large-scale shift to other means of production.

On the other hand, the pandemic has brought to the forefront a number of issues that have already been identified within the GVC model, from the need to engage a wide range of countries in promoting widespread development, to the importance of resilience to shocks. Technological change, such as the rise of the services economy with accompanying digitalization and automation, certainly poses challenges for low-income countries still in the early stages of industrialization. They will need to adapt to these new realities, but the general model of joining GVCs, rather than developing full domestic supply chains, still offers important potential advantages. Critically, developing capacity to produce and use services and new technologies will shape the ability of firms to join and move up in GVCs. From a policy perspective, it will be important to invest heavily in human capital development through education and training systems, as well as to ensure basic service provision, including internet connectivity. While low labour costs represent a source of comparative advantage, increasing incomes necessarily undermine it and make it all the more important to shift towards a skill-based labour market.

In addition, ensuring openness to trade and investment flows, along with developing social safety nets and redistribution mechanisms, will help align human development and economic objectives but will also ensure continued support for this development model in a political economy sense. Low- and middle-income countries face a key challenge: learning from successful examples of rapid income growth and sustained poverty reduction, including those that have made strategic use of GVC integration in the service of broader development objectives. Viet Nam is perhaps the best example in point; it has engaged rapidly with GVCs in a broadening list of sectors and has succeeded in reducing poverty and moving a significant number of people into the global middle class (World Bank, 2018). Of course, backsliding on these advances poses a real risk given the size of the economic shock associated with the COVID-19 pandemic. But there is nothing to suggest that restricting movements of goods, services and capital across borders will aid in recovery. Rather, it is likely that supporting an open, rules-based trading system remains a key economic policy objective, particularly for smaller low-and middle-income countries, as it provides them with a source of external demand to aid in the recovery effort. Ensuring openness to services as well as goods has emerged as a policy priority for many of these countries, in particular those that suffer from geographical disadvantages, such as being landlocked. Borchert et al. (2017) show that policy barriers in 'connectivity services,' such as telecommunications and transport, serve to increase the isolation of geographically disadvantaged countries from world markets.

Accounting for trade in intermediates – a key feature of the GVC model – makes clear that the economic losses from protectionist trade policies are higher than previously thought (Ossa, 2015). Using trade policy to attempt to re-shore substantial portions of GVC activity would therefore involve major economic costs, in particular since the evidence suggests that production-sharing is relatively robust under trade policy changes, at least in proportional terms when it comes to tariffs. As such, while unilateral actions by large countries undoubtedly pose real challenges to the rules-based multilateral trading system, they do not appear to have fundamentally changed the ability of GVCs to operate as they have become accustomed to do in recent years.

Similarly, it would not be appropriate to frame GVC-related policies too strongly in reference to the COVID-19 pandemic and accompanying economic shock. The shock is an unusual one in that it brought strongly correlated country-level shocks, at least in the early days of the pandemic. More commonly, country-level economic shocks are much less strongly correlated; in this case, the ability to diversify risk by relying on multiple suppliers in multiple countries becomes an advantage of the GVC system, not a negative feature. While the private sector continues to reassess its approach to resilience – looking in particular at building in redundancies that can better respond to major economic shocks – the public sector does not yet have an obvious mandate to impose a particular vision of risk management from the outside. Of course, a much stronger case exists for using public-sector resources to maintain inventories of critical equipment in circumstances where the private sector cannot do so optimally. But that would involve forward-looking purchase arrangements between governments and GVCs, not policy involvement in the planning decisions of GVCs as such.

While the pandemic has posed real challenges to economies in all regions and at all development levels, the widespread availability of safe and effective vaccines should support a return to more favourable conditions. Against that background, there is every reason to expect that GVCs will continue to play an important role in global trade, and that developing countries will continue to successfully adopt outward-oriented growth strategies.

NOTES

1. For the World Bank 2021 fiscal year, low-income economies are defined as those with a gross national income (GNI) per capita, calculated using the World Bank Atlas method, of US$1,035 or less in 2019; lower middle-income economies are those with a GNI per capita between $1,036 and $4,045; upper middle-income economies are those with a GNI per capita between $4,046 and $12,535; high-income economies are those with a GNI per capita of $12,536 or more (World Bank, 2021a).

2. See Shepherd (2020) for a review of the methodological issues.

3. For instance, Xing (2020) uses such an approach to show that Chinese firms contribute about 25 per cent of the value-added in the iPhone X, with 45 per cent coming from Japan, the Republic of Korea and other economies, and a significant proportion from the United States as well.

REFERENCES

Acemoglu, D. and Restrepo, P. 2019. 'Automation and New Tasks: How Technology Displaces and Reinstates Labor'. *Journal of Economic Perspectives* 33(2), 3–30.

Alfaro-Urena, A., Manelici, I. and Vasquez, J. 2020. *The Effects of Joining Multinational Supply Chains: New Evidence from Firm-to-Firm Linkages*. Chicago: The Weiss Fund for Research in Development Economics, the University of Chicago. https://3768255e-bb38-4e95-9575-269a322cc0d4.filesusr.com/ugd/c7b5dd_50cb1a69cd824e5aa3abf6e7d6a23f63.pdf.

Association for Professionals in Infection Control and Epidemiology (APIC). 2016. 'National Survey Shows Dire Shortages of PPE, Hand Sanitizer across the U.S.' Association for Professionals in Infection Control and Epidemiology, Inc., Arlington, VA. apic.org/news/national-survey-shows-dire-shortages-of-ppe-hand-sanitizer-across-the-u-s/.

Autor, D., Dorn, D. and Hanson, G. 2016. 'The China Shock: Learning from Labor-Market Adjustment to Large Changes in Trade'. *Annual Review of Economics* 8(1), 205–240.

Baldwin, R. 2011. 'Trade and Industrialization after Globalization's Second Unbundling: How Building and Joining a Supply Chain are Different and Why It Matters'. NBER Working Paper No. 17716, National Bureau of Economic Research, Cambridge, MA.

Blattman, C. and Dercon, S. 2017. 'The Impacts of Industrial and Entrepreneurial Work on Income and Health: Experimental Evidence from Ethiopia'. *American Economic Journal: Applied Economics* 10(3), 1–38. papers.ssrn.com/sol3/papers.cfm?abstract_id=2843595.

Borchert, I., Gootiiz, B. and Mattoo, A. 2017. 'Services Trade Protection and Economic Isolation'. *World Economy* 40(3), 632–652.

Borin, A. and Mancini, M. 2019. *Measuring What Matters in Global Value Chains and Value Added Trade*. Washington, DC: The World Bank Group.

Brambilla, I., Depetris Chauvin, N. and Porto, G. 2017. 'Examining the Export Wage Premium in Developing Countries'. *Review of International Economics* 25(3), 447–475.

Cattaneo, O., Gereffi, G., Miroudot, S. and Taglioni, D. 2013. *Joining, Upgrading, and Being Competitive in Global Value Chains: A Strategic Framework*. Washington, DC: The World Bank Group.

Feenstra, R. and Sasahara, A. 2018. 'The "China Shock", Exports, and US Employment: A Global Input–Output Analysis'. *Review of International Economics* 26(5), 1053–1083.

Frederick, S. 2016. *Concept and Tools*. Durham, NC: Duke University. globalvaluechains.org/concept-tools.

Grossman, G. and Rossi-Hansberg, E. 2008. 'Trading Tasks: A Simple Theory of Offshoring'. *American Economic Review* 98(5), 1978–1997.

Helble, M. and Shepherd, B. 2019. *Leveraging Services for Development: Prospects and Policies*. Manila: Asian Development Bank.

Hoekman, B. and Shepherd, B. 2017. 'Services Productivity, Trade Policy, and Manufacturing Exports'. *World Economy* 40(30), 499–516.

International Trade Center (ITC). 2017. *Small and Medium Enterprises Competitiveness Report: The Region – A Door to Global Trade*. Geneva: International Trade Center.

Low, P. and Pasadilla, G. 2016. *Services in Global Value Chains: Manufacturing-Related Services*. Singapore: World Scientific.

Organisation for Economic Cooperation and Development (OECD). 2020. 'Shocks, Risks, and Global Value Chains: Insights from the OECD METRO Model'. Organisation for Economic Cooperation and Development, Paris. oecd.org/trade/documents/shocks-risks-gvc-insights-oecd-metro-model.pdf.

Ossa, R. 2015. 'Why Trade Matters After All'. *Journal of International Economics* 97(2), 266–277.

Park, C.-Y. 2020. *Global Shortage of Personal Protective Equipment amid COVID-19: Supply Chains, Bottlenecks, and Policy Implications*. Manila: Asian Development Bank.

Reuters. 2016. 'Thai Hard Disk Drive Exporters See Silver Lining in Cloud Storage – For Now'. 24 April. reuters.com/article/thailand-technology/thai-hard-disk-drive-exporters-see-silver-lining-in-cloud-storage-for-now-idUSL3N176035.

Rocha, N. and Winkler, D. 2019. *Trade and Female Labor Participation: Stylized Facts Using a Global Dataset*. Washington, DC: The World Bank Group.

Rodrik, D. 2015. 'Premature Deindustrialization'. *Journal of Economic Growth* 21(2015), 1–33.

Saxena, S. 2020. *Labor, Global Supply Chains, and the Garment Industry in South Asia: Bangladesh after Rana Plaza*. London: Routledge.

Shepherd, B. 2018. *Global Value Chains and Women's Labor: Firm-Level Evidence*. Jakarta: Economic Research Institute for ASEAN and East Asia.

———. 2019. 'Productivity and Trade Growth in Services: How Services Helped Power "Factory Asia"'. In *Leveraging Services for Development: Policies and Prospects*, ed. M. Helble and B. Shepherd. Manila: Asian Development Bank, 215–233.

———. 2020. *Measuring Participation in Global Value Chains and Developing Supportive Policies: A User Guide*. Bangkok: United Nations Economic and Social Commission for Asia and the Pacific. unescap.org/resources/gvc-analysis-guide.

Stolper, W. and Samuelson, P. 1941. 'Protection and Real Wages'. *Review of Economic Studies* 9(1), 58–73.

United Nations Conference on Trade and Development (UNCTAD). 2012. *Corporate Social Responsibility in Global Value Chains*. New York: United Nations Conference on Trade and Development.

Winkler, D. 2019. 'Productivity Spillovers from Services Firms in Low- and Middle-Income Countries: What Is the Role of Firm Characteristics and Services Liberalization?' In M. Helble and B. Shepherd, eds., Leveraging Services for Development: Policies and Prospects. Manila: Asian Development Bank, 173–214.

World Bank. 2018. 'Vietnam Continues to Reduce Poverty, According to WB Report'. The World Bank Group, Washington, DC. worldbank.org/en/news/press-release/2018/04/05/vietnam-continues-to-reduce-poverty-according-to-world-bank-report.

———. 2020. *World Development Report 2020: Trading for Development in the Age of Global Value Chains*. Washington, DC: The World Bank Group.

———. 2021. 'World Bank Country and Lending Groups'. The World Bank Group, Washington DC. datahelpdesk.worldbank.org/knowledgebase/articles/906519-world-bank-country-and-lending-groups.

World Trade Organization (WTO). 2021. 'Trade Datasets'. World Trade Organization, Geneva. wto.org/english/res_e/statis_e/trade_datasets_e.htm.

Xing, Y. 2020. 'How the iPhone Widens the US Trade Deficit with China: The Case of the iPhone X'. *Frontiers of Economics in China* 15(4), 642–658.

5 | Is Southeast Asia Falling into a Latin American–Style Middle-Income Trap?

José Gabriel Palma and Jonathan Pincus

> Productivity isn't everything, but in the long run, it's almost everything.
> —Paul Krugman (1997)

INTRODUCTION

The first generation of East Asian newly industrializing countries and territories (NICs-1), including Hong Kong SAR (China), the Republic of Korea, Singapore and Taiwan (Province of China), like Japan in the post-war period, and China and India since 1980, have raised the bar for other developing economies. Second-tier Southeast Asian NICs (NICs-2), including Indonesia, Malaysia, Thailand and Viet Nam, have not yet been able to replicate the NICs-1 long-term growth of gross domestic product (GDP) or labour productivity, partly because – barring Viet Nam – they never properly recovered from the 1997 Asian financial crisis.[1] If Malaysia and Thailand, for example, had been able to sustain their pre-crisis growth rates into the 21st century, output per person could have reached US$18,900 and $17,000, respectively, ranking them among the most successful developing economies of the post-war period.[2] However, because of slower growth from 2000 to 2019, Malaysia's GDP per capita was 70 per cent lower and Thailand's 50 per cent lower than prospective numbers, leaving both NICs-2 well below the $20,000 per capita threshold (Figure 5.1).[3] Is it possible that Indonesia, Malaysia and Thailand are showing signs of an economic and productivity growth slowdown similar to the slowdowns in Argentina, Brazil, and Mexico?

The term 'middle-income trap' was coined by Gill et al. (2007), who predicted that growth in Asia would inevitably taper off as capital–labour ratios rose as economies approached the global technological frontier, which they define as the most advanced technology currently in use (Kharas and Gill, 2015). In countries with few or no natural resources, the trap manifests when middle-income countries

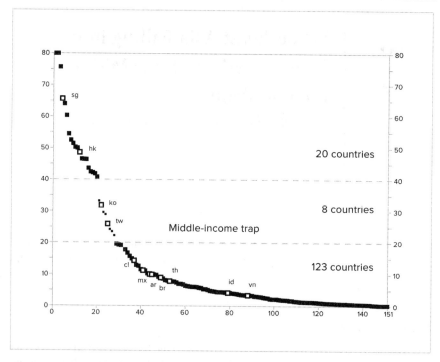

Figure 5.1   The middle-income trap in terms of GDP per capita, 2019 (US$ '000)
Source: International Monetary Fund (2021).
Note: Throughout this chapter, abbreviations for countries are identical to their internet domains. The top two countries in the ranking are Switzerland and Ireland, which have a GDP per capita above the range of the Y axis ($85,686 and $80,482, respectively).

are priced out of labour-intensive activities by cheap-labour competitors, but cannot yet challenge more technologically advanced countries because of lagging productivity levels. In countries rich in natural resources, the trap tends to manifest when they exhaust their merely extractive development model and do not move to processing their commodities.

Operating within mainstream new growth theory, Gill et al. view increasing returns to scale as a positive externality that stems from research and development activities outside of the firm. Although these growth models posit that research-intensive activities generate increasing returns, as single sector models they do not associate increasing returns with the level of output or investment in manufacturing. Furthermore, the models do not allow for manufacturing to have specific effects on research and development (R&D) activities, except for allowing that investment in *any* sector could complement R&D by affecting research profitability. Therefore, these growth models have no room for the idea that manufacturing is special because of unique growth-inducing properties that set manufacturing apart from any other productive activity (Kaldor, 1966; 1978), nor for Kaldorian-style effects concerning investment embedding or embodying technical change (Palma, 2005).[4]

Instead, Gill et al. theorize that middle-income countries can escape the trap by adopting orthodox economic policies, such as the liberalization of trade and finance, the retreat of the state to a subsidiary role relative to the market, the enforcement of intellectual property rights, and higher levels of investment in education and skills. Using these strategies, middle-income countries should, in theory, be able to specialize in niche industries and products that benefit from knowledge spillovers, and thereby realize increasing returns (Gill et al., 2007).

At first glance, the empirical evidence from Latin America and Southeast Asia appears to give some support to this mainstream view (Paus, 2014; Tran Van Tho, 2013). However, in contrast to the Gil et al. hypothesis, we show that in Argentina, Brazil, Chile, Mexico and the NICs-2, a growth slowdown set in at labour productivity levels far removed from the technological frontier (considered to be the productivity level of the United States [US], the global benchmark). Labour productivity in Latin American and Southeast Asian middle-income countries, such as Chile[5] and Malaysia, hit a glass ceiling at 50 per cent or less of average US labour productivity levels; this contrasts with a first-generation NIC, such as the Republic of Korea, which has already achieved 65 per cent of US labour productivity, as seen in Figure 5.2.

The appearance of symptoms of the middle-income trap at relatively low levels of labour productivity casts doubt on the original formulation of the theory, which hypothesizes that growth would slow down *only* as countries neared the technological frontier. However, as seen in Figure 5.1, the data highlights the fact that only 10 out of 151 countries have broken through the $20,000 per capita GDP threshold since 1950, which makes them statistical outliers. These 10 countries (four NICs-1 and six from the European periphery) have managed to progress further towards higher per-capita-GDP status, which brings them closer to the technological frontier.[6]

As indicated in Figure 5.2 with Chile, labour productivity growth in Argentina, Brazil and Mexico has also failed to catch up with the technological frontier, and, like Malaysia, the other Asian NICs-2 have not be able to sustain their pre-1997 growth trajectories. Lagging productivity in both regions, but especially in Latin America, suggests that rapid growth is more difficult to sustain at higher and more complex stages of the catching-up process.

This chapter explores the middle-income trap thesis from the perspective of major Latin American and Southeast Asian middle-income countries. We argue that the productivity slowdown in these countries was not an inevitable result of rising capital-labour ratios as these countries neared the technological frontier, since productivity slowed at the half-way mark at best. Matching the performance

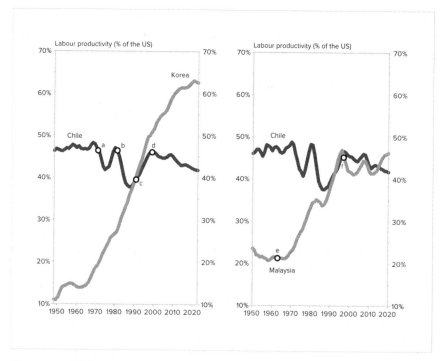

Figure 5.2 NIC-1 Korea, NIC-2 Malaysia and Latin America's Chile relative to catching up with the United States, 1950–2020 (% of US labour productivity)
Source: The Conference Board (2021).
Note: a = 1970 election of President Salvador Allende in Chile; b = 1982 financial crisis; c = 1990 Chile's return to democracy after 17 years of dictatorship; d = 1998 end of Chile's rapid period of recovery and catching up; e = 1963 Malaysian independence; f = 1997 Asian financial crisis. The original data is expressed in 2019 US$ purchasing power parity (PPP).

of the NICs-1 requires more than progress along a production function; instead, a conscious, national-level strategy is necessary to promote investment in activities with higher long-term potential for productivity growth, especially manufactured exports, to realize economies of scale across a wide range of industries. In both Latin America and Southeast Asia, governments have doubled down on their prevailing development strategies long after they exhaust their potential to drive a sustained increase in productivity growth. The growth collapse is deeper and has persisted for far longer in Latin America than in Southeast Asia, contributing to the former's notoriously high levels of inequality, caused by high labour concentrations in low productivity-growth activities.[7] When Chile's neo-liberal reforms began in 1973, the share of employment in low productivity-growth services and construction was 55 per cent; by 2019, it reached 86 per cent (Palma, 2019a). Furthermore, there are signs that the growth strategies in NICs-2, based on a combination of commodity exports and foreign direct investment in assembly operations, are also nearing their limits. Breaking free from the middle-income country pack in both regions will require departing from orthodox laissez faire economic policies and static comparative advantage to promote manufactured exports (including commodities with manufacturing value added) and invest in related industries.

We begin by explaining that the 'more-of-the-same-but-better' supply-side-strategy that many current policies focus on is the wrong solution; instead, Latin American and Asian NICs-2 economies require the reengineering of existing development strategies. The second section explains issues such as how Latin America and Southeast Asia should leverage natural resource-based industrialization in order to increase their productivity growth. The third section describes how Latin American countries and Asian NICs-2 persist with their prevailing growth model despite having exhausted their potential to drive productivity growth. In the fourth section, we describe how Latin America's growth model is 'dual-extractive' in that commodities are the main driver of productivity growth while all job creation is confined to less dynamic activities in services and construction; therefore, no single sector in Latin America has managed to generate both productivity growth and jobs. Section five explains how Southeast Asian economies are still capable of generating both employment and productivity growth; however, their manufacturing labour productivity growth has slowed following the 1997 Asian financial crisis. The chapter concludes with policy recommendations on how Southeast Asian and Latin American countries can revisit their dominant growth strategies to reignite labour productivity growth.

THE PROBLEM WITH MORE-OF-THE-SAME-BUT-HOPEFULLY-BETTER

Conventional policy recommendations favour what we might call a 'more-of-the-same-but-hopefully-better' supply-side strategy of trying to cultivate competitive advantage in more technologically sophisticated subsectors through financial liberalization, training, education, and investment protections, such as strict intellectual property rights regulation. Drawing on endogenous growth theory, conventional policies assume that international trade and investment flows will spontaneously generate rapid labour productivity growth as domestic producers benefit from technological spillover effects (Roemer, 1990; Lucas, 1988). Therefore, slow productivity growth must either be an indication of supply constraints (human capital or finance), or domestic market distortions created by government intervention or corruption that can only be overcome through more market liberalization.

Current trade agreements, such as the Comprehensive and Progressive Agreement for Trans-Pacific Partnership (commonly known as the TPP-11), clearly point in this more-of-the-same-but-hopefully-better direction – provided that any change is achieved by incentives that create private sector investment opportunities and not by changes in policy or regulation that would create different forms of compulsions for firms to take up opportunities. In other words, the goal is for countries to become more attractive for foreign direct investment (FDI) in a highly competitive international environment. In our view, this is a misdiagnosis of the problem and the wrong solution: what Latin American and Asian NICs-2 economies actually require is a reengineering of existing development strategies. Expecting these countries to leap from a mid-table ranking to world leader through policies that are based on the same strategies that landed them mid-table is not a realistic solution.

The supply-side orientation of mainstream economists obscures the ways that market power blocks an upgrading of development strategies. Contrary to the beliefs of endogenous growth theorists, technology is not an external benefit that flows costlessly between firms. Rather, technology is increasingly dominated by massive global companies that use their market power to create and acquire new technologies and to apply pressure on suppliers to cut costs and accelerate the pace of innovation. Financialization (the steady increase in the size and dominance of the financial sector relative to the non-financial sector, as well as the diversification towards financial activities in non-financial corporations since the 1980s) has fuelled concentration of ownership, inequality, rising household and corporate debt, and the formation of asset bubbles in financial, land and currency markets. In the developing world, financialization has redirected investment from production to speculation; in Latin America and Southeast Asia, investment rates have fallen over the past decade as the private debt burden has increased (Palma, 2009).[8]

These are not problems that will be easily fixed by supply-side remedies like training more computer scientists or easing the regulatory burden on venture capitalists. Policymakers must also look to the demand side: to upstream and downstream linkages and to the competitiveness of domestic firms in international markets. Export demand is essential to enable domestic firms to acquire technology and realize economies of scale, the two processes that generate demand for domestically produced and more technologically sophisticated goods.

MANUFACTURING AS THE ENGINE OF PRODUCTIVITY GROWTH

Decades before endogenous growth theory rediscovered increasing returns to scale for a neoclassical economics audience, Nicholas Kaldor (1966; 1978) fashioned an alternative theory of economic growth grounded on the capacity of manufacturing operations to generate increasing returns. He expressed his theory in the form of three empirical regularities, or laws. The first states that the rate of output growth in the non-manufacturing sector is related to the rate of growth in manufacturing because of the movement of labour from low to higher productivity activities, such as from agriculture to manufacturing, and because of within-sector productivity gains in manufacturing associated with increasing returns. The relationship is robust for the NICs-1 and middle-income countries in Latin America and Southeast Asia from 1980 to 2018 (Figure 5.3). Countries that achieved rapid growth of manufacturing also recorded high rates of growth in other sectors, as predicted by Kaldor, thus raising their economies' overall GDP.

Kaldor's second law posits that the rate of within-sector productivity growth in manufacturing is related to the rate of growth of manufacturing output.[9] The acceleration of output growth generates static returns to scale, or declining fixed costs, while dynamic returns are derived from learning by doing and technological innovation. The data show that productivity growth is most rapid in countries in which manufacturing value added has increased fastest, especially in the NICs-1, and slower in Latin America, where output growth lags (Figure 5.4). The usual objection

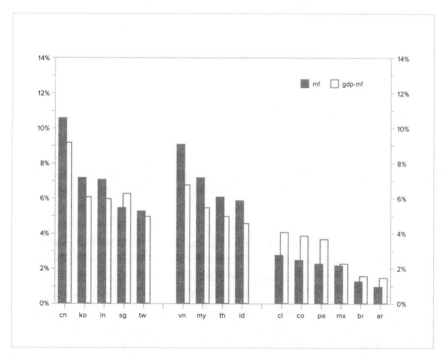

Figure 5.3   The relationship between the growth rates of manufacturing value added and non-manufacturing value added in NICs-1, NICs-2 and Latin America, 1980–2018
Source: de Vries et al. (2021).
Note: The dataset, at 2015 prices, only spans from 1990 to 2018. This was brought back to 1980 with the rate of growth from a previous version of this dataset, at 2005 prices. mf = manufacturing GDP; gdp-mf = non-manufacturing GDP.

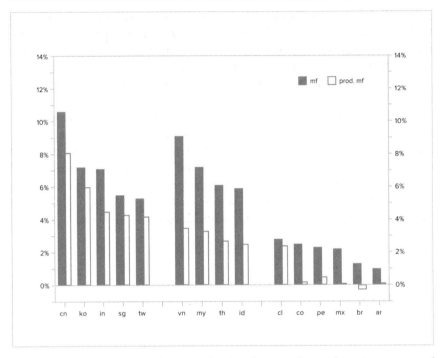

Figure 5.4   The relationship between the growth rates of manufacturing output and manufacturing labour productivity, 1980–2018
Source: de Vries et al. (2021).
Note: The dataset, at 2015 prices, only spans from 1990 to 2018. This was brought back to 1980 with the rate of growth from a previous version of this dataset, at 2005 prices. mf = manufacturing GDP; prod. mf = manufacturing labour productivity.

to Kaldor's second law is that correlation is not causation: It could be that productivity growth is driving output growth, not the other way around, and as overall productivity accelerates, demand for manufactured goods also rises. This would suggest, however, that productivity growth is autonomous, or unrelated, to the rate of investment and effective demand. This is clearly not the case. For example, productivity has increased faster in the automobile industry in China than in India, partly due to the rate of growth of output and exports (Lopez Acevedo et al., 2017: 119).

Kaldor's third and final law posits a positive relationship between the rates of output growth of the manufacturing sector and that of labour productivity in the non-manufacturing sector, including labour-sending sectors, including agriculture and traditional services, such as petty trade and domestic labour. There is nothing automatic about this relationship; it depends on enlightened government policy to provide and maintain productive physical infrastructure, such as irrigation works, drainage, roads and electricity, and to promote technological change through nonphysical infrastructure, such as support for research and financing for capital equipment.

The movement of labour from agriculture to industry, if sufficiently rapid, has the potential to raise rural wages and stimulate investment in labour-saving technologies if the necessary infrastructure is in place. This third law also applies to the capacity of manufacturing to drive productivity growth in services and construction, which, as non-tradables, depend crucially on domestic demand factors. Figure 5.5 confirms that countries with rapidly growing manufacturing also record higher rates of productivity growth in agriculture, mining, and services than countries like Argentina, Brazil, Chile and Mexico, where the performance of manufacturing has been poor.

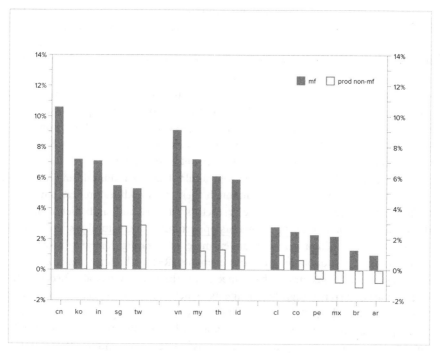

Figure 5.5   The relationship between the growth rates of manufacturing output and non-manufacturing labour productivity, 1980–2018
Source: de Vries et al. (2021).
Note: The dataset, at 2015 prices, only spans from 1990 to 2018. This was brought back to 1980 with the rate of growth from a previous version of this dataset, at 2005 prices. mf = manufacturing GDP; prod non-mf = non-manufacturing labour productivity.

Kaldor strongly emphasizes the role of demand in economic growth. Countries that are not rich in natural resources must quickly learn to export consumer goods because, in most cases, the domestic market is too small to accommodate a rapid expansion of industrial output, even under an import-substitution regime. Competing internationally also forces domestic manufacturers to improve quality and reduce costs, driving further productivity gains. Countries that are rich in resources should upgrade their merely extractive activities. Domestic investment is another source of demand, but backward linkages will not automatically arise if production is limited to the domestic market or to the extractive stage of commodities. In this sense, industrial output growth is ultimately determined by export growth and the domestic capacity to adopt investment opportunities created by export markets. In turn, the sustainability of GDP growth is determined by the differential between the income elasticities of import and export demand (Thirlwall, 2015: 337). These elasticities will largely depend on the composition of a country's imports and exports.

Growth in the Latin American commodity sector (agriculture, crude oil, gas and mining) has not induced (or is not associated with) productivity growth in the rest of the economy. In contrast to emerging Asia, Argentina, Brazil, Chile and Mexico have not invested in the processing of commodities or in industries producing technologically sophisticated inputs for extractive industries, thereby failing to create forward linkages between commodity production and manufacturing. In fact, Chile is actually going in reverse: The percentage of its refined copper or partially refined blister copper exports in terms of all copper exports have declined from close to 100 per cent in 1973 to 44 per cent in 2018 (United Nations, 2017). Similarly, Brazil has not capitalized on its iron ore or soybean production.[10]

The NICs-2 should take note to avoid similar failures: Indonesia and Malaysia process palm oil and natural gas, although these commodities are less amenable to forward linkages. The commodity sectors in Thailand and Viet Nam are diverse and dynamic, offering numerous opportunities for natural resource-based industrialization. China provides an example of creating forward linkages by imposing an export quota on rare earth elements (REE). China is a major exporter of REE ores and concentrates, but, since 2012, the country has also become the largest manufacturer of high-tech magnets, which is one of the main uses of REE (Medeiros and Trebat, 2017: 504). China's move to restrict exports of commodities with a potential for high-tech manufacturing, and processing them domestically in order to export high-value products, is a transferable lesson, and one that will find applications in both Latin America and in Southeast Asia.

NEOPHOBIA AND THE PRODUCTIVITY GLASS CEILING

The NICs-1 were unusual in their capacity to close the productivity gap with the world's leading economies. As seen earlier, with Chile and Malaysia (Figure 5.2), it appears there is a threshold at which output per person stalls, a 'productivity glass ceiling' that manifests at about 50 per cent of the United States' levels, and which is quite a distance from the technological frontier. Figure 5.6 shows that the labour productivity levels of Brazil, Mexico, Indonesia and Viet Nam, like those of Chile and Malaysia, lag well below the glass ceiling. Argentina and Thailand labour productivity levels reflect similar lags (The Conference Board, 2021). Indeed, since ending their import-substitution strategies, the Latin American countries have been falling behind rather than catching up with the technological frontier.

In Latin America, neophobia, or the fear of the new, has led Argentina, Brazil, Chile and Mexico to persist with the prevailing growth model – whether import-substituting industrialization before 1980, or reliance on extractive industries since then – long after the potential to drive productivity growth was exhausted (Palma, 2019a). The countries did not lack options: backward and forward linkages from extractive activities, including the processing of primary exports from agriculture,

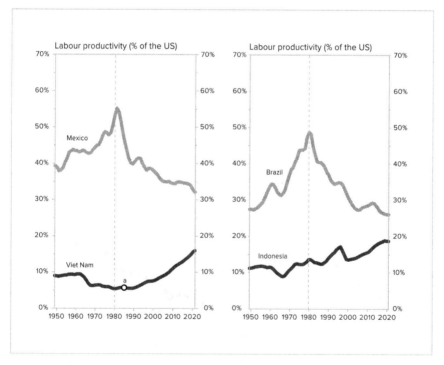

Figure 5.6   Mexico versus Viet Nam and Brazil versus Indonesia catching up with the United States, 1950–2020 (% of US labour productivity)
Source: The Conference Board (2021).
Note: a = 1986 economic reforms begin in Viet Nam. Mexico's employment data before 1993 underestimates informal employment; therefore, instead of showing productivity relative to the US, Mexico shows relative income per capita.

oil and mining; investment in renewables, clean energy and production systems; and digitalization of the non-tradeable sector were all realistic possibilities. Instead, these Latin American countries continued to export unprocessed commodities despite a clear loss of productivity-growth momentum, reaching the productivity glass ceiling and then moving into a reverse, catching-up mode.

However, during the same period, NICs-2 economies, such as Viet Nam and Indonesia, showed respectable productivity gains and grew much faster (Figure 5.6). For example, despite a temporary slowdown after the 1997 Asian financial crisis, the contribution of labour productivity growth to Malaysia's and Thailand's GDP growth also increased in each successive period since 1950. Labour productivity contributed nearly 60 per cent of GDP growth in Thailand from 1950 to 1980; 70 per cent from 1980 to 1997; and 76 per cent from 1998 to 2019. In Indonesia, productivity growth contributed 44 per cent of GDP growth from 1950 to 1966; 55 per cent from 1967 to 1997; and 58 per cent from 1998 until 2019 (The Conference Board, 2021).

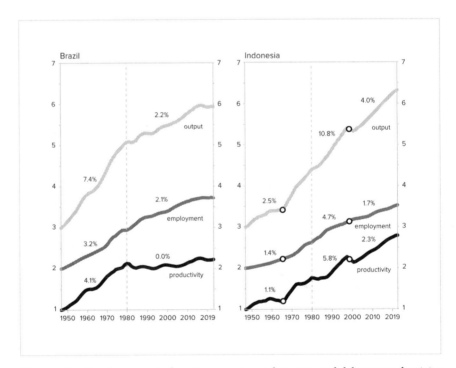

Figure 5.7   Brazil versus Indonesia output, employment and labour productivity, 1950–2019

Source: de Vries et al. (2021).

Note: Each series is an index number of a 3-year moving average (in log-scale), with base 1 in 1950 for productivity, 2 for employment, and 3 for output. Productivity = output per worker; employment = total employment; output = GDP.

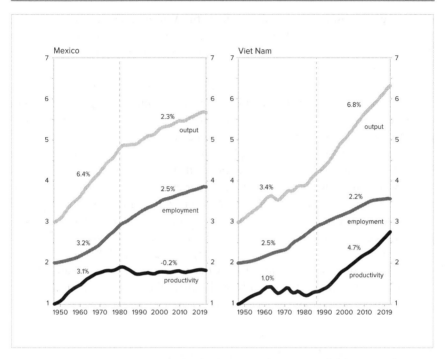

Figure 5.8 Mexico versus Viet Nam output, employment and labour productivity, 1950–2019

Source: de Vries et al. (2021).

Note: Each series is an index number of a 3-year moving average (in log-scale), with base 1 in 1950 for productivity, 2 for employment, and 3 for output. Productivity = output per worker; employment = total employment; output = GDP.

As productivity growth in Latin America faltered, output growth in Argentina, Brazil, Chile and Mexico (except in Chile on its return to democracy in 1990) has depended entirely on employment growth since the 1980s. During the same period, the NICs-2 economies combined productivity gains and output growth with steady employment increases, as seen in the comparison between Brazil and Indonesia (Figure 5.7) and Mexico and Viet Nam (Figure 5.8).

Meanwhile, the productivity of the average worker in Argentina, Brazil and Mexico, which together represent well over 80 per cent of Latin America's GDP (a share that has risen since the collapse of the Venezuelan economy), remains the same today as it was in 1980. Employment generation has been confined to sectors having little or no potential for long-term productivity growth. The extractive sector, which posted rapid productivity gains for a while, has not created jobs. Notably, overall productivity growth in Brazil came to an abrupt halt in 1982 with the end of the import-substitution period and the Latin American debt crisis. Since then, Brazil has sustained productivity growth at the expense of the devastation of the Amazon rainforest, and GDP growth has been entirely due to employment creation in services and construction.

However, Brazil's rapid increase in demand for labour (reaching more than twice the rate of population growth) did little to increase the income share of the bottom 40 per cent of the population (Palma, 2011, 2019b, 2020). Instead, slow productivity growth in sectors that have the capacity to generate employment results in a lower wage share and higher returns to capital, which in turn results in greater wealth inequality. For example, Oxfam (n.d.) estimates that the six richest Brazilians control the same amount of wealth as the bottom 50 per cent of the population. According to *Forbes* magazine, since Latin America's neoliberal reforms, no other region of the world has created as many millionaires, centimillionaires and billionaires; even under successive Workers' Party governments, the number of Brazilian millionaires and billionaires trebled (Andrade, 2020). Today there are more billionaires in Brazil than in the Republic of Korea and more in Chile than in Saudi Arabia (Palma, 2019). We examine this progression towards wealth inequality and stagnation of overall productivity growth in more detail in the next section.

LATIN AMERICA'S DUAL-EXTRACTIVE MODEL

Palma (2019a) describes Latin America's growth model as 'dual-extractive': extractive because commodities are the main (often only) driver of productivity growth (at least until the extractive drive gets exhausted); and dual because while productivity growth takes place only in commodity production, all job creation is confined to activities that have no productivity-growth dynamics, such as services and construction. As the productivity growth potential of extractive industries has begun to fade in Latin America (except for Brazil) and as these economies have failed to generate new sources of productivity growth, employment creation in services and construction has become the sole driver of GDP growth. In contrast to emerging Asia, no single sector in Latin America has been able to generate both productivity growth and jobs (Figure 5.9).

The slowdown of manufacturing in Latin America since the 1980s has been a significant drag on labour productivity growth and, compounded by Venezuela's manufacturing collapse, has reduced the region's share of emerging market manufacturing output from over half of all manufacturing production in 1980 to only one-tenth in recent years (Palma 2019a). In fact, in manufacturing, China's relative rise is nearly the reverse image of Latin America's decline (Palma, 2011).

Old and new orthodox theories of international trade would predict that trade liberalization and competition from emerging Asian manufacturing

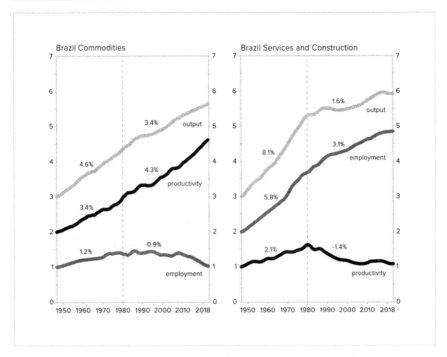

Figure 5.9 Brazil output, employment and productivity in commodities and services and construction, 1950–2018
Source: de Vries et al. (2021).
Note: Each series is an index number of a 3-year moving average (in log-scale), with base 1, 2 or 3 in 1950 for its respective variable. Productivity = output per worker; employment = total employment; output = GDP; Commodities = agriculture, oil, gas and mining.

would lead to the offshoring of Latin American labour-intensive (and frequently lower productivity) manufacturing activities (or segments of value chains) and the retention of more productive (and productivity-enhancing) activities. Concentration on higher value added and more dynamic activities in manufacturing would generate more rapid productivity growth through specialization and increasing returns. From a simple, arithmetical point of view, therefore, deindustrialization in Latin America should have resulted in an increase in average productivity growth as, in relative terms, growth in manufacturing employment would fall more rapidly than in output.

Yet, the opposite took place: In Argentina, Brazil, and Mexico, three economies with advanced manufacturing sectors in 1980, manufacturing employment continued to grow while productivity stalled, as shown in the examples of Brazil and Mexico (Figure 5.10). In fact, in addition to some labour-intensive activities,

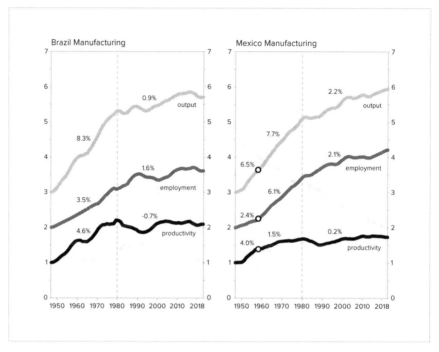

Figure 5.10   Brazil and Mexico output, employment and productivity in manufacturing, 1950–2018

Source: de Vries et al. (2021).

Note: Each series is an index number of a 3-year moving average (in log-scale), with base 1 in 1950 for productivity, 2 for employment, and 3 for output. Productivity = output per worker; employment = total employment; output = GDP.

the industries that were transferred from Latin America to Asia were more mobile, or 'footloose', but not necessarily less productive, including consumer durables, garments, footwear and other goods that diversified extensively under import substitution (Palma, 2011).

At the same time, falling transport costs allowed manufacturing activities previously tied to the geographical source of their main input to be transferred to Asia, such as the processing of bulky raw commodities. This deindustrialization process causes unnecessary pollution and significantly contributes to global warming. For example, as seen earlier, Chile exports of copper concentrates to Asia includes the transportation of copper slag, which accounts for 70 per cent of the volume of the product experted (Palma, 2019a; Sturla-Zerene et al., 2020).

MANUFACTURING LOSES STEAM IN THE NICS-2

As we saw earlier, unlike in Latin America, manufacturing in the large Southeast Asian economies is still capable of generating both employment and productivity growth. However, these countries, with the exception of Viet Nam, have not managed to sustain the high rates of manufacturing output and productivity growth that they recorded prior to the Asian financial crisis.

Prior to the crisis, Southeast Asia enjoyed a decade of exceptionally rapid investment, exports, and output growth as countries incorporated their manufacturing into Japanese production networks for both exports and import substitutes. Following the Plaza Accord in 1985, the value of the yen rose sharply against the dollar, prompting Japanese firms to relocate to China and Southeast Asia – a preferred destination because of the region's combination of cheap labour and currencies effectively pegged to the US dollar.

Japanese FDI in Indonesia, Thailand, the Philippines and Malaysia increased 66 per cent in real terms from 1970 to 1985 and more than nine-fold from 1985 to 1996 (UNCTAD, n.d.). Similarly, from 1985 to 1996, manufactured exports from the Association of Southeast Asian Nations (ASEAN)[11] countries rose nine-fold. Governments built export processing zones and transport and logistics infrastructure to attract investment, while also deploying local content requirements and other instruments to boost domestic value added and upgrade technological capabilities, such as in the Thai and Indonesian automobile industries. However, the boom had already begun to lose momentum by the early 1990s as Japan's prolonged recession deepened, and the 1997 Asian financial crisis brought it to an abrupt end.

Donors and international agencies offered only modest financial assistance to distressed NICs-2, and, to make matters worse, made their support conditional on the NICs-2 adopting orthodox adjustment policies, ostensibly to tackle the crony capitalism donors blamed for the severity of the crisis.[12] The result was a severe contraction in output, employment, and domestic demand and a delayed recovery. Reversing the boom seen prior to 1997, private and public investment in Indonesia, Malaysia and Thailand declined and remained subdued, not just in the years immediately after the crisis, but also for the next two decades (Figure 5.11), while Viet Nam withstood the direct effects of the Asian financial crisis, buffered by a closed capital account and limited overseas commercial borrowing.

Southeast Asia's productivity growth slowdown after the Asian financial crisis signalled the exhaustion of the post-Plaza Accord boom, which was based on Japanese inward investment in manufacturing. After the crisis, China emerged as the benchmark for low-cost production and simultaneously managed to upgrade its managerial and technological capabilities across a broad range of industries. The NICs-2, especially Malaysia and Thailand, were priced out of many labour-intensive

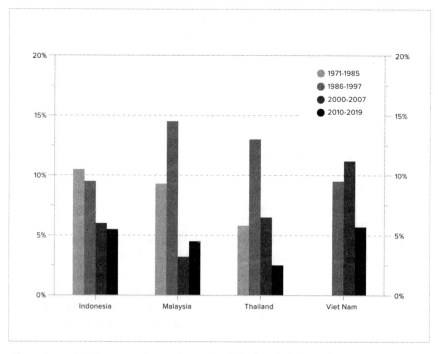

Figure 5.11 NICs-2 annual rate of growth of fixed capital formation, 1971–2019
Source: World Bank WDI (2021).
Note: The crisis years of 1998, 1999, 2008 and 2009 omitted as investment contracted in these years.

activities and were unable to keep pace with China's drive into capital- and technology-intensive operations; this remained the case despite years of incentive schemes and complementary public investments (Figure 5.12). Indonesia lost competitiveness during the 2004 to 2013 commodity boom when surging prices for coal, palm oil and metals led to exchange rate appreciation and rising real wages in manufacturing. There was even talk of 'premature' deindustrialization in Indonesia, Thailand and Malaysia (Rasiah, 2020).[13] Manufactured exports lost momentum, no longer growth engines except in Viet Nam, which assumed the role of low-cost assembler for foreign companies moving out of China. The absence of large national firms and heavy reliance on multinationals for technology and access to markets has imposed limits on the potential for Southeast Asian economies' productivity growth.

Furthermore, like the Latin American countries, Malaysia, Thailand and Indonesia have been unable to reengineer their growth strategies so as to penetrate markets for more sophisticated manufactured goods or to increase domestic value

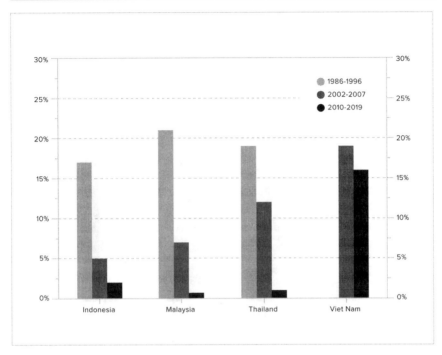

Figure 5.12   NICs-2 manufactured exports, 1986–2019
Source: World Bank WDI (2021).
Note: The crisis years of 1998, 1999, 2008 and 2009 omitted as trade contracted in these years.

added in foreign assembly operations. This leaves them increasingly reliant on legacy industries from the Plaza Accord era, such as automobile and electronics assembly (Malaysia and Thailand), or processing commodities, like palm oil, that have few upstream or downstream linkages (Indonesia and Malaysia). As seen in Figure 5.13, growth of export volumes fell sharply after the Asian financial crisis and have not recovered in Indonesia, Malaysia and Thailand, and unit export values declined in the past decade, except in Viet Nam.

Indonesia experienced two periods of rapid productivity growth in manufacturing before the Asian financial crisis. The first, from 1971 to the mid-1980s, was driven by state investment in basic industries financed by oil revenues. After oil prices declined, Indonesia devalued the rupiah and attracted investment in labour-intensive manufactures for export including garments, footwear and electronics. Import substitution was maintained in key industries like auto assembly and electrical machinery. Between 1971 and 1997, manufacturing output grew 10.9 per cent per annum, and labour productivity increased at an average

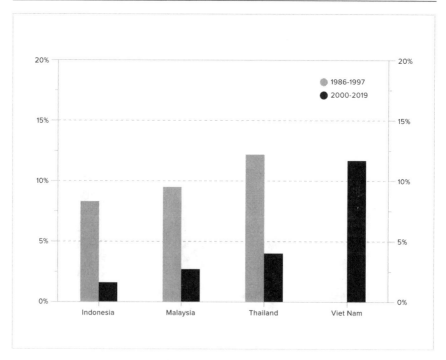

Figure 5.13   NICs-2 average annual rate of growth of trade volumes, 1986–2019
Source: UNCTAD (n.d.).
Note: The crisis years of 1998 and 1999 omitted as trade contracted in these years.

rate of 5 per cent. Industry contracted during and after the Asian financial crisis, and investment in manfacturing remain subdued during the commodity boom from the early 2000s to 2013. Productivity growth in manufacturing slowed to 2.1 per cent for the post-crisis period (Figure 5.14). The Indonesian services sector is diverse, encompassing high value added financial and business services alongside domestic services and petty trade; the latter two act as a reservoir for underemployed labour.

Malaysia pursued export-oriented industrialization from the 1970s, attracting foreign investment in electronics, which have accounted for the largest share of manufactured exports ever since. The government launched a new heavy industry strategy in the early 1980s, including a national automobile project, but had to reverse course within a few years as a fall in global commodity prices threatened a balance of payments crisis (Lall, 1996: 151). A renewed effort to attract inward investment coincided with the post-Plaza Accord surge in Japanese FDI and rapid growth of manufactured exports. After the crisis, both employment and productivity growth

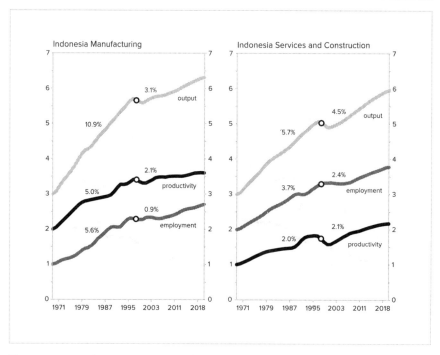

Figure 5.14   Indonesia output, employment and productivity in manufacturing and services and construction, 1971–2018

Source: de Vries et al. (2021).

Note: The circles = 1997 Asian financial crisis. Each series is an index number of a 3-year moving average (in log-scale), with base 1, 2 or 3 in 1950 for its respective variable. Productivity = output per worker; employment = total employment; output = GDP.

slowed as Malaysia lost competitiveness relative to China and Viet Nam in labour-intensive assembly operations, but did not succeed in moving into more technology-intensive phases of production (Figure 5.15).

For many years, Thailand combined development of import-substituting industries, most notably automotive assembly, with export-oriented manfacturing of electronics and other labour-intensive goods. Growth of manufacturing productivity accelerated to 4.9 per cent per annum after the Plaza Accord, but decelerated after the Asian financial crisis, and to an even greater extent after the global financial crisis of 2008 (Figure 5.16). Thailand has lost competitiveness with rising wages and a strengthening currency, and domestic political instabiltiy also deters foreign investment. Thailand's service sector, like Indonesia's, spans the full range of activities from finance and luxury tourism to low-paid jobs sought by seasonal migrants.

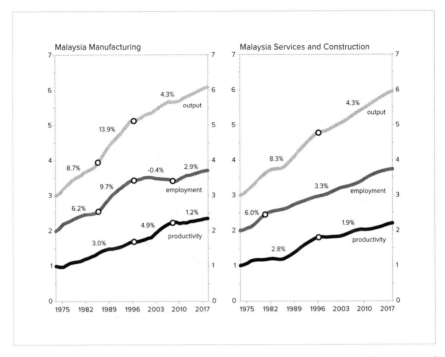

Figure 5.15   Malaysia output, employment and productivity in manufacturing and services and construction, 1975–2018

Source: de Vries et al. (2021).

Note: Each series is an index number of a 3-year moving average (in log-scale), with base 1 in 1950 for productivity, 2 for employment, and 3 for output. Productivity = output per worker; employment = total employment; output = GDP.

Viet Nam, still at a relatively early stage of industrialization, is the outlier in the region. Viet Nam's low wages and improving infrastructure have encouraged massive foreign investment in the manufacture of electronics, garments, and footwear, allowing Viet Nam to nearly recapture its pre-1997 6.2 per cent manufacturing productivity growth rate with 5.8 per cent by 2018 (Figure 5.17). Productivity growth dipped during the global financial crisis of 2007–2008 as the government subsidized employment, but, since 2015, FDI in electronics assembly, which comprises 35 per cent of exports, has driven an employment and productivity boom. Legacy products, such as garments and footwear, still make up 25 per cent of exports, but are growing more slowly. However, Viet Nam's boom in productivity growth is largely due to the movement of labour from low productivity occupations to manufacturing, with little evidence of productivity growth within assembly operations (Ohno et al., 2020).

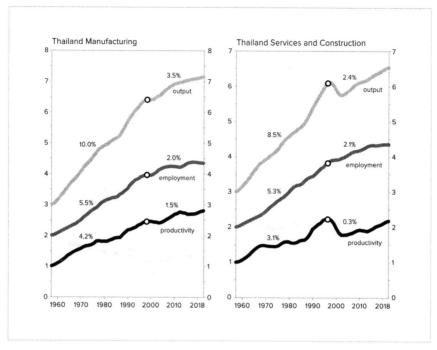

Figure 5.16   Thailand output, employment and productivity in manufacturing and services and construction, 1960–2018
Source: de Vries et al. (2021).
Note: The circles = 1997 Asian financial crisis. Each series is an index number of a 3-year moving average (in log-scale), with base 1 in 1950 for productivity, 2 for employment, and 3 for output. Productivity = output per worker; employment = total employment; output = GDP.

To revive exports, Southeast Asian countries have sought to integrate more deeply into regional production networks, entering into a vast array of overlapping regional and bilateral trade and investment agreements. In 1997, no country in the region was party to more than two or three such agreements, but, by 2020, Indonesia had signed 45 such agreements, Thailand 40, Malaysia 36, and Viet Nam 26 (ADB, 2021). These agreements promise to ease access to foreign markets, but also contain provisions on patents and trademarks, non-tariff or other trade barriers, government procurement, limits to the scope of state-owned enterprises, the opening of domestic financial markets, and compensation to multinationals in case any policy or regulatory change (for example, in industrial policies or in environmental regulation) affects their profitability – no matter how reasonable the change may be.[14]

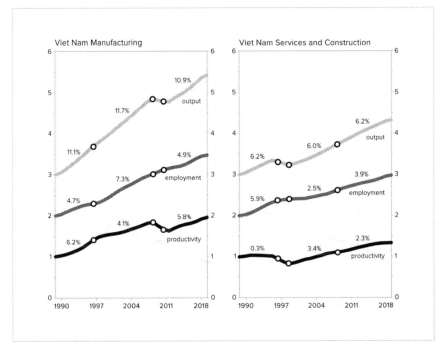

Figure 5.17   Viet Nam: output, employment and productivity in manufacturing and services and construction, 1990–2018

Source: de Vries et al. (2021).

Note: Each series is an index number of a 3-year moving average (in log-scale), with base 1 in 1950 for productivity, 2 for employment, and 3 for output. Productivity = output per worker; employment = total employment; output = GDP.

POLICY RECOMMENDATIONS AND OTHER ACTIONS

The main policy implication of this analysis is that both regions – Latin America and Southeast Asia – must urgently revisit their current growth strategies to reignite labour productivity growth. The former by processing (adding value to) their commodity exports while strengthening backward linkages to their extractive activities; the latter by deepening their assembly operations in manufacturing. In the 1960s, decades before neoclassical economics rediscovered increasing returns to scale, Nicholas Kaldor provided a theoretical account of the unique role of manufacturing as the engine of economic growth. Because manufacturing has demonstrated greater scope to realise increasing returns to scale and therefore more rapid productivity growth, the overall rate of growth of output and productivity (as well as wage growth) both within and outside of manufacturing depends on the rate of growth of output in the manufacturing sector. However, because increasing returns are the source of productivity growth, domestic demand emerges as a key driver of growth. Therefore, Kaldor emphasised the rate of growth of manufactured exports and domestic investment as essential to the achievement of rapid economic growth. We provided support for this relationship in Latin America and Southeast Asia, demonstrating the continuing relevance of Kaldor's analysis to the situation of middle-income countries in their quest to break through their productivity glass ceilings and escape the middle-income trap.

Additionally, middle-income countries need to recognise that the dominant growth strategy is the present-day cause of the middle-income trap, not the escape route: as noted earlier, mere commodity extraction and pure assembly operations in manufacturing have run their course in the more advanced Latin American countries and most of emerging Asia. Mid-table countries need to deploy every available instrument to deepen manufacturing across the full range of subsectors with backward and forward linkages. Of course, many of the traditional policies used to achieve this objective in the past are no longer available, or at least not to the degree they were available to the NICs-1; selective tariff protection, local content rules, domestic preference in government procurement, investment restrictions, and backward engineering of imported goods are explicitly ruled out under multilateral and bilateral trade and investment agreements. However, even under existing agreements there are still significant degrees of freedom, and these countries are not without choice.

In addition to moving from exporting raw commodities to processing them into exportable products, fiscal linkages are also important in countries where natural resource rents account for a large percentage of GDP, such as Chile and Malaysia.[15] Palma (2019a) suggests applying a 'differentiated' royalty to natural resources: Chile, for example, should apply a high royalty rate on copper concentrates (one that could reach up to a one-third of export values at current prices), a much lower rate for refined cooper bars, and reduce the royalty rate further if copper is exported as wire or a similar manufactured product.

Under pressure from the COVID-19 pandemic and mounting evidence of the human and economic costs of climate change and inequality, the political consensus sustaining neoliberal policies in advanced countries has begun to waver. Whether 'levelling up' in the United Kingdom or 'building back better' in the United States, activist economic policy is back in vogue. A similar ideological shift is playing out in the developing world: Every country has its own pandemic recovery plan and a Green New Deal to accelerate the transition to renewable energy and net zero carbon emissions, promote digitalization of commerce and government services, and train the citizenry for the jobs of the future. While most of the attention has centred on these plans' financial constraints, the main obstacles are likely to be political. Plans will remain on the drawing board if governments cannot persuade or compel domestic elites to accept a larger state role in the mobilization and allocation of capital. Governments can make greater use of fiscal and other levers to encourage productive investment and discourage speculative investment. Taxes will have to rise to finance essential public investment in physical and nonphysical infrastructure, and, in some countries, strategic use of capital controls will be necessary. Latin American, NICs-2 and foreign corporations, which for many years have been offered generous investment incentives but have never experienced compulsion, are likely to object strenuously.

CONCLUSION

This chapter has presented an alternative explanation to the middle-income trap experienced in both Latin American and Southeast Asia. The situation is more dire in Latin America, which has performed poorly in comparison to NICs-1 countries and relative to the second-tier NICs in Southeast Asia. Latin American countries have pursued a dual-extractive model, relying on a combination of raw commodity exports and low productivity services and construction. While the former one delivered productivity growth, it has not generated any employment gains. Conversely, services and construction have created almost all jobs but have shown limited or no scope for productivity growth. Furthermore, with productivity growth nearly grinding to a halt in commodity extraction in all countries except Brazil (at the expense of the devastation of the Amazon rainforest), and as extractive industries approach the technological frontier and face diminishing returns, output growth has become restricted to the rate of growth of low-wage employment in services and construction. Notably, further employment opportunities but little or no productivity growth derives from assembly manufacturing in Mexico under the North American Free Trade Agreement (NAFTA) or foreign-owned factories for exports in Central America.

The situation in the NICs-2 differs because (except for Malaysia) they are further from the technological frontier than their Latin American peers and still register productivity and employment growth from their manufacturing-based development strategies. However, there are early signs that their prevailing growth strategy, one based on FDI and manufactured exports, is losing steam. This is not, however, because their production processes have closed the gap with the technological frontier (as is the case with many commodities in Latin America), but because assembly-style manufacturing is not delivering opportunities to deepen productive structures in their domestic economies. Using Hirschman's terminology (1972), the backward and forward linkages that could set in motion a more self-propelling growth have not materialized.

From the Plaza Accord in 1985 until the Asian financial crisis in 1997, Southeast Asian countries were integrated into manufacturing systems organised around Japanese conglomerates, producing exports and import substitutes. But when the

Japanese economy faltered in the early 1990s, the centre of regional manufacturing shifted to China. Unlike Japan, China competed directly with Southeast Asian NICs-2 for inward investment in manufacturing, forcing the region into low-wage activities, such as garments and electronics assembly, or legacy industries, like semiconductors and automotive parts. NICs-2 newcomers, like Viet Nam and Cambodia, still enjoy rapid growth of assembly-manufacturing for exports, but this is no longer the case in the more mature economies, Thailand and Malaysia.

An argument often heard these days is that while manufacturing used to be the engine of growth, as demonstrated by countries like Japan, Republic of Korea, Taiwan (Province of China), China, India and Singapore, it no longer is. One example of this type of thinking is the famous 'smiling curve,' which is a graphical depiction of how value added varies across the different stages of bringing a manufactured product onto the market, especially in the information technology sector. First proposed in the early 1990s by Stan Shih, the founder of Acer Inc., in the personal computer industry, the two ends of the value chain, which are conception, R&D, design and branding on one end, and distribution, marketing, sales and service on the other, command higher returns than the middle component of the value chain, which is assembly manufacturing (Shih, 1996). This holds because the two ends are where all rents are generated.

Other commentators have pointed out that new technologies have blurred the distinction between manufacturing and services, and that automation will destroy some labour-intensive jobs in manufacturing. Even the World Bank, long a champion of the growth-promoting effects of labour-intensive manufactured exports, now has one foot on the 'end of manufacturing' bandwagon, even if it is not yet ready to climb on board fully (Hallward-Driemeier and Nayyar, 2018).[16]

It is true that products and services are changing, but this was always the case, and the use of machines to replace human power is not a new phenomenon. The evidence presented in this chapter shows that manufacturing is still an important contributor to labour productivity and GDP growth, at least in the two regions that we examine. Historically, low- and middle-income countries that have achieved more rapid growth of manufacturing have grown more quickly. And we believe that they will continue to do so – provided they rise to the challenge of continuously upgrading their development strategy. Moreover, since they are still far from the technological frontier, middle-income countries must seek to exploit every opportunity to accelerate labour productivity growth across the full range of sectors. While many of the traditional tools of industrial policy are no longer available, or at least not to the same extent as before the 1980s economic reforms, governments still have considerable scope to support research and development; develop strategic infrastructure; use fiscal policies, public investment, and finance to promote manufactured exports; and facilitate forward and backward linkages within industry and between sectors. Insisting on the more-of-the-same-but-hopefully-better is a tacit acceptance of permanent mid-table status.

Notes

1. Cambodia and the Philippines are often grouped with the second-tier NICs, but we do not include them in this report because the timing and duration of their growth episodes differ from that of the other large Southeast Asian countries for reasons that take us beyond the scope of this chapter. See Jomo (2001).

2. From 1989 to 1996, real growth per capita was 5.6 per cent in Malaysia and 7.3 per cent in Thailand. The corresponding figures for 2000–2019 were 2.9 per cent and 3.2 per cent. Per capita income growth in Indonesia slowed from 5.5 per cent to 3.7 per cent, starting from a lower base: Indonesia's actual GDP per capita in 2019 was only $4,200. Data from International Monetary Fund (2021).

3. Figure 5.1 excludes high-income, oil-producing countries in the Middle East (Qatar, United Arab Emirates, Kuwait, Bahrain, Saudi Arabia and Oman) because of the distorting impact of high oil price instability. GDP per capita in US$ figures is reported in 2019 current US dollars.

4. Endogenous growth models, following Romer (1990) and Lucas (1998), altered the standard assumptions of traditional neoclassical growth theory to incorporate increasing returns to scale. For an early critique from the NICs-1 perspective, see Pack (1994). On the contrasting nature of different development strategies (that is, Solow-type neo-classical models, new growth theories, and Kaldorian/structuralist theories of growth as 'sector specific'), see Palma (2005, 2008).

5. Note that the end of Chile's recovery and catching-up period in 1998 was not marked by a political or financial crisis or natural disaster. Chile's economy simply ran out of steam, which also characterizes the end of all periods of rapid growth in every Latin American country since the Second World War, thus suggesting the inability to sustain periods of 'catching up' (Palma, 2011, 2019a).

6. Of the 10, 8 are in the $20,000 to $40,000 per capita GDP group: Republic of Korea, Taiwan (Province of China), Italy, Spain, Slovenia, Estonia, Czech Republic and Portugal. Only Singapore and Hong Kong SAR (China) have broken into the over $40,000 per capita group as well (IMF, 2021).

7. For example, the headcount poverty rates in Mexico and Viet Nam, using the World Bank's $5.50 per day poverty line, are virtually identical even though income per capita is nearly three times greater in Mexico (in international dollar purchasing power parity). On Latin America's inequality, see Palma (2019b).

8. Private debt to GDP increased and gross fixed capital formation decreased in Brazil, Mexico, Malaysia, Thailand and Viet Nam from 2007 to 2019 (World Bank WDI, 2021).

9. Kaldor referred to this second growth law as Verdoorn's Law after the Dutch economist who published the first statistical tests of the relationship.

10. For example, Brazil's steel exports were equal to one-third of its unrefined iron ore exports in 1980, but the corresponding figure for 2019 was 3 per cent. In the 1980s, Brazil exported roughly the same value of soybeans and soybean oil, but, by 2019, soybean oil was 2 per cent of soybean exports by value (United Nations, 2017).

11. ASEAN member states include Thailand, Malaysia, Indonesia, Singapore, the Philippines, Brunei, Viet Nam, Cambodia, Myanmar and the Lao People's Democratic Republic.

12. The International Monetary Fund and the US government had aggressively promoted financial market and capital account liberalization in affected countries in the years prior to the crisis, trumpeting the benefits of capital inflows while downplaying the macroeconomic risks. As the Asian financial crisis unfolded, both argued that the cause of the crisis was excessive government intervention leading to overinvestment and the misallocation of capital as its main cause – in other words, too much government, not too little (Singh, 1998; Palma, 2012).

13. For the concept of 'premature' deindustrialization, see Palma (2005).

14. A key characteristic of recent trade agreements (like the so-called TPP-11) is to introduce the concept of 'indirect expropriation': any change of policy or regulation (no matter the reason) that may affect the profitability of multinationals (or large domestic conglomerates that qualify as multinationals) would be subject to compensation, and the amount of this will be determined by international courts.

15. In 2018, natural resource rents were 8 per cent and 12 per cent of GDP in Malaysia and Chile, respectively. In Chile, they exceeded 20 per cent in the previous super cycle of commodity prices (World Bank WDI, 2021) and should return to that level with the current export-price bonanza.

16. Unsurprisingly, the World Bank sees the problem only from the supply side, and thus proposes only better governance, human capital, and connectivity as solutions.

References

Andrade, J. 2020. '10 maiores bilionários brasileiros em 2020' (10 more Brazilian billionaires in 2020). *Forbes*, 17 September. forbes.com.br/listas/2020/09/10-maiores-bilionarios-brasileiros-em-2020/#foto6.

Asian Development Bank (ADB). 2021. 'Asian Regional Integration Centre'. Asian Development Bank, Manila. aric.adb.org/database/fta.

de Vries, G., Arfelt, L., Drees, D., Godemann, M., Hamilton, C., Jessen-Thiesen, B., Kaya, A. I., Kruse, H., Mensah, E. and Woltjer, P. 2021. 'The Economic Transformation Database (ETD): Content, Sources, and Methods'. WIDER Technical Note 2021/2. UNU-WIDER, Helsinki. wider.unu.edu/database/etd-%E2%80%93-economic-transformation-database

Gill, I. S., Kharas, H. J. and Bhattasali, D. 2007. *An East Asian Renaissance: Ideas for Economic Growth*. Washington, DC: International Bank for Reconstruction and Development and the World Bank Group. openknowledge.worldbank.org/handle/10986/6798.

Hallward-Driemeier, M. and Nayyar, G. 2018. *Trouble in the Making? The Future of Manufacturing-led Development*. Washington, DC: The World Bank Group. worldbank.org/en/topic/competitiveness/publication/trouble-in-the-making-the-future-of-manufacturing-led-development.

International Monetary Fund (IMF). 2021. 'World Economic Outlook Database'. International Monetary Fund, Washington, DC. imf.org/en/Publications/WEO/weo-database/2021/October.

Jomo, K. S. 2001. *Introduction: Growth and Structural Change in the Second-Tier Southeast Asian NICs*. In K. S. Jomo, ed., *Southeast Asia's Industrialization*. London: Palgrave Macmillan, 1–29. doi.org/10.1057/9781137002310_1.

Kaldor, N. 1966. *Causes of the Slow Rate of Economic Growth of the United Kingdom: An Inaugural Lecture*. Cambridge: Cambridge University Press.

Kaldor, N. 1978. *Further Essays on Economic Theory*. Teaneck, NJ: Holmes & Meier.

Kharas, H. J. and Gill, I. S. 2015. *The Middle-Income Trap Turns Ten*. Washington, DC: The World Bank Group. openknowledge.worldbank.org/bitstream/handle/10986/22660/The0middle0income0trap0turns0ten.pdf?sequence=1&isAllowed=y.

Krugman, P. 1997. *The Age of Diminished Expectations*. Cambridge, MA: MIT Press.

Lall, S. 1996. *Learning from the Asian Tigers: Studies in Technology and Industrial Policy*. London: Palgrave Macmillan.

Lopez Acevedo, G., Medvedev, D. and Palmade, V., eds. 2017. *South Asia's Turn: Policies to Boost Competitiveness and Create the Next Export Powerhouse*. Washington, DC: The World Bank Group.

Lucas, R. E. 1988. 'On the Mechanics of Economic Development'. *Journal of Monetary Economics* 22(1988), 3–42.

Medeiros, C. A. D. and Trebat, N. M. 2017. 'Transforming Natural Resources into Industrial Advantage: The Case of China's Rare Earths Industry'. *Brazilian Journal of Political Economy* 37(3), 504–526. doi.org/10.1590/0101-31572017v37n03a03.

Ohno, K., Thanh, N. D., Anh, P. T., Huong, P. T. and Linh, B. T. T. 2020. *Vietnam Productivity Report*. Washington, DC: Devex. grips.ac.jp/forum/pdf20/[EN]VNProductivityReport_PreliminaryFinal2020_0904.pdf.

Oxfam. No date. 'Brazil: Extreme Inequality in Numbers'. Oxford International, Nairobi. oxfam.org/en/brazil-extreme-inequality-numbers.

Pack, H. 1994. 'Endogenous Growth Theory: Intellectual Appeal and Empirical Shortcomings'. *Journal of Economic Perspectives* 8(1), 55–72.

Palma, J. G. 2005. 'Four Sources of De-Industrialization and New Concept of the Dutch Disease'. In J. A. Ocampo, ed., *Beyond Reforms: Structural Dynamics and Macroeconomic Vulnerability*. Washington, DC: The World Bank Group, 71–116. openknowledge.worldbank.org/bitstream/handle/10986/7378/344340PAPER0Be101official0use0only1.pdf?sequence=1&isAllowed=y.

–––––. 2008. 'Entry for *De-industrialisation, Premature De-industrialisation and the Dutch Disease*'. In S. N. Durlauf and L. E. Blume, eds., *The New Palgrave Dictionary of Economics*, 2nd edition. London: Palgrave Macmillan, 1297–1306.

–––––. 2009. 'The Revenge of the Market on the Rentiers: Why Neo-liberal Reports of the End of History Turned out to Be Premature'. *Cambridge Journal of Economics* 33(4), 829–869. econ.cam.ac.uk/research-files/repec/cam/pdf/cwpe0927.pdf.

–––––. 2011. 'Why Has Productivity Growth Stagnated in Most Latin-American Countries since the Neo-liberal Reforms?' In J. A. Ocampo and J. Ros, eds., *The Oxford Handbook of Latin American Economics*. Oxford: Oxford University Press, 568–606. www.repository.cam.ac.uk/handle/1810/257180.

–––––. 2012. 'How the Full Opening of the Capital Account to Highly Liquid Financial Markets Led Latin America to Two and a Half Cycles of "Mania, Panic and Crash"'. In G. Epstein and M. H. Wolfson, eds., *The Handbook on the Political Economy of*

Financial Crises. Oxford: Oxford University Press, 248–295. www.econ.cam.ac.uk/research-files/repec/cam/pdf/cwpe1201.pdf.

———. 2019a. 'The Chilean Economy Since the Return to Democracy in 1990. On How to Get an Emerging Economy Growing, and Then Sink Slowly into the Quicksand of a "Middle-Income Trap"'. Cambridge Working Papers in Economics, 1991. econ.cam.ac.uk/research-files/repec/cam/pdf/cwpe1991.pdf.

———. 2019b. 'Behind the Seven Veils of Inequality: What If It's All about the Struggle within Just One Half of the Population over Just One Half of the National Income?' *Development and Change* 50(5), 1133–1213. doi.org/10.1111/dech.12505.

———. 2020. 'Why the Rich Always Stay Rich (No Matter What, No Matter the Cost)'. *CEPAL Review* 132(12), 93–132. doi.org/10.17863/CAM.62839.

Paus, E. 2014. *Latin America and the Middle Income Trap*. Santiago: Economic Commission for Latin America and the Caribbean. repositorio.cepal.org/bitstream/handle/11362/36816/1/S2014300_es.pdf.

Rasiah, R. 2020. 'Industrial Policy and Industrialization in Southeast Asia'. In A. Oqubay, C. Cramer, H.-J. Chang and R. Kozul-Wright, eds., *The Oxford Handbook of Industrial Policy*. Oxford: Oxford University Press, 681–715.

Romer, P. 1990. 'Endogenous Technical Change'. *Journal of Political Economy* 91(1990), S71–S102.

Shih, S. 1996. *Me Too Is Not My Style: Challenge Difficulties, Break Through Bottlenecks, Create Values*. Melbourne: Australian Council for Educational Research.

Singh, A. 1998. '"Asian Capitalism" and the Financial Crisis'. CEPA Working Paper Series III, Centre for Economic Policy Analysis. economicpolicyresearch.org/scepa/publications/workingpapers/1998/cepa0310.pdf.

Sturla-Zerene, G., Figueroa B, E. and Sturla, M. 2020. 'Reducing GHG global emissions from copper refining and Sea Shipping of Chile's Mining Exports: A World Win-Win Policy'. *Resources Policy* 65(101565). doi.org/10.1016/j.resourpol.2019.101565.

The Conference Board. 2021. 'Total Economy Database Data'. The Conference Board, New York. conference-board.org/data/economydatabase/total-economy-database-productivity

Thirlwall, A. P. 2015. 'A Plain Man's Guide to Kaldor's Growth Laws'. In A. P. Thirlwall. *Essays on Keynesian and Kaldorian Economics*. London: Palgrave Macmillan, 326–338. doi.org/10.1057/9781137409485_15.

Tho, T. V. 2013. *The Middle-Income Trap: Issues for Members of the Association of Southeast Asian Nations*. Manila: Asian Development Bank. think-asia.org/bitstream/handle/11540/1183/2013.05.16.wp421.middle.income.trap.issues.asean.pdf?sequence=1.

United Nations (UN). 2017. 'UN Comtrade Database'. New York: United Nations. comtrade.un.org.

United Nations Conference on Trade Development (UNCTAD). No date. 'UNCTADStat'. United Nations Conference on Trade Development, New York. unctadstat.unctad.org/EN/.

World Bank, World Development Indicators (WDI). 2021. 'Data Bank. World Development Indicators'. The World Bank Group, Washington, DC. databank.worldbank.org/source/world-development-indicators.

6 Equality of Opportunity as a Measure of Development

Avidit Acharya and John E. Roemer

INTRODUCTION: DEVELOPMENT ENTAILS EQUALIZING OPPORTUNITIES

A society – even one that has achieved a high level of average income, education and public health outcomes – cannot be considered developed if its ordinary citizens do not believe that life is fair. But what exactly is fairness? However varied, most answers have their root in some notion of equality – equality before the law, equality of representation in politics, and so on. Building upon the work of one of the present authors (Roemer, 1996, 1998) we propose that fairness means that citizens have equal opportunities to achieve their goals. We will define the roles played by choices and circumstances in the origins of inequality and go on to propose metrics for measuring, and policies for achieving, equality of opportunity. We will conclude with a set of recommendations for policymakers.

We consider the goals of citizens as those that prior work in development has identified as important and influential in policy: Individuals seek to achieve a high income, good health, the empowerment afforded by education and other such objectives as measured and reported in past United Nations Development Programme (UNDP) *Human Development Reports*.[1] We will refer to these goals as the objectives of individuals.

What does it mean for individuals to have equal opportunities to achieve these objectives? We postulate three categories of inputs that determine their success in achieving these objectives. The first set of factors are the individual's choices, which includes the effort she puts in, the decision of which sector to work in, and so on. The second set includes those that we call the individual's circumstances, which are outside her control. This includes all individual-specific factors relevant for success but which the individual did not choose. For example, individuals do not choose the ethnic group to which they belong, the socioeconomic status of their families of origin, their rural or urban background, or their gender. But it is evident that these things will matter at least to a degree in determining their lot in life. Individuals ought to be held responsible for their choices, but not their circumstances. The final category is public policy which shapes the economic and social environment in which individuals live, the benefits they receive and, importantly, the relative importance of their circumstances versus their choices.

Good public policy, we argue, blunts the effect of circumstances, while amplifying the relative importance that choices have in an individual's success. When individuals consider fairness, they think not just about what they and their fellow citizens are entitled to, but also what they are responsible for. Circumstances, as we have defined them, are the aspects of their situations or environments for which individuals cannot be held accountable, whereas choices are, up to a degree, their direct responsibility. Many will consider inequality due to circumstances to be unfair, but not inequality due to choices. Why, after all, should children born to poor, uneducated parents belonging to a disadvantaged ethnic group have fewer opportunities than those born to wealthy, educated parents belonging to an advantaged ethnic group? On the other hand, if a pair of twins who received the same opportunities in life earn differential rewards because one was lazy while the other worked hard, it is harder to justify what we might term 'correcting' the inequality in some way.[2]

What we are saying is that the reason, or source, of inequality matters. In the introduction to his influential book, *Capital in the 21st Century*, Thomas Piketty (2014) wrote: "Inequality is not necessarily bad in itself: the key question is to decide whether it is justified, whether there are reasons for it." We then go on to learn that much contemporary inequality in industrialized countries arises from inherited wealth and, thus, rests on circumstance. Most people find this more disturbing than if the data had shown that essentially all inequality depends on differences in earnings rather than inheritance; that would indicate perhaps that choices play a more important role than circumstances (although, of course, we could find other circumstances beyond parental inheritance as objectionable sources of inequality).

When opportunities are equal, how well individuals do in achieving their commonly held objectives does not depend at all on their circumstances. If opportunities are not equal, then public policy can seek to equalize them by neutralizing the effects of the circumstances on the objective. When public policy succeeds, then how well an individual did in achieving the objective depends entirely on the choices she has made and for which she should be held responsible, and not on her circumstances, for which she should not.

The United Nations should guide policymakers toward policies that equalize opportunities in their societies. It is not enough for developing countries to raise their average levels of income, health status and education, or lower the percentage of individuals living below the poverty line. They must also move towards creating a fairer society for their citizens. The way to do this is by implementing policies that equalize opportunities for all citizens.[3]

How Do We Identify Circumstances?

We have our own personal views as to which attributes define circumstances – those factors that individuals do not choose and for which they should not be held responsible. But, as a methodological matter, an important component of the equality-of-opportunity approach is cultural deference on this question. What serves as circumstance for some may prove a choice for others, and this may vary across cultures.

Consider, for example, religion. An individual's faith can affect her success in pursuing an objective because members of some religions may face greater societal discrimination than others. In some cultures, religion may be a circumstance, whereas in others it is a choice. When individuals of a particular religious background cannot avoid the discrimination that comes with it, even by converting to another religion or abandoning religion altogether, then religion constitutes a circumstance. In other societies where this is not the case, we might consider religion to be a choice.

Another difficult question is whether we should consider even personal choices as completely determined by circumstances, because all choices may arise from mental or psychological states of mind outside the control of the individual. The materialist thesis says that any action a person takes has a correlated physical state in his or her brain. A person's thinking and actions, in principle, can be read from physical brain states. Compatibilists say that the materialist thesis and the postulate of meaningful responsibility are mutually consistent. One can believe the materialist thesis and still assert that there are actions for which it makes sense to hold a person responsible. Incompatibilists say the two are inconsistent: if the materialist thesis is true, responsibility makes no sense. For an incompatibilist, everything is circumstance; there are no such things as choices.[4]

Most philosophers are compatibilists. What thinking supports the compatibilist view? If one has contemplated an action and undertaken it in a calm and sober state, with intact powers of thought, then one becomes responsible for the action. The fact that the action and the thought that preceded it have physical correlations in the brain does not permit a person to say, "Don't hold me responsible, my synapses did it."[5]

Of course, a society may, over time, hold people responsible for a smaller set of actions than it did earlier in history, as it learns how circumstances cause behaviour – that is, as social science advances. A compatibilist holds persons responsible for actions that they appear to have arrived at by calm, conscious thought, even though she recognizes that those actions may eventually appear as due to circumstances beyond the individual's control. A compatibilist will recognize that what counts as a circumstance will not only vary across cultures; it will also change over time.

Finally, at what age should society start holding individuals responsible for their choices? Should children be held responsible in the same way that adults are? A child is an adult in the process of formation. As such, children should not be held responsible for anything, as far as equality of opportunity policies are concerned.[6] Whatever the child does or accomplishes results from nature and/or nurture, and the child cannot be considered responsible for either. Nurture entails the circumstance of parental education – and, of course, if we have more data on the environment in which the child was raised, those details comprise circumstances as well. A child is not responsible for her nature: it was the luck of the birth lottery that endowed her with the talents and abilities that she has.[7]

This view implies that up to a certain point that we call the age of moral consent, everything that a child does should be considered as due to circumstances. Each society sets the age of moral consent – often sometime in adolescence. Ideally, if we measure inequality of income opportunity in, say, a society of adults with 16 as the age of moral consent, then we should consider as 'circumstance' the entire biography of the individual up to that age! Some might object: if this were the case, then would not society end up holding adults responsible for very little, because the adult's path is in large part determined by who he or she is at age 16? Perhaps, but this only means that society must invest a great deal in children under 16, and particularly in disadvantaged children, so that they have an equal starting point to others at 16 years of age. The alternative, of holding children responsible for their behaviour at age 8 (for example) is not acceptable, if we understand childhood as a period for learning what comprises morality and responsibility, and if we fix the age of moral consent at 16.

We have said that it is up to each society, given its culture, to decide what counts as a circumstance and what does not. Importantly, this implies that a planner who desires to measure inequality of opportunity in a society should decide upon the set of circumstances and the associated partition of the population into types, according to the theory of responsibility that the society itself endorses: the age of moral consent in that society, whether or not that society considers religion to be a circumstance or a choice, and so on. Of course, different people in society will hold different theories of responsibility, calling for eventual compromise on these points. Many developing countries today tend to accept four circumstances as uncontroversial: parental income or educational level, ethnicity, gender and upbringing in a rural versus urban household. The first three are important circumstances in industrialized countries and the fourth – urban/rural status – may be as well.[8]

MEASURING EQUALITY OF OPPORTUNITY

As we have said, the important factors outside an individual's control that determine her success will vary by society, and so the data and measures of inequality of opportunity will also vary. In India, for example, membership in a high caste makes it easier for one to succeed in life. But individuals cannot choose their caste, so it is a circumstance; they cannot be held responsible for its effect on their incomes. On the other hand, in a country like Iceland, we cannot consider caste a circumstance because it does not shape discrimination. But some circumstances will be common to all societies. In virtually every society, the children of wealthier and more educated parents have an advantage. Children do not choose their parents, so again they cannot be held responsible for any disadvantage that comes with poorer or less educated parents; therefore, the wealth and education of one's parents become part of one's circumstance.

Consider the following hypothetical scenario. Sangeeta is a Dalit woman in rural India from a poor background. She has worked hard to support herself and achieved a modest yearly income that is at the 80th percentile of income among all rural Indian Dalit women. Gopal is a Brahmin man living in Mumbai who comes from a privileged background, and whose income is much higher than that of Sangeeta's. Gopal too has worked hard in life, and his income also sits at the 80th percentile of income among all urban Indian Brahmin men. If caste, urban-rural status, and gender are the factors that determine success in earnings, then the inequality in income between Gopal and Sangeeta is due entirely to factors outside their control. This would call for policies that equalize their incomes.

But what if Gopal worked much harder than Sangeeta to get to the same 80th percentile among his group? What if he put in more long workdays and sleepless nights? We can only attribute this additional effort to his circumstance as a high-caste urban male; perhaps membership in this category teaches children to work harder. But if Gopal sits at the 90th percentile of income among urban Brahmin males, then part of the inequality between him and Sangeeta would be due to the choices that they have made. In this case, a policy that fully equalizes opportunities across members of Indian society would give Gopal a higher income than Sangeeta. Correspondingly, if Gopal sits at the 70th percentile among his circumstance category, but still earns more than Sangeeta, who is at the 80th percentile among her circumstance category (what we will call a 'type' from here on), a policy that equalizes opportunities would give Gopal a lower final income than Sangeeta.

The claims that we make in the preceding two paragraphs rest on four important ideas. First, we characterize every individual as belonging to a type, a group of people who share the same circumstances. In the above example, Sangeeta is a member of the (female, rural, low caste) type and Gopal belongs to the (male, urban, high caste) type. Second, we define the degree of effort of an individual as his or her place (centile position) on the income distribution of his or her type. Third, we understand that the distribution of income of a type is itself a circumstance of that type: That is, it is a fact about society, determined by social policy, not by any individual. Therefore, it is a circumstance for that type and, as such, we should not hold persons responsible for belonging to a type with a low distribution of income or effort – a distribution with, let us say, a low mean. Fourth, given these terms, we say that the equal-opportunity ideal at which policy should aim is to equalize the type-distributions of income. In particular, the income differences between those at the same centile of income across types should be minimized by crafting policies that raise the income of those in the most disadvantaged types.

Opportunity maps

What does this imply about how we measure inequalities in opportunity? Suppose for the sake of illustration, that the only factor that affects an individual's expected income besides that individual's effort is parental educational level. Consider Figures 6.1 and 6.2, which present what we call 'opportunity maps' for Indonesia and Germany, respectively.

Figure 6.1 presents the distributions of (pre-tax) income among three types of individuals, defined by the levels of education of their two parents. The most disadvantaged types are those whose parents did not complete primary school, and the most advantaged type are those where at least one parent has at least a secondary education. We see that the distributions of income among the types in Indonesia are perfectly ordered.[9] The left-most curve represents the income distribution of the most disadvantaged type.

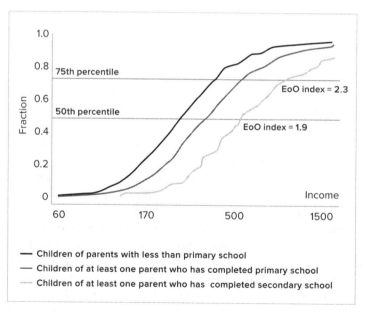

Figure 6.1 Cumulative distribution function of three parental-education types on individuals' incomes in Indonesia (IDR, monthly)
Source: Calculations by Akmal Abdurazakov based on Central Bureau of Statistics (BPS) of Indonesia (2007).

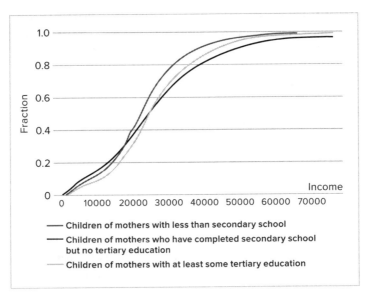

Figure 6.2 Cumulative distribution function of three maternal-education types on individuals' incomes in Germany (EUR, annual)
Source: Eurostat (2005).

This is not the case in Germany; its opportunity map focuses on three levels of maternal education. We see that the three distributions of income in Germany fall much closer together (Figure 6.2). The distribution of income among persons of a given type precisely summarizes the income opportunities available to its members. Inequality of opportunity for income appears to be a good deal higher in Indonesia than in Germany around a similar time.

Of course, these inferences rest on the assumption that parental education is the only relevant circumstance in both societies, which is an unlikely scenario. Many more circumstances will play a part, and these will vary by country. In many developing societies, such as China, urban-rural status may prove an important circumstance, if children born and raised in rural areas become disadvantaged with respect to those from urban areas. In Figures 6.3 and 6.4, we present the evidence for this. Figure 6.3 shows the income distribution in the rural and urban parts of Southwest China, while Figure 6.4 shows the same distributions for Central China. We see that, although urban status confers an advantage in both regions, the advantage appears greater in Southwest China than in Central China.

In determining how to construct the most informative opportunity map, each society's citizens and policymakers should determine which circumstances it considers the relevant ones for which they do not hold individuals responsible. With these taken into account, the kinds of opportunity maps shown here for Indonesia,

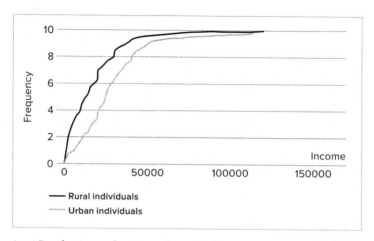

Figure 6.3 Rural versus urban type shows significant impact on individuals' income distribution in Southwest China (RMB, annual)
Source: Author calculations based on Peking University (2014).

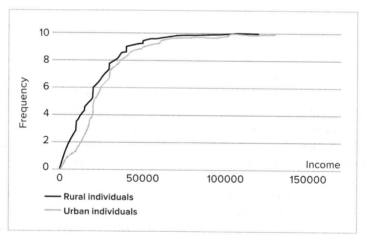

Figure 6.4 Rural versus urban type shows little impact on individuals' income distribution in Central China (RMB, annual)
Source: Author calculations based on Peking University (2014).

Germany and China can provide a clear picture of inequalities of opportunity. In Appendix 6A.A, we suggest a survey that can gather the information necessary to produce such opportunity maps, assuming the four circumstances that we have suggested here (parental education, ethnicity, gender and rural/urban status) will define the main types.

Indices

Consider again the opportunity maps for Indonesia and Germany (Figures 6.1 and 6.2). These opportunity maps suggest less inequality of opportunity in Germany because the distributions for Germany appear tighter (to the extent that the mother's income can be safely assumed as the only relevant circumstance – an assumption that we have already questioned). How can we formalize this to produce a simple measure of inequality of opportunity? One could measure the ratio of median income among the most disadvantaged type to the median income among the most advantaged type. We may infer that the higher the measure, the more equal the opportunities.[10]

In Indonesia, for example, we see that the median income of the most disadvantaged type is between 170 and 500 Indonesia rupiah (IDR), while that of the most advantaged type is about IDR 500. In fact, we calculate the ratio of these two numbers to be 1/1.9 = 0.53. We refer to this as the equality of opportunity ratio (EOR). For Germany, the most advantaged type has a median income of 27,000 euros (EUR) while the most disadvantaged type has EUR 23,000. Therefore, in Germany, EOR = 23,000/27,000 = 0.85. By this measure, Germany appears significantly more developed than Indonesia.

Of course, this simple measure discards much information that becomes available in the opportunity map, which depicts the extent of inequality of opportunity – with the caveat that parental education is only one of several important circumstances that determine individual income, so that the figures presented here tell only part of the story. The EOR measure simply tells us how far apart the objective's distributions are across a pair of types. It does not have any qualitatively interpretable meaning beyond that. But it may still prove a useful statistic that can guide policy evaluation and help track improvements in opportunity equality over time and across countries. For example, the Czech Republic has a corresponding EOR for median income of 0.57, allowing us to assert that the Czech Republic fares slightly better than Indonesia but worse than Germany.

Similarly, suppose that the government of Indonesia starts adopting policies that improve equality of opportunity, and the EOR measure 10 years from now climbs from 0.53 to 0.7. We would be able to say that Indonesia has made substantial progress in equalizing opportunities and surpassing where the Czech Republic was, although it still has some way to go before it reaches the level we see in Germany.

We must emphasize that this measure discards the fuller picture derived from the opportunity maps, and that the latter themselves may not tell the whole story; they surely do not consider all of the immutable circumstances that we know contribute to individual success, and that vary across societies. Since UNDP produces region- and country-specific Human Development Reports in addition to the global report, it could collect the data necessary to provide a more tailored picture of inequality in opportunity through regional and country-level opportunity maps, ones that account for important region- and country-specific circumstances. EORs can then be computed easily from the data in these maps. Another measure of inequality of opportunity that has a clearer interpretation is the fraction of inequality due to any given set of circumstances. We explain how to compute this measure in Appendix 6A.B.

Comparison with other inequality measures

Our (in)equality of opportunity measures can play a vital role in public policy by complementing other measures of inequality such as Gini coefficients (for income, landownership, and so on) or even the inequality-adjusted Human Development Index (IHDI) that the UNDP has published in recent years.[11]

To see why equality of opportunity measures have such relevance, let us return to Gopal and Sangeeta whom we introduced earlier. If despite their different backgrounds, Gopal and Sangeeta truly had equal opportunities in life but Gopal became twice as successful as Sangeeta simply because he worked much harder, we would have a difficult time justifying public policies that compensated Sangeeta for her low performance (particularly if they came at Gopal's expense). But if Gopal is twice as successful as Sangeeta mainly due to his status as a high-caste urban male, where Sangeeta is a low-caste rural female, then it becomes easier, we would argue, to justify public policies that compensate Sangeeta for her disadvantage.

The conventional measures of inequality such as the Gini (and for that matter the IHDI) do not distinguish between these two very different causes of inequality: The overall level of inequality is the same in both. But the equality of opportunity approach does distinguish between them: Inequality of opportunity is nil in the former and substantial in the latter. And we argue that distinguishing between these causes matters if the purpose of studying inequality is to create a fairer society. It is precisely this view that guides our distinction between circumstances and choices, and we encourage policymakers to consider this distinction when they think about the right policies, as we discuss in the following section.[12]

What Policies Reduce Inequality of Opportunity?

Equality-of-opportunity policy should aim to mitigate the effect of circumstance on an individual's ability to achieve her objectives, and it should make her success or failure depend entirely (or at least more) on individual choices – in particular, individual effort.[13] Naturally, the policies that improve equality of opportunity will depend on the relevant circumstances, which, as we have said, will vary by society. Nevertheless, we can generalize that certain circumstances are likely to be important in all developing societies. These fall into four broad categories:

1. Status advantage that comes from belonging to a social category, such as a privileged ethnic or caste group (for example, Brahmins in India), a group with the right ancestry (for example, those of European descent in many Latin American countries), or membership in some kind of recognized nobility.

2. Socioeconomic advantage that comes from having successful parents who invest in their children. Even in a society with a homogenous ethnic group and no nobility or other notable divisions, individuals can derive advantage from having parents, family members and friends who support them in their objectives more than those who do not have this privilege.

3. Network and positional advantages that come from social connections, and from happening to be at the right place at the right time. We can see a special case of this in China know as *guanxi*, through which individuals exploit their social networks and personal relationships for gains in business. In some cases, these networks come into being as a result of the choices that people make, but often they are derived from inherited connections, in which case they form part of an individual's circumstances. For example, through these networks, people born and residing in a booming city may have an advantage compared to those who happen to be living in depressed economic areas. Moreover, with the local economic environment as an important factor determining an individual's success, geography itself can become a significant circumstance, particularly when moving is costly.

4. Biological advantage that comes with the absence of mental or physical disabilities. Individuals who suffer from these disabilities, through no fault of their own, may become inherently disadvantaged if they cannot perform as effectively in certain jobs, or if they face societal discrimination on the basis of their disabilities, in life and work, alike.

In Western countries, the rise of capitalism, which replaced feudalism, sought to eliminate the status advantages of category 1. But in many developing countries, status advantages akin to those of European feudalism remain quite prevalent. Policies that seek to eliminate these advantages also seek to abolish social discrimination.[14] This includes abolishing titles; implementing laws that make it illegal to discriminate on the basis of race, ethnicity and social category; and adopting affirmative action policies and minimum quotas for disadvantaged groups in education, politics and the economy.

Additionally, even in the societies that have adopted capitalism, the structure of property ownership has preserved or even exacerbated the socioeconomic and network advantages of categories 2 and 3. For example, if wealthy individuals can bequeath their wealth to their children, this can give the children advantages that others do not have – not because of any choices they made, or effort they applied, but simply because they had the right parents. Even where wealth cannot be easily transferred from one generation to the next (because of, say, high estate taxes), successful parents may still pass down their knowledge, skills and social networks to their children, or invest more in their children's education and human capital. Again, these advantages do not arise from the choices and effort applied by these children, but by virtue of their having the right parents.

Similarly, geography can provide advantage. Raj Chetty and his collaborators show in the case of the United States, how social mobility varies considerably by region (Chetty et al, 2014). Presumably, this occurs because opportunities to climb the economic ladder are more plentiful in some places than others. We have no reason to doubt that other countries besides the United States also display regional variation in economic opportunities. In fact, we have already demonstrated that in China, a rural background is a source of disadvantaged circumstance as compared to an urban background.

Policies that target resources to the children of disadvantaged parents help reduce the socioeconomic advantages of category 2. This includes investment in public education and public health targeted to low-income families. These policies aid human capital formation, and alleviate inequalities in human capital. As James Heckman and his collaborators have argued, investments in early childhood education are likely to have the highest returns (Heckman et al., 2013). Similarly, policies that encourage the spread of economic activity across regional geographies, or that promote geographic mobility in the labour market, can alleviate the network advantages of category 3.

Lastly, policies designed to take care of those disadvantaged by physical and mental disability address the inequality in circumstances described in category 4. These include special needs education, access to mental healthcare, and supportive infrastructure that enables those with physical and mental disabilities to contribute and participate as active members of society.

Since every society has a distinct economic and social structure, the set of relevant circumstances (and the relative importance of any pair of circumstances) also differs in each. As a result, experts in each society ought to develop tailored policies that meet the needs of their society, and eliminate the inequality in outcome caused by circumstances. This includes the circumstances mentioned earlier, but also any others specific to that society.

CONCLUSIONS AND RECOMMENDATIONS

As we have said, we cannot consider any society developed if its ordinary citizens remain steeped in a deep sense of unfairness – believing that the 'system is rigged'. We have argued that fairness entails equalizing opportunities rather than equalizing something else. Since one of the present authors began work on the topic in the early 1990s, research on equality of opportunity has exploded; we provide a partial bibliography of this literature as an addendum (Appendix 6A.C). But most of this prior work has focused on industrialized countries that have collected data in order to measure inequalities in opportunity and look at their various facets. We strongly recommend that UNDP collect this kind of data for developing countries as well.

Fairness concerns are not the sole province of industrialized countries; they are just as important in developing countries, if not more.

An effective research programme, we propose, would proceed via the following steps:

1. UNDP should convene in each country a group of its philosophers, public intellectuals, government officials, expert economists and other social scientists to determine the relevant set of 'circumstances' for its citizens and their 'objectives', as we have defined these terms. We have suggested the following three objectives: income, education and health status. We have also suggested starting with the following four circumstances: parental income or education, ethnicity, urban/rural status and gender. But these circumstances must be tailored to each country, and any given country will no doubt have more of them to consider.

2. Based on the set of circumstances as defined in Step 1, the UNDP, along with country governments and local partners, should collect data on how distribution of achievement in each of the objectives varies with the circumstances, using the kind of step-by-step data-collection procedure that we describe in Appendix 6A.A. This calls for creating the kinds of 'opportunity maps' that we depicted in Figures 6.1–6.4.

3. After examining these opportunity maps, the same group of experts mentioned in Step 1 above should craft the policies that they think would prove most effective in reducing inequalities of opportunity in each country. We have mentioned general policies that eliminate status advantages, socioeconomic advantages, network advantages and biological advantages. But, again, these policies require tailoring to the needs of each society – hence the importance of convening local experts to craft them.

APPENDIX 6A.A   GATHERING THE DATA TO MEASURE EQUALITY OF OPPORTUNITY

As we have said, each society must determine which circumstances are important and how to categorize individuals accordingly. But suppose, for the sake of illustration, that we take the principal circumstances as the four that we have proposed: ethnicity, parental education, urban/rural status and gender. Suppose we categorize individuals into two ethnic groups: majority and minority. For parental education, let us focus on the education level of the mother and classify individuals into four groups: those whose mothers have no education, those whose mothers have only primary education, those with secondary education and those with at least some tertiary education. We consider urban/rural status as a binary category, and let us take gender as binary for the purpose of this illustration (although, of course, all societies have many members with nonbinary genders). The number of types of individual is then $2^3 \cdot 4 = 32$. Each type comprises a group with the same set of circumstances.

Suppose we collect data from a sample of 10,000 individuals. On average, then, there will be approximately 300 individuals in each type. Let us suppose that we asked these individuals questions regarding their objectives, of which we consider two: income and education.

From these data, we can create opportunity maps for income and education by type, like the ones we depicted in the main text. These opportunity maps give us a picture of inequality of opportunity: disadvantaged types will have distributions of income and education that are overall worse than the those of advantaged types – just as how, in the main text, we saw opportunity maps showing the rural type in China, particularly in the Southwest, as disadvantaged relative to the urban type.

How should we run the survey? The following are some sample questions:

1. What is your age?
2. What is your ethnicity?
3. How many years of schooling did your mother have?
4. How many years of schooling did your father have?
5. Were you raised up to the age of 16 primarily in a rural area (for example, village, small rural town) or urban area (for example, large town, major city)?
6. Please select your gender: Male, Female, Other/Nonbinary.
7. What is your approximate monthly income?
8. How many years of schooling have you attained?

These questions are merely suggestions. For example, in many developing countries, individuals cannot report their incomes, so the survey must ascertain their income or wealth status indirectly. In addition, we have asked individuals to self-report their urban/rural background, assuming that the age of moral consent is 16. However, it may be a better idea to simply ask them where they were born, where they lived when they were 10, and so on, and then code their urban/ rural status later. (The age of moral consent itself may vary according to what that society considers appropriate.) For the ethnicity question, giving the respondents a set of options may produce more precise results. Expert surveyors will do better than we have in framing these questions, but the sample questions above provide a basic idea of the information needed. The survey should also collect data on any additional circumstances relevant to that country, beyond the four proposed.

After creating the opportunity maps, one can measure the extent of inequality of opportunity using the equality of opportunity ratios (EORs) described in the main text, or by measuring the extent of inequality due to circumstance. A method of estimating this appears in Appendix 6A.B.

APPENDIX 6A.B   ESTIMATING THE FRACTION OF INEQUALITY IN
INCOME DUE TO UNEQUAL OPPORTUNITIES

Let there be T types. Let F be the cumulative distribution function of income for the society. Let F^t be the income cumulative distribution function (cdf) in type $t = 1, \ldots T$. Let the fraction of type t in the population be f^t.

For any distribution F, let $\Phi(F)$ be the 'smoothed distribution'; this is a hypothetical distribution in which every member of a type is assigned the average income of that type, denoted μ^t. The cdf $\Phi(F)$ is a step function with T steps. In the distribution $\Phi(F)$, it is as if every member of a given type has expended identical effort: The inequality in $\Phi(F)$ is due *only* to circumstances, that is, to the individual's type.

Let the mean log deviation (MLD) of a distribution F be denoted $m(F)$. The ratio

$$r = \frac{m\,[\Phi(F)]}{m(F)}$$

is the fraction of inequality (as measured by the MLD) ascribed to circumstances. In fact, there is a nice formula:

$$m(F) = m\,[\Phi(F)] + \sum_{t=1}^{T} f^t m(F^t)$$

That is, the MLD of F is equal to the MLD of the smoothed distribution plus the weighted sum of MLDs of the type distributions. This formula implies that the MLD is *decomposable*. (The Gini coefficient, in particular, is not decomposable. That is if we substituted 'Gini' for 'm' in this formula, the two sides would not be equal.)

To calculate r, one would need the following data:

- The fraction of each type in the population
- The mean income of each type, and
- The income distribution in the aggregate population.

APPENDIX 6A.C   PARTIAL BIBLIOGRAPHY OF RECENT EMPIRICAL
LITERATURE ON EQUALITY OF OPPORTUNITY

Björklund, A., Jäntti, M. and Roemer, J. 2012. 'Equality of Opportunity and the Distribution of Long-Run Income in Sweden'. *Social Choice and Welfare* 39(2/3), 675–696.
Brunori, P., Ferreira, F. H. G. and Peragine, V. 2013. 'Inequality of Opportunity, Income Inequality and Economic Mobility: Some International Comparisons'. In E. Paus, eds., *Getting Development Right*. New York: Palgrave Macmillan, 85–115.

Brunori, P., Palmisano, F. and Peragine, V. 2016. 'Inequality of Opportunity in Sub-Saharan Africa'. World Bank, Policy Research Working Paper 7782.

Brunori, P., Guidi C. F. and Trannoy, A. 2020. 'Ranking Populations in Terms of Inequality of Health Opportunity: A Flexible Latent Type Approach'. Working Paper No. 01/2020, University of Florence.

Bourguignon, F., Ferreira, F. H. G. and Menendez, M. 2007. 'Inequality of Opportunity in Brazil'. *Review of Income and Wealth* 53(4), 585–618.

Charma, C. 2018. 'Inequality of Opportunity and Economic Performance: Empirical Evidence from Indian States'. *Economic Issues* 23(1), 65–88.

Checchi, D. and V. Peragine, 2010. 'Inequality of Opportunity in Italy'. *Journal of Economic Inequality* 8, 429-450.

Corak, M. 2013. 'Income Inequality, Equality of Opportunity, and Intergenerational Mobility'. *Journal of Economic Perspectives* 27(3), 79–102.

Ferreira, F.H.G. and Gignoux, J. 2011. 'The Measurement of Inequality of Opportunity: Theory and an Application to Latin America'. *Review of Income and Wealth* 57(4), 622–657.

Ferreira, F.H.G, Gignoux, J. and Aran, M. 2011. 'Measuring Inequality of Opportunity with Imperfect Data: The Case of Turkey'. *Journal of Economic Inequality* 9, 651–680.

Jones, A., Roemer, J. and Rosa Dias, P. 2014. 'Equalising Opportunities in Health through Educational Policy'. *Social Choice and Welfare* 43, 521–545.

Jusot, F., Tubeuf, S. and Trannoy, A. 2013. 'Circumstances and Efforts: How Important Is Their Correlation for the Measurement of Inequality of Opportunity in Health?' *Health Economics* 22(12), 1470–1495.

Lee, W. and J. Cho, 2017. 'Inequality of Opportunity in South Korea'. Department of Economics, Korea University.

Paes de Barros, R., Ferreira, F. H. G., Molinas Vega, J. R. and Khandvi, J. S. 2009. *Measuring Inequality of Opportunities in Latin America and the Caribbean*. Washington, DC: World Bank.

Peragine, V. and Serlenga, L. 2008. 'Higher Education and Equality of Opportunity in Italy'. *Research on Economic Inequality* 16, 67–96.

Pervaiz, Z. and Akram, S. 2018. 'Estimating Inequality of Opportunities in Punjab (Pakistan): A Non-Parametric Approach'. *Pakistan Journal Commerce and Social Sciences* 12(1), 136–152.

Ramos, X. and Van de gaer, D. 2016. 'Approaches to Inequality of Opportunity: Principles, Measures, and Evidence'. *Journal of Economic Surveys* 30(5), 855–883.

Roemer, J. 2014. 'Economic Development as Opportunity Equalization'. *World Bank Economic Review* 28(2), 189–209.

Roemer, J. and Trannoy, A. 2016. 'Equality of Opportunity: Theory and Measurement'. *Journal of Economic Literature* 54(4), 1288–1332.

Rosa Dias, P. 2009. 'Inequality of Opportunity in Health: Evidence from a UK Cohort Study'. *Health Economics* 18(9), 1057–1074.

Singh, A. 2010. 'The Effect of Family Background on Individual Wages and an Examination of Inequality of Opportunity in India'. *Journal of Labor Research* 31(3), 230–246.

Song, Y. and Zhou, G. 2019. 'Inequality of Opportunity and Household Educational Expenditure: Evidence from Panel Data in China'. *China Economic Review* 55(6), 85–98.

Trannoy, A., Tubeuf, S., Jusot, F. and Devaux, M. 2010. 'Inequality of Opportunities in Health in France: A First Pass'. *Health Economics* 19(8), 921–938.

Van de Gaer, D., Vandenbossche, J. and Figueroa, J. L. 2016. 'Children's Health Opportunities and Project Evaluation: Mexico's Oportunidades Program'. World Bank, Policy Research Paper no. 6345.

NOTES

1. Since 1990, the UNDP has published *Human Development Reports* (HDRs) most years; see hdr.undp.org/en/humandev.

2. Actually, a fourth factor that we did not mention also contributes to determining an individual's success: 'episodic luck'. Two individuals with the same circumstances who worked equally hard may reap different rewards simply because one got lucky in life and the other did not. Developed societies are often ambivalent about accepting this kind of inequality and implement social insurance policies to insure individuals against bad luck. Standard veil-of-ignorance arguments going back to the philosopher John Rawls (1971) are used to justify social insurance policies, besides the fact that there is a market demand for such insurance.

3. See Appendix 6A.C for further reading on research into equality of opportunity.

4. Often, the language of 'freedom of the will' is used. Having free will means persons are responsible (to some degree at least) for their actions. An incompatibilist says this is impossible if the materialist thesis holds. A compatibilist does not consider the two to be inconsistent.

5. A few years ago, one of us was writing a paper measuring inequality of opportunity in several countries, and one of our collaborators proposed using brain scans of persons that were available in our data set as circumstances. We strongly opposed doing so. Why? As compatibilists, we believe that every action a person takes, for which she is responsible or not, has an associated brain state. Thus, showing that particular brain states were associated with an action tells us nothing about whether we should hold the person responsible for the action. Brain scan data are not irrelevant, but, at present, we believe that using such data to excuse an individual from responsibility is only permissible if we have a causal theory of action. If we have a plausible theory of causation, in which the causes of the action are agreed to be circumstances beyond the individual's control, then she should not be held responsible.

6. The reason that we say children should not be held responsible as far as equality of opportunity policies are concerned is that, when raising children, we do hold them responsible for their behaviour and actions, as a way of teaching them what is acceptable. This is a pedagogical strategy and does not imply that children are indeed morally responsible for their actions.

7. The terminology here is that talent is an inborn trait and skill is the output when education and training are applied to talent.

8. It is clear that parental income and education matter everywhere. Ethnicity is often the focus of discrimination, and should be delineated as circumstances. The same goes for gender.

9. In the language of statistics, the three income distributions are ordered perfectly by first order stochastic dominance.

10. Since we are comparing distributions, a best and worst distribution may or may not exist, but in practical applications, we have found in most cases the distributions of the objective across types can be ordered from worst to best according to the ordering induced by first order stochastic dominance

11. See hdr.undp.org/en/content/inequality-adjustedhuman-development-index-ihdi.

12. Another critical point: the inequality of opportunity measures we propose are not utilitarian metrics along the lines of per capita gross domestic product (GDP) and the unadjusted HDI. (The introduction of the HDI made literacy and life expectancy important components of development in addition to per capita income, but the HDI is still an average of the whole society; in that sense, it remains a modified utilitarian measure. It does not record how well the most disadvantaged in the society are doing.) Like other measures of inequality, our equality of opportunity measures embody a special moral concern for the most disadvantaged members of society – in this case, those who have the most disadvantaged circumstances. In this sense, it is a Rawlsian measure that implicitly guides policymakers to maximize the average value of the objective for the most disadvantaged type: the one with the worst distribution of the objective.

13. We do not support 'levelling down' – that is, reducing the average income of advantaged types simply to reduce the differences between average incomes of all types. It is more accurate to say that equality of opportunity policy compensates disadvantaged types through policies that increase their incomes.

14. In the United States – seen as a bastion of capitalism – naturalized citizens must renounce any titles of nobility, and the 1810 Titles of Nobility Amendment to the Constitution strips American citizenship from anyone who accepts a title from "any emperor, king, prince or foreign power".

References

Central Bureau of Statistics (BPS) of Indonesia. 2007. 'National Socio-Economic Survey (NSES) of Indonesia'. Government of Indonesia, Jakarta. catalog.ihsn.org/index.php/catalog/4851.

Chetty, R., Hendren, N., Kline, P., and Saez, E. 2014. 'Where Is the Land of Opportunity? The Geography of Intergenerational Mobility in the United States'. *Quarterly Journal of Economics* 129(4), 1553–1623.

European Statistical Office (Eurostat). 2005. 'European Union Statistics on Income and Living Conditions'. European Commission, Brussels. ec.europa.eu/eurostat/web/microdata/european-union-statistics-on-income-and-living-conditions.

Heckman, J., Pinto, R. and Savelyev, P. 2013. 'Understanding the Mechanism through Which an Early Childhood Program Boosted Adult Outcomes'. *American Economic Review* 103(6), 2052–2086.

Peking University. 2004. 'China Family Panel Studies'. Peking University, Beijing. isss.pku.edu.cn/cfps/en/index.htm.

Piketty, T. 2014. *Capital in the Twenty-First Century*. Translated by A. Goldhammer Cambridge, MA: Harvard University Press.

Rawls, J. 1971. *A Theory of Justice*. Cambridge, MA: Harvard University Press.

Roemer, J. 1996. *Theories of Distributive Justice*. Cambridge, MA: Harvard University Press.

———. 1998. *Equality of Opportunity*. Cambridge, MA: Harvard University Press.

7 | Insights for Policymaking from the Multidimensional Poverty Index

Sabina Alkire and Alexandra Fortacz

INTRODUCTION

The human development approach is holistic and freedom-based, reflecting the richness of human lives. Human development aims to expand all people's freedoms by directly enhancing human capabilities and creating conditions for decent and fulfilling lives. The global Multidimensional Poverty Index (MPI) identifies and profiles the situations of those who face acute deprivations in three foundational aspects of human development: health, education and standard of living (Box 7.1). The human development approach and the reduction of multidimensional poverty share common roots in Amartya Sen's capability approach and theory of development as freedom and draw upon three fundamental features: people, participation and policy.

People   The human development approach emerged out of an understanding that economic or monetary indicators do not sufficiently measure progress in human flourishing; they do not reflect the richness of people's lives and the diversity of their well-being. Drawing on Sen's capability approach, the objective became the expansion of human freedom and reduction of disadvantages of many kinds. In other words, development aims to improve and enlarge human capabilities, along with actual achieved levels of well-being (Deneulin, 2004: 26). The assessment criteria reflect "the things people can do and be in their lives, now and in the future" – or what Sen called 'functionings' or 'beings and doings' (Deneulin, Shahani and International Development Research Centre, 2009: 23). This means that human development and poverty are inescapably multidimensional (Sen, 2000).

Participation and empowerment   Participation serves as a key principle of the human development approach, as articulated by Mahbub ul Haq (Deneulin, 2004). Amartya Sen argues that people should be not seen as patients or beneficiaries of development, but as active agents, both as groups and individuals (Sen, 1985, 1999). The human development approach seeks to empower and support people as agents who determine their own life and the life of their communities (Deneulin, Shahani and International Development Research Centre, 2009).

Participation and empowerment also have an instrumental role in poverty reduction. Indeed, the "Moving Out of Poverty Study" interviewed persons who had exited poverty to ascertain what they perceived as the most important cause of their success: assistance from kinship networks; actions by government or nongovernmental organisations (NGOs), faith-based groups, or businesses; transferred or earned income, and so on. In fact, over three-quarters of the respondents (77 per cent) responded that their exit from poverty primarily depended on their own initiative (Narayan et al., 2009).

Policy   The human development approach is ultimately concerned with change – specifically, with expanding capabilities. Metrics contribute to this end. As this chapter shows, the MPI provides a unique tool for expanding human development among the poor at the bottom of the distribution, who lack basic necessities. Policy analysts use the MPI not only to identify those in poverty, but to understand how they are poor (thus which deprivations to focus upon), and where they live (hence where to target interventions). For example, the global MPI 2021 is disaggregated by age group, for rural and urban areas and for 1,283 subnational regions, with other studies disaggregating by ethnicity and disability status; all disaggregations include information on deprivation profiles by indicator. This extensive information platform allows for the design of integrated and multi-sectoral policies in budgeting, targeting, coordination, monitoring and evaluation – providing the means to effectively address multidimensional poverty and expand human development. Alongside the global MPI, national MPIs also have extensive roles in policymaking.[1]

The 2010 United Nations Development Programme (UNDP) *Human Development Report* succinctly stated the relationship between human development and multidimensional poverty: human development proposes a "systematic examination of a wealth of information about how human beings in each society live and what substantive freedoms they enjoy" (UNDP, 2010). Multidimensional poverty measurement, as represented by the MPI, goes one step further: It provides a focused and specific examination of a rich information platform – one that demonstrates the who, how and where of deprivations in basic capabilities and freedoms. When stakeholders and policymakers[2] take action to alleviate poverty, this decreases the MPI, empowers the poor and raises the floor of basic capabilities distribution, directly reducing the most egregious part of overlapping inequalities.

Box 7.1 How the global MPI is constructed

The first global MPI was developed by Alkire and Santos in 2010 in collaboration with the UNDP's Human Development Report Office (HDRO). The most recent global MPI 2021 covers 109 countries and 5.9 billion people in developing regions for which comparable and accessible data are available (out of 194 universally recognized countries and a world population of 7.7 billion). It also includes a discussion of trends of multidimensional poverty among 5 billion people in 80 countries (UNDP and OPHI, 2021).

The global MPI captures acute and joint deprivations, using the 10 indicators described in Table 7.1 across the three dimensions of education, health, and living standards. Each dimension is equally weighted, and the indicators within each dimension are also equally weighted (Figure 7.1). The Alkire-Foster method is used to compute a single metric that reflects multidimensional poverty in its depth and magnitude.

The global MPI 2021 draws data from 45 Demographic and Health Surveys (DHS), 51 Multiple Indicator Cluster Surveys (MICS), three Pan Arab Population and Family Health Surveys, and 10 national surveys.

The first step is identifying those in poverty. This entails ascertaining the specific deprivations they experience and combining them into a deprivation score: a weighted sum of deprivations for each individual. The MPI defines any person with a deprivation score of one-third or more as multidimensionally poor. From this, the number of those in poverty and the incidence or headcount ratio of poverty (H) can be calculated. This represents the percentage of the population who fit the MPI definition of poverty. Next, the breadth of deprivation is assessed by calculating the intensity of poverty (A). The intensity of poverty shows the average percentage of weighted deprivations that poor people experience – their average deprivation score. Finally, the MPI or adjusted headcount ratio is calculated by multiplying H by A. The MPI changes if either incidence or intensity change. The MPI value ranges from 0 to 1. It shows the percentage of possible deprivations across all dimensions actually experienced by poor people. A higher value implies higher poverty.

MULTIDIMENSIONAL POVERTY IN THE ASIA AND PACIFIC REGION

In the Asia and Pacific Region (APR), the global MPI 2021 data covers 21 countries (Tables 7.2 and 7.3). The MPIs for each country in the region vary from 0.002 for Thailand (2019 survey) and 0.003 for the Maldives (2016-2017 survey) to 0.263 in Papua New Guinea (2016–2018 survey) and 0.272 in Afghanistan (2015–2016 survey). This section will shine light on what lies behind these headline figures and provide crucial information on levels and trends in multidimensional poverty in the APR.

Table 7.1   Global MPI 2021: Dimensions, indicators, deprivation cut-offs and weights

Dimensions of poverty	Indicator	Deprived if...	Weight
Health	Nutrition	Any person under 70 years of age for whom there is nutritional information is **undernourished.** Children under 5-years-old (60 months and younger) are considered undernourished if their z-score of either height-for-age (stunting) or weight-for-age (underweight) is below -2 standard deviations from the median of the reference population. Children aged 5–19 years (61–228 months) are identified as deprived if their age-specific body mass index (BMI) cutoff is below -2 standard deviations. Adults older than 19 to 70 years (229–840 months) are considered undernourished if their BMI is below 18.5 m/kg^2.	1/6
	Child mortality	A child **under age 18 has died in the household in the five-year period preceding the survey.** The child mortality indicator of the global MPI is based on birth history data provided by mothers aged 15–49. In most surveys, men have provided information on the occurrence of child mortality, as well, but this lacks the date of birth and death of the child. Hence, the indicator is constructed solely from mothers. However, if data from the mother are missing, and if the male in the household reported no child mortality, then we identify no child mortality in the household.	1/6
Education	Years of schooling	**No eligible household member has completed six years of schooling.** If all individuals in the household are in an age group where they should have formally completed six or more years of schooling, but none have this achievement, then the household is deprived. However, if any individuals aged 10 years and older reported six years or more of schooling, the household is not deprived.	1/6

(Continued)

Table 7.1 *(Continued)*

Dimensions of poverty	Indicator	Deprived if...	Weight
	School attendance	Any school-aged **child is not attending school up to the age at which they would complete class 8.** The data sources for the age children start compulsory primary school are the DHS or MICS reports, and data.uis.unesco.org.	1/6
Living Standards	Cooking fuel	A household **cooks using solid fuel,** such as dung, agricultural crop, shrubs, wood, charcoal or coal. If the survey report uses other definitions of solid fuel, we follow the survey report.	1/18
	Sanitation	The household has **unimproved or no sanitation facility** or it is improved but shared with other households. A household is considered to have access to improved sanitation if it has some type of flush toilet or latrine, or ventilated improved pit or composting toilet, provided that it is not shared with other households. If survey report uses other definitions of adequate sanitation, we follow the survey report.	1/18
	Drinking water	The household's source of **drinking water is not safe or safe drinking water requires a 30-minute or longer round-trip walk** from home. A household has access to clean drinking water if the water source is any of the following types: piped water, public tap, borehole or pump, protected well, protected spring or rainwater, and it is within a 30-minute walk, round trip. If the survey report uses other definitions of clean or safe drinking water, we follow the survey report.	1/18
	Electricity	The household has **no electricity.** If a country does not collect data on electricity because of 100 per cent coverage, we identify all households in the country as non-deprived in electricity.	1/18

(Continued)

Table 7.1   *(Continued)*

Dimensions of poverty	Indicator	Deprived if...	Weight
	Housing	The household has **inadequate housing materials in any of the three components: floor, roof** or **walls.** Inadequate materials are as follows: if the floor is made of natural materials or if the dwelling has no roof or walls or if either the roof or walls are constructed using natural or rudimentary materials. The definition of natural and rudimentary materials follows the classifications used in country-specific DHS or MICS questionnaires.	1/18
	Assets	The household does **not own more than one of these assets:** radio, TV, telephone, computer, animal cart, bicycle, motorbike or refrigerator, and does not own a car or truck.	1/18

Source: Edited version from Alkire, Kanagaratnam and Suppa (2021: 8).

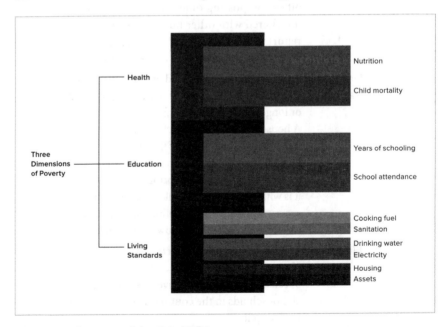

Figure 7.1   Structure of the global MPI
Source: Alkire and Kanagaratnam (2018).

Table 7.2   Overview of the MPI in the Asia and Pacific Region and detail of South Asia and East Asia Pacific distributions

		MPI	H (%)	A (%)	Vulnera-bility (%)	Severe Pov-erty (%)	Population (2019)
APR	Proportion	0.074	16.46	42.74	16.30	5.34	
	Number (000)		642,947		636,619	208,711	3,905,129
EAP	Proportion	0.023	5.37	40.99	14.52	1.00	
	Number (000)		111,232		300,485	20,762	2,069,832
SA	Proportion	0.131	28.97	44.72	18.31	10.24	
	Number (000)		531,715		336,134	187,950	1,835,298

Source: Authors, based on Alkire, Kanagaratnam and Suppa (2021).
Note: APR = Asia and Pacific Region; SA = South Asia; EAP = East Asia Pacific.

Table 7.2 shows the global MPI covers more than 3.9 billion people in the APR, with 16.54 per cent (more than 602 million people) identified as poor. In other words, nearly half of the developing world's poor people live in Asia. Four in five of these poor live in South Asia (531 million), despite its smaller population, while 111 million live in East Asia and the Pacific (EAP).

How many poor? Measuring the extent and intensity of poverty

According to the global MPI 2021, 1.3 billion people (21.7 per cent of the population of the 109 countries measured by the Index) live in multidimensional poverty (UNDP and OPHI, 2021) (see Box 7.1). The APR is home to 3.9 billion of the 5.9 billion measured, and to just under half of the poor people. A poor person faces 41 per cent of all deprivations measured in East Asia and the Pacific and 44.7 per cent in South Asia. But the region has tremendous diversity at the national level. In none of the 10 indicators do all South Asian countries have higher (or lower) censored headcount ratios, or percentage contributions, than the East Asia and Pacific countries. We return to this in Figure 7.3.

The incidence of multidimensional poverty varies across countries (Table 7.3). Thailand (0.58 per cent as of 2019) and the Maldives (0.77 per cent as of 2016–2017) have the lowest prevalence of multidimensionally poor people in the region. The intensity of poverty in the Maldives (34.4 per cent) is the lowest in the region. Thailand's poor face a similar but slightly lower level of intensity (36.7 per cent) as do the poor in Tonga, Sri Lanka, Indonesia or Mongolia (39 per cent). The multidimensionally poor people of Pakistan experience the highest levels of intensity: on average, 51.7 per cent of all deprivations (2017–2018 survey).

Table 7.3 Global MPI 2021 values in the Asia and Pacific Region

Country	Region	Survey	Year	MPI data source	Multidimensional poverty								
					Multidimensional Poverty Index (MPI = H*A) Range 0 to 1	Headcount ratio (H) Population in multidimensional poverty % Population	Intensity (A) average share of deprivation among the poor Average % of weighted deprivations	Vulnerable to poverty (experience 20–33.32% of deprivations) % Population	In severe poverty (experience 50% or more of deprivations) % Population	Inequality among the poor (variance)	Total Population 2019 Thousands	MPI Poor People 2019 Thousands	Data source is missing for Indicator(s)
Afghanistan	SA	DHS	2015–2016		0.272	55.91	48.60	18.14	24.86	0.0203	38,042	21,269	Nutrition
Bangladesh	SA	MICS	2019		0.104	24.64	42.23	18.21	6.48	0.0097	163,046	40,176	
Bhutan	SA	MICS	2010		0.175	37.34	46.83	17.68	14.68	0.0161	763	285	
Cambodia	EAP	DHS	2014		0.170	37.19	45.81	21.13	13.21	0.0149	16,487	6,131	
China	EAP	CFPS	2014		0.016	3.89	41.36	17.45	0.32	0.0052	1,433,784	55,703	Housing
India	SA	DHS	2015–2016		0.123	27.91	43.95	19.27	8.77	0.0135	1,366,418	381,336	
Indonesia	EAP	DHS	2017		0.014	3.62	38.71	4.74	0.44	0.0063	270,626	9,794	Nutrition

Country	Region	Survey	Year								
Kiribati	EAP	MICS	2018–2019	0.080	19.80	40.48	30.22	3.53	0.0059	118	23
Lao PDR	EAP	MICS	2017	0.108	23.07	46.95	21.18	9.56	0.0158	7,169	1,654
Maldives	SA	DHS	2016–2017	0.003	0.77	34.38	4.84	0.00	...*	531	4
Mongolia	EAP	MICS	2018	0.028	7.26	38.75	15.50	0.78	0.0042	3,225	234
Myanmar	EAP	DHS	2015–2016	0.176	38.32	45.89	21.92	13.84	0.0147	54,045	20,708
Nepal	SA	MICS	2019	0.074	17.50	42.50	17.84	4.86	0.0098	28,609	5,008
Pakistan	SA	DHS	2017–2018	0.198	38.33	51.72	12.92	21.47	0.0227	216,565	83,014
Papua New Guinea	EAP	DHS	2016–2018	0.263	56.63	46.49	25.26	25.79	0.0160	8,776	4,970 Nutrition
Philippines	EAP	DHS	2017	0.024	5.80	41.84	7.26	1.27	0.0097	108,117	6,266 Nutrition
Sri Lanka	SA	SLDHS	2016	0.011	2.92	38.29	14.33	0.26	0.0038	21,324	623
Thailand	EAP	MICS	2019	0.002	0.58	36.70	6.15	0.03	0.0028	69,626	402
Timor-Leste	EAP	DHS	2016	0.222	48.25	45.91	26.83	17.38	0.0143	1,293	624
Tonga	EAP	MICS	2019	0.003	0.87	38.14	6.40	0.02	...*	104	1
Viet Nam	EAP	MICS	2013–2014	0.019	4.90	39.50	5.62	0.73	0.0095	96,462	4,722 Nutrition

Source: Alkire, Kanagaratnam and Suppa (2021).

Note: Five countries are missing nutrition data, and one does not have housing information. In these cases, the remaining indicator(s) in the dimension concerned are reweighted to sum to one third. Region: SA = South Asia, EAP = East Asia and the Pacific.

In Pakistan, 38.3 per cent of the population are MPI poor, almost 20 percentage points less than in Afghanistan and Papua New Guinea with 55.9 per cent (2015–2016 survey) and 56.6 per cent (2016–2018 survey), respectively.[3] Nevertheless, in numbers, Pakistan houses more than 83 million MPI-poor people – almost three times the number of poor in Afghanistan (21 million) and Papua New Guinea (5 million) combined. According to the most recent available data for India (2015–2016 survey), the highest number of MPI poor people in the APR lived in India (381 million), amounting to 27.9 per cent of its population.

Overall, the levels of poverty incidence and intensity across the APR vary significantly, requiring caution in comparisons between countries. Moreover, variance exists in both population size and in the information available to compute the MPI in terms of data and indicator coverage. On average, the MPI for the APR is 0.074, which is equivalent to Nepal's MPI. This translates to a regional percentage of 16.5 per cent MPI poor, and these experience on average 42.7 per cent of all possible deprivations – just a little bit more than the intensity for Nepal.

Three poverty lines

For the global MPI, a poverty cut-off of one-third determines who is multidimensionally poor. This defines a person as poor if they are deprived in one-third (33.33 per cent) of the 10 weighted indicators. Two additional poverty cut-offs are also applied in order to provide a 'gradient' across countries. A higher cut-off of 50 per cent identifies people in 'severe' multidimensional poverty, experiencing half or more of weighted deprivations. Moreover, anyone with a deprivation score of 20 to 33.33 per cent of the 10 weighted indicators is categorized as 'vulnerable'. People vulnerable to poverty currently have a lower deprivation profile than the MPI-poor people, but would become poor with one or two additional deprivations.

These additional poverty lines offer further information on the multiple deprivations faced by poor people. They make visible, for example, that while the MPI headcount ratio for Sri Lanka (2016 survey) is only 2.9 per cent and only around 0.3 per cent of the population experiences severe poverty, 14.3 per cent of the population falls into the vulnerable category. In Kiribati (2018–2019 survey), almost a third (30.2 per cent) of the population experiences vulnerability. More than half of Papua New Guinea's population (2016–2018 survey) is multidimensionally poor, with another quarter of the population (25.3 per cent) vulnerable to poverty. Furthermore, a similar proportion of the population (25.8 per cent) lives in severe poverty.

Overall, while more than 642 million people experience multidimensional poverty in the APR, more than 636 million more fall into the 'vulnerable' category. South Asia and East Asia and the Pacific each have more than 300 million people who experience vulnerability – in addition to those identified as poor.

However, while severe poverty has an incidence of less than 1 per cent in East Asia and the Pacific, it affects around 11 per cent of people in South Asia. Overall, nearly one-third of all poor people in the APR region – 32.5 per cent and 209 million people – are severely multidimensional poor. This suggests that pockets of severe poverty exist in these contexts; such left-behind groups need dedicated attention.

Where do they live?

A more detailed picture of where the multidimensionally poor live emerges when the MPI is disaggregated by subnational region and when we consider differences between rural and urban areas. Figure 7.2 shows where the MPI poor people live. However, one should note that the data for APR countries come from different years. For example, India's data covers 2015–2016, whereas Pakistan's covers 2017– 2018, China 2014, Bangladesh 2019 and Afghanistan 2015–2016. Hence, surveys in the region that include global MPI indicators should be updated every three years, at a minimum.

How are they poor, according to each indicator?

The MPI technology also allows a breakdown by indicator in order to assess how much each contributes to the overall poverty level. Figure 7.3 presents the indicator composition of MPI by country, with the countries within each sub-region ranked from least poor to poorest. The region has a striking diversity of poverty patterns by indicator. Here, the MPI provides new information that can shape policy responses.

Nutritional data are, unfortunately, the most frequent missing indicator, unavailable for Afghanistan, Indonesia, Papua New Guinea, the Philippines and

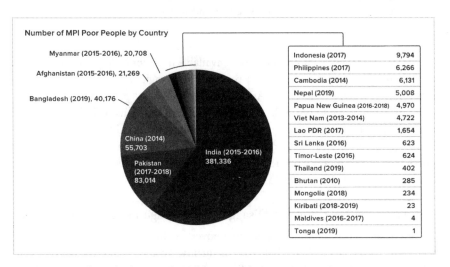

Figure 7.2 Where do the poor live? (thousands)
Source: Authors, based on Alkire, Kanagaratnam and Suppa (2021).

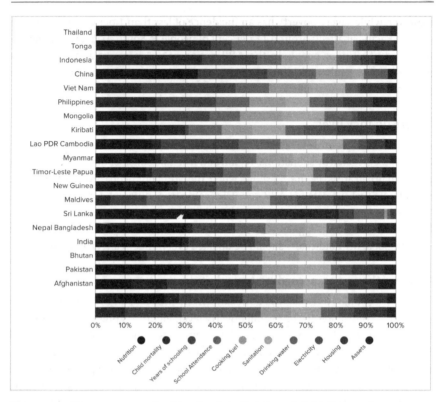

Figure 7.3   Percentage contribution of each indicator to global MPI 2021 by country
Source: Authors, based on Alkire, Kanagaratnam and Suppa (2021).

Viet Nam. Yet across APR countries with available nutritional data, this proves one
of the strongest contributors to MPI poverty. This single indicator accounts for a
contribution of 26 per cent in East Asia and the Pacific and 25 per cent in South Asia –
a significant finding. Other indicators with high contributions include insufficient
years of schooling, as well as deprivations in cooking fuel and housing among the
living-standards indicators. Understanding the composition and experience of
poverty helps one identify priority areas for policy action. As we see, these can vary
between countries, despite similar levels of poverty.

Inequalities within countries: Disaggregation by age and geographic region

An important aspect of multidimensional poverty is inequality. As we have already
seen, the global MPI sheds light on inequality by differentiating degrees and
intensities of poverty. Additionally, disaggregation by region and age establishes
a better understanding of existing inequalities. Subnational MPI data can help to

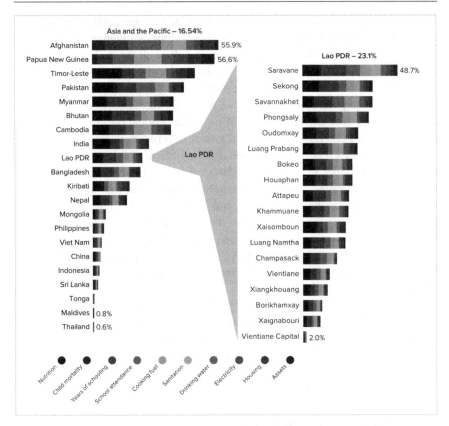

Figure 7.4   Going beyond national averages reveals inequalities within countries
Source: Authors, based on Alkire, Kanagaratnam and Suppa (2021).

uncover inequalities in poverty levels within countries. For example, Indonesia (2017 survey) has a national poverty incidence of 3.62 per cent. However, while almost all subnational regions have an incidence of poverty below 10 per cent, (often even below 5 per cent), two regions, East Nusa Tenggara and Papua, have multidimensional poverty rates of 16.12 per cent and 17.93 per cent respectively.

Figure 7.4 shows the information-rich content of the global MPI and starkly illuminates the contrasts. Overall, the APR's MPI is 0.074 and 16.5 per cent of its people are poor, with a range from 0.6 per cent in Thailand to 56.6 per cent in Papua New Guinea. But if we look at Lao PDR, the national MPI is 0.108 and 23.1 per cent of people are poor – a bit above the APR average. Yet Lao PDR mirrors a similar diversity found throughout the region. When disaggregating the data to the subnational level, the incidence of poverty ranges from 2.0 per cent to 48.7 per cent. Furthermore, the MPI itself represents the weighted sum of the deprivations poor people experience, as shown by the stripes in Figure 7.4.

Disaggregation by age offers another way to identify inequalities among those affected by multidimensional poverty. The recent global MPI report highlights the fact that children aged 0 to 17 years make up half of all the multidimensionally poor (Alkire et al., 2021). In the APR, children comprise only 29 per cent of the population but account for 43 per cent of the poor. This means that children are disproportionately affected by poverty. In Nepal, for instance, children below the age of 10 years have the highest rate of multidimensional poverty compared to other age groups (10 years and older) (Government of Nepal, National Planning Commission and OPHI, 2021). More than a fifth of children in South Asia (22.7 per cent) under the age of five also experience intrahousehold inequality in nutrition – meaning that some but not all children in the same household experience malnourishment (UNDP and OPHI, 2019a). Here as elsewhere, however, stark variations recur across the region. For example, in Pakistan, intrahousehold inequality affects over one-third of children under the age of five (UNDP and OPHI, 2019a). In South Asia, 10.7 per cent of school-aged girls are multidimensionally poor, but in Afghanistan, the rate goes up to 44.0 per cent (Alkire, Ul Haq and Alim, 2019).

Finally, the global MPI report also publishes a measure of inequality based on variance. It demonstrates that Pakistan has the highest level of inequality, followed by Afghanistan, even though Pakistan has a lower percentage of multidimensionally poor people. Whilst multidimensional poverty in, for example, Bangladesh affects one quarter of the population (and the MPI value is close to Pakistan), it has much more moderate levels of inequality.

Leaving no one behind: Reducing poverty

The United Nations Sustainable Development Goal (SDG) 1 aims to end poverty in all its forms. In 2021, the global MPI report looked at the progress made in this regard. Information on changes over time is considered here for 12 countries in the APR (Table 7.4). For most countries, the trend analysis focuses on changes between two data points; three out of the 12 have three data points available.

Within the APR, the poorer countries had the most rapid poverty reduction in absolute terms,[4] Timor-Leste (2009–2010 to 2016 survey) and Lao PDR (2011–2012 to 2017 survey) reduced MPI the fastest, followed by India (2005–2006 to 2015–2016 survey) and Nepal (2011 to 2016 survey); the latter continued to reduce poverty from 2016 to 2019, cutting its poverty rate by more than half. India witnessed by far the largest reduction in the number of MPI poor. It also cut its MPI value by half between 2006 and 2016, both nationally and among children, with 271 million people moving out of poverty. In contrast to the years prior to 2006, India's poverty reduction between 2005–2006 and 2015–2016 had a 'pro-poor' character. That means that the poorest states, caste groups, age groups and religious groups

Table 7.4 MPI change over time in the Asia and Pacific Region

		MPI Data Source				Multidimensional Poverty Index (MPI_T)		Annualized change[b]		Total population at survey year[a]				Number of MPI poor people		Data source is missing for Indicator(s)
Country	Region	Survey	Year 1	Survey	Year 2	Year 1	Year 2	Absolute (p.p.)	Relative (%)	Thousands	Year 1	Thousands	Year 2	Thousands	Thousands	
Bangladesh	SA	DHS	2014	MICS	2019	0.175	0.101	-0.015	-10.36	154,517	2014	163,046	2019	58,040	39,236	
Cambodia	EAP	DHS	2010	DHS	2014	0.228	0.170	-0.014	-7.04	14,312	2010	15,275	2014	6,827	5,680	
China	EAP	CFPS	2010	CFPS	2014	0.041	0.018	-0.006	-19.10	1,368,811	2010	1,399,454	2014	129,675	58,914	Housing
India	SA	DHS	2005-2006	DHS	2015-2016	0.283	0.123	-0.016	-8.02	1,165,486	2006	1,324,517	2016	642,484	369,643	
Indonesia	EAP	DHS	2012	DHS	2017	0.028	0.014	-0.003	-12.86	248,452	2012	264,651	2017	17,076	9,514	Nutrition
Lao PDR	EAP	MICS	2011-2012	MICS	2017	0.210	0.108	-0.018	-11.30	6,445	2012	6,953	2017	2,593	1,604	
Mongolia	EAP	MICS	2013	MICS	2018	0.056	0.039	-0.003	-6.92	2,882	2013	3,170	2018	385	315	
Mongolia	EAP	MICS	2010	MICS	2013	0.081	0.056	-0.008	-11.72	2,720	2010	2,882	2013	533	385	
Nepal	SA	DHS	2016	MICS	2019	0.111	0.075	-0.012	-12.22	27,263	2016	28,609	2019	7,010	5,065	
Nepal	SA	DHS	2011	DHS	2016	0.185	0.111	-0.015	-9.75	27,041	2011	27,263	2016	10,583	7,010	

(Continued)

Table 7.4 (Continued)

Country	Re-gion	\<MPI Data Source\>				\<Multidimensional Poverty Index (MPI$_T$)\>				\<Total population at survey year[a]\>				\<Number of MPIT poor people\>		Data source is miss-ing for Indi-cator (s)
		Sur-vey	Year 1	Sur-vey	Year 2	Year 1	Year 2	Abso-lute (p.p.)	Rela-tive (%)	Year 1	Thou-sands	Year 2	Thou-sands	Thou-sands	Thou-sands	
Thailand	EAP	MICS	2015-2016	MICS	2019	0.003	0.002	0.000	-11.60	2016	68,971	2019	69,626	578	402	
Thailand	EAP	MICS	2012	MICS	2015-2016	0.005	0.003	-0.001	-12.06	2012	67,836	2016	68,971	943	578	
Timor-Leste	EAP	DHS	2009-2010	DHS	2016	0.362	0.215	-0.023	-7.68	2010	1,094	2016	1,219	761	572	

Source: Alkire et al. (2021).
Notes: [a] UNDESA (2019).
[b] In cases in which the survey was conducted over two years, the second year of the survey was used to compute the annualized changes.
[c] In surveys that were fielded across two years the number of poor is estimated using the population data from the second year of the survey.

experienced the fastest absolute reduction of MPI. China (2010 to 2014 survey) and Indonesia (2012 to 2017 survey) came close to halving their respective MPI.

A second way to measure change examines poverty reduction relative to the starting point. This approach usually profiles the achievements of less-poor countries.[5] In relative terms, China (2010 to 2014 survey) and Indonesia (2012 to 2017 survey) led the way in poverty reduction, followed by Nepal (2016-2019) and Thailand (2012 to 2015–2016 survey). China, for example, managed an annual relative reduction of over 19 per cent, lifting more than 70 million people out of poverty in just four years. In Bangladesh (2014 to 2019 survey), nearly 19 million people moved out of poverty over only five years. Happily, the recent global MPI analysis demonstrated that multidimensional poverty among children (aged 0–17) – the poorest group in Bangladesh – reduced fastest. Reductions in poverty per region also show a pro-poor trend. Pakistan reduced its poverty headcount by almost 4 million people. Even in less-populated countries, such as Nepal, almost 5.5 million people moved out of poverty between 2011 and 2019, cutting the number of poor in half. In Indonesia, 8 million people moved out of poverty between 2013 and 2017, with reductions in each of the MPI indicators. In 2017, the great majority of Indonesia's multidimensionally poor people (77 per cent) faced only between 33.3 and 39.9 per cent of deprivations. Furthermore, in keeping with the SDG pledge to leave no one behind, the poorest regions reduced multidimensional poverty most rapidly.

These recent trends in poverty reduction are promising. Overall, as per the global MPI report assessment, all APR countries included in the report except Pakistan are on track to halve multidimensional poverty by 2030 (Alkire et al., 2020).

FROM GLOBAL TO NATIONAL

Today, the global MPI measures multidimensional poverty in ways that offer comparisons across developing countries; national MPIs can offer countries a means to measure and address domestic poverty. In addition, Latin America and the Arab States have regional MPIs, but for simplicity we will focus on the national and global MPIs. The distinction between them offers an analogy to the difference between a US$1.90/day international poverty measure and those that apply at the national level. Both have their specific characteristics, role and added value in understanding and addressing multidimensional poverty. This section will outline them briefly.

Global MPI   The global MPI is a measure of acute poverty, produced by the Oxford Poverty and Human Development Initiative (OPHI) and the United Nations Development Programme (UNDP) since 2010, and revised in 2018 to better align with the SDGs. Standing as a complement to the $1.90/day poverty measure and related monetary metrics, the global MPI and its linked information platform show acute deprivations in 10 core non-monetary deprivations (Box 7.1). Going beyond the $1.90/day measure, the global MPI offers extensively disaggregated data, for example by subnational regions and rural and urban areas. Together with the $1.90/day monetary poverty measure, the global MPI provides international comparisons, identifying patterns of poverty and progress made toward the SDGs. It supports the SDG 1 'to end poverty in all its forms' because its component indicators provide information on advancements or shortcomings related to SDGs 2, 3, 4, 5, 6, 7 and 11. The global MPI directly reflects the SDG emphasis on understanding interlinked deprivations and responding with integrated policies.

National MPI   In the APR, over a dozen countries have launched their own national MPI, or are in the process of designing one. A national MPI provides an official permanent statistic of multidimensional poverty that usually complements the national monetary poverty measure. Mexico (2009) pioneered a multidimensional poverty measure and Bhutan (2010) and Colombia (2011) released the first national MPIs using the Alkire-Foster methodology.

The national MPIs have different dimensions and indicators, weights and cut-offs, thereby tailoring them to national definitions of poverty, datasets and priorities. For example, while Pakistan's MPI has the same dimensions as the global MPI, Viet Nam has opted for a total of five dimensions: education, health, housing, clean water and sanitation, and access to information. Figure 7.5 displays the relative frequency various dimensions are selected in the APR. The dimension selection process often involves a variety of inputs: experts; documents, such as the national plan;

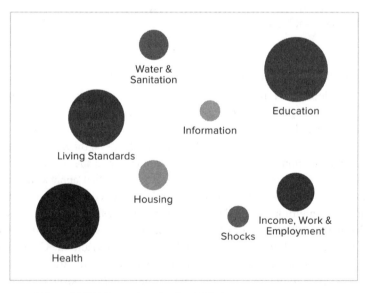

Figure 7.5   Selected MPI dimensions in the APR
Source: Authors, based on MPPN (2020).
Note: The larger the bubble the more often the specific dimension was chosen.

Table 7.5 At-a-glance comparison of global and national MPIs

	Global MPI	National MPI
Headline poverty statistic (MPI)	✓	✓
Incidence of poverty (H)	✓	✓
Intensity of poverty (A)	✓	✓
Disaggregation by population groups and geographical areas	✓	✓
Indicator composition of MPI	✓	✓
Reflects SDGs	✓	✓
Uses the Alkire-Foster methodology	✓	✓
Dimensions	3	Nationally defined
Indicators	10	Nationally defined
Weights	Equal nested	Nationally defined
Poverty cut-off	33.33% (+20% and 50%)	Nationally Defined
Comparable across countries	✓	✗
Tailored to country context	✗	✓

Source: Authors.

international agreements, such as the SDGs; civil society; participatory exercises with poor communities, and so on. All these efforts aim to define poverty in a manner that reflects the experiences of the nation's poor and that creates consensus around policy priorities. But all of them still use the Alkire-Foster method and have an overall national headline accompanied by a detailed and policy-relevant information platform. In this way, differences across countries become readily intelligible. Moreover, the national MPI offers comparable data over time for the same country, providing an excellent tool for dynamic analysis. Table 7.5 summarises key similarities and differences between national MPIs and the global (or regional) MPIs.

THE NATIONAL MPI AND POLICY

Multidimensional poverty has become a key issue in national contexts around the globe, manifested in national development plans, participatory exercises, the SDGs and policy priorities. In the APR, as noted earlier, over a dozen countries have equipped themselves with multidimensional poverty measurement as a complementary official national measure of poverty, or are in the process of designing it (Table 7.6). In the APR, Bhutan was the first to do so in 2010; a diverse cohort of countries followed, including

Afghanistan, Malaysia, Nepal and Viet Nam (Table 7.6 profiles countries in the APR with a national MPI). This section provides a discussion of the construction, purpose and use of a national MPI as a measurement and policy tool.

The national MPI as a measurement tool

A national MPI aims to establish a permanent official non-monetary, multidimensional poverty index, one with which accurate information can guide policy over time and across changes of government or political party. One of the core features and advantages of national MPIs is that ownership lies with national governments. The MPI technology offers flexibility, as the dimensions, indicators, poverty cut-offs and weights can be altered according to the specific context. The national MPIs are developed locally and tailored to the situation and values of the respective country. These factors make the development process of a national MPI a technical, political, and participatory one.

Technical development processes

The national MPI requires reliable and valid data. The availability of data nearly always constrains the choice of dimensions and indicators for a national MPI. While some countries use the Demographic and Health Surveys (DHS) or the Multiple Indicator Cluster Surveys (MICS), other countries use national surveys (UNDP and OPHI, 2019b). For instance, Pakistan chose the Pakistan Social and Living Standards Measurement (PSLM) survey, as it provided additional information on the quality of education and had more frequent updates, while supplying the necessary data at the national, provincial and district level (Tiwari, 2019). In some cases, as, for example, in the Philippines, two datasets, the 2016 and 2017 Annual Poverty Indicator Survey (APIS) and Labor Force Survey (LFS), were merged because they used the same enumeration units (UNDP and OPHI, 2019b).

Furthermore, construction of a robust, replicable, and reliable measure requires participation by technical experts and statisticians. In the end, the quality of the data and the rigor of the analysis determine the credibility of the MPI estimations, and credibility is a key requirement for the MPI to become a successful measurement tool (UNDP and OPHI, 2019b).

Political development processes

The MPI development process often gains a political dimension, since the highest levels of government or other government institutions and stakeholders may need to endorse the national MPI in order to ensure effective implementation and concrete action. A strong leader or political champion who has the support of high-level officials will also have the ability to push the process ahead (UNDP and OPHI, 2019b). In addition, many countries stress the importance of dialogues and

Table 7.6   Some national MPIs in South Asia and Southeast Asia

Country	Region	Launched in	Dimensions	Number of Indicators	Poverty cut-off
Afghanistan	SA	2019	Health, Education, Living Standards, Work, Shocks	18	40%
Bhutan	SA	2010	Health, Education, Living Standards	13	30.7%
Andhra Pradesh (India)	SA	2018	Health, Education, Living Standards	10	33.33%
Malaysia	SEA	2015	Health, Education, Living Standards, Income	11	30%
Maldives	SA	2020	Health, Education & Information, Living Standards	8	34%
Nepal	SA	2017	Health, Education, Living Standards	10	33.33%
Pakistan	SA	2016	Health, Education, Living Standards	15	33.33%
Philippines	SEA	2016/18	Health & Nutrition, Education, Housing, Water & Sanitation, Employment	13	33.33%
Viet Nam	SEA	2014/15	Education, Health, Housing, Clean Water & Sanitation, Access to Information	10	33.3%

Source: Tiwari (2019).

Note: SA = South Asia; SEA = South East Asia. In some instances, efforts to develop and commute a national MPI take place outside the government, as in Lao PDR and Indonesia. China's International Poverty Reduction Centre, together with OPHI, have written a case study showing internationally valid insights from China's multidimensional poverty reduction 2012–2020. Mongolia has also taken the first steps to develop its own national MPI.

discussions when they introduce new measures, such as the national MPI, to better inform a wider set of actors. With deeper consultation, the process of developing a national MPI may require more time, but may result in greater ownership among stakeholders.

One of the earliest steps in this process is articulating the purpose of the MPI, as this clarifies the reasons for developing it. Critically, this stage must involve input from various stakeholders, sufficient information, and transparency (Box 7.2).[6]

Box 7.2	Examples of the purpose of national MPIs in the Asia and Pacific Region
Bhutan	To design, monitor and evaluate national and regional programs for the poor and to allocate resources.
Pakistan	To track poverty and improve targeting and the evaluation of public policies, improve allocations and support the design and implementation of more effective social policies to reduce poverty.
Viet Nam	To measure the levels of deprivation on access to basic social services and to identify the beneficiaries of poverty reduction and social protection policies; to propose programs and policies for socio-economic development of the whole country, in each region and sector; and to use the result to advise the government on developing policies and plans to reduce deprivation and poverty.

Source: UNDP and OPHI (2019b).

Naturally, each of the normative exercises requires a complementary assessment of data availability. As the next section discusses, inputs from participatory exercises with poor communities may supplement expert consultations and may rightly attain a similar prominence.

Participatory development processes

In many countries, the development and selection processes took on a participatory approach involving multiple stakeholders, particularly those affected by multidimensional poverty.

For example, in El Salvador and Panama, direct participatory work enhanced the validity of the national MPIs, both in structure and content (UNDP and OPHI, 2019b).[7] Nepal's 2018 MPI report noted that prior participatory exercises had proved particularly helpful in affirming some of the proposed MPI indicators, and in highlighting crucial aspects not yet included in the global MPI, such as the inclusion of roofing material. Viet Nam conducted discussions with various government and nongovernmental stakeholders, as well as national and international experts, to identify dimensions and indicators (Tiwari, 2019). The process of developing the MPI took about two years and included activities such as "(i) initial studies on multidimensional poverty measurement concepts and methodologies, proposing feasible measures and providing initial information on multidimensional poverty in Viet Nam […] and (v) consultation and testing of the procedures and the tools at the commune/ward levels" (MPPN, 2021a).

The overarching aim is to find a definition of poverty that reflects the actual experiences of the poor and can create consensus about policy priorities.

The national MPI: A complementary and permanent measure of poverty

The national MPI has an important complementary function for understanding and measuring poverty. Monetary poverty measures offer an important but incomplete picture. They do not reflect the joint portfolio of deprivations that many poor people face, nor can they identify those who face deprivations in key areas of their lives, such as education, housing, or health. A study in Bhutan has demonstrated that the monetary-poor population does not always coincide with the multidimensionally poor. In 2012, a similar percentage of the Bhutan's population fell into income (12 per cent) and multidimensional (12.6 per cent) poverty. However, only 3.2 per cent of the population was simultaneously income and multidimensionally poor. In 2017, that figure had fallen to 1 per cent (UNDP and OPHI, 2019b). Introducing the MPI in Pakistan demonstrated that, with an incidence of 38.8 per cent, multidimensional poverty is more common than income-based poverty, with an incidence of 24.3 per cent (Tiwari, 2019).

Furthermore, monetary poverty measures do not fully capture the impact of public policy efforts focused on, for example, education, infrastructure and housing (UNDP and OPHI, 2019b). Due to its multidimensional character and technology, the MPI serves as a tool to measure and capture improvements in various areas of people's lives. For this reason, countries in the APR, such as Afghanistan, Bhutan, Malaysia, Pakistan, the Philippines, Nepal, Thailand and Viet Nam, have adopted the MPI as an official poverty measure next to their official monetary measure.[8]

To recapitulate: a national MPI aims to represent a permanent official multidimensional poverty measure; it calls for a design sustainable over time and across governments, and gains its credibility through a nonpartisan technical process and overall transparency. The institutional set-up will depend on national political realities, but it calls for arrangements that ensure sufficient, continuously available capacity and budget.[9]

The national MPI as a policy tool

A national MPI can become a key tool for policy, as it can be adapted to the national values and specific contexts of poverty; it also supports crucial steps in poverty reduction efforts – namely identification and understanding, goal setting and targeting, policy and resource planning and coordination, monitoring and accountability, and communication.

Construction and ownership

The process of constructing a national MPI can build ownership and legitimacy by drawing on key national documents and monitoring their priorities. Afghanistan's MPI drew on the National Peace and Development Framework (2017–2021) and the National Citizen's Charter, as well as consultations. For this, Afghanistan added two additional dimensions, work and shocks, creating an MPI based on 18 indicators in five dimensions. While these dimensions are equally weighted, certain indicators within the dimensions received a higher weight due to their importance. One of these indicators is security, covering the vital aspect of personal security from violence. Furthermore, Afghanistan created a gendered adult schooling indicator to illuminate gender disparities in education. In Afghanistan, the indicator with the highest deprivation level of all is 'Female Schooling,' with 48 per cent of the population are poor and deprived in this indicator; in other words, the censored headcount ratio of female schooling is 48 per cent (National Statistics and Information Authority, 2019).

Other examples abound. The Philippines added the dimension of employment, including indicators on underemployment and working children, to reflect the importance of these issues in the country. Due to the centrality of agriculture and transportation, Bhutan's national MPI included indicators on road access, land and livestock. Similarly, Pakistan included an indicator on land and livestock and one on overcrowding under the living-standard dimension, as well as an indicator on the quality of education – all of which reflected active policy priorities (Tiwari, 2019).

There is room for some diversity in the construction and structure of national MPIs. When the final product aligns with national priorities, advancing any of the linked national priorities will reduce the MPI figure, and vice versa. In this way, a synergy between public commitments and poverty statistics becomes visible.

Identification and goal setting

Effective policymaking and implementation require, in the first instance, accurate identification and understanding of the poor and their composition of poverty. This was one of the main rationales for introducing the MPI in, for example, Viet Nam and Andhra Pradesh State (India) (Tiwari, 2019). While other social statistics and poverty measures do not identify which people face overlapping or 'joint' deprivations, with a national MPI, policymakers can detect whether multidimensionally poor people facing, for example, educational deprivations are also those who lack adequate sanitation facilities. It reveals the complexity of simultaneous deprivations and how they contribute to the experience of multidimensional poverty.

This was one of the reasons why the Philippines introduced a national MPI in 2018 (UNDP and OPHI, 2019b). The Philippines trial MPI captures deprivations in the dimensions of education, health and nutrition, housing, water and sanitation, and employment, using 13 indicators. Deprivations in education contributed the most to poverty. Indeed, in 2017, 5 out of 10 poor families had at least one member aged 18 or above who had been unable to finish basic education (MPPN, 2021b). These findings rippled out to affect education policies.

The MPI also contributes to results-based policy frameworks for poverty reduction. For example, in 2017, Nepal's SDG strategy document set the clear target "to reduce multi-dimensional poverty to 11.5 percent by 2024" (Government of Nepal, National Planning Commission 2021: 1). Bhutan's documents articulated the aim to reduce the poverty incidence to below 10 per cent by 2018 – a target it met in 2017.

Individual and geographical targeting

One prominent use of the MPI in the APR is identifying individuals, households, or groups for targeted interventions. Targeting becomes particularly important with resource scarcity: when universal provision might not prove necessary, or targeting would offer more efficient and appropriate means of addressing various deprivations. Due to the detailed depiction of poverty that the MPI and its technology offer, this becomes relatively straightforward.

Group or geographical targeting draws on disaggregation by groups (such as between urban and rural areas, subnational regions, gender, age groups, indigenous groups and disability status). Disaggregation showed that in Nepal, every second person in the two poorest provinces (2 and 6) faced multidimensional poverty. This information crucially showed where resources needed to go. Malnutrition and insufficient years of schooling were the strongest contributors to multidimensional poverty and became recognised as priorities in the 2018 MPI report (Government of Nepal, National Planning Commission and OPHI, 2018). Between 2014 and 2019, six out of seven provinces in Nepal significantly reduced multidimensional poverty and incidence; Province Two, the second poorest, saw the fastest reduction (Government of Nepal, National Planning Commission and OPHI, 2021).

Viet Nam also used the MPI as a component of their precise targeting at the commune level. Individual targeting requires data collection from all eligible individuals and assessment of their poverty status. In Viet Nam, eligibility rests on registry data that include multidimensional poverty indicators along with some others. Such people are entitled to certain public benefits, such as free health care services, exemption from tuition fees in primary and secondary schooling, cash transfers for electricity use, or credit priority for housing, clean water, hygienic toilets and economic activities (Tiwari, 2019).

Targeting vulnerable social groups is also essential. In 2018, Viet Nam presented a detailed analysis of multidimensional poverty among various ethnic groups that revealed important differences in their experience of poverty. For example, only 6.4 per cent of the Kinh majority faced multidimensional poverty, as opposed to 76 per cent among the Hmong. Such information reveals inequalities that well-targeted policies can address.

In Pakistan, the MPI 2004–2005 provided the first directly disaggregated poverty data at the district level. This information received media attention and proved useful for policy targeting and for SDG localization. Its 12th Five Year Plan 2018–2023 identified less-developed areas (67 districts of four provinces) on the basis of their multidimensional poverty incidence of more than 50 per cent. Thus, the ability to see the composition of poverty in a disaggregated manner can support more efficient policy design, policy coordination, targeting and allocation of resources. The province of Punjab incorporated the MPI in its growth strategy. They estimated that an additional year of schooling can reduce their MPI by 5 per cent; this led to an investment prioritisation in human capital. Furthermore, the province worked in cooperation with the UNDP to create a targeted regional SDG plan for the districts most affected by multidimensional poverty (Tiwari, 2019).

During its first decade, Bhutan used the national MPI to design, monitor and evaluate national and regional programmes that targeted the poor in different ways at the household level. For instance, the MPI compiled data at the gewog level in 2010 to locate poverty incidence by area and households. Together with a transport cost index, MPI calculations allowed Bhutan to develop Resource Allocation Formula (RAF) criteria. These became instrumental in the implementation of the Rural Economy Advancement Program (REAP) and the Targeted Household Poverty Program (THPP) in 2014, as well as the National Rehabilitation Program for landless and destitute people, developed in order to stem the country's growing inequalities (Royal Government of Bhutan, 2018).

Budget allocation

In one of its most frequent uses around the world, the MPI informs budget allocation across regions and sectors. It does not serve as a stand-alone input – population size, monetary poverty and universal priorities may also contribute to budget formulae. But, because the MPI provides a direct measure of key policy priorities and often differs from monetary poverty, it is explicitly included in the budget allocation process. For example, in 2013 Bhutan started using the MPI for appropriate budget allocation to *dzongkhags* and *gewogs*, with a priority weight of 45 per cent. Nepal's planning documents include the intention to use the MPI for targeting resources to those most in need, in order to accelerate reduction in poverty. This will include multisectoral policies, monitoring and evidence-based policy adjustment.

Policy planning and coordination

Effective reductions in multidimensional poverty will require integrated multisectoral policies. But coordination often poses a challenge. In Latin America, the MPI regularly serves as a tool of coordination and management; it may also become so in the APR.

In light of the current COVID-19 pandemic, coordination efforts have gained even more importance and urgency. Effective and efficient policies and strong resilience after crises and shocks make cooperation between ministries, government levels and different stakeholders indispensable. The national MPI can serve to bring together and coordinate efforts among these institutions and other stakeholders.

Beyond coordination and management, the MPI can inform cross-cutting policies for outside institutions. The Asian Development Bank's project, Scoping Potential Economic Corridors in Pakistan, used the MPI estimates as a criterion in their effort to increase regional connectivity and trade among districts with high MPIs, through investment in trade and public-private partnerships (Tiwari, 2019).

Monitoring and accountability

With regular data updating, the MPI can make visible any reduction of any deprivation, down to the level of the individual; all such reductions will decrease the MPI value. Thus, the MPI can become a powerful tool to monitor positive change. It can also serve as a tool for accountability in the case of less-evident changes. Overall, using the MPI to monitor poverty trends can also provide incentives for policymakers to leave no one behind and to reach the furthest behind first. The impact of these efforts will, in turn, become visible in changes to the official multidimensional poverty headline figure. This means that the national MPI serves as a monitoring and tracking tool to measure and evaluate changes in poverty levels over time and across a country.

For example, Nepal, which uses the global MPI as its national one, reduced the MPI rate from just over 30 per cent in 2014 to 17.4 per cent in 2019 – a change "driven by statistically significant reduction in each of the 10 component indicators" (Government of Nepal, National Planning Commission, 2021: iv). Pakistan's disaggregation of MPI estimates to a district level proved particularly useful in visualizing and evaluating the changes made in each region: it found that the poorest region in the country had made the fastest progress in a decade's time (2004–2005 to 2014–2015). Bhutan's progress in reducing poverty from

12.7 to 5.2 per cent within a mere five years (2012–2017) resulted from considerable improvements in access to water and sanitation (99 per cent and 66 per cent, respectively), clean energy for 99.9 per cent of all households, and almost 100 per cent school enrolment with gender parity at the secondary levels (Royal Government of Bhutan, 2018).

Viet Nam determined that "the proportion of households who are multidimensionally poor and deprived in each of the indicators […] decreased for almost all indicators" (Figure 7.6) (Duc, 2019: 7). For example, sanitation showed a decrease of more than 2 percentage points in 2018 as compared to 2016 (Duc, 2019). Additionally, as shown in Figure 7.7 Viet Nam made considerable progress in those regions most affected by multidimensional poverty. For instance, the poverty headcount ratio in the central highlands dropped from 19.5 per cent to 13.4 per cent (Duc, 2019).[10] While these are impressive accomplishments that deserve separate attention, the MPI also provides a figure to represent the overall improvements in multidimensional poverty. Energised by this success, in 2020 Viet Nam has moved to update the MPI not only annually, but quarterly. This kind of information can catapult the MPI into becoming a sensitive tool for management and for mid-course corrections.

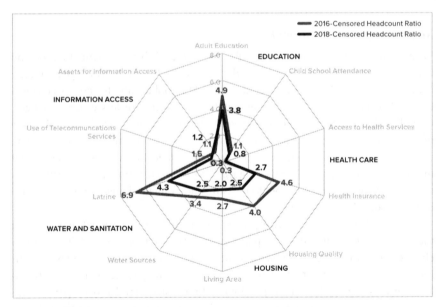

Figure 7.6   Viet Nam's censored headcount of each indicator (%)
Source: Duc (2019: 6).

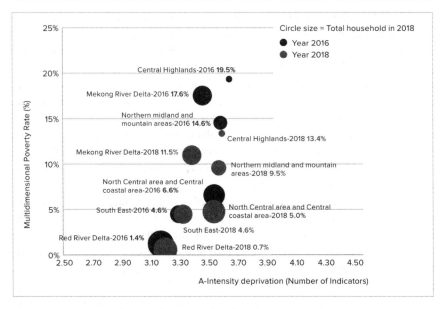

Figure 7.7   Viet Nam's multidimensional indices by region and year
Source: Duc (2019: 7).

It becomes easier to see outcomes with measurement and tracking of changes. As a result, the MPI serves as a tool of accountability for government and citizens and to demonstrate the impact of government work.

Communication with all actors

The multidimensional poverty rate, or incidence of MPI, is an intuitive statistic, like the familiar monetary poverty rate, and often rightly appears as such in media communication: used to open a story, and then supplemented by information on the numbers of poor people, MPI value, intensity and the composition of poverty. But for important reasons, most governments use the MPI as the official national statistic. The MPI offers a headline figure that can announce the official level of multidimensional poverty, because it captures two kinds of change: changes in the poverty rate or incidence and changes among people who remain poor, but have become 'less poor' – have a lower deprivation score – than before. In this way, the MPI better reflects the SDG goal of leaving no one behind. It provides government officials, the media, and other stakeholders with an enhanced high-level view of the state of multidimensional poverty in their country. It also tends to move more rapidly than other metrics. For example, India halved its MPI between 2005–2006 and 2015–2016 but did not halve its incidence.

The 'MPI information platform' is a term that we use to describe the system of coherent and interlinked statistics about the MPI (incidence, intensity, indicator censored headcount ratios and contributions to the MPI). MPI reports usually provide these at the national level and then disaggregate them by rural and urban areas, subnational regions, age cohorts and other groups. This means that the MPI provides a broadly available portfolio of crucial information for good communication about poverty levels, trends, efforts and their impact. For example, the state-level media may focus on comparing their results to their immediately neighbouring states; a student may write a winning essay on MPI using their district-level figures; an international health NGO may decide to focus activities in the poorest region with high health deprivations, and so on.

To communicate the MPI to a plethora of potential actors, adopting countries often develop an outreach strategy for all government and civil society stakeholders, along with journalist resources or training (UNDP and OPHI 2019b). Several countries have demonstrated the importance of such an outreach strategy. For example, training for media editors and journalists improved the quality of MPI reporting in Colombia, and, in Mexico, statisticians physically travelled to each state to explain their MPI and how to reduce it (Botello, 2020). Costa Rica and Panama commissioned public relations firms to help them draft a media strategy for the initial launch of the MPI, enabling more cost-effective communication of key information up-front. Some countries received support from international donors for this stage. While planning is vital, a certain degree of flexibility and creativity, alongside clear lines of authority in terms of communication, helped to make the most of unexpected opportunities and allowed adjustment to changing circumstances (UNDP and OPHI, 2019b). Countries also stress the importance of translating information into local languages (for example infographics, visuals and other materials).

Fundamentally, the MPI cannot serve its purpose unless officials at multiple levels of government understand it and use it in their work. So, for example, countries such as Costa Rica, Chile and El Salvador, among others, briefed different political parties on multidimensional poverty in the run-up to elections. This can ensure that all understand, and use, the MPI to end poverty. At the same time, different political parties have room to formulate their own action plans and strategies on how to advance this overarching goal. As they articulate their plans on the campaign trail, they create more understanding and awareness of the MPI, which then becomes an important permanent tool of policy communication (UNDP and OPHI, 2019b).

The national MPI as an SDG reporting tool

SDG Reporting

In many ways, multidimensional poverty has taken centre stage in national and international poverty and development efforts. That is as it should be. It aligns tightly with a key goal of the SDGs, 'to leave no one behind', and also with the first goal, SDG 1: 'to end poverty in all its forms'. In fact, the national MPI appears as indicator 1.2.2 in the SDGs. Since 2020, all countries with official MPIs in the APR have reported them in the global SDG database.

Because of this alignment, one motivation for countries to develop a national MPI has been their commitment to report progress on the SDG indicators and to meet the SDGs by 2030. And not only is the national MPI a reporting tool, it is the only one of the 232 global-level SDG indicators that the country owns directly. Yet as the last section covered, reporting alone does not determine the MPI's success, but rather its use as a tool at different phases of the planning cycle. Still, at-a-glance views on how APR countries report on their MPI have their use, as well.

In the APR, many countries report the national MPI in the global SDG database and use it in their Voluntary National Reviews to report their progress in accomplishing the SDGs (Table 7.7). Nepal offers one example (Government of Nepal, National Planning Commission and OPHI, 2018; UNDP and OPHI, 2019b). Other countries, such as Pakistan, have also used the MPI for monitoring the SDG

Table 7.7   Voluntary national reviews that mention multidimensional poverty

Year	South Asia
2021	Bhutan
	China
	Indonesia
	Lao PDR
	Malaysia
	Thailand
2020	Bangladesh
	India
	Nepal
2019	Sri Lanka
	Tonga
2018	Bhutan
	Viet Nam
2017	Bangladesh
	India
	Indonesia
	Nepal
2016	Philippines

Source: Authors, based on UN (2021).

target 1.2. They mention that the MPI has the advantage of a clear headline figure that can present the overall progress, as well as more detailed analysis of the situation of the poor, one that reflects multiple deprivations and SDGs. The specific functions of the MPI, such as disaggregation and indicator breakdown, allow countries to showcase their respective efforts and improvements in the various dimensions, as well as define clear focus areas and strategies for future actions.

Multidimensional Poverty Peer Network (MPPN)

In 2013, the rising application of multidimensional poverty indices within national contexts, and their unusual position of spanning statistical offices and policy actors, gave rise to the Multidimensional Poverty Peer Network (MPPN), a growing global community of 60 countries and 19 organizations. The MPPN holds annual meetings, active online calls and interchanges, and publishes the magazine *Dimensions*. It hosts high-profile events at the UN General Assembly with heads of states, ministers and heads of agencies, and at the UN Statistics Commission with Statistician Generals. The MPPN steering committee includes Bangladesh, China, Colombia and South Africa, as well as OPHI at the University of Oxford, which acts as its Secretariat. Ministers and senior officials from 14 APR countries take part in MPPN (Figure 7.8).

The MPPN website (mmpn.org) provides a platform and a repository of detailed national MPI reports for each country as well as resources for capacity-building,

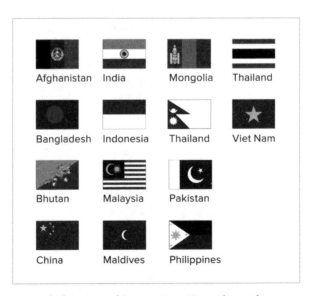

Figure 7.8   APR Multidimensional Poverty Peer Network members
Source: MPPN (2021c).

technical support and dialogue; it fosters exchanges on measuring multidimensional poverty, relevant policy efforts and strategies, and experiences and lessons learned in participant countries. The bilingual MPPN magazine *Dimensions*, annual meetings and round-robin conference calls (in English and Spanish) enable further exchanges between early adopters and newcomers to multidimensional poverty measurement. Informally, the MPPN enables countries to access peer-to-peer technical, statistical and policy support, as well as input into the design and institutional arrangements for successful multidimensional poverty eradication (MPPN, 2021c). As the MPPN mission statement puts it:

> Through meetings, knowledge sharing and informal exchange, the MPPN supports policymakers in developing more effective poverty eradication policies that are grounded in multidimensional measures of poverty. Its vision is a world in which poverty in all its forms is measured, tracked over time, and eventually eliminated. (MPPN, 2021c)

CONCLUSION

The work in the APR on multidimensional poverty is by no means new. But the use of new metrics to design integrated policies and to manage and measure change remains in its initial phase. As the many analyses in this document have shown, countries in the APR have the potential to innovate quickly and skilfully using such metrics. The APR could become a field leader in truly ending acute and abject conditions while empowering impoverished persons and communities as agents and leaders. If such momentous improvement in human development occurs, it will serve both impacted nations and the entire world.

ACKNOWLEDGEMENTS

This research applies the global Multidimensional Poverty Index (MPI) 2021 microdata and conducts analysis for 21 countries included in the 2021 global MPI database. The microdata were cleaned, standardized and produced for further analysis by Alkire, Kanagaratnam and Suppa (2021). The microdata harmonization formed part of the global MPI 2021 project that tracked changes over time in 80 countries (Alkire et al., 2021). We are thankful to Usha Kanagaratnam and Nicolai Suppa, as well as Fanni Kovesdi, Corinne Mitchell, Monica Pinilla-Roncancio and Sophie Scharlin-Pettee for their tremendous work in preparing the data we analysed. We are grateful to Christian Oldiges and Ross Jennings for comments.

Notes

1. Official statistics are computed regularly, using national or internationally comparable survey data and updated by a designated institution, often the National Statistics Office. Poverty statistics, both monetary and multidimensional, should be permanent and independent. The custom is to update their design (poverty lines, indicators) every decade and, in the year of updating, provide both the old and new estimates for transparent comparability.
2. Including governments, nongovernmental organizations, faith-based organizations, businesses, and so on.
3. Please note that Afghanistan and Papua New Guinea are both missing information on nutrition.
4. The difference in a poverty measure between two years, divided by the number of years between surveys (annualised).
5. The compound rate of change per year. It shows the percentage by which the previous year's poverty has changed (annualised).
6. See UNDP and OPHI (2019b: 21) for a list of country's purposes.
7. For more information on El Salvador, see Moreno (2016).
8. While the MPI is, first and foremost, a measure to reflect nonmonetary poverty, some countries, such as Malaysia, have incorporated income as one of the dimensions.
9. For more elaboration, see UNDP and OPHI (2019b: 36).
10. For a more detailed, yet older, demonstration of how the MPI can be used, see MOLISA et al. (2018).

References

Alkire, S. and Kanagaratnam, U. 2018. *Global Multidimensional Poverty Index 2018: The Most Detailed Picture to Date of the World's Poorest People*. Oxford: University of Oxford.

Alkire, S., Conceição, P., Calderon, M., Dirksen, J., Evans, M., Hall, J. and Jahic, A. 2020. *The 2020 Global Multidimensional Poverty Index (MPI)*. Oxford: Oxford Poverty and Human Development Initiative, University of Oxford.

Alkire, S., Kanagaratnam, U. and Suppa, N. 2021. 'The Global Multidimensional Poverty Index (MPI) 2021'. *OPHI MPI Methodological Notes*, 51. Oxford Poverty and Human Development Initiative, University of Oxford.

Alkire, S., Kovesdi, F., Mitchell, C., Pinilla-Roncancio, M. and Scharlin-Pettee, S. 2020. *Changes over Time in the Global Multidimensional Poverty Index*. Oxford: Oxford Poverty and Human Development Initiative, University of Oxford.

Alkire, S., Ul Haq, R. and Alim, A. 2019. *The State of Multidimensional Child Poverty in South Asia: A Contextual and Gendered View*. Oxford: Oxford Poverty and Human Development Initiative, University of Oxford.

Botello, S. 2020. *MPPN Policy Briefing: How to Explain the Measurement of Multidimensional Poverty to the General Public: Workshop for Journalists in Colombia*. Oxford: Oxford Poverty and Human Development Initiative.

Deneulin, S. 2004. 'Examining Sen's Capability Approach to Development as Guiding Theory for Development Policy'. University of Oxford, Oxford. ora.ox.ac.uk/objects/uuid:1c357bd8-5e83-48df-a748-f71745304ac1.

Deneulin, S, Shahani, L. and International Development Research Centre. 2009. *An Introduction to the Human Development and Capability Approach: Freedom and Agency*. Sterling, VA: Earthscan.

Duc, L. T. 2019. 'Multidimensional Poverty in Vietnam'. *Dimensions* 8(12), 4–9. mppn. org/wp-content/uploads/2019/12/Dimensions8_EN_webversion-4.pdf.

Government of Nepal, National Planning Commission, and Oxford Poverty and Human Development Initiative. 2018. *Nepal's Multidimensional Poverty Index: Analysis Towards Action*. Kathmandu: Government of Nepal. ophi.org.uk/wp-content/uploads/VF-Nepal_2018_vs9_21Dec-2_online.pdf.

―――. 2021. *Nepal's Multidimensional Poverty Index: Analysis Towards Action*. Kathmandu: Government of Nepal. mppn.org/wp-content/uploads/2021/08/MPI_Report_2021_for_web.pdf.

Ministry of Labor, Invalids and Social Affairs (MOLISA), Centre for Analysis and Forecast, General Statistics Office (GS), Multilateral Debt Relief Initiative (MDRI) and United Nations Development Programme (UNDP) Vietnam. 2018. *Multidimensional Poverty in Vietnam. Reducing Poverty in All Its Dimensions to Ensure a Good Quality Life for All*. Hanoi: United Nations Development Programme Vietnam.

Moreno, C. 2016. 'How Did El Salvador Choose Its National MPI Dimensions?' *Dimensions* 16(1), 16–20.

Multidimensional Poverty Peer Network (MPPN). 2020. 'Some National Measures'. Oxford Poverty and Human Development Initiative, Oxford. mppn.org/applications/national-measures/.

―――. 2021a. 'Multidimensional Poverty in Vietnam: Sustainable Poverty Reduction 2016–2020'. MPPN. Oxford Poverty and Human Development Initiative, Oxford. mppn.org/multidimensional-poverty-viet-nam/.

―――. 2021b. 'Philippines Launches a National MPI'. Oxford Poverty and Human Development Initiative, Oxford. mppn.org/mpiphilippines/.

―――. 2021c. 'Multidimensional Poverty Peer Network (MPPN)'. Oxford Poverty and Human Development Initiative, Oxford. mppn.org/about-us/mppn-en/.

Narayan, D., Pritchett, L. and Kapoor, S. 2009. *Moving Out of Poverty: Volume 2, Success from the Bottom Up*. Washington, DC: The World Bank and Palgrave Macmillan.

National Statistics and Information Authority. 2019. *Afghanistan Multidimensional Poverty Index 2016–2017*. Kabul: National Statistics and Information Authority.

Royal Government of Bhutan. 2018. *Sustainable Development and Happiness: Bhutan's Voluntary National Review Report on the Implementation of the 2030 Agenda for Sustainable Development*. Thimphu: Royal Government of Bhutan.

Sen, A. 1985. 'Well-being, Agency and Freedom: The Dewey Lectures 1984'. *Journal of Philosophy* 82(4), 169–221.

―――. 1999. *Development as Freedom*. New York: Alfred Knopf.

Tiwari, B. N. 2019. *Multidimensional Poverty Measures as a Policy Tool for Achieving the Sustainable Development Goals: A Review of MPI Measurement and Uses in Asia and the Pacific*. New York: United Nations Development Programme.

United Nations (UN). 2021. 'Sustainable Development Knowledge Platform'. United Nations, New York. sustainabledevelopment.un.org/vnrs/.

United Nations Department of Economics and Social Affairs (UNDESA). 2019. 'World Population Prospects: The 2019 Revision'. United Nations Department of Economics and Social Affairs, New York. population.un.org/wpp.

United Nations Development Programme (UNDP). 2010. *Human Development Report 2010: The Real Wealth of Nations - Pathways to Human Development*. New York: United Nations Development Programme. http://hdr.undp.org/sites/default/files/reports/270/hdr_2010_en_complete_reprint.pdf.

United Nations Development Programme (UNDP) and Oxford Poverty and Human Development Initiative (OPHI). 2019a. *Global Multidimensional Poverty Index 2019: Illuminating Inequalities*. New York: United Nations Development Programme.

———. 2019b. *How to Build a National Multidimensional Poverty Index (MPI): Using the MPI to Inform the SDGs*. New York: United Nations Development Programme. undp.org/content/undp/en/home/librarypage/poverty-reduction/how-to-build-a-national-multidimensional-poverty-index.html.

———. 2021. *Global Multidimensional Poverty Index 2021 – Unmasking Disparities by Ethnicity, Caste and Gender*. New York: United Nations Development Programme. hdr.undp.org/sites/default/files/2021_mpi_report_en.pdf.

8 | COVID-19 and Human Security
A. K. Shiva Kumar

INTRODUCTION

The COVID-19 pandemic has made one thing clear: nothing matters more to people than security in their daily lives. The helplessness and lack of preparedness among individuals, families, communities and governments during the pandemic has underscored the need to focus on human security – an idea first introduced in the 1994 *Human Development Report* and later articulated in the 2003 *Report of the Commission on Human Security*, chaired by Sadako Ogata and Amartya Sen (UNDP, 1994; Commission on Human Security, 2003).

This chapter revisits the idea of human security by examining efforts made over the past 25 years by Asian-Pacific nations to promote human development and assessing the impact of the COVID-19 pandemic on the outcomes. Despite considerable progress, the COVID-19 pandemic has exposed the fragility of the development foundations of most countries in the region. An important lesson emerges: While promoting human development remains essential, it cannot guarantee prosperity unless it also prioritizes human security. Looking ahead, nations need to re-envision their human development strategies to prioritize building resilience and empowerment that can overcome the sense of helplessness – one that not only dominates everyday lives but becomes worse in the event of an unforeseen crisis.

THE IDEA OF HUMAN SECURITY

Human security has many dimensions: economic, food, health, environmental, personal, community and political. Manifestations of insecurity include lacking a steady source of income, suffering from hunger, needing medical attention without the means of paying for it, living in fear of abuse and feeling persecuted for belonging to a particular race or religion. As the 1994 *Human Development Report* states:

> In the final analysis, human security is a child who did not die, a disease that did not spread, a job that was not cut, an ethnic tension that did not explode in violence, a dissident who was not silenced. Human security is not a concern with weapons-it is a concern with human life and dignity. (UNDP, 1994)

Of the many dimensions and features of human security, four have prescriptive importance and will inform the rest of the discussion. First, human security means an end to deprivations. At a minimum, this requires a guaranteed, steady source of income, freedom from hunger, good quality education and affordable healthcare, prevention of child abuse and domestic violence, and insurance of equal participation and non-discrimination. Second, human security entails upholding rights and freedoms. Crises such as the pandemic erode freedom from fear and freedom from want, but can also aggravate threats to democracy and human rights through the stifling of voices and dissent.[1] Third, human security is intentionally protective. Individual states, therefore, need to create policies and programs that protect people from uncertainties and unpredictable events that could threaten their peaceful survival and dignity. For example, these policies should protect people from financial crises, natural disasters that destroy property and leave families homeless, and from future pandemics or health crises. Fourth, human security and human development complement each other. Human development has an inherently optimistic quality, given its focus on expanding freedoms, enhancing capabilities, increasing opportunities and guaranteeing human rights. Human security complements human development by focusing on protection from unforeseen downside risks.

This chapter begins by assessing the current state of human development in Asian-Pacific countries and the immediate effects of the COVID-19 crisis before identifying a set of priority actions urgently needed to promote human security.

HUMAN DEVELOPMENT IN THE ASIA AND THE PACIFIC REGION

Discussions of development in the Asia-Pacific Region (APR) often overlook one of its distinct achievements. Between 1990–2019, South Asia and East Asia and the Pacific recorded the highest annual rates of increase in the Human Development Index (HDI) (Table 8.1). Prior to the COVID-19 pandemic, Asia and the Pacific had emerged as the world's fastest-growing region, leading the world in poverty reduction. Incomes expanded over the past three decades and pulled millions out of poverty. Impressive improvements in access to goods and services have resulted in significant gains in child survival, life expectancy and standards of living.

Table 8.1   Human Development Index trends, 1990–2019

	Human Development Index (HDI)							Average annual HDI growth (%)
	Value							
Regions	1990	2000	2010	2014	2015	2017	2018	2019	1990-2019
South Asia	0.437	0.501	0.580	0.612	0.620	0.635	0.637	0.641	1.330
East Asia and the Pacific	0.517	0.595	0.688	0.718	0.724	0.735	0.740	0.747	1.280
Sub-Saharan Africa	0.404	0.426	0.501	0.530	0.535	0.542	0.544	0.547	1.050
Arab States	0.556	0.614	0.676	0.687	0.691	0.699	0.702	0.705	0.820
Latin America and the Caribbean	0.632	0.690	0.736	0.756	0.759	0.762	0.764	0.766	0.670
Europe and Central Asia	0.662	0.675	0.739	0.772	0.775	0.785	0.787	0.791	0.620
World	0.601	0.644	0.699	0.720	0.724	0.732	0.734	0.737	0.710

Source: UNDP (2020a).
Note: Regions have been ranked in descending order of the 1990–2019 average annual HDI growth.

Despite these achievements, many countries in the APR continue to face serious human development challenges. In 2019, 31 out of the 46 countries in the APR fell in the category of low- and middle-income countries (LMICs). Only 15 were high-income countries.[2] Levels of human development also vary widely within the region. In 2019, Hong Kong SAR (China) ranked fourth in the Human Development Index (HDI), while Afghanistan – a low human-development country – ranked 169th out of 189 countries. 22 countries fell into the category of 'very high' and 'high' human development, whereas 14 were in the 'medium' human development category (UNDP, 2020a).

The backlog of human deprivations in the APR remains large. The benefits of economic growth have reached only a few, and not the poorest and most vulnerable: An estimated 400 million continue to live in extreme poverty. Unequal economic growth has, in many instances, worsened the power asymmetries between rich and poor, weakened social cohesion and undermined stability. Large disparities continue to prevent millions of families from leading secure lives and living in dignity. Despite gains in health, access to healthcare and other basic services remains unequal and far from universal. Gender inequality continues to hamper development. A rising proportion of older people risk social exclusion, and a growing number of persons with disabilities face marginalization. Migrant workers and their families remain highly vulnerable.[3]

A recent analysis by the United Nations Development Programme (UNDP) reaffirms that policies in many Asian-Pacific countries have failed to translate high economic growth into tangible benefits for people in terms of better health, improved education, cleaner environments, or better access to basic social services. Even prior to the COVID-19 pandemic, the APR was on an unsustainable development trajectory. Rapid demographic growth, migration, high population density, displacement of animals and changes in land use had created ripe conditions for the rise of zoonotic diseases and their transmission to humans. The high dependence of growth on fossil fuels, as well as unsustainable production and consumption patterns, had begun to push against planetary boundaries. Rising inequality within most countries had exacerbated social tensions and several countries were experiencing protracted conflicts (UNDP, 2020c).

Children's lives in South Asia remain insecure in many different ways (UNICEF, 2021). More than 60 per cent of deaths in South Asia among children younger than 5 occur during the first month of life. Of the 144 million children who are stunted worldwide, 56 million, or nearly two in five, live in South Asia. Maternal mortality rates also vary widely with Afghanistan being among the countries with the highest rates globally. In 2017, South Asia had the second highest share of children living in extreme poverty (at 10.2 per cent) and accounted for 18 per cent of the world's extremely poor children (Silwal et al., 2017).

Young girls in most parts of South Asia lack the freedom to pursue their ambitions. Early marriage, in particular, remains a stumbling block. Levels of child marriage vary greatly across South Asia, with the highest prevalence in Bangladesh – home to 38 million child brides married before their 18th birthday, including 13 million who married before the age of 15 (UNICEF, 2020a).

The backlog of human deprivations in the APR suggests that the region has not been able to convert economic expansion into tangible benefits and increased security in the lives of its peoples. Among the many reasons for the region's under-performance in advancing human development and human security, six stand out:

1. *Failure to create decent jobs*
    Although the APR has seen robust economic growth, many governments have proven unable to create sufficient job opportunities, especially for the more than 700 million young people in the region. According to the International

Labour Organisation (ILO), 20 per cent of the region's workers aged between 15 and 24 account for almost half the jobless (ILO, 2021a). A majority of the employed young people (about 300 million) do not have decent[4] jobs. For many, the option of staying unemployed does not exist. As a result, they often have no choice but to take up jobs that offer poor pay, poor conditions and poor prospects. As a consequence, they struggle for economic security and dignity, and to build a secure future for their families. The youth employment challenge is made more complex given the interconnections between economic development, child labour, rural livelihoods, urban and trans-border migration, gender, poverty and vulnerability.

2. *The neglect of health justice*

Most of the countries in the APR have yet to fully embrace the idea of universal health coverage. More than 40 years after the 1978 Alma Ata Declaration, health is still not recognized as a fundamental right, and national governments, as well as the world community, have not taken the necessary actions to protect and promote the health of all (WHO, 1978). The 1978 Declaration underscored gross inequalities in health status across and within countries as politically, socially and economically unacceptable. They remain a concern even now. The Declaration had called for attaining 'Health for All' by the year 2000 – a goal that required making primary healthcare (PHC) the cornerstone of health systems. The reach of primary healthcare remains extremely limited in many countries. For instance, in 2016 and 2017, the proportion of fully immunized children 12-23 months old was 49 per cent in Timor-Leste, 59 per cent in Indonesia, 62 per cent in India, 66 per cent in Pakistan, 70 per cent in the Philippines, 77 per cent in the Maldives, 78 per cent in Nepal and 86 per cent in Bangladesh (GDS, Ministry of Health and ICF, 2018; BKKBN et al., 2018; IIPS and ICF, 2017; NIPS and ICF, 2019; PSA and ICF, 2018; MOH Maldives and ICF, 2018; MOH Nepal, New ERA and ICF, 2017; NIPORT and ICF, 2020). State underinvestment in healthcare has also resulted in extremely high private out-of-pocket expenditures in the APR. Such expenditures run as high as 50–60 per cent in Nepal, Pakistan and Sri Lanka, 62 per cent in India and 74–75 per cent in Afghanistan and Bangladesh (WHO, 2021a). These private health costs have emerged as a major cause of impoverishment.

3. *The neglect of basic education*

Education is a valuable achievement in itself and a key component of a flourishing life, regardless of whether the individual earns an income or not. Education also has instrumental significance. It contributes to health and wealth and adds to a person's freedom to do the many things they value. Education develops civic skills, particularly important for strengthening responsible citizenship, promoting public participation and deepening democracy. Finally, education has powerful empowerment and distributive roles – the ability to resist oppression, to organize politically, and to negotiate better conditions, even within families.[5] Despite the significant role that education plays in society, many countries in the APR have failed to provide universal quality school education to children. The mean years of schooling in South Asia (6.5 years) is only marginally higher than in Sub-Saharan Africa (5.8 years) and considerably lower than the average in the Arab region (7.3 years) and the world (8.5 years) (UNDP, 2020d). Insufficient investment in teacher education and training, as well as in school infrastructure, has hampered quality education provision. Curricula often tend to be outdated and do not align with the needs of future labour markets.

4. *Gender inequality and lack of women's economic empowerment*
    Sustainable and inclusive societies must prioritize women's equal access to ownership and control of land, property and other resources. A study by the McKinsey Global Institute estimated that with gender parity, Asian countries as a whole could gain US$4.4 trillion of additional gross domestic product (GDP) by 2025 if they matched the fastest-improving country in the region; the full potential could go even higher.[6]

    Women in most Asian-Pacific countries do not enjoy the same freedoms as women living in other parts of the world. In societies without systematic discrimination against girls and women, women outnumber men in the total population. In South Asia, except for Nepal and Sri Lanka, men outnumber women in the total population – indicating the antifemale biases that still dominate society. These biases deny girls and women equal opportunities to study, work, or even marry when and whom they choose to. This reflects the dominant patriarchal character of most Asian-Pacific societies.

    Girls in many Asian-Pacific countries face more educational deprivation than boys. Except in Sri Lanka, the youth literacy rate (15–24 years) is lower for girls than for boys in all countries of South Asia. In Afghanistan, for instance, the female youth literacy rate is only 32 per cent against the male rate of 62 per cent.

    Attitudes towards the abuse of wives also capture the subordinate position of women. According to the Demographic Health Surveys,[7] in Afghanistan, for instance, 8 in 10 ever-married women and more than 7 in 10 men agree that a husband may be justified in hitting or beating his wife (CSO, MoPH and ICF, 2017). Thirty-two per cent of women and 17 per cent of married men in Indonesia consider wife-beating justified in at least one of the five specified circumstances (National Population and Family Planning Board et al., 2018). In India, the percentages run to 42 per cent of men and 52 per cent of women (IIPS and ICF, 2017).

5. *Weak social protection programmes*
    Despite economic progress, precariousness characterizes the lives of a majority of workers in the region, especially women. Most countries in the APR have

weak social protection systems that fail to offer comprehensive universal coverage.[8] Typically, poverty-targeted schemes fail to reach the poorest families. Maternity, unemployment, sickness and disability benefits accrue only to a small proportion of workers employed in the formal sector. In the absence of universal health coverage in many countries, unforeseen and catastrophic medical expenditures continue to impoverish a large number of families that do not have access to affordable treatment, and push vulnerable households back into poverty. Even where pension schemes exist, the amount individuals receive is insufficient to cover basic needs. Significant underinvestment in social protection bears much of the responsibility for the situation. According to United Nations Economic and Social Commission for Asia and the Pacific (UNESCAP) and ILO (2021), excluding health, many countries in the region spend less than two per cent of GDP on social protection, compared to the global average of 11 per cent.

The limited coverage of social protection programs in the APR also arises from the employment of a large workforce in the informal sector. More than 80 per cent of all South Asia's workers, for instance, engage in informal activities, and more than 90 per cent of the region's businesses are informal (Bussolo, Sharma and Timmer, 2020). Even in many formal firms, a large proportion of employment consists of informal workers, for instance in Bangladesh and Pakistan. Women make up a disproportionate percentage of workers in the informal sector and remain particularly vulnerable because they typically work for lower wages and in unsafe conditions.

Migrant workers face particularly bad conditions in many countries. For instance, according to the *Thailand Migration Report 2019*, there were approximately 3.9 million (non-Thai) migrant workers in Thailand, constituting almost 10 per cent of the workforce (Harkins, 2019). Of these, some 21 per cent undertook so-called irregular work (working without work permits). Persistent labour abuses against migrant workers of any gender in regular and irregular work continues, including forced labour, such as deceptive recruitment practices and withholding wages. Most migrant workers find themselves denied fundamental rights, including access to basic social services. Migrant sex workers in Thailand, in particular, experience stigma and live in constant fear of harassment and arrest, as well as uncertainty in their family-supporting incomes.

6.   *Neglect of the most disadvantaged*

Most of the countries in the APR have failed to ensure that benefits of economic expansion accrue to the most disadvantaged groups in society. The list is long and includes broad categories of vulnerable women, children (including children in care institutions), youth and adolescents (particularly girls), older persons and people with disabilities. Economic insecurities concentrate not only among those in poverty, but also those with insecure incomes, low-income and informal economy workers, including those in the gig economy, internal migrant workers and migrant workers in foreign countries. People infected with COVID-19 and those in quarantine and their families, healthcare providers and frontline workers (especially during pandemics) face severe health insecurity, as do those living with HIV/AIDS and other chronic medical conditions, those in need of mental health and psychological support, those with general medical needs, and people with alcohol dependence and substance abuse disorders. Several groups also experience physical insecurity. These typically include ethnic and religious minorities, people living with diverse sexual orientation and gender identities, indigenous people and tribal communities, refugees, internally displaced persons (IDPs), refugee returnees and asylum seekers, people in detention or deprived of their liberty, and Stateless populations. Other groups also face environmental insecurity, including, for instance, climate-vulnerable and disaster-affected people and those living in water-scarce and drought-prone areas.

This picture of unsustainable growth and unequal human development, coupled with high levels of vulnerability, has meant widespread and unequal impacts from the economic and health crises caused by COVID-19.

THE SOCIOECONOMIC IMPACTS OF COVID-19

The COVID-19 pandemic exposed the fragility of the APR's development efforts. Several recent reports have documented the devastating impacts of the COVID-19 pandemic on the lives and livelihoods of millions of people in the APR.[9] Only a small minority of privileged has escaped relatively unscathed. A recent UNDP report on the APR (2020) identifies three major adverse impacts of the pandemic:

1. *Global value chains and the supply and demand shock*
    Governments face twin supply- and demand-side shocks. Loss of livelihoods and higher unemployment have greatly reduced the demand for goods and services. At the same time, the pandemic has severely disrupted global value chains, halted production and reduced the supply of goods and services. The adverse effects on economies highly integrated in value chains, such as China, have negatively impacted the closely integrated economies of other countries in the region, including Cambodia, Hong Kong SAR (China), Japan, Malaysia, Singapore, the Republic of Korea, Thailand and Viet Nam. Moreover, restrictions on cross-border movements – and associated delays and cost increases – are likely to amplify the impact on value chains, affecting China and much of East and Southeast Asia. These shocks severely affect small and medium enterprises (SMEs) in particular, because of their limited access to

resources and working capital; these firms account for more than 96 per cent of all businesses and for two thirds of private sector jobs.

2.   *The social crisis*

The cascading effects of the pandemic on employment in Asia and the Pacific have drastically cut production and increased trade barriers, reduced global demand and imposed restrictions on movement. As a result, the situation has worsened in many countries such as Bangladesh, Cambodia, India, Myanmar and Viet Nam that had already faced crises in employment and job losses even before the pandemic. While poverty has substantially declined in Asia and the Pacific, its rate of reduction has slowed down since 2010, and the COVID-19 pandemic will likely reverse a considerable part of these gains. The World Bank expects over 11 million people in East Asia to fall into poverty in 2020, with many more likely to do so across South Asia (World Bank, 2020a).

3.   *The gender impacts*

A third type of crisis has also emerged: the crisis in caregiving, severely impacting the already high gender inequality in the APR. Although large-scale evidence, specifically from Asia-Pacific, remains limited, it is clear that women have experienced a particularly adverse impact from COVID-19, given the gendered nature of the health workforce and the accompanying risks that predominantly female health workers face, as well as their lower wages, higher share of unpaid care and the burden of domestic work. Additionally, the workload on women has risen steeply compared to normal times because of school closures affecting over 850 million learners in the APR. Moreover, women principally shoulder the increased need for care of elderly relatives more at risk for COVID-19-related complications.[10] Recent evidence points to a marked rise in domestic violence, and in discrimination at the workplace, as employers may see women overloaded with care obligations as less competitive and committed than male colleagues.

The crisis triggered by the COVID-19 pandemic had, in the initial phase of the lockdown, brought South Asia in particular to a near-standstill. Reports on the impact of the pandemic pointed out, for instance, that the economic disruption was visible from space. South Asia had darkened between March and August 2020, and night-time light intensity had declined in more than three quarters of South Asia's districts (World Bank, 2020b). The temporary school closures in South Asian countries had kept an estimated 391 million students out of school in primary and secondary education. The pandemic may cause up to 5.5 million students to drop out of the education system altogether. In 2020, an additional 3.9 million children in South Asia under the age of five could suffer from wasting – and therefore become dangerously undernourished – as a result of the socioeconomic impact of the COVID-19 pandemic (Headey et al., 2020). Additionally, approximately 29 million babies that were expected to be born in South Asia in the approximately nine months since the World Health Organization (WHO) declared COVID-19 a pandemic on 11 March 2020, risked having no access to primary healthcare due to stress on existing health systems and medical supply chains (UNICEF, 2020b).

LESSONS LEARNED

We can learn much from the experience of countries and territories in the APR, both those more and less successful in promoting human development and reducing insecurities (especially those exacerbated by the COVID-19 pandemic). A number of Asian-Pacific countries and territories have received global recognition for their successes in handling the pandemic. These include Japan, New Zealand, Hong Kong SAR (China), Republic of Korea, Thailand, Viet Nam, Singapore and Bhutan.

Japan does not have large national public health agencies, such as the Centers for Disease Control and Prevention (CDC) in the United States, that it can draw on for technical support during pandemics. Instead, Japan was able to minimize the adverse impacts of COVID-19 through its unique model of regionalized public health delivery. This consisted of local public health centres (PHCs), *hokenjo* in Japanese, that doubled as 'miniature CDCs' within their respective communities (Hamaguchi et al., 2020). While PHCs illustrate the importance of strong local public health institutions, capable of swift adaptation to their local context, it is notable that these centres proved unable to facilitate testing.

New Zealand demonstrated the importance of continued surveillance. It also pioneered a social bubble model that allowed a defined group of people to have close physical contact with each other while practising physical distancing rules with others outside of that group (Cook et al., 2020).

Hong Kong SAR (China), Japan and the Republic of Korea had an advantage: the habit of mask-wearing by people with respiratory conditions – already widespread before the COVID-19 pandemic as a way of protecting others from seasonal viruses or as a reaction to air pollution. After making mask-wearing mandatory in April 2020, Singapore's government provided reusable cloth masks to the entire population (Han et al., 2020).

Several factors seem to have underpinned Thailand's success: a combination of government action, social responsibility and community solidarity ensured continued vigilance. Thailand also adopted a whole-of-society approach and ramped-up testing as borders reopened and full economic activities resumed (Sabharwal, 2020).

Viet Nam's successful tackling of the COVID-19 pandemic highlights the importance of preparedness in dealing with infectious diseases, critical for protecting people and minimizing their insecurities. Viet Nam had the advantage of an existing long-term plan for coping with public health emergencies, built on its previous experience with disease outbreaks, such as severe acute respiratory syndrome (SARS). To that extent, Viet Nam's success in dealing with the COVID-19 outbreak rests, at least in part, on the investments made during pre-pandemic 'peacetime'. Collectively, early preparedness, contact tracing, isolation and mass molecular (polymerase chain reaction [PCR]) testing, coupled with timely border closure, physical distancing and community adherence, have determined the success of Viet Nam's control of COVID-19 (Malhotra, 2020; Van Tan, 2021).

Several similar factors have contributed to Bhutan's success in containing the spread of the pandemic (Drexler, 2021). The country prioritized investing in preparedness, and, as early, as mid-January 2020, had drafted and put in place its National Preparedness and Response Plan. A rigorous and altruistic state and public health response was accompanied by genuine civic compassion and engagement from King Jigme Khesar Namgyel Wangchuck, the Queen Mother, Bhutan's monastic community, cabinet ministers, political leaders, government officials and ordinary citizens, including farmers, volunteers, hoteliers and others. The government drew on its existing strengths and enhanced its capacities by shifting technicians from livestock-health and food-safety programs to its COVID-19 testing corps and by instructing non-specialist doctors and nurses in the clinical management of respiratory infections and WHO protocols.

Notably, these exemplary governments also made it possible for citizens to follow public health guidance by providing those required to quarantine with economic and social support.

Building trust through honest and effective communication has also emerged as another critical factor in controlling the adverse effects of such pandemics. Viet Nam's success owes much to the trust built up through real-time, transparent communication from the Ministry of Health, supported by WHO and other UN agencies (Malhotra, 2020; Van Tan, 2021). In the Republic of Korea, the government's highly transparent communication strategy helped gain public participation by disclosing detailed information on infected patients via government websites and text alerts. New Zealand's Prime Minister and the Director General of Health have also won credit for their firm yet empathetic direct communications with the public (Han et al., 2020).

In Singapore, close to 95 per cent of confirmed cases appeared among migrant workers living in overcrowded dormitories. The government responded by immediately improving disinfection regimens, establishing medical facilities onsite and shielding workers older than 45 years by moving them to less dense accommodation (Han et al., 2020).

Beyond these successes lie the broader challenges of ensuring human security. But most countries today do not yet have in place the needed institutions, policies and priorities. This needs to change. The Commission on Human Security has proposed mobilizing a global initiative to place human security at the top of local, national, regional and global agendas. This initiative would aim to prevent conflict and advance human rights and development; protect and empower people and their communities; deepen democratic principles and practices; and overall, promote a human security culture and framework.

Promoting human development must go hand-in-hand with enhancing human security through measures that focus on protecting and expanding freedoms during downturns as well as in prosperity. Countries needs to fulfil its legal obligations to protect and promote human rights, including the right to social security, and ensure their exercise without discrimination. Governments should create the enabling conditions and forge partnerships with civil society organizations and other stakeholders, both to safeguard people from threats, and simultaneously empower them to take charge of their own lives (Commission on Human Security, 2003).

The Way Forward

The three pillars of human development – embedding values, enhancing capabilities and promoting agency – spotlighted by the 2020 *Human Development Report* (UNDP, 2020a) have an equally central role in guaranteeing human security (Figure 8.1).

Embedding values

A new approach to development must begin with reaffirming human values enshrined in the constitutions of countries. These would include, for example, adherence to

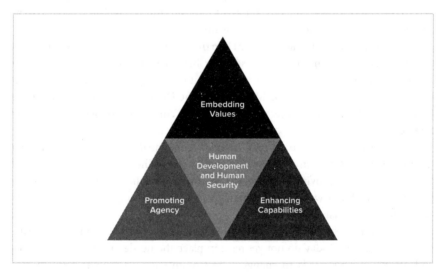

Figure 8.1   Three pillars for promoting human development and human security
Source: Adapted from UNDP (2020a).

social, economic, cultural and political justice, liberty of thought, expression, faith, belief and worship, equality of status and opportunity, and solidarity assuring the dignity of the individual as well as the unity and integrity of the nation. The United Nations 2030 Agenda for Sustainable Development foregrounds these values as central to transforming the world. There are, of course, numerous instances where communities in different countries of the APR came forward to help stranded migrant workers and others who lost their sources of livelihood. Nevertheless, states and societies, as a whole, will need to commit much more conscious investment to instilling a sense of community, non-discrimination and solidarity. This might require revisiting how school education inculcates values in the young, and also finding new mechanisms and platforms that can proactively strengthen actions by community organisations and others to build social solidarity and social cohesion.

Enhancing capabilities

The following priorities have a particularly critical role in developing human and institutional capabilities:

Establishing effective social protection systems
An effective social protection umbrella implements three main social-security systems: (1) universal social protection that includes benefits for sickness, unemployment, occupational injury and survivorship; (2) a social protection floor that ensures availability, continuity and accessibility in public services, such as housing, water and sanitation, education, health including maternal and childcare as well as family planning services, and family-focused social work support; and (3) social transfers in cash and in kind that are paid to the poor, older persons and the vulnerable to enhance food security and nutrition, and to provide a minimum-income security, particularly in cases of sickness, unemployment and disability.

This will call for correcting the historical under-investment and prioritizing the provision of basic social services, with the following as primary goals:
Universal health coverage
Progress towards universal health coverage will require renewed political commitment, adequate investments in people and infrastructure, as well as an effective regulatory framework to ensure accountability. An increase in public spending will be necessary to reduce the burden of private out-of-pocket expenditures on healthcare. Community-based health initiatives will need to be strengthened to ensure access to primary healthcare for all.
Universal basic education
This will require investing in many well-known measures, including supporting girls' education and making schools adaptable to their needs; committing significant resources to schooling and school feeding programmes;

empowering parents, community committees and other stakeholders to hold schools accountable for the quality of education; and encouraging states and school authorities to ensure a safe and secure learning environment, free from discrimination, health hazards and violence. The COVID-19 pandemic has opened the potential of using online learning and teaching methods in education. These require judicious deployment to ensure that the digital divide does not amplify the educational divides in society.

Providing minimum living standards

The present moment seems opportune for revisiting the Commission on Human Security's recommended approach to work and work-based security. Secure livelihoods depend on finding sustained and creative ways of ensuring both income and meaningful work. This will require addressing issues of access to land, credit, training and education, especially for poor women. Equally critical measures would ensure a social and economic minimum for all, including the working poor and those in unpaid work. Special measures should increase protections for those in chronic poverty as well as those most vulnerable to economic hardship during economic downturns, disasters and crises, including women, children, people with disabilities and the elderly.

Promoting agency

Individual states and societies must make concerted efforts to ensure four conditions that can promote agency and empowerment:

- A well-educated society in which everyone has the freedom to express their views without fear.
- A free press whose reporting on the failures of the ruling administration or the sufferings faced by the poor does not stand compromised because of pressures from the government in power.
- A culture of open public discussion where opinions can be expressed without fear and in the true spirit of encouraging public debate.
- A listening government open to engaging and learning in an effort to come up with solutions – as opposed to a government that uses its majority to pass legislation without a debate and discussion.

Fulfilling these conditions will go a long way toward deepening democracy and establishing a supportive framework for other security needs.

Conclusion

Even as nations step up to mitigate and reverse the negative impacts of the COVID-19 pandemic, it becomes necessary to re-envision the role of state governments.

Governments must play a proactive role in enhancing capabilities, building people's agency and promoting human security by providing sufficient protection against downside risks. Three concerns should provide a focus. The first addresses the disconcerting absence of serious public discussion on the role of the state vis-à-vis the private sector in the provision of basic social services. In a number of countries (and in South Asia in particular), governments appear to have abdicated their responsibilities to assure adequate protection to citizens. No country in the world has managed to provide universal healthcare or universal schooling without the dominant presence of the public sector. It is, therefore, disturbing to see a sharp increase in the share of both health and education delivery now in the hands of the private sector – along with a possibly unwitting withdrawal by the public sector.

Second, governments in many nations appear to have reached their limit in evolving strategies to 'leave no one behind.' Differentiated strategies under the umbrella of universal coverage could ensure that the most disadvantaged groups also gain access to basic social services and social protection benefits. Third, states often appear overly preoccupied with promoting economic growth. Policymakers need to pay equal attention – if not more – to creating conditions for human development, including deepening of democracy, mitigating and preventing the human impacts of climate change, reducing human insecurities, decreasing inequalities and addressing social injustices.

At the same time, states and societies should promote more active engagement with the public and ensure greater involvement of different stakeholders in public decision-making. Many schisms in society have roots in misconceptions and entrenched belief systems that obstruct the building of social cohesion and social solidarity. Advocates fighting violence against women and children, for instance, have called for changing social norms, but progress in changing behaviours has not kept pace with recorded economic gains. The available means and media for influencing social norms and behaviours have increased phenomenally over the past two decades. Whereas the role of traditional communications media seems to have declined, the expansion in social media has brought phenomenal disruption. One could cite many instances of social media platforms used effectively in critical public health outreach. At the same time, the misuse of these platforms has also propagated hate speech and violence.

Addressing these gaps in development requires proactive measures to change social norms and behaviours. Towards this end, the *2020 Human Development Report* recommends promoting learning and ensuring an alignment between self-interest and common goals (UNDP, 2020a). Governments need to create more favourable conditions: making behavioural change feasible, attractive and profitable for the majority of people, promoting agency through participatory approaches, and introducing laws and incentives that encourage desirable behaviour and innovation. Much remains to be learned about which efforts in this area will work best. Careful design and execution of such efforts, along with documentation and disseminating outcomes, will foster that learning.

One final, crucial lesson: The COVID-19 pandemic has shown that high incomes alone cannot guarantee health security. The Global Health Security (GHS) Index 2019[11] benchmarks 195 countries according to the Index's definition of their level of 'preparedness' for dealing with epidemics or pandemics (Table 8.2). High-income countries filled the list of the GHS top five 'most prepared' countries, with Thailand a lower-income outlier (GHS rank 6). The United States and the United Kingdom ranked first and second, respectively, for pandemic preparedness on the GHS Index, but by 15 April 2021, the two countries showed among the poorest rankings for preventing deaths due to COVID-19 per 100,000 population.

Looking at preparedness in terms of actually being able to prevent pandemic deaths instead of using the GHS-defined preparedness, of the 178 countries that had COVID-19-related cases and deaths as of 15 April 2021, the United States and United Kingdom rank 164th and 167th – in other words, they registered the 14th and 11th highest death rates, respectively. This disastrous real-world performance compares especially poorly to lower-GHS-ranked but higher-death-preventing countries in Asia, such as the global leaders, Viet Nam (49th on GHS versus 1st for low death rate), or Bhutan (83rd on GHS versus 4th for low death rate). Only Thailand ranked highly for both pandemic preparedness and performance.

Rich nations were perhaps overly confident and unprepared when the COVID-19 virus was detected. Both the United States and the United Kingdom (at least initially) floundered in their response, and their handling of the pandemic proved far worse than that of many much poorer nations. Many Western nations prioritised capacities, such as economic activity and equipment, and not capabilities, such as effective quarantining and efficient contact tracing (Yong, 2020). The poor handling of the COVID-19 pandemic reveals that many rich nations had little experience in deploying their enormous capacities, in contrast to East Asian and sub-Saharan countries that regularly deal with epidemics.

The future of the pandemic remains uncertain, but its conclusions for development policy remain firm. These pandemic results imply that countries do not have to become rich first to reduce vulnerabilities, enhance security, and promote the dignity of human lives. It is possible for LMICs to protect people from downside risks. What seems less clear is how to do so, especially in a world undergoing rapid transformation led by the technology and communication revolutions. At the same time, the COVID-19 pandemic has exposed the fragility of the development foundations of most countries of the APR. A new ethic rooted firmly in human values should now guide policymaking. Such an ethic should recognize the importance of promoting and protecting not just economic and social freedoms, but civil, cultural and political freedoms, as well. Human insecurity stands heightened by increasing economic uncertainty, rising social inequalities and reduced mobility, all going

Table 8.2 GHS Index 2019 predicted pandemic preparedness rankings versus actual pandemic death prevention rankings as of 15 April 2021 (top and bottom)

GHI predicted pandemic preparedness rank	Country	2019 Overall Score[1]	2019 GNI per capita, Atlas Method (current US$)[2]	2019 World Bank country classifications by income level	Cumulative total COVID-19 deaths per 100,000 population[3] 15 April 2021	Actual pandemic death prevention rank 15 April 2021
1	United States	83.5	65,850	High Income	168.88	164
2	United Kingdom	77.9	42,220	High Income	187.36	167
3	Netherlands	75.6	53,100	High Income	96.86	137
4	Australia	75.5	55,100	High Income	3.57	48
5	Canada	75.3	46,370	High Income	62.12	120
49	Viet Nam	49.1	2,590	Lower-middle Income	0.04	1
83	Bhutan	40.3	3,140	Lower-middle Income	0.13	4
6	Thailand	73.2	7,260	Upper-middle Income	0.14	5
23	Singapore	58.7	59,590	High Income	0.51	11
34	New Zealand	54.0	42,760	High Income	0.54	12

Sources: 1 = Global Health Security (2021); 2 = World Bank (2021); 3 = WHO (2021b).
Note: Of the GHS 195 ranked countries, this table excludes countries in the WHO database that reported zero cumulative deaths per 100,000 population, therefore these GHS rankings have been recalculated for the remaining 178 countries.

hand-in-hand with increasing social fragmentation, growing authoritarianism and regressing democracy.

The evaluative evidence remains limited, on what works, when and why, and for whom in different cultures and contexts, across and within nations. Tapping existing knowledge, encouraging innovations and generating new evidence will become critical in reimagining the approach to enhanced human security and accelerated human development.

NOTES

1. See, for example, the text of Amartya Sen's acceptance speech of 18 October 2020 after being awarded the Peace Prize of the German Book Trade (*DW*, 2020).
2. Low-income economies are defined as those with a gross national income (GNI) per capita, calculated using the World Bank Atlas method, of US$1,035 or less in 2019; lower middle-income economies are those with a GNI per capita between $1,036 and $4,045; upper middle-income economies are those with a GNI per capita between $4,046 and $12,535; high-income economies are those with a GNI per capita of $12,536 or more (World Bank, 2021).
3. The discussion on the backlog of deprivations in the APR draws on UNESCAP (2017).
4. According to ILO: "Decent work sums up the aspirations of people in their working lives. It involves opportunities for work that is productive and delivers a fair income, security in the workplace and social protection for families, better prospects for personal development and social integration, freedom for people to express their concerns, organize and participate in the decisions that affect their lives and equality of opportunity and treatment for all women and men" (ILO, 2021b).

    A joint ILO-Eurofound report identifies the following seven dimensions of job quality: the physical environment, work intensity, working time quality, the social environment, skills and development, prospects, and earnings (ILO, 2019).
5. For a discussion on the many roles of education, see Drèze and Sen (1995).
6. Gender parity score based on 15 indicators, with equal weighting of all indicators, calculated an aggregate score at the country level to measure each country's distance from full gender parity (Woetzel et al., 2015).
7. The Demographic and Health Surveys (DHS) collect, analyse and disseminate representative data on population, health, HIV and nutrition in over 90 countries. The methodology and survey questions are standardised across countries. Attitudes towards justification of wife-beating are based on response to a set of five questions regarding the conditions under which hitting or beating one's wife would be justifiable. The five questions are: (1) if she goes out without telling her husband; (2) if she argues with her husband; (3) if she neglects the children; (4) if she refuses to have sexual intercourse with her husband; and (5) if she burns food (Guide to DHS Statistics, n.d.).
8. See, for example, the discussion in UNESCAP and ILO (2021).
9. See, for example, UNDP (2020b).
10. See, for instance, the discussions in Wenham, Smith and Morgan (2020), UNESCO (2020) and UN Women (2020a, 2020b).

11. The Global Health Security (GHS) Index, developed by the Johns Hopkins Center for Global Health Security, the Economist Intelligence Unit and the Nuclear Threat Initiative, is the first comprehensive assessment and benchmarking of health security and related capabilities across 195 countries. The measure aims to gauge the capacity of national health systems in contributing to global health security. The GHS Index uses 140 questions to make this assessment, organised across six categories: prevention of the emergence or release of pathogens; early detection and reporting for epidemics of potential international concern; rapid response to and mitigation of the spread of the epidemic; sufficient and robust health system to treat the sick and protect health workers; commitments to improving national capacity, financing plans to address gaps, and adhering to global norms; overall risk environment and country vulnerability to biological threats. Among its 140 questions, the GHS Index prioritizes not only country capacities, but also the existence of functional, tested, proven capabilities for stopping outbreaks at the source (GHS, 2021).

REFERENCES

Bussolo, M., Sharma, S. and Timmer, H. 2020. 'COVID-19 Has Worsened the Woes of South Asia's Informal Sector'. World Bank Blogs, 7 December.

Central Statistics Organization, Ministry of Public Health and ICF. 2017. *Afghanistan Demographic and Health Survey 2015*. Kabul: Central Statistics Organization. dhsprogram.com/pubs/pdf/FR323/FR323.pdf.

Commission on Human Security. 2003. *Human Security Now*. Beirut: United Nations Economic and Social Commission for Western Asia. reliefweb.int/sites/reliefweb.int/files/resources/91BAEEDBA50C6907C1256D19006A9353-chs-security-may03.pdf.

Cook, L. Y. H., Teo, Y. Y., Heymann, D., Clark, H., McKee, M. and Legido-Quigley, H. 2020. 'Lessons Learnt from Easing COVID-19 Restrictions: An Analysis of Countries and Regions in Asia Pacific and Europe'. *The Lancet* 396(10261), 1525–1534. doi.org/10.1016/S0140-6736(20)32007-9.

Drexler, M. 2021. 'The Unlikeliest Pandemic Success Story: How Did a Tiny, Poor Nation Manage to Suffer Only One Death from the Coronavirus?' *The Atlantic*, 10 February. theatlantic.com/international/archive/2021/02/coronavirus-pandemic-bhutan/617976/.

Drèze, J. and Sen, A. 1995. *India: Economic Development and Social Opportunity*. Oxford: Clarendon Press.

General Directorate of Statistics (GDS), Ministry of Health, and ICF International. 2018. *Timor-Leste Demographic and Health Survey 2016*. Fairfax, VA: ICF International.

Global Health Security. 2021. *Global Health Security Index*. Baltimore, MD: Johns Hopkins Center for Global Health Security, Economist Intelligence Unit and Nuclear Threat Initiative. ghsindex.org/.

Demographic and Health Surveys (DHS). No date. 'Attitude towards Wife Beating'. Washington, DC: United States Agency for International Development. dhsprogram.com/data/Guide-to-DHS-Statistics/Attitude_towards_Wife_Beating.htm.

DW. 2020. 'Amartya Sen Wins Peace Prize of the German Book Trade'. 19 October. dw.com/en/amartya-sen-wins-peace-prize-of-the-german-book-trade/a-55320479.

Hamaguchi, R., Negishi, K., Higuchi, M., Funato, M., Kim, J.-H. and Bitton, A. 2020. 'A Regionalized Public Health Model to Combat COVID-19: Lessons from Japan'. *Health Affairs*, 22 July. healthaffairs.org/doi/10.1377/hblog20200721.404992.

Han, E., Tan, M. M. J., Turk, E., Sridhar, D., Leung, G. M., Shibuya, K., Asgari, N., Oh, J., García-Basteiro, A. L., Hanefeld, J., Cook, A. R., Hsu, L. Y., Teo, Y. Y., Heymann, D., Clark, H., McKee, M. and Legido-Quigley, H. 2020. 'Lessons Learnt from easing COVID-19 Restrictions: An Analysis of Countries and Regions in Asia Pacific and Europe'. *The Lancet*, 396(10261),1524–1534. doi.org/10.1016/S0140-6736(20)32007-9.

Harkins, B., ed. 2019. *Thailand Migration Report 2019*. Bangkok: United Nations Thematic Working Group on Migration in Thailand. reliefweb.int/sites/reliefweb.int/files/resources/Thailand%20Report%202019_22012019_LowRes.pdf.

Headey, D., Heidkamp, R., Osendarp, S., Ruel, M., Scott, N., Black, R., Shekar, M., Bouis, H., Flory, A., Haddad, L. and Walker, N. 2020. 'Impacts of COVID-19 on Childhood Malnutrition'. *The Lancet* 396(10250), 519–521. doi.org/10.1016/S0140-6736(20)31647-0.

International Institute for Population Sciences (IIPS) and ICF International. 2017. *National Family Health Survey (NFHS-4), 2015–16*. Mumbai: International Institute for Population Sciences.

International Labour Organisation (ILO). 2019. 'Job Quality of Concern to All Workers'. International Labour Organization, Geneva. ilo.org/global/about-the-ilo/newsroom/news/WCMS_696146/lang--en/index.htm.

———. 2021a. 'Youth Employment in Asia-Pacific'. International Labour Organization, Geneva. ilo.org/asia/areas/WCMS_117542/lang--en/index.htm.

———. 2021b. 'Decent Work'. International Labour Organization, Geneva. ilo.org/global/topics/decent-work/lang--en/index.htm.

Malhotra, K. 2020. 'Game Changers in Vietnam's Successful COVID-19 Response'. *UN Chronicle*, 30 August. un.org/ar/node/97757.

Ministry of Health (MOH) Maldives and ICF International. 2018. *Maldives Demographic and Health Survey 2016-17*. Fairfax, VA: ICF International.

Ministry of Health (MOH) Nepal, New ERA and ICF International. 2017. *Nepal Demographic and Health Survey 2016*. Kathmandu: Ministry of Health Nepal.

National Institute of Population Research and Training (NIPORT) and ICF International. 2020. *Bangladesh Demographic and Health Survey 2017–18*. Dhaka: National Institute of Population Research and Training and Fairfax, VA: ICF International.

National Institute of Population Studies (NIPS) Pakistan and ICF International. 2019. *Pakistan Demographic and Health Survey 2017–18*. Islamabad: National Institute of Population Studies and Fairfax, VA: ICF International.

National Population and Family Planning Board, Statistical Indonesia, Ministry of Health Kemenkes and ICF International. 2018. *Indonesia Demographic and Health Survey 2017*. Fairfax, VA: ICF International. dhsprogram.com/pubs/pdf/FR342/FR342.pdf.

Philippine Statistics Authority (PSA) and ICF International. 2018. *Philippines National Demographic and Health Survey 2017*. Fairfax, VA: ICF International.

Sabharwal, G. 2020. 'Thailand's COVID-19 Response an Example of Resilience and Solidarity'. *UN News*, 4 August. news.un.org/en/story/2020/08/1069191.

Silwal, A. R., Engilbertsdottir, S., Cuesta, J., Newhouse, D. and Stewart, D. 2017. 'Estimate of Children in Monetary Poverty: An Update'. The World Bank Group, Washington, DC. documents1.worldbank.org/curated/en/966791603123453576/pdf/Global-Estimate-of-Children-in-Monetary-Poverty-An-Update.pdf.

UN Women. 2020a. 'COVID-19 and Its Economic Toll on Women: The Story Behind the Numbers'. UN Women, New York. unwomen.org/en/news/stories/2020/9/feature-covid-19-economic-impacts-on-women.

———. 2020b. 'The Shadow Pandemic: Violence Against Women During COVID-19'. UN Women, New York. unwomen.org/en/news/in-focus/in-focus-gender-equality-in-covid-19-response/violence-against-women-during-covid-19.

United Nations Children's Fund (UNICEF). 2020a. *Ending Child Marriage: A Profile of Progress in Bangladesh.* New York: United Nations Children's Fund.

———. 2020b. 'Millions of Pregnant Mothers and Babies Born During COVID-19 Pandemic Threatened by Strained Health Systems and Disruptions in Services'. United Nations Children's Fund, New York. unicef.org/rosa/press-releases/millions-pregnant-mothers-and-babies-born-during-covid-19-pandemic-threatened.

———. 2021. *Progress towards UNICEF South Asia's Headline and Complementary Results (2018–2021).* New York: United Nations Children's Fund. unicef.org/rosa/media/10671/file/Progress%20towards%20UNICEF%20South%20Asia%E2%80%99s%20Headline%20and%20Complementary%20Results%20(2018%E2%80%932021).pdf.

United Nations Development Programme (UNDP). 1994. *Human Development Report 1994.* New York: United Nations Development Programme. hdr.undp.org/en/content/human-development-report-1994.

———. 2020a. 2020 *Human Development Perspectives, COVID-19 and Human Development: Assessing the Crisis, Envisioning the Recovery.* New York: United Nations Development Programme. hdr.undp.org/sites/default/files/covid-19_and_human_development_0.pdf.

———. 2020b. *Synthesis of Socioeconomic Impact Assessments (SEIAs) of COVID-19 in Asia Pacific.* New York: United Nations Development Programme.

———. 2020c. The Social and Economic Impact of Covid-19 in the Asia-Pacific Region. New York: United Nations Development Programme. undp.org/content/undp/en/home/librarypage/crisis-prevention-and-recovery/the-social-and-economic-impact-of-covid-19-in-asia-pacific.html.

———. 2020d. 'Human Development Data Center'. United Nations Development Programme, New York. hdr.undp.org/en/data.

United Nations Economic and Social Commission for Asia and the Pacific (UNESCAP). 2017. *Sustainable Social Development in Asia and the Pacific: Towards a People-Centred Transformation.* Bangkok: United Nations Economic and Social Commission for Asia and the Pacific. unescap.org/sites/default/files/publications/Sustainable%20Social%20Development%20in%20A-P.pdf.

United Nations Economic and Social Commission for Asia and the Pacific (UNESCAP) and International Labour Organization (ILO). 2021. *The Protection We Want: Social Outlook for Asia and the Pacific.* Bangkok: United Nations Economic and Social Commission for Asia and the Pacific. unescap.org/sites/default/d8files/knowledge-products/Social_Outlook_Report_v10.pdf.

United Nations Educational, Scientific and Cultural Organization (UNESCO). 2020. '"Half of World's Student Population Not Attending School". UNESCO Launches Global Coalition to Accelerate Deployment of Remote Learning Solutions'. United Nations Educational, Scientific and Cultural Organization, New York. en.unesco.org/news/half-worlds-student-population-not-attending-school-unesco-launches-global-coalition-accelerate.

Van Tan, L. 2021. 'COVID-19 Control in Vietnam'. *Nature Immunology*, 22(261). doi. org/10.1038/s41590-021-00882-9.

Wenham, C., Smith, J. and Morgan, R. 2020. 'COVID-19: The Gendered Impacts of the Outbreak'. *The Lancet*, 6 March. doi.org/10.1016/S0140-6736(20)30526-2.

Woetzel, J., Madgavkar, A., Ellingrud, K., Labaye, E., Devillard, S., Kutcher, E., Manyika, J., Dobbs, R. and Krishnan, M. 2015. *Power of Parity: How Advancing Women's Equality Can Add $12 Trillion to Global Growth*. Chicago, IL: McKinsey & Company. mckinsey. com/featured-insights/employment-and-growth/how-advancing-womens-equality-can-add-12-trillion-to-global-growth#.

World Bank. 2020a. *East Asia and Pacific in the Time of COVID-19: Overview*. Washington, DC: The World Bank Group. openknowledge.worldbank.org/bitstream/handle/10986/33477/211565ov.pdf?sequence=26&isAllowed=y.

———. 2020b. *Beaten or Broken? Informality and COVID-19*. Washington, DC: The World Bank Group. openknowledge.worldbank.org/bitstream/handle/10986/34517/9781464816406.pdf.

———. 2021. 'World Bank Country and Lending Groups'. The World Bank Group, Washington, DC. datahelpdesk.worldbank.org/knowledgebase/articles/906519-world-bank-country-and-lending-groups.

World Health Organization (WHO). 1978. 'Declaration of Alma Ata: The International Conference on Primary Healthcare'. World Health Organization, Geneva. euro.who. int/__data/assets/pdf_file/0009/113877/E93944.pdf.

———. 2021a. 'Global Health Expenditure Database'. World Health Organization, Geneva. apps.who.int/nha/database/Select/Indicators/en.

———. 2021b. 'WHO Coronavirus (COVID-19) Dashboard'. World Health Organization, Geneva. covid19.who.int/.

Yong, E. 2020. 'Where Year Two of the Pandemic Will Take Us'. *The Atlantic*, 29 December. theatlantic.com/health/archive/2020/12/pandemic-year-two/617528/.

9 | Making COVID-19 Vaccines Universally Accessible

Partha Mukhopadhyay

> Of all the products in the world you don't want to use market-based prioritization, it's gotta be vaccines.
>
> —Bill Gates (*Financial Times*, 2021)

INTRODUCTION

Sometime in the first week of February 2021, the global number of vaccinations exceeded the number of identified cases of COVID-19. As of this writing (13 March 2021), the number of cases has passed 118 million, while the number of vaccine doses administered exceeds 345 million. On average, the daily recorded global cases tally around 400,000, and each day also sees more than 8 million vaccine doses administered – a ratio of 20:1. However, 90 per cent of these vaccinations took place in only 11 countries – almost three-fourths of which in the United States, European Union (EU), United Kingdom, China and India, although, the first batch of supplies from the COVID-19 Vaccines Global Access (COVAX) have also arrived in Ghana and Cote-d'Ivoire (WHO, 2021d; *Bloomberg*, 2021).[1]

This journey is only one-year old. In March 2020, Yan et.al (2020) published an article detailing the interaction between the now famous spike protein of the SARS-CoV-2 virus and the ACE 2 receptor in human cells to which it binds – the expression of COVID-19 infection at the molecular level. Most of the vaccines now being developed, especially the mRNA and protein antigen viruses, aim to prevent this binding from taking place. The ability to move from a molecular understanding of the virus infection to multiple vaccines in less than nine months is an exceptional affirmation of human ingenuity.

Not all the news is good, however. The case fatality rate (CFR) for February 2021 was about 2.8 per cent, much higher than the cumulative CFR of around 2.2 per cent, although the CFR returned to the average level in March 2021. Also, the progress of vaccination appears very inequitable. Figure 9.1 shows the relationship of deaths normalized as a share of the urban population over age 65 to doses administered as a share of the urban population. A large number of countries that have high death rates have yet to vaccinate a discernible proportion of their populations, while the first countries to begin mass-scale vaccination programmes, such as the United States and United Kingdom, have gone far ahead. Yet both these countries and some European nations remain the most in need, as measured by current fatalities, represented by square markers. So, while one must try to rectify the situation in the high-death/low- or zero-vaccination countries, this cannot divert supplies from the high-death countries. Indeed, given the logistics infrastructure and the health

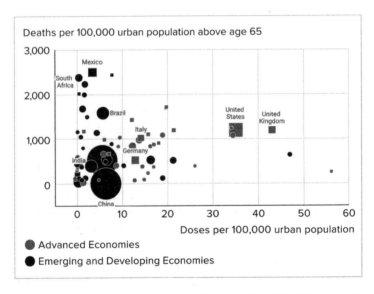

Figure 9.1 Vaccine doses administered and fatalities from COVID-19, as of 10 March 2021

Sources: Our World in Data (2021); World Bank (2019).

Note: The size of the markers refers to population. Square markers indicate a country in the top quartile of deaths per 100,000 urban population aged over 65 in 2021. For countries with zero vaccinations, only those with a death rate (as defined here) above 100 are included. United Arab Emirates and Israel, which have vaccinated the highest proportions of their population, do not appear in order to keep the scale of the others discernible.

systems in some of these countries, one might question the feasibility of their rolling out the mRNA vaccines currently in use in the United Kingdom and the United States.[2] Fortunately, many more suitable vaccine options have become available, with others on the way, as discussed later.

This chapter outlines the key challenges in making COVID-19 vaccines universally accessible, highlighting decisions that governments will need to make along the way. While a private individual good, the vaccine offers enormous potential positive externalities: decreases in virus transmission, risk of illness and fears of infection and death, and the consequent ability to return to pre-pandemic practices of living and economic production (Cakmakli et al., 2021). The scale of these potential benefits has led most governments to provide the vaccine as a free good. The world has the ability to produce and the capacity to pay for sufficient vaccines to vaccinate all the eligible persons on the planet. The challenge lies in the organization and implementation of such a global programme and, critically, in convincing people to get vaccinated.

This claim has the following premises: First, a number of vaccines are swiftly securing regulatory approval. Second, the production capacity across the varieties of vaccine currently or imminently in use appears sufficient to vaccinate the 5.8 billion people aged 16 years and older in the global population. Of these, about 1 billion reside in high-income countries. Of the population aged 65 or more, approximately 225.6 million live in 82 high-income countries, 286.2 million in 56 upper-middle-income countries, 164.3 million in 50 lower-middle-income countries, and just 21.9 million in 29 low-income countries (of which 23 are in sub-Saharan Africa). Box 9.1 shows that a relatively small number of vaccines can help vaccinate the vulnerable in poorer and smaller countries. Third, the logistics infrastructure has the capacity to transport the vaccines to delivery points – especially now that only one vaccine requires an ultra-cold chain (see note 1), other vaccines can be transported and stored under normal refrigeration. Fourth, on the demand side, vaccines have become available at various price points and they appear broadly affordable for public procurement, even for lower-income countries, especially with support from initiatives such as the COVAX Advance Market Commitment (AMC). Where offered for private sale, the indicative prices remain affordable for some segments of the population. Fifth, a large segment of the world population will certainly agree to get vaccinated. However, as of now, an unacceptably large cohort may prove unwilling to do so. As long as a sufficiently large pool of unvaccinated people exists, the virus will have a human reservoir (and non-human reservoirs) to draw upon. The challenge would then include convincing the doubters, but also considering policy options if persuasion fails.

Box 9.1   Vaccinating the elderly in poorer and smaller countries

The 29 low-income countries (of which 23 in sub-Saharan Africa) have a combined elderly (over 65) population of less than 22 million; only Ethiopia, Democratic Republic of the Congo and Sudan, and possibly Afghanistan, have more than 1 million people aged over 65. Ensuring that these countries receive sufficient vaccines for their elderly population should therefore not prove difficult. Just 1 million doses of a single-dose vaccine, such as that of Johnson and Johnson (Janssen), would suffice to vaccinate the entire elderly population of 41 small countries that have fewer than 1 million inhabitants. A broader group of small countries below 10 million in population accounts for only 4.5 per cent of global population but 8 per cent of the world's cases; their disease burden runs substantially higher than the global average. They also find it difficult to negotiate with vaccine manufacturers, which prioritize the larger countries with more demand. This discrepancy became one of the rationales underpinning COVAX. Protecting the vulnerable in the smaller countries thus appears eminently feasible within a relatively short time. Indeed, the COVAX allocations through May 2021, released in early March, would – if fulfilled – suffice to vaccinate all vulnerable elderly people in 82 countries (Appendix 9A.1).[3]

SUPPLY CONSIDERATIONS AND CONSTRAINTS

Regulatory approval

Regardless of vaccine availability, most countries require regulatory approval prior to their purchase and use. While countries such as the United States and United Kingdom have placed orders conditional on regulatory approval, leaving them with a possible oversupply of committed vaccines, other countries have shown more reticence (Wintour, 2021). Indeed, one could argue that even the EU, acting on behalf of sovereign governments, may have shown excessive caution (*Deutsche Welle*, 2021; Davies, 2021). However, at present, a number of vaccines have secured regulatory approval in different countries, and the World Health Organization (WHO) has also granted an emergency use listing to three vaccines as of 13 March 2021: Pfizer-BioNTech (mRNA), AstraZeneca Oxford & Serum Institute of India (viral vector) and single-dose Janssen (viral vector). Six more are in the pipeline for approval by April 2021, including Moderna (mRNA) and Novavax (protein subunit) from the United States,[4] Sputnik V (viral vector) from Russia, and CanSino (single-dose viral vector), Sinopharm and Sinovac (both inactivated virus) from China. In addition, India has already begun using its domestically developed vaccine, Covaxin (inactivated virus), even though only interim (albeit positive) Phase 3 results are available (Bharat Biotech, 2021).

Production capacity

Will sufficient production capacity be available? The answer seems affirmative over the course of 2021, especially as the number of approved vaccines grows, with another six candidates (in addition to those listed earlier) in Phase 3 trials and five in Phase 2/3 trials (WHO, 2021b). A number of manufacturers for the listed vaccines have made arrangements for producing large volumes, many of them in countries like India. An estimated 12 billion doses should become available by the end of the year, if all these plans are realized (Van Gogh et al., 2021).

Manufacturers also expect to build additional capacity going forward. For example, the United States International Development Finance Corporation (2021) recently announced support for the Indian manufacturer Biological E Ltd. in its effort to produce at least 1 billion doses by the end of 2022. This will include production of the Janssen vaccine, for which the firm already has an arrangement with Johnson and Johnson.[5] Many manufacturers have also collaborated with competitors to expand production capacity. For example, Sanofi, a large vaccine manufacturer without an existing approved vaccine candidate for COVID-19, has offered to help Pfizer-BioNTech and Johnson and Johnson expand capacity, as has Merck (Sagonowsky, 2021a; Sanofi, 2021; Brubaker, 2021). Countries, such as the United States, have invoked wartime legislation (Defense Production Act) to assist vaccine manufacturers in smoothing supply-chain problems (Lupkin, 2021).

In developing countries, Brazil will manufacture and/or 'fill and finish'[6] the Sputnik V, Sinopharm and AstraZeneca vaccines (Boadle, 2021). Thailand has signed a manufacturing agreement with AstraZeneca, and the United Arab Emirates with Sinopharm (Bio Spectrum, 2021; Elbahrawy, 2021). South Africa is seeking to manufacture domestically, as well (Thukwana, 2021). An effort has also begun in the World Trade Organization (WTO) to suspend intellectual property (IP) rights protection for the duration of the pandemic, in order to expand manufacturing capacity in less-developed countries (Quinn, 2021).

From the point of view of a country that does not manufacture vaccines, these plans remain a variable outside its control, although sufficient options should become available within the year for physical production capacity to prove less of a binding constraint. Note that these vaccine options do not equate to shots in arms, because inoculation requires separate procurement, logistics and delivery.

However, international organizations may find possible points of intervention, such as the initiative under consideration at the WTO. Other barriers may arise through export limitations of essential inputs that prevent expansion of global capacity, as a country seeks to insure domestic production capacity against input bottlenecks, such as supplies of giant plastic bags used in bioreactors (Kansteiner, 2021; Kuchler and Miller, 2021). The good offices of international organizations could help mitigate these problems.

Some other caveats may also be in order. First, as with materials, so with vaccines. Manufacturers may commit themselves to supply particular governments, either in their host country or because of contractual commitments. The chief executive of Serum Institute of India (SII), the firm manufacturing AstraZeneca vaccines in India, recently announced that the firm had been "directed to prioritize the huge needs of India and along with that, balance the needs of the rest of the world".[7] Concomitantly, however, 600,000 doses of vaccine from the firm arrived in Ghana as the first African delivery from the COVAX initiative.[8] SII production accounts for a significant part of COVAX's global supply (WHO, 2021c) and COVAX has announced that deliveries of vaccines produced by SII will face delays due to a new wave of COVID-19 infections in India (WHO, 2021f). This is noteworthy because AstraZeneca's is also the least expensive vaccine – reportedly US$3 a dose, according to GAVI (n.d.) – thereby reducing the funding needed for COVAX. Similarly, in an abundance of caution, the United States is holding on to its stock of AstraZeneca vaccines, although it has yet to authorize it for use; given the recent authorization of the Janssen vaccine, the United States may never need AstraZeneca's vaccine (Wingrove and Ring, 2021).

Second, vaccine policy changes in one country could affect other countries significantly. On 21 April 2021 the Government of India announced that it would expand vaccination to 18–45-year-olds (MoHFW, 2021), leading to increased demand from India and possibly a reduction in international supplies from manufacturers based in India over the medium-term. Third, significant differences in productivity may occur across sites, especially in the initial stages. The yield of biological manufacturing processes more closely resembles the yield from planting, rather than a predictable chemical reaction. Already, production problems have led to friction between AstraZeneca and the EU on meeting supply commitments (Guarascio, 2021).

Price

On the issue of price, at least two vaccines with relatively large production capacities – namely AstraZeneca and Janssen – seem to cost less than or equal to $10 a person (Table 9.1). Prices vary by country and buyer: Sinovac reportedly costs $106 in Thailand, AstraZeneca $14 in Uganda, and Sinopharm $36 in Hungary (Setboonsarng, 2021; Nakkazi, 2021; Vaski, 2021). One of the major issues of universal access is the variance in prices and the secrecy associated with the contracts between manufacturers and countries. Even the prices paid by COVAX have remained confidential, with its chief executive stating: "In terms of the individual agreements with manufacturers, that is proprietary information and not something that we're planning on sharing, given the nature of those types of commercial and legal agreements" (Beaubien, 2021). In addition to price, there may be other non-price conditions that add to cost, of which the most important is indemnity of the manufacturer, which can involve protracted negotiations (Box 9.2).

Table 9.1 How much do vaccines cost?

Vaccine	Platform	Price (US$)
Two-dose vaccines		$ per person
Pfizer-BioNTech	mRNA	38
Moderna	mRNA	30 to 74
Gamaleya (Sputnik V)	viral vector	20
Oxford/AstraZeneca-Serum Institute of India	viral vector	4 to 14
Sinopharm and Sinovac	inactivated virus	61 (RMB 200)
Novavax	protein subunit	32
Bharat Biotech (Covaxin)	inactivated virus	8
One-dose vaccines		$ per person
Janssen (Johnson and Johnson)	viral vector	8.5
CanSino	viral vector	3 to 4

Sources: Sagonowsky (2021b); *The Guardian* (2020); Junaidi and Azeem (2021); *Global Times* (2020); Hooker and Palumbo (2020); PIB Mumbai (2021).

Box 9.2   Indemnity for vaccine manufacturers

In addition to price, vaccine makers usually seek protection from damages as part of their supply agreements. Most governments offer indemnity, meaning if a citizen wins a claim against a vaccine company, the government will bear the cost. This offers protection against very rare adverse effects that may only emerge once millions of people have been vaccinated. Authorizing a vaccine is a judgment call by the government, which thereby agrees to bear the consequences. COVAX also requires that recipient governments offer such indemnification to the vaccine manufacturer, and has negotiated indemnification agreements for this purpose. However, some firms have reportedly asked for additional indemnity beyond rare adverse effects, such as from manufacturing defects, and have requested new legislation and physical collateral such as government buildings and other assets, even in countries that have hosted Phase 3 trials for the vaccine (Davies et al., 2021). Navigating and negotiating such legal terrain can delay or impede universal access to vaccines.

Affordability

One can analyse affordability from both the private and public perspective. Table 9.2 examines vaccine affordability at a cost of $10 per person, as measured in terms of the share of government expenditure and of per capita public health expenditure. For all but four countries, the additional expenditure on vaccination is less than 5 per cent

Table 9.2 Public affordability of the cost of vaccines in select Asian countries, as of March 2021

Country	Cases	Deaths	Case fatality rate	Population (million)	Death per mn	Cases per mn	Government final consumption expenditure ($ bn)	Vaccine cost at $10* per person ($ bn)	Vaccine cost as share of government expenditure	Per capita government health expenditure (PCGHE) $	Increase in PCGHE at $10 per person
Afghanistan	47,516	1900	4.00%	38.9	48.8	1221	2.51	0.39	15.50%	3.4	294.12%
Bangladesh	479,743	6874	1.40%	164.7	41.7	2913	17.42	1.65	9.45%	6.1	163.93%
Bhutan	432		0.00%	0.8	-	560	0.42	0.01	1.90%	72.1	13.87%
Brunei	151	3	2.00%	0.4	6.9	345	3.28	0.004	0.12%	636.7	1.57%
Cambodia	350		0.00%	16.7	-	21	1.21	0.17	13.80%	19.5	51.28%
China	93,670	4746	5.10%	1439.3	3.3	65	2297.62	14.39	0.63%	249.8	4.00%
India	9,703,770	140,958	1.50%	1380	102.1	7032	300.94	13.80	4.59%	18.8	53.19%
Indonesia	581,550	17867	3.10%	273.5	65.3	2126	93.88	2.74	2.91%	55.6	17.99%
Lao PDR	41		0.00%	7.3	-	6	2.21	0.07	3.30%	21.8	45.87%
Malaysia	74,294	384	0.50%	32.4	11.9	2295	42.86	0.32	0.76%	194.3	5.15%
Myanmar	100,431	2132	2.10%	54.4	39.2	1846	13.94	0.54	3.90%	8.6	116.28%
Nepal	241,995	1614	0.70%	29.1	55.4	8305	3.39	0.29	8.58%	10.7	93.46%
Pakistan	423,179	8487	2.00%	220.9	38.4	1916	36.85	2.21	5.99%	14.1	70.92%

Philippines	441,399	8572	1.90%	109.6	78.2	4028	41.77	1.10	2.62%	42.4	23.58%
Rep. of Korea	38755	552	1.40%	51.3	10.8	756	277.61	0.51	0.18%	1310	0.76%
Singapore	58,273	29	0.00%	5.9	5	9961	37.51	0.06	0.16%	1262.3	0.79%
Sri Lanka	28,580	142	0.50%	21.4	6.6	1335	8.07	0.21	2.65%	68.5	14.60%
Thailand	4126	60	1.50%	69.8	0.9	59	81.81	0.70	0.85%	188.1	5.32%
Timor-Leste	31		0.00%	1.3	-	24	0.87	0.01	1.49%	54.9	18.21%
Viet Nam	1367	35	2.60%	97.3	0.4	14	15.87	0.97	6.13%	63	15.87%

Sources: (a) Cases, deaths and population as of 7 December 2020, Our World in Data (2021); (b) Government final consumption expenditure (current US$) as of 2018, World Bank WDI (2021); (c) PCGHE (current US$) as of 2017, World Bank WDI (2021).

Note: mn = million; bn = billion. *The estimate of $10 per person is based on two doses at a per dose cost of $3 for AstraZeneca and $2 for domestic distribution and international cargo.

of the government's final consumption expenditure, and for all but three of them, the increase in per capita government expenditure on health is less than 10 per cent.

From the point of view of global support, at this average $10 per person price, the COVAX AMC initiative should also be able to meet its 20 per cent target and perhaps expand it, even at current funding levels of $7.5 billion, with expected recipient country contributions (Prime Minister's Office, Govt. of United Kingdom, 2021). Individual countries have set aside significant amounts in their government budgets. The Indian government, for example, has committed an amount close to $5 billion for the 2021 fiscal year.

In addition, one should expect private spending on vaccination since some countries may not offer the vaccine for free. To date, few countries, including India, have decided to charge for the vaccine, although the Philippines, Thailand and Pakistan seem to be moving in that direction.[9] A fuller discussion of this appears later. Using a measure of 1 per cent of median annual income, about 30 per cent of the global population falls below the affordability level (Figure 9.2). However, using the same 1 per cent cut-off point, large, if minority, segments of the population may be able to afford a vaccination cost of between $5 and $50 per person, especially in middle-income countries.

Logistics

The final aspect of supply – logistics – comprises three parts: first, the issue of a temperature-controlled delivery chain; second, the actual transportation of vaccines;

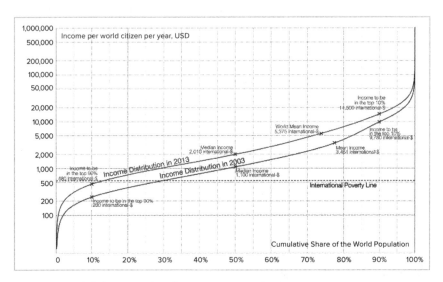

Figure 9.2   Global income distribution in 2003 and 2013
Sources: Hellebrandt and Mauro (2015); Roser (2021).

and third, the transportation of incidentals necessary for vaccination. Initial reports on requirements of mRNA vaccines made it appear that the temperature-controlled logistics chain would pose a near-insurmountable challenge in developing countries. However, recent developments in other newly available vaccines, as well as new information about the temperature requirements of both Pfizer-BioNTech and Moderna vaccines, offer positive news in this regard. It now appears that, although Pfizer-BioNTech does require ultra-cold-chain storage for the longer term, it can withstand storage for two weeks in normal food-grade freezers, such as frozen food or ice cream storage facilities, or even the freezer compartments of refrigerators. Similarly, the Moderna vaccine appears to allow storage in a normal refrigerator for up to 30 days (Kiefer, 2021). This indicates that these vaccines may work in developing-country conditions, especially in cities. The other vaccines in Table 9.1 all allow for normal refrigeration, although Sputnik requires food-grade refrigeration for reconstitution (it comes in a dry form). Therefore, the temperature control requirements for transportation and storage of vaccines now appears much more feasible.

On the second issue of vaccine transport, although some countries have established manufacturing facilities as noted earlier, there remains the daunting challenge of moving vaccines from limited production sites across the globe (mostly in India, China, Europe and the United States) to a vast number of countries that must distribute them within an acceptable time frame. Figure 9.3 illustrates the possible movements for such vaccines.

This may call for bringing in global cooperation and utilizing surplus airplane capacity currently lying idle due to limited international passenger traffic. One also needs to ensure security of supply chains to protect vaccines from diversion or substitution. The less scarce the supply, the less the likelihood of such security threats.

A more voluminous challenge, though one lacking the cold-chain issues, is that of supplying complementary items needed for vaccination: Personal protection equipment (PPE), syringes, gloves, needles and post-vaccination disposal arrangements for these items and for the used vials.

DECISIONS UNDERLYING DEMAND

The demand for vaccines thus far has come from national governments. Indeed, vaccine manufacturers have been reluctant to deal with entities other than national governments, which, in turn, have generally not allowed sub-national governments to transact directly with vaccine producers (Higgins, 2021). This may change if private involvement increases. At this time, when many countries are scrambling for any vaccines at all, it may seem premature to think about procurement choices that governments need to make while deciding among vaccines. But, given

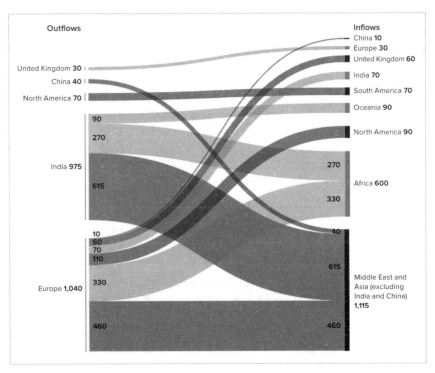

Figure 9.3 COVID-19 vaccine flows from producing to consuming countries (millions of doses)
Source: Van Gogh et al. (2021).

the growing number of available options, this will soon become an important consideration.

Authorization

The first decision for governments is accepting or rejecting applications for vaccine authorization. This decision rests on the vaccine candidate's safety, immunogenicity and efficacy (Appendix 9A.2). At present, the WHO has advised an absolute (rather than relative) benchmark of 50 per cent efficacy, with proven safety and immunogenicity. But the efficacy across vaccines and trials may vary for a number of reasons unrelated to the underlying efficacy of the vaccine (Box 9.3). Without effective communication of the reasons for such differences, this lack of uniformity adds to confusion around the regulatory approval for vaccines – leading some people, in Europe, for example, to refuse to take the AstraZeneca vaccine on offer and instead demand the Pfizer-BioNTech vaccine (Kresge et al., 2021).

Frequently, the information needed for this decision has either remained unavailable or is not transparent and commensurate. For example, since China's vaccines could not undergo Phase 3 trials in China due to the paucity of cases, the trials took place in other countries, including Brazil, United Arab Emirates, Pakistan and others. The information from such Phase 3 trials has not come together in an organized manner and has limited comparability across these countries, given that infection patterns and the nature of the virus varies from one to another. Similarly, India authorized Covaxin for emergency use "in clinical trial mode" in early January 2021, even with the Phase 3 trials still in progress. Subsequently, India removed the clinical trial mode restriction in early March, after the manufacturer submitted promising but interim Phase 3 results (*The Wire*, 2021). The AstraZeneca vaccine – granted emergency use listing by the WHO, comprises the mainstay of COVAX, and is currently in extensive use in India, the United Kingdom and Europe – has yet to gain authorization in the United States, where the Food and Drug Administration (FDA) awaits submissions from an ongoing Phase 3 domestic trial.

Single- or two-dose

For governments, the next key choice is between a single- or a two-dose vaccine. From the point of view of delivery logistics, even when a two-dose vaccine costs less per person than a single-dose one (two doses of AstraZeneca cost around $6, compared to a single dose of Janssen at $10), the complication of administering two doses might outweigh the additional base cost. Flexibility in the interval between doses can mitigate this. Instead of having to ensure that the vaccinated person receives the second dose at a precise interval after the first, a relatively long interval now appears possible – 4 to 6 weeks according to the WHO, up to 12 weeks in the United Kingdom and up to four months in Canada (Gillies, 2021) – which enhances the feasibility of vaccination in developing countries. Where the single-dose vaccine costs less than a two-dose option (Janssen is less expensive per person than any other two-dose vaccine except AstraZeneca), it will likely receive preference, subject to availability.

However, there are only two single-dose vaccines currently in use: the Chinese CanSino vaccine, used in Mexico and expected to expand to Pakistan (which recently reported Phase 3 trial results); and the Janssen vaccine, granted emergency use listing by the WHO. Although Janssen contracted with the United States for its initial dose rollout, its production capacity has rapidly expanded and may reach 1 billion within the year. CanSino has the capacity to produce 500 million doses, as well (Wei, 2021). Depending on their availability, each country must choose the quantity and timing of purchase for single- and two-dose vaccines.

Dosing schedule for two-dose vaccines[10]

A third and related choice concerns the schedules between different doses, which currently vary greatly between Europe, the United Kingdom and the United States.

In Europe, the regulator has recommended a three-week interval between the doses of Pfizer-BioNTech's Comirnaty vaccine, but individual countries may make different decisions.[11] The United Kingdom, on the other hand, has allowed up to 12 weeks for the administration of the second dose for both the Pfizer-BioNTech and AstraZeneca vaccines, even though the Pfizer–BioNTech Phase 3 trial did not feature a 12-week interval. The United States has retained the relatively strict adherence to the interval between doses used during the Phase 3 trial, although some immunologists have pushed for a longer interval (Plotkin and Halsey, 2021). This kind of major difference becomes difficult to interpret – especially with relatively little public communication to clarify it, apart from reassurances that justified the decisions in the respective countries. In the United Kingdom, practising doctors (GPs) initially pushed back against the extended dosing schedule and in response, a number of immunologists tried to justify the decision; in the United States, some immunologists have also suggested an extended dosing schedule. One advantage of so-called latecomer countries is that they have more evidence to evaluate the arguments on both sides of the debate, and decide accordingly on the appropriate strategy.

The trade-offs in this appear relatively well-defined. Even without vaccine scarcity, if the initial vaccination offers a high degree of protection for an extended period, with the second dose adding relatively little, then it would seem reasonable to maximize the percentage of the population receiving the first dose, so as to spread out a relatively high degree of immunity among the largest number as quickly as possible. If, on the other hand, the first dose did not offer a very high degree of protection, and if that protection lasted a relatively short time, then it may make sense to ensure giving the second dose as soon after eligibility as possible – unless, as appears the case with AstraZeneca, increasing the interval between doses raises the effectiveness of the second one. In this context, it is important to point out that the degree of protection or efficacy of the vaccine is difficult to measure in a comparable manner across vaccines and trials for a variety of reasons (see Box 9.3).

Duration of protection

Information remains scarce on the length of immunity, but it seems clear that cell-mediated immunity, that is, the body's ability to retain memory of the infection/immunization, may continue even if the levels of antibody in the blood (humoral immunity) decline over time (Sette and Crotty, 2021). Immunologists appear to agree that the human body does respond to longer intervals between doses, a finding also supported by the dosing schedule of vaccines other than those against SARS-CoV-2. However, response to infection based on memory in the T-cells could induce a mild infection before the body could prepare itself to respond effectively to the virus.

In this context, recent results indicate that a single standard dose of the AstraZeneca vaccine provided 76 per cent protection, which is very high among

---

Box 9.3   Comparing efficacy across vaccines

The media often highlight differences in efficacy among vaccines. However, these differences may arise from differences in trials as well in vaccines. Some causes of trial variation include:

(a) Different definitions of illness: Most trials only check for symptomatic infections, but some, such as the Sinopharm trial in Brazil, also check for mild or asymptomatic infections, which requires frequent testing. The Sinopharm vaccine in Brazil was only 50.4 per cent effective when measured for mild infections, but 78 per cent effective when measured for illness requiring medical attention (not necessarily hospitalization). In the trial, seven infections requiring medical attention occurred among 4,653 vaccinated and 31 in 4,599 unvaccinated. Including mild infections, however, 78 additional cases occurred in the vaccinated group (for a total of 85) and 136 more in the placebo group (a total of 167).[12]

(b) The nature of the virus can differ depending on the time and place of the trial. For example, for the Janssen vaccine, the "level of protection against moderate to severe COVID-19 infection was 72 percent in the United States, 66 percent in Latin America and 57 percent in South Africa, 28 days post-vaccination", possibly due to the presence of variant strains in Brazil (P.1) and South Africa (B.1.351) that may have affected the immune response (Johnson & Johnson, 2021).

(c) The age-structure and gender composition of the volunteers in the trial, such as more elderly men, may push the number of severe cases higher; ergo, such participant factors may influence results (Global Health 5050, 2021).

(d) The quality of the trial: The AstraZeneca trial had considerable variation in the dosing and the interval between doses. This proved fortuitous in this case, as it later gave the basis for justifying the 12-week gap between doses in the United Kingdom, but uniformity is generally associated with better quality trials.

(e) The underlying efficacy of the vaccine: Some may simply prove better than others.

---

current (not just COVID-19) vaccines, against primary symptomatic illness 22 to 90 days after inoculation. However, the efficacy appears to drop after 90 days, and the vaccine did not provide protection against asymptomatic infection in the same period, although the sample size was very small (Voysey et al., 2021).

Transmission

The evidence to date on the degree of protection from disease transmission provided by vaccines remains inconclusive and continues to evolve. One can surmise that if vaccines cannot prevent mild or moderate infection, they may also be unable to prevent transmission; but the evidence emerging from countries such as Israel and the United Kingdom indicates that vaccines may slow transmission by, inter alia, reducing the viral load in patients (Appendix 9A.3) (Mallapaty, 2021). A second dose appears to support an increased ability to prevent transmission (Lovett, 2021), although this aspect also appears more complex with the Delta variant's increased transmissibility.

Dosing schedule and hoarding

The adoption of a single- or two-dose schedule, along with a flexible dose interval, will also affect the number of doses that authorities hoard in order to ensure the availability of the second dose. Under normal circumstances, with no expected supply disruptions, there would be no reason for holding vaccines. Under the current circumstances, however, public health authorities may deem it prudent to hold some doses as insurance against supply failures, even in countries such as the United States (LaFraniere et al., 2021). This hoarding becomes unhelpful in the event that supply disruptions do not occur, because it reduces the number of people who receive the first dose. With a single dose, there is no need to hoard. A flexible dose interval may also mitigate hoarding incentives, since dispensing authorities can manage temporary supply disruptions by altering the date of the second dose or even consider doing away with the second dose altogether (Box 9.4).

Box 9.4   Can two-dose vaccines be used as single-dose vaccines?

Another somewhat radical possibility has emerged: that current vaccines approved as two-dose vaccines may actually confer substantial protection when used as single doses. However, many unknowns remain on this score – critically, the length of protection afforded by the single dose. In ordinary times, no advanced country would contemplate the use of a single-dose regimen for a vaccine approved as a two-dose vaccine. However, the imperative of the pandemic and the growing need to provide protection, even if partial, to as large number of people as possible, as quickly as possible, has led countries, such as the United Kingdom, to go ahead with dosing schedules substantially different from the Phase 3 trials. In the United States, although the FDA has not followed the United Kingdom's precedent, respected experts in the field have also suggested an extended dosing schedule, so as to accelerate the number of people who would receive at least partial protection from infection from the first dose as early as possible. The data appear to support a relatively high extent of protection from this practice, which may make it possible to consider these vaccines as single-dose vaccines without the booster shot, if the extent of protection proves long-lasting enough.

In such a situation, the number of vaccines classifiable and usable as single-dose vaccines would increase considerably. This would reduce the cost of vaccination, making it more feasible and also retaining the option of a later booster dose with a modified vaccine designed to be more effective against variants. Survey evidence in the United States also indicates that a single dose may also induce some of the currently sceptical to agree to vaccination (Hamel et al., 2021).

To sum up, the evidence remains relatively sparse but appears to indicate that the first dose confers a reasonably high degree of protection against severe disease, hospitalization and death, with less clear evidence on the extent of protection from mild to moderate disease. The duration of protection and extent of protection from variants remain less well-understood, and the second dose may also reduce transmission of infection. Thus, a country has to choose the dosing schedule to adopt for two-dose vaccines, with an evolving information base on which to base the decision.

Variants, old and new vaccines

A growing risk has appeared in the rapid spread of new mutations that allow the virus to escape immunity gained either from natural infection or from vaccination (Appendix 9A.3). It also appears that while one dose does not suffice to generate an antibody immunity against immune-escape variants even though it may generate sufficient cell-mediated immunity to avoid severe disease, a second dose does lead to a stronger antibody response to combat the infection and potentially work against such variants (Geddes, 2021). It may also turn out that traditional inactivated whole-virus vaccines, as compared to the newer mRNA and protein antigen vaccines that generate antibodies against specific antigens, such as the spike protein, may provide broader protection against variants. But these questions remain unresolved. In such a situation, rapid development of booster doses incorporating elements of the new variant seems feasible, especially for the mRNA, viral vector, and the protein antigen vaccine platforms, but this may involve considerable financial and logistical burdens. Boosters may become available as early as the summer of 2021.[13] However, demand for such new booster doses from countries that have had extensive vaccinations may affect production targeted for unvaccinated countries, and, as such, might slow down the global process of vaccination. Such a situation calls for collective action to reduce our collective risk. The question becomes the following:

> Should governments delay pursuing approximately 80 per cent protection against severe COVID-19 for unvaccinated populations in order to permit an approximately 30 per cent increase in protection against mild COVID-19 among the already vaccinated? This assumes a diversion of manufacturing capacity toward booster doses. Note that this also increases the probability of newer variants in unvaccinated populations.

A radical choice for governments would be to wait for newer, improved versions of vaccines to commence vaccination, instead of using the existing vaccines that confer protection against severe infection. Governments would also need to adopt stronger border-control measures in terms of testing, quarantine, and so forth for arrivals from countries with variants. Governments could also decide to continue existing forms of non-pharmaceutical intervention, such as mask-wearing and physical distancing. This could work in countries where community infection is low and economic activity has returned to near-normal levels, albeit without international travel.

Vaccine hesitancy

Despite the best efforts of governments to make sensible choices, there remains a critical unknown: How many people will voluntarily accept vaccination? Sensible choices and transparent information-sharing by governments about their rationales can increase trust in vaccines among their citizens.

In recent times, vaccine hesitancy has appeared as a growing phenomenon (Lazarus et al., 2021). Surveys in several countries on COVID-19 vaccines have found that the population falls into three main groups: those who will take the vaccine as soon as it is available; those who will wait and see and then decide whether to take it; and people who say they will not take the vaccine. The proclivity towards vaccines varies in different ways across countries. In some countries with more politicized responses to the pandemic, it reflects the political polarization of that nation (Owens, 2021; Verma et al., 2021). Other countries, such as France, Japan and the Philippines, have had historically high levels of hesitancy, often linked to specific incidents (Du and Huang, 2020; Alfonso et al., 2021; Vignaud, 2021). But these are not immutable categories. Over time, as the pandemic accelerated and as vaccines became less hypothetical and more imminent, the extent of vaccine hesitancy declined.[14] However, in countries that have had more effective pandemic management, the inclination towards vaccination may remain low, since fewer people have experienced adverse effects. China could become one such example, as could Australia (Standaert, 2021; Biddle et al., 2021). In countries not extensively affected by the pandemic, hesitancy opens up an immunity gap, leaving them more vulnerable.

Concerns include the process through which the vaccine development occurred; the speed and manner of vaccine approval in some countries; the nature of the mRNA vaccine, which 'persuades' the body to make the requisite protein, which raises misplaced fears in some that it might change the body's genetic code; and the lack of previous vaccines on similar platforms. It has become the norm to expect a broadly similar process for vaccine approval and administration among developed countries. However, the marked differences observed across countries in this pandemic may mean that those with some education tend more towards hesitancy, even if this declines with higher education (Lew, 2021; Hamel et al., 2021). In India, healthcare and frontline workers in many states have been slow to take up the vaccine, and even the second dose if they have received the first dose; a third of younger military personnel in the United States have declined vaccination altogether

(Steinhauer, 2021).[15] A major challenge for all governments is convincing citizens to seek vaccination, sometimes using both carrots and sticks (Box 9.5). Vaccine hesitancy can also be enhanced by reports of adverse events following immunization (AEFI) that emerge during a large-scale vaccination exercise. For example, clotting incidents following vaccination by AstraZeneca and Janssen vaccines, which share the viral vector platform, is one such example (Quinn, 2021); even though the AEFI appears to have an incidence of one in a few hundred thousand vaccinations, it may deter people from getting vaccinated. Regulators have advised that both vaccines should now carry a warning indicating the low possibility of such clotting. In sum, vaccine hesitancy risks leading to large unvaccinated segments of populations, which creates a pool from which the virus can re-emerge.

Box 9.5   Penalties and rewards to promote vaccination

In Israel, at present the country with the largest vaccinated share of its population, people receive incentives to encourage them to accept vaccination. On the other hand, there have also been reports of penalties imposed on those who do not want the vaccine, such as suspending salaries of government workers, denying services to unvaccinated people, or levying fines upon them (Yoon, 2021; Reuters, 2021b). The effectiveness of such measures will depend on their impact on the 'wait and watch' group of people – will they turn into people willing to be vaccinated or become no longer willing at all? This group usually represents quite a large segment of the population – up to half – in many countries; as such, their mindset will determine the success or failure of the vaccination programme. Such stick-rather than-carrot initiatives may backfire, especially among those with low levels of trust in the government and the perception of such coercive measures as practices imposed by the government against the population's self-interest. It is not clear that the adoption of coercive measures will favourably influence the vaccine hesitant.

ADMINISTRATION OF THE VACCINE

Sequencing of vaccination

Almost all countries started with vaccinating health care workers and frontline workers, then moved to the elderly population and then to other age groups. However, Indonesia has adopted a strategy of vaccinating the more mobile young population first, on the grounds that they are more likely to transmit infection than an elderly population tending to remain relatively safe at home (Lane, 2021). This inversion of sequence, Indonesia argues, will allow for faster economic revival and thereby reduce the distress among the poorer segments of the population. This strategy presumes that vaccinations will lead to a significant effect on transmission, as discussed earlier; otherwise, this mobile population will continue to carry the virus to other more vulnerable segments. Moreover, only 6 per cent of the population is over 65 in Indonesia, while the share of those aged 15–64 runs to about two thirds.

Indeed, many developing countries around the world have relatively small numbers of older people as a proportion of the population. For the least-developed countries, the proportion of people over 65 is 3.6 per cent and that of people between 15 and 64 is about 57.3 per cent, with the rest younger than 15. In the initial stages of a vaccination programme, therefore, vaccinating the younger population poses the greater challenge.

The other factor to take into account is that vulnerability in terms of serious death or disease may vary across countries. For example, in India, 47 per cent of the deaths from confirmed cases have occurred among those under 60, while in Chile that figure is less than 13 per cent (*The Wire*, 2020; Undurraga et al., 2021). In terms of case fatality rate, the situation appears much starker. In Chile, the case fatality rate for those aged less than 60 is 0.5 per cent versus 16.1 per cent for those over 60. In India, for patients with co-morbidities, the case fatality rate is 8.8 per cent for those under 45 and 24.6 per cent for those over 60; for those without comorbidities the fatality rates are 0.2 per cent and 4.8 per cent respectively. Thus, in India, the decrease in vulnerability among younger people is less than in Chile.

Co-morbidity

In addition to age, a range of so-called 'co-morbidities' act as indicators of adverse outcomes – for example, hypertension and diabetes. In some countries with established universal healthcare systems, such as the United Kingdom and Israel, GPs (the first point of contact for most patients) and healthcare providers will have this information, and vaccine candidates can be prioritized accordingly. Countries that do not have such an established tradition may find it difficult to introduce this as a qualifying characteristic. India has tried to prioritize by requiring a registered medical practitioner to certify comorbidity,[16] but this may add to complexity and inequity, privileging the rich who have easier access to doctors and can afford to pay the fees for such a certification (Sheriff, 2021). If a country performs vaccination as part of a one-time health campaign, it may find it easier to use fewer characteristics to prioritize candidates, even in developed countries (Carlesso and Phaneuf, 2021). However, integrating this campaign into an established health system with an extensive history of engagement may allow for more fine-tuned sequencing in prioritizing specific categories.

Spatial sequencing

Large countries, however, also face the critical choice of geographical prioritization. Given limitations on how many vaccinations can take place within a given period of time – based on the availability of vaccinators, if not the availability of vaccines themselves – countries must decide which areas will receive vaccines first.

Should areas with a high incidence of cases go first because they pose the highest risk of infection? On the other hand, one could argue that such areas, usually large cities, tend to have inhabitants with relatively better personal resources, and may also have substantial immunity from undetected asymptomatic infections in the population, as evidenced by high sero-positivity in sample studies (Banaji, 2021; Muanya, 2021). Thus, areas that have not seen high infection so far, and often have concentrations of poorer inhabitants, should receive vaccination priority. Especially at present, if the pandemic appears spatially concentrated, as is the case in India and even internationally (Box 9.6), the use of geographical sequencing to prioritize vaccination becomes an important consideration. Indonesia is one country that has explicit provision to prioritize certain high-infection areas (Government of Indonesia, 2021). The government should evaluate the factors of age, co-morbidity, and the history and current extent of local infections in determining the sequence of vaccination.

Box 9.6   How should COVAX prioritize vaccine distribution?

The overall allocations of COVAX have been determined broadly in terms of population and allocation decisions are made keeping availability, readiness and representation in mind. This begs the question as to whether the sequencing should stay uniform across all regions or whether it should take into account the stage of the pandemic in different countries and prioritize accordingly. Should the higher numbers of cases and deaths in Latin America (at present) give that region greater consideration than Asia or Africa, which currently have lower numbers (barring a few instances)? Should less of the initial supply from COVAX go to poor countries, such as Ghana and Cote d'Ivoire, and more to richer but more afflicted countries, such as Mexico, which is currently dealing with a surge? Mexico would not get more than its quota in total, but would get it earlier, at a time when it is most needed. At this juncture, with the pandemic raging in some countries and quiet in others, could the COVAX stakeholders have a conversation on revisiting allocation principles?

Vaccine to the people or people to the vaccine?

In a situation where a substantial minority of people remain hesitant to take the vaccine, requiring them come to a potentially hard-to-reach vaccination centre imposes additional costs and may deter more people. At least one United States' state has offered vaccination to otherwise ineligible persons if they accompany an eligible (older than 75) close friend or family member to a centre (Barry, 2021). Would it be better to bring the vaccine to the people, by, for example, enabling vaccination at their familiar place of care, such as a neighbourhood doctor's office or pharmacy, even though door-to-door vaccination may prove impractical except in exceptional cases? This vaccination through proximity becomes much more feasible with extensive healthcare institutions that interface regularly with the community, as seen in the United Kingdom with its

National Health Service and GP delivery of vaccinations, as well as in Israel with its universal healthcare. However, with less-extensive interfaces between the population and health services, vaccination may call for dedicated touch points – a sort of pop-up vaccination centre in a fixed location, staffed from time to time but with hours limited by the availability of vaccinators (Box 9.7). Even the United Kingdom has now begun this practice (Haringey Council, 2021). Note that any strategy that does not imply vaccinating everyone in a certain locality means that the programme will not complete its work without multiple visits. Thus, such centres will have to 'pop up' multiple times if the government decides to vaccinate different segments of the population at different points in time, tilting the balance against multiple categories of people. This approach might also entail what we might call 'mop-up' vaccination centres that cater to those not vaccinated as part of the mainstream programme.

Box 9.7   Increasing vaccinator capacity

The availability of trained vaccinators creates a critical supply bottleneck in mass vaccination programmes. Could vaccinators be trained in a short period of time to serve large segments of the population? This entails much more than simply putting needles into arms, because these vaccines do not yet come in pre-filled syringes, as is usually the case. Given that it would take much longer to produce prefilled syringes with given vaccines, manufacturers have opted to produce multi-dose vials. However, this implies a more advanced level of vaccinator skill, including the ability to maintain an aseptic environment, practice in filling multiple doses from the same vial and discarding syringes and needles, as appropriate. Indeed, in the case of certain vaccines, such as those from Sputnik V and Pfizer-BioNTech, it also includes the complex process of preparing the vial, which may require thawing and then diluting before administration. These skills, and especially the awareness and ability to maintain safe practices, require time for inculcation, and therefore do not suit training within a very short time frame. Thus, the greater the use of freshly trained vaccinators, the greater the risk of gaps in these procedures. These gaps may have limited consequences in terms of not adequately protecting the vaccinated person from improper vaccine preparation or administration; in more extreme situations, they could lead to an adverse event for the recipient, such as sepsis. Any publicity, including on social media, surrounding such events, even if only anecdotal, could increase vaccine hesitancy in the population and therefore reduce the number of people willing to be vaccinated. The use of freshly trained vaccinators thus comes with a trade-off. It can increase the pace of vaccination but at the risk of increasing vaccine hesitancy. These risks will depend on the nature of the specific vaccine and the complexity of the process itself. The more complex the process, the higher these risks. Depending on the nature of the pandemic in a country, it may therefore prove safer to vaccinate over a longer time frame, with lower risk. Thus, there is no obvious correct choice for countries as to whether they should rapidly ramp up the number of vaccinators using modern training tools.

In the United States, the extremely decentralized nature of delivery has meant that individuals must try to make appointments at multiple delivery points – much like choosing the shortest queue out of the many checkout counters in front of you, with no guarantee that the counter will not close before you get to the head of the queue. The federal government has now initiated a consolidated informational website, but it too offers a two-step process, providing information about possible vaccination sites that reportedly have open slots available (Robbins and Stolberg, 2021). Therefore, booking a vaccination appointment is not easy (Buell, 2021). India, too, has adopted a web-based and app-based system to schedule appointments (Government of India, 2021); after initial hiccups, it seems to be functioning relatively well. This complicated and frustrating online process for seeking vaccination not only poses impediments for those still hesitating, it also excludes those uncomfortable with technology. However, in countries with relatively lesser vaccine supply problems, on-site registration can supplement the online service, thus allowing a substantial proportion of walk-ins at vaccination centres. In India, of the 132.9 million registered (who were not healthcare or frontline workers) for vaccination on the CoWin site (https://dashboard.cowin.gov.in/) as of 29 April 2021, 71 per cent (94.4 million) were walk-in (on-site) registrations.

Data and decentralization

The two-dose structure of most COVID-19 vaccines makes record-keeping an essential function of vaccination providers. The logistics of maintaining the records – who has received the first shot, how to ensure they receive the second – will pose one of the more complex administrative tasks of the vaccine rollout. One option, as currently attempted in India, would be a national digital app or website, where an individual can register and receive referral to a vaccination centre. This creates a national digital system that records every vaccinated person on a common database, with the app informing both the person and the vaccination system about when the first and second doses need to take place. This approach raises concerns connected to the digital divide and inability of vulnerable populations – older and less literate – to access and interface with digital devices. More relevantly, countries will have to decide their response if a person does not show up for the second vaccination. In India, many healthcare and frontline workers have missed their second dose, but as employees, they can be easily traced. If this phenomenon recurs in the general population, then the problem will become more severe.

Without a strong community link, keeping track of those needing second doses becomes a large-scale challenge. A more localized structure, with record-keeping handled at the community level along with responsibility for monitoring, search, and delivery, could offer an alternative or supplementary system. The local delivery organization could take responsibility for updating a common national information system recording such vaccinations (subject to audits), or the national system could share information with the local entities (subject to concerns regarding data privacy). That would enable local follow-up and delivery of the actual vaccination, especially the second dose; meanwhile, other levels of government responsible for procuring and distributing vaccines would also have visibility into the progress of the vaccination initiative, in order to, for example, determine how many vaccines to supply and in what time frame.

Such local community-level institutions could also help address vaccine hesitancy; research has found that people may prove more willing to trust local providers of information, such as the local doctor or a paramedic with whom the community engages on a regular basis, than common national-level messaging (Paterson et al., 2016).

Private vaccination

India was the first country to announce a widespread involvement of private hospitals in the vaccination delivery process, with a fixed but relatively small fee of $3.40 (Sheriff, 2021). This was not a scheme for the private procurement and delivery of vaccines. Rather, it aimed to expand the number of vaccination sites; the government supplies vaccines to the hospitals. Though the incentive for hospitals remains unclear, given the low margin, their participation has meant that 65 per cent of vaccinations initially occurred in the private sector.[17] Since a few months after their initial roll-out in mid-January 2021, however, the vaccinations have been overwhelmingly public, probably because they became free of cost for ever-larger groups of people (Radhakrishnan, 2021).

Hitherto, national governments have made all purchase decisions, although there have been reports of private firms procuring vaccines (Lopez and Reuters, 2021; Setboonsarng, 2021). This practice rests on the understanding of equity within nations and the buying power of nations as an aggregate to smaller sub-national entities. However, some countries have adopted a different path. Indonesia has started Vaksini Mandiri, a programme where the private sector can import vaccines through a central procurement agency, Bio Farma, to vaccinate its workers and family members, free or at a regulated price. Bio Farma has reportedly placed an order for 20 million vaccine doses (Reuters, 2021a; Dewi, 2021). The Philippines reportedly has a tripartite structure with a private-sector partner, local government and national government as part of the purchase process. Private firms can procure vaccines if they donate an equivalent number to the public vaccination programme – a buy-one, give-one structure (Kabagani, 2021; ABS-CBN News, 2021). They must offer the vaccinations to their workers for free (Coloma, 2021). Concomitantly, there are also reports of queue-jumping in Philippines (Esguerra, 2021). Pakistan has allowed the private sector to import and distribute vaccines (Baloch, 2021). Even in the United Kingdom, there are 'clubs' offering what effectively amount to vaccine vacations by arranging for travel to the United Arab Emirates, vaccination and stay (Wills, 2021).

There are two ways of looking at this. On the one hand, as the vaccine market sees new suppliers and different vaccines appear as more or less suitable for certain groups (for example, a number of European countries did not administer the AstraZeneca vaccine to older individuals, age 55 and over in some countries, 65 and over in others), one could argue that the value of buying power will decrease and the benefits of a more decentralized delivery system would increase. Indeed, one could also argue that individuals with financial or social resources, whether money and/or connections, would subvert the public delivery system and jump to the front of the queue anyway. The private channel brings this into the open.[18] If it adds to the vaccine supply and does not divert vaccines from the public sector, which may not procure certain vaccines either because of technical limitations, such as the need for an ultra-cold chain, or lack of financial resources to buy more expensive vaccines, it actually improves the welfare of the poorer population: It increases their vaccine supply by reducing demand and may even add to supply, as seen in the Philippines, and allows the government to divert saved resources toward accelerated procurement. Thus, an expansion in the private-sector supply would improve population immunity and accelerate vaccine delivery.

On the other hand, a real possibility exists that a private market would squeeze out a free public market, as private firms offer incentives (bribes) to divert supply or slow down public distribution – a zero-sum game that hurts the poorer individual, and would become more likely if vaccine supply remains scarce. In India, it remains to be seen whether the waiting times at free public institutions for the second dose will prove longer than those at private vaccination sites. To add to all this, allowing richer individuals to receive vaccination early means a further capitulation to the march of what Michael Sandel calls a market society: a "way of life where market values seep into every aspect of human endeavour [...] where social relations are made over in the image of the market" (Sandel, 2012). Indeed, in Indonesia, Rosan Roselani, the chair of KADIN (Indonesian Chamber of Commerce) has been quoted as saying: "It's like going to the Disneyland [...] if you want to go faster, there's a priority pass, but you must pay more" (Jefriando and Widianto, 2021).

A single uniform prioritization system does have its merits, but will be difficult to implement without a prior functioning public health system, as in Europe and the United Kingdom, where the individual's primary caregiver calls to schedule vaccination appointments. India's common web (cowin.gov.in) and app-based (through Aarogya Setu) registration and scheduling system for vaccination offers a test case of much interest, especially to see whether it can substitute for the information advantages of the former system. The choice of allowing the private sector to enter the system (and to what extent) will depend on the rapidity with which the public sector can actually expand vaccination: If expansion in the private sector significantly reduces the time to vaccinate the population as a whole, it may prove a worthwhile trade-off, especially if vaccine costs remain low relative to income, or if the private sector itself subsidizes vaccine delivery to accelerate resumed production, as in the Philippines and Indonesia. Governments must therefore decide whether to allow private vaccination, and if so, under what circumstances.

Conclusion

What does the future hold? Will it be enough to get through this first global vaccination campaign, or will such campaigns need repeating year after year, as the Moderna chief executive expects (*Financial Times*, 2021)? Would we have the resources and the delivery capacity to do so? What levels of vaccination would persuade the world's countries to open up to each other? As long as substantial numbers remain unvaccinated, a reservoir will remain for the virus to fester and to develop variants that could overcome immunity from existing vaccinations. Even if human hosts become unavailable, animal hosts may prove sufficient. One expert claims, "There is no disease in the history of humankind that has disappeared from the face of the Earth when zoonotic disease was such an important part of, or played a role in, the transmission" (Michael Osterholm, quoted in Phillips, 2021: 384). In a *Nature* poll of 119 disease experts from 23 countries, 89 per cent felt that SARS-CoV-2 was either likely or very likely to become endemic (Phillips, 2021). Figure 9.4 provides a schematic illustration of the possible future of COVID-19.

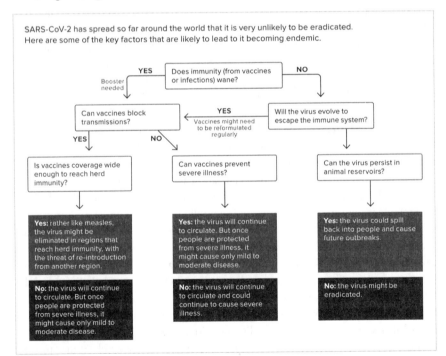

Figure 9.4   Coronavirus: Here to stay?
Source: Phillips (2021).

If COVID-19 does indeed become endemic, will the same degree of global cooperation displayed in manufacturing and distributing the first-generation vaccines go into administering them to holdout populations and convincing populations of the benefits, if necessary? Or, faced with the challenge of another global vaccination campaign, will we decide to accept living with another virus that causes as many or fewer deaths as influenza or tuberculosis do today?[19] Such questions may prove premature, and SARS-CoV-2 may not become endemic, or even if it does, it may become less virulent than it appears today. But, then again, it might become more debilitating or lethal. The precautionary principle requires us to consider this question about the future, and to ask how we can build on our successes even as we combat the pandemic of today.

EPILOGUE

Since April 2021, when this chapter was initially written, to present (November 2021), the number of doses administered worldwide has increased from under 350 million to more than 7 billion – a 20-fold increase. One can expect 9 billion doses will have been administered by the end of 2021. So far, it does not appear that storage, logistics, or other constraints have been a problem in distribution, though most of Africa, the most challenging geography, remains to be vaccinated.

The highly transmissible Delta variant spread widely during 2021, becoming predominant globally. But the vaccines are working – significantly reducing the likelihood of hospitalization and deaths, even among the elderly. Instances of AEFI have been very rare. However, the vaccines have been less successful at preventing infection and it appears that vaccinated persons can transmit the disease, even to other vaccinated persons (Singanayagam et al., 2021). Currently, the WHO has approved eight vaccines, the most recent being Covaxin, an inactivated viron vaccine from an Indian firm.

Vaccine supply

In March 2021, 11 countries accounted for 90 per cent of the vaccinated but, as of November 1, China and 89 other countries, comprising 44 per cent of the global population recorded more vaccines administered than their population. Large countries, such as Bangladesh, India, Indonesia, Mexico, Philippines, Pakistan, Nigeria and Russia, have yet to reach that milestone, but all except Nigeria and Russia are making progress. The share of fully vaccinated to total population is 44 per cent in Asia and 65 per cent in the European Union, *but only 6 per cent in Africa*. Nigeria, with 200 million people, has administered less than 10 million doses. Globally, fully vaccinated people that have received booster shots exceed the number of fully vaccinated people in Africa.[20] This is the face of vaccine inequity.

COVAX, which was supposed to provide doses, inter alia, to countries in Africa, has supplied about 450 million doses, that is less than 7 per cent of all doses administered globally. India was supposed to be a major supplier to COVAX, but it prioritized all vaccine production for domestic use beginning in the second quarter of 2021. The fourth quarter should see external deliveries resume and progressively rise as India completes its vaccination programme. After some initial hiccups, India has so far administered over a billion doses. India's *sui generis* portal, CoWin, is performing well, enabling people to arrange to get vaccinated at any location in the country.

Vaccine hesitancy

In Russia, the problem is demand, not supply. Ostensibly, a lack of faith in the domestically manufactured Sputnik vaccine, even though WHO-approved, delayed vaccination campaigns and now the pandemic is sweeping through the country with daily caseloads at 30,000 and deaths at 1,000, all-time highs. Cases are at or near all-time highs elsewhere too, for example, Germany and United Kingdom, but deaths in these countries are a fraction – one eighth or so – of past peaks, due to vaccination. Russia is an extreme case, but hesitancy exists elsewhere too. In the United Kingdom, over September and October 2021, the share of vaccinated for the 55–59 age group increased only a fraction, from 88.5 per cent to 88.8 per cent and from 81.1 per cent to 81.8 per cent for the 45–49 age group. That contrasts, for example, with Sao Paulo, Brazil, where 99 per cent of the eligible population has been fully vaccinated (Freelon, 2021). Hesitancy can also mean missing the second dose, as in India, where over 103.4 million individuals, about a quarter of those eligible, have not taken their second dose (PIB Delhi, 2021). It is unclear if India's unusually long gap between doses (12 to 16 weeks) is responsible for this situation.

Private sector involvement

While the private sector has been substantially involved in vaccine distribution, it has not been as successful in procuring vaccines. In the Philippines and Indonesia, the private sector has not significantly added to supply.[21] India has a separate track for private procurement from domestic vaccine firms, but demand at the price set ($10.00 to $20.00), has been limited in the presence of a free public alternative.

Endemic phase

The United Kingdom's experience with the removal of physical-distancing restrictions and other non-pharmaceutical interventions indicates that infections can persist even after a widespread vaccination programme. In this context, the start of child vaccination,[22] the confirmation of the safety of mixing vaccines (Callaway, 2021), and the approval of the first anti-viral drug (Aripaka, 2021) together with encouraging results from other antiviral trials (Chappell, 2021) provides welcome news for managing the advent of COVID-19's endemic phase.

Appendix 9A.1   The Difference COVAX Makes

On 2 March 2021, COVAX released the first round of vaccine allocations to 142 COVAX Facility participants, targeted for use through May 2021 (UNICEF, 2021). The organization has provided detailed information on the distribution of around 187 million doses of the AZ-Oxford vaccine, manufactured by AstraZeneca and by Serum Institute of India under license, and about 1 million vaccines from of Pfizer-BioNTech. One may compare these allocations with the population over the age of 65, the most vulnerable persons in a given country, as available in the World Development Indicators, which has information for 129 of the countries in the COVAX list (World Bank, 2019). Since both vaccines require two doses, a two-dose regimen was assumed. Figure 9.A.1 shows the number of countries where at least a certain share of the population over 65 could become fully vaccinated. For example, the expected COVAX supply by May 2021 could vaccinate at least 60 per cent of the vulnerable population in 101 countries and 100 per cent the vulnerable population in 82 countries. In other words, vaccination could extend to other age groups as early as May 2021, if vaccination supplies materialise or whenever supplies are made available, as some delays have been indicated (WHO, 2021f).

This calculation does not account for the need to vaccinate healthcare workers, nor does it allow for vaccine wastage, which would increase quantity requirements

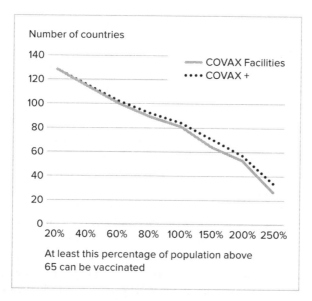

Figure 9A.1   How many people can the first allocation of COVAX vaccines reach?
Sources: UNICEF (2021); World Bank (2019).

(though wastage in countries like India has been minimal). Conversely, it also does not consider the reduction in requirements due to vaccine hesitancy, since some (hopefully small) part of the population will choose not to receive a vaccine. Some countries, such as Indonesia, will not follow a policy of prioritizing the older population. In the United States, as well, considerable variation occurs across the states despite uniform recommendations from the Centers for Disease Control (CDC) (Stacey and Burn-Murdoch, 2021). Nevertheless, a very large number of countries were supposed to be able to vaccinate their vulnerable elderly populations as early as May or when supplies were provided, if COVAX had been able to deliver on its allocation plan. However, COVAX was unable to deliver and all countries, such as India, did not exclusively prioritize their elderly over other populations in vaccination campaigns.

Appendix 9A.2   Regulatory Approval Process for Vaccines

The regulatory approval process for vaccines involves three phases after preclinical testing on non-human subjects. Once past this pre-clinical stage, regulators give approval for a Phase 1 safety test on human subjects. The objective of this study is to see whether the vaccine has any immediate or medium-term adverse effects. Phase 2 testing assesses whether the vaccine generates sufficient antibodies after administration (immunogenicity). This will usually be checked a few days after administration of the first dose and then again after administration of the second dose. In this pandemic, many firms ran combined Phase 1 and Phase 2 trials, reducing the effort of recruiting volunteers and also accelerating the time taken to complete the trial. The second phase is a critical one because it shows whether the vaccine will induce appropriate immune response in the body. The final Phase 3 trial tests for efficacy, that is, whether the vaccine gives protection from disease in a statistically measurable way.

This final phase usually recruits a large population in the tens of thousands. A certain portion of these subjects, the control group, receives a placebo while the rest receive the vaccine. Usually, the trial continues until a pre-decided number of infections (the primary endpoint) appear in the entire group of volunteers. For example, in India, the Phase 3 trial for Covaxin, with around 25,800 volunteers, was scheduled to close when 130 symptomatic infections occurred. These trials are usually double-blinded, which means neither the person administering the trial nor the person receiving the injection knows its status – vaccine or placebo.

This state of ignorance continues until the trial reaches the primary endpoint, after which an independent group checks how many of the infections appeared in the placebo group and how many in the vaccinated one. The difference in the two ratios is the measure of efficacy of the vaccine. For example, if there are two groups of 13,000 subjects each in the Covaxin vaccine trial, and if 100 of the infections came from the placebo group and 30 infections came from the vaccinated group, then we say that the vaccine is 70 per cent effective because without the vaccine, one would expect about 100 infections in a group of 13,000, based on the experience with the control (placebo) group. Since the total number of infections is relatively small, the number of infections within specific age groups becomes even more limited; for example, in the 65 and over (or 75 and over) age groups of the Pfizer-BioNTech trials, 1(0) infections occurred among the 3848 (774) vaccinated and 19 (5) among the 3880 (785) given the placebo (Polack et al., 2020). During this pandemic, vaccine manufacturers have released interim information during the Phase 3 trial for a smaller number of infections and regulators have taken such information into consideration, helping to speed up the regulatory process.

The vaccines were developed with unprecedented speed compared to any predecessors, and while the speed of delivery has its appreciators, it has also fostered suspicion in others about corner-cutting during the process. Obviously, some aspects of safety, such as the long-term effects of the vaccine, remain unknown because not enough time has elapsed to study them. This also applies to rare adverse events following immunization, which are only seen during large-scale (multi-million) administrations of the vaccine. Since over 7 billion vaccines have been administered as of November 2021, the data on AEFI is now extensive and the vaccines appear safe. Moreover, other aspects of vaccine effectiveness, such as the basic safety studied as part of Phase 1 trials and immunogenicity as part of Phase 2 trials, have been shared and published in peer-reviewed journals. Vaccine manufacturers have compressed trials by doing Phases 1 and 2 together and maintaining concurrent records during the process of Phase 3. This has allowed them to compile the data and submit it to independent analysts and outside regulators on an ongoing basis in the minimum time possible, without compromising on the quality of the evaluation.

The three-phase process is conducted for particular populations, such as adults with or without co-morbidities. For significantly different populations, such as children, the process would usually have to be repeated. However, for populations of different ethnicities, the full process may not be needed and only the safety and immunogenicity trials (Phases 1 and 2) may be conducted.

APPENDIX 9A.3   VARIANTS AND VACCINATION EFFECTIVENESS

In the final quarter of 2020, specific variants began to dominate cases in the United Kingdom (B.1.1.7), South Africa (B.1.351) and Brazil (P.1), since named Alpha, Beta, and Gamma respectively. The detection of variants requires a widespread genomic sequencing programme that is available in the United Kingdom and, to a lesser extent, in South Africa, but is otherwise limited, even in the United States.[23] The key mutations of interest appear to be N501Y and E484K; both appear to make the virus more transmissible, and in the case of E484K, which is present in both the South African and Brazilian variants and now spreading in the United Kingdom, may reduce the antibody response to infection, either from earlier infection of other varieties of SARSCoV-2 or from recent immunization. In the recent explosion of cases in India, a new variant, B.1.617 has come into the limelight and has been classified as a variant of interest (VOI). It has three characteristic mutations, L452R, similar to the VOI, B.1.427/B.1.429 (California variant), E484Q and P681R. Its contribution to the rise in cases in India is still under investigation (WHO, 2021g). Since then, this variant, B.1.617.2, also known as AY and now named Delta, has become the predominant variant globally. It has proved more transmissible, and it has been able to infect fully vaccinated people and those with prior infections, especially from other variants.

In February 2021, South Africa paused administration of the AstraZeneca vaccine following results from a small trial where it failed to prevent the emergence of mild or moderate (not requiring hospitalization) disease (Vecchiatto and Sguazzin, 2021). The protection of the vaccine against serious disease in this trial was indeterminate. Nevertheless, the WHO subsequently backed the AstraZeneca vaccine for global rollout, including among the elderly; it is the protocol now followed in the United Kingdom and India.[24]

Subsequently, both the Pfizer-BioNTech and Moderna vaccines have been tested against synthetic versions of the viruses containing the N501Y and E484K mutations; for both vaccines, the results indicated a reduced generation of antibodies. This reduced level may still provide sufficient protection, although no consensus yet exists on the relationship between the level of antibodies and the extent of protection. The Janssen single-dose protein antigen vaccine candidate was also tested in South Africa as part of its Phase 3 trial, and its "level of protection against moderate to severe COVID-19 infection was [...] 57 percent in South Africa, 28 days post-vaccination". The new VOI B.1.617 (Delta) has been found to be neutralized by recipients of the Indian vaccine BBV152 (Yadav et. al., 2021). The experience since then indicates that vaccines may not prevent mild or moderate infection, but can protect substantially against severe infection and death.

In Israel, the Pfizer-BioNTech vaccine appears to have reduced transmission substantially. Even the United Kingdom, which uses a mix of Pfizer-BioNTech and AstraZeneca vaccines, appears to have seen a substantial post-vaccination drop in transmission (Wise, 2021; London School of Hygiene and Tropical Medicine, 2021). This effect appears weaker with the Delta variant.

It therefore appears that vaccines do have reduced efficacy against the variants carrying both the N501Y[25] and E484K mutations and the Delta variant. Even if vaccination cannot prevent mild or moderate infections, since vaccination may reduce virus transmission and substantially reduces severe infection and the risk of fatality, it will reduce the burden on the health system.

NOTES

1. World Health Organization (WHO) African Region, 24 Febrary 2021, Twitter, twitter. com/WHOAFRO/status/1364487485842161664.

2. This is especially true for the Pfizer-BioNTech mRNA vaccine, which needs an ultra-cold chain for long-term storage (as discussed under logistics, the vaccine can be stored at food-grade refrigeration for shorter periods) and trained vaccinators who can thaw the vaccine and then mix it with diluent before vaccine administration by gently inverting, not shaking, ten times prior to and after adding diluent. The Pfizer vaccine also requires a special low-dead-space syringe to use the full six doses in its vial. This means that even a country famed for advance preparation, such as Japan, may waste hundreds of thousands of doses because it has not procured sufficient quantities of these syringes in time (Pfizer Inc. and BioNtech, 2021). However, these are not characteristics of mRNA vaccines in general. Moderna's version can be stored in regular refrigerators for 30 days and does not need dilution before administration.

3. Vaccinating larger countries, such as Bangladesh, India, Indonesia Pakistan, Peru, Brazil and Mexico – many severely affected by the disease – poses a challenge of a different magnitude and scale.

4. Janssen's approval had been projected for May or June 2021, but was approved on 12 March 2021 (WHO, 2021a).

5. This was announced during the first summit meeting of the 'Quad' group of countries, United States, Japan, India and Australia (DFC, 2021). See also Johnson & Johnson (2020).

6. Fill-finish facilities are industrial plants that package vaccine in vials and prepare them for distribution; such plants have an important role in increasing supply, since sterile facilities may be scarce. They also account for a substantial portion of the cost of the vaccine. For example, in the case of the Janssen vaccine, "[o]f the US$10 that the federal government has agreed to pay for a dose of Johnson & Johnson's vaccine, the drug substance itself accounts for only about 30 cents, federal officials said. The rest is the so-called fill and-finish cost" (LaFraniere and Weiland, 2021).

7. A. Poonawalla, 20 February 2021, Twitter, twitter.com/adarpoonawalla/ status/ 1363346341275967488. Also see Gettleman, Schmall and Mashal (2021).

8. WHO African Region, 24 Febrary 2021, Twitter, twitter. com/WHOAFRO/ status/1364487485842161664.

9. The Indian vaccination scheme has both public centres for free vaccination and private hospitals and clinics where people will pay a pre-fixed charge of US$3.5 per dose (PIB Mumbai, 2021). This may become more differentiated under a revised vaccination policy (MoHFW, 2021).

10. There is now the possibility of a triple-dose vaccine. The United Arab Emirates is already administering a third dose of Sinopharm, and India has started trials (Al Nowais, 2021; Raghavan and Mukul, 2021).

11. "Considering the option of delaying the administration of the second dose to ensure the highest possible coverage of the first dose […] and considering the vaccination course included in current EMA [European Medicines Agency] product information for Comirnaty (two doses 21 days apart) and COVID-19 vaccine Moderna (two doses 28 days apart), and WHO's recommendation based on currently available clinical trial data that the interval between vaccine doses may be extended up to 42 days (six

weeks), most countries replied that for the time being they will not extend the timing between the first and second dose (14 countries), or that the decision is still pending (six countries). Two countries have extended the 21-day dose interval for Comirnaty (one of them to 28 days and the other to up to 42 days); one other country is also planning to extend the timing between the first and second dose" (ECDPC, 2021).

12. H. Bastian, 12 January 2021, Twitter, twitter.com/hildabast/status/ 1349042451298754563.

13. The FDA has promised expedited approval without an extensive phase three trial for such booster doses, and firms such as Moderna are already ready to test a version targeted to the B.1.351 variant (Burton, 2021; Loftus, 2021).

14. For example, among Republicans, who are among the most vaccine hesitant in the United States, the share of those who will take the vaccine as soon as possible or that have already taken it rose from 25 per cent in December 2020 to 41 per cent in February 2021, as people shifted from hesitancy to more confidence (Hamel et al., 2021).

15. Centre for Policy Research (CPR) India, 13 March 2021, Twitter, twitter.com/ CPR_India/status/1370736410601328640.

16. As of 13 March 2021, about 15 per cent of those vaccinated are in this category, implying that about 10 per cent of the population in the 45–59 age group have been certified as having these comorbidities.

17. Centre for Policy Research (CPR) India. 12 March 2021, Twitter, twitter.com/CPR_ India/ status/1370246598245052420.

18. In addition, such richer individuals are more likely to be mobile and able to travel internationally, and thus more likely to be infected and then infect others. As such, if vaccination priority rested on the probability of becoming infected, as in Indonesia, the rich would go to the head of the queue in any case.

19. Paget et al. (2019) estimate that "an average of 389,000 (between 294,000 and 518,000) respiratory deaths were associated with influenza globally each year [...] corresponding to ~ 2% of all annual respiratory deaths" whereas 1.4 million people died from tuberculosis in 2019 (WHO, 2020).

20. Despite evidence of cell-mediated immunity (see, for example, Cho et. al., 2021), infections of vaccinated individuals and decaying antibody levels over time, especially among the old, have led to the early use of boosters.

21. In the Philippines, as of 22 October 2021, of 94.7 million total doses, 58.7 million were procured directly by the national government, 24.3 million came through COVAX, 3.6 million from bilateral donations, and 8 million doses were purchased by the private sector (see Kabagani, 2021b). The Indonesian case of Vaksinasi Gotong Royong, a vaccination programme intended for employees and their families that is provided free of charge from the company where they work, is similar (Surianta, 2021).

22. The CDC has approved vaccines for children above age 5. It remains to be seen if the immunity will be long-lasting or similar to that of adults (CDC, 2021).

23. The 677 mutation and the so-called California variant B.1.427/B.1.429 (with the L452R mutation, later found in 19 other countries) were expected to become variants of concern (VOCs) owing to their spread and rising share in genomically sequenced cases (Hodcroft et al., 2021; Wadman, 2021). WHO provides a regularly updated variant tracker at: who.int/en/activities/tracking-SARS-CoV-2-variants/.

24. The trial only consisted of younger South African health care workers, who were less likely to develop serious disease; no such cases developed either in the placebo group or the vaccinated group (WHO, 2021e).
25. The Pfizer-BioNTech vaccine has been effective against the B.1.1.7 variant with only the N501Y mutation (*The Guardian*, 2021).

References

ABS-CBN News. 2021. 'First Batch of AstraZeneca COVID-19 Vaccine for Private Sector Arriving in Q2'. *Concepcion*, 5 March. news.abs-cbn.com/business/03/05/21/first-batch-of-astrazeneca-covid-19-vaccine-for-private-sector-arriving-in-q2-concepcion.

Al Nowais, S. 2021. 'First Booster Shots of Covid-19 Vaccine Administered in UAE'. *The National*, 9 March. thenationalnews.com/uae/health/first-booster-shots-of-covid-19-vaccine-administered-in-uae-1.1180482.

Alfonso, C., Dayrit, M., Mendoza, R. and Ong, M. 2021. 'From Dengvaxia to Sinovac: Vaccine Hesitancy in the Philippines'. *The Diplomat*, 8 March. thediplomat.com/2021/03/from-dengvaxia-to-sinovac-vaccine-hesitancy-in-the-philippines/.

Baloch, S. M. 2021. 'Fears over Covid Vaccine Access in Pakistan as Private Imports Sanctioned'. *The Guardian*, 15 February. theguardian.com/global-development/2021/feb/15/pakistan-allow-private-firms-import-coronavirus-vaccines.

Banaji, M. 2021. 'COVID-19: What the Third National Sero-Survey Result Does and Doesn't Tell Us'. *The Wire*, 5 February. science.thewire.in/health/third-national-seroprevalence-survey-icmr-covid-19-rural-prevalence-test-positivity/.

Barry, E. 2021. 'Will Massachusetts's Vaccine Buddy System Work? Well. It's Worth a Shot'. *New York Times*, 12 February. nytimes.com/2021/02/12/us/covid-vaccine-caregivers-massachusetts.html.

Beaubien, J. 2021. 'Price Check: Nations Pay Wildly Different Prices for Vaccines'. National Public Radio, 19 February. npr.org/sections/goatsandsoda/2021/02/19/969529969/price-check-nations-pay-wildly-different-prices-for-vaccines.

Bharat Biotech. 2021. 'Bharat Biotech Announces Phase 3 Results of COVAXIN'. Bharat Biotech International Limited, Hyderabad. bharatbiotech.com/images/press/covaxin-phase3-efficacy-results.pdf.

Biddle, N., Edwards, B., Gray, M. and Sollis, K. 2021. 'Change in Vaccine Willingness in Australia: August 2020 to January 2021'. *medRxiv*, 17 February. doi.org/10.1101/2021.02.17.21251957.

Bio Spectrum. 2020. 'Thailand Triggers Production of COVID-19 Vaccine for 2021'. *Bio Spectrum Asia Edition*, 19 October. biospectrumasia.com/news/56/16953/thailand-triggers-production-of-covid-19-vaccine-for-2021.html.

Bloomberg. 2021. 'COVID Vaccine Tracker: Global Distribution'. 18 November. bloomberg.com/graphics/covid-vaccine-tracker-global-distribution/.

Boadle, A. 2021. 'Russian Vaccine Could Be Fully Produced in Brazil by April - Company Executive'. Reuters, 12 January. reuters.com/article/us-health-coronavirus-brazil-russia-idUSKBN29Q2AS.

Brubaker, H. 2021. 'Merck Plant in Montgomery County Will Help Produce J&J's COVID-19 Vaccine'. *Philadelphia Inquirer*, 11 March. inquirer.com/business/drugs/merck-west-point-jj-covid-19-vaccine-20210311.html.

Buell, S. 2021. 'An Insider's Guide to Getting a Vaccine Appointment in Massachusetts'. *Boston Magazine*, 24 March. bostonmagazine.com/news/2021/02/23/massachusetts-vaccine-online-tips/.

Burton, T. M. 2021. 'FDA Looks to Quickly Authorize Covid-19 Vaccine Booster Shots as New Variants Emerge'. *Wall Street Journal*, 22 February. wsj.com/articles/fda-looks-to-quickly-authorize-covid-19-vaccine-booster-shots-as-new-variants-emerge-11614028763.

Cakmakli, C., Demiralp, S., Kalemli-Özcan, Ş. and Yildirim, M. A. 2021. *The Economic Case for Global Vaccinations*. Paris: International Chamber of Commerce. iccwbo.org/publication/the-economic-case-for-global-vaccinations/.

Callaway, E. 2021. 'Mix-and-match COVID Vaccines Ace the Effectiveness Test'. *Nature*, 21 October. doi.org/10.1038/d41586-021-02853-4.

Carlesso, J. and Phaneuf, K. M. 2021. 'Breaking with National Recommendations. Lamont Says Connecticut's Vaccine Rollout Will Now Be Prioritized by Age'. *CT Mirror*, 22. February. ctmirror.org/2021/02/22/breaking-with-national-recommendations-lamont-says-connecticuts-vaccine-rollout-will-now-be-prioritized-by-age/.

Cho, A., Muecksch, F., Schaefer-Babajew, D., et al. 2021. 'Anti-SARS-CoV-2 Receptor Binding Domain Antibody Evolution after mRNA Vaccination'. *Nature*. doi. org/10.1038/s41586-021-04060-7.

Coloma, A. 2021. 'COVID-19 Vaccinations in Private Firms Should Be Free'. ABS-CBN News, 13 March. news.abs-cbn.com/business/03/13/21/covid-19-vaccinations-in-private-firms-should-be-free-dole.

Davies, G. 2021. 'Has the UK Really Outperformed the EU on Covid-19 Vaccinations?' The London School of Economics and Political Science, London. blogs.lse.ac.uk/europpblog/2021/03/25/has-the-uk-really-outperformed-the-eu-on-covid-19-vaccinations/.

Davies, M., Furneaux, R., Ruiz, I. and Langlois, J. 2021. '"Held to Ransom": Pfizer Demands Governments Gamble with State Assets to Secure Vaccine Deal'. *Mail and Guardian*, 23 February. mg.co.za/health/2021-02-23-held-to-ransom-pfizer-demands-governments-gamble-with-state-assets-to-secure-vaccine-deal/.

Deutsche Welle. 2021. 'EU Chief Admits COVID Vaccine Blunders'. 5 February. dw.com/en/eu-chief-admits-covid-vaccine-blunders/a-56462522.

Dewi, R. K. 2021. 'Menkes terbitkan aturan soal vaksin mandiri. ini penjelasan lengkapnya' (Minister of health issues regulations about independent vaccines. This is the complete explanation). *Kompas*, 3 January. kompas.com/tren/read/2021/03/01/121500965/menkes-terbitan-aturan-soal-vaksin-mandiri-ini-penjelas-l completed/.

Du, L. and Huang, G. 2020. 'Japan's Bitter Vaccine History Creates Hurdle in COVID-19 Fight'. *Japan Times*, 23 December. japantimes.co.jp/news/2020/12/23/national/japan-vaccine-history-coronavirus/.

Elbahrawy, F. 2021. 'UAE to Start Manufacturing Sinopharm Vaccine This Year'. *Bloomberg*, 6 January. bloomberg.com/news/articles/2021-01-06/uae-to-start-manufacturing-sinopharm-vaccine-this-year-national.

Esguerra, A. 2021. 'Vaccine Line-Jumping in the Philippines Is Getting So Bad That WHO Might Punish the country for It'. *Vice*, 26 March. vice.com/en/article/dy8njq/vaccine-line-jumping-is-so-bad-in-the-philippines-that-who-could-punish-it.

European Centre for Disease Prevention and Control (ECDC). 2021. 'Overview of the Implementation of COVID-19 Vaccination Strategies and Vaccine Deployment Plans in the EU/EEA'. European Centre for Disease Prevention and Control, Stockholm. ecdc.europa.eu/sites/default/files/documents/Overview-of-COVID-19-vaccination-strategies-deployment-plans-in-the-EU-EEA.pdf.

Financial Times. 2021. 'Covid-19 and the Business of Vaccines'. 9 March. ft.com/video/e6f487f4-a7d9-4e90-b9cb-ef8d25803bec.

Gavi. No date. 'New Collaboration Makes Further 100 Million Doses of COVID-19 Vaccine Available to Low- and Middle-Income Countries'. Gavi, the Vaccine Alliance, Geneva. gavi.org/news/media-room/new-collaboration-makes-further-100-million-doses-covid-19-vaccine-available-low.

Geddes, L. 2021. 'Pfizer Vaccine Found to Give Strong Immune Response to New Covid Variants'. *The Guardian*, 11 February. theguardian.com/world/2021/feb/11/pfizer-vaccine-strong-response-new-covid-variants.

Gettleman, J., Schmall, E. and Mashal, M. 2021. 'India Cuts Back on Vaccine Exports as Infections Surge at Home'. *New York Times*, 27 March. nytimes.com/2021/03/25/world/asia/india-covid-vaccine-astrazeneca.html.

Gillies, R. 2021. 'Canada Vaccine Panel Recommends 4 Months between COVID Doses'. ABC News, 4 March. abcnews.com/International/wireStory/canada-vaccine-panel-recommends-months-covid-doses-76239947.

Global Health 5050. 2021. 'The Sex, Gender and COVID-19 Project'. Global Health 5050, London. globalhealth5050.org/the-sex-gender-and-covid-19-project/.

Global Times. 2020. 'Government to Pay 200 Yuan per Dose of Chinese COVID-19 Inactivated Vaccines'. *Global Times*, 16 December. globaltimes.cn/content/1210093.shtml.

Government of India. 2021. 'Citizen Registration and Appointment for Vaccination: User Manual Version 1.1'. Government of India, New Delhi. mohfw.gov.in/pdf/UserManualCitizenRegistration&AppointmentforVaccination.pdf.

Government of Indonesia. 2021. 'Peraturan Menteri Kesehatan Republik Indonesia Nomor 10 Tahun 2021'. Government of Indonesia, Jakarta. covid19.go.id/p/regulasi/peraturan-menteri-kesehatan-republik-indonesia-nomor-10-tahun-2021.

Guarascio, F. 2021. 'AstraZeneca to Miss Second-Quarter EU Vaccine Supply Target by Half - EU Official'. Reuters, 24 February. reuters.com/article/health-coronavirus-eu-astrazeneca/exclusive-astrazeneca-to-miss-second-quarter-eu-vaccine-supply-target-by-half-eu-official-idINKBN2AO07O.

Hamel, L., Sparks, G. and Brodie, M. 2021. 'KFF COVID-19 Vaccine Monitor'. *KFF*, 26 February. kff.org/coronavirus-covid-19/poll-finding/kff-covid-19-vaccine-monitor-february-2021/.

Haringey Council. 2021. 'Pop-Up Vaccination Clinics Coming to Haringey'. Haringey Council, 12 March. haringey.gov.uk/news/pop-vaccination-clinics-coming-haringey.

Hellebrandt, T. and Mauro, P. 2015. *The Future of Worldwide Income Distribution*. Washington DC: Peterson Institute for International Economics. piie.com/publications/working-papers/future-worldwide-income-distribution.

Higgins, T. 2021. 'White House Says U.S. States Can't Directly Purchase Covid Vaccine under Emergency Use Authorization'. CNBC, 24 January. cnbc.com/2021/01/24/white-house-says-states-cant-purchase-covid-vaccine-directly.html.

Hodcroft, E. B., Domman, D. B., Oguntuyo, K., Snyder, D. J., Van Diest, M., Densmore, K. H., Schwalm, K. C., Femling, J., Carroll, J. L., Scott, R. S., Whyte, M. M., Edwards, M. D., Hull, N. C., Kevil, C. G., Vanchiere, J. A., Lee, B., Dinwiddie, D. L., Cooper, V. S. and Kamil, J. P. 2021. 'Emergence in Late 2020 of Multiple Lineages of SARS-CoV-2 Spike Protein Variants Affecting Amino Acid Position 677'. Cold Spring Harbor Laboratory, New York. medrxiv.org/content/10.1101/2021.02.12.21251658v1.full-text.

Hooker, L. and Palumbo, D. 2020. 'Covid Vaccines: Will Drug Companies Make Bumper Profits?' British Broadcasting Corporation, 18 December. bbc.com/news/business-55170756.

Jefriando, M. and Widianto, S. 2021. 'Indonesia May Allow Private Sector to Buy and Distribute Vaccines'. Reuters, 14 January. reuters.com/article/us-health-coronavirus-indonesia-vaccine-idUSKBN29J1ET.

Johnson & Johnson. 2020. 'Statement on Johnson & Johnson's Collaboration in India with Biological E to Expand Manufacturing Capabilities for its COVID-19 Vaccine Candidate'. Johnson & Johnson, New Brunswick, NJ. jnj.in/about-jnj/company-statements/statement-on-johnson-johnsons-collaboration-in-india-with-biological-e-to-expand-manufacturing-capabilities-for-its-covid-19-vaccine-candidate.

———. 2021. 'Johnson & Johnson COVID-19 Vaccine Authorized by U.S. FDA For Emergency Use – First Single-Shot Vaccine in Fight against Global Pandemic'. Johnson & Johnson, New Brunswick, NJ. jnj.com/johnson-johnson-announces-single-shot-janssen-covid-19-vaccine-candidate-met-primary-endpoints-in-interim-analysis-of-its-phase-3-ensemble-trial.

Junaidi, I. and Azeem, M. 2021. 'Clinical Trial of Covid-19 Vaccine Completes This Week'. *Dawn*, 8 January. dawn.com/news/1600340.

Kabagani, L. J. 2021. 'Gov't Assures Transparency, Accountability in Vaccine Procurement'. Philippine News Agency, 16 January. pna.gov.ph/articles/1127616.

Kansteiner, F. 2021. 'U.S. Focus on Pfizer Production Could Delay Manufacturing of Other COVID-19 Vaccines, Serum Institute CEO Warns'. *Fierce Pharma*, 5 March. fiercepharma.com/manufacturing/u-s-focus-pfizer-production-could-delay-manufacturing-other-covid-19-vaccines-serum.

Kiefer, P. 2021. 'Storing the Pfizer Vaccine Could Get a Lot Simpler in Coming Weeks'. *Popular Science*, 19 February. popsci.com/story/health/pfizer-vaccine-stored-normal-freezer/.

Kresge, N., Loh, T. and Rogers, I. 2021. 'AstraZeneca's Vaccines Go Unused in EU as Mutants Spread'. *Bloomberg Quint*, 17 February. bloombergquint.com/business/astrazeneca-s-covid-19-vaccines-are-going-unused-in-germany.

Kuchler, H. and Miller, J. 2021. 'Shortage of Giant Plastic Bags Threatens Global Vaccines Rollout'. *Financial Times*, 17 February. ft-com.btpl.idm.oclc.org/content/b2f4f9cf-af80-428f-a198-2698ceb4c701.

LaFraniere, S. and Weiland, N. 2021. 'For Biden a New Virus Dilemma: How to Handle a Looming Glut of Vaccine'. *New York Times*, 26 March. nytimes.com/2021/03/26/us/biden-coronavirus-vaccine.html.

LaFraniere, S. Stolberg, S. G. and Goodnough A. 2021. 'Short of Vaccine States Find Hidden Stashes in Their Own Backyards'. *New York Times*, 19 February. nytimes.com/2021/02/19/us/coronavirus-vaccines.html.

Lane, M. 2021. 'Indonesia's Vaccination Policies Seem to Favour the Young and Rich'. Channel News Asia, 8 March. channelnewsasia.com/news/commentary/covid-19-indonesia-vaccine-program-worker-mandiri-jokowi-sinovac-14341636.

Lazarus, J. V., Ratzan, S. C., Palayew, A., Gostin, L. O., Larson, H. J., Rabin, K., Kimball, S. and El-Mohandes, A. 2021. 'A Global Survey of Potential Acceptance of a COVID-19 Vaccine'. *Nature Medicine* 27(2), 225–228.

Lew, L. 2021. 'China's Public Hesitant to Take Covid-19 Vaccines, Another Survey Suggests'. *South China Morning Post*, 19 February. scmp.com/news/china/science/article/3122418/chinas-public-hesitant-take-covid-19-vaccines-another-survey.

Loftus, P. 2021. 'Moderna Says Covid-19 Vaccine for South Africa Strain Is Ready for Human Testing'. *Wall Street Journal*, 24 February. wsj.com/articles/moderna-says-covid-19-vaccine-for-south-africa-strain-is-ready-for-human-testing-11614201000.

London School of Hygiene and Tropical Medicine. 2021. 'COVID-19 Vaccine Linked to a Reduction in Transmission'. London School of Hygiene and Tropical Medicine, London.   lshtm.ac.uk/newsevents/news/2021/covid-19-vaccine-linked-reduction-transmission.

Lopez, E. and Reuters. 2021. 'Philippines Set to Roll Out Sinovac Covid-19 Jabs, but Some Businesses Can't Wait'. *South China Morning Post*, 26 February. amp.scmp.com/week-asia/health-environment/article/3123303/philippines-set-roll-out-sinovac-covid-19-jabs-some.

Lovett, S. 2021. 'UK's Coronavirus Vaccines Dramatically Cut Transmission, New Study Suggests'. *Independent*, 12 March. .independent.co.uk/news/health/covid-vaccines-uk-spread-latest-b1816586.html.

Lupkin, S. 2021. 'Defense Production Act Speeds up Vaccine Production'. National Public Radio, 13 March. npr.org/sections/health-shots/2021/03/13/976531488/defense-production-act-speeds-up-vaccine-production.

Mallapaty, S. 2021. 'Can COVID Vaccines Stop Transmission? Scientists Race to Find Answers'. *Nature*, 19 February. doi.org/10.1038/d41586-021-00450-z.

Ministry of Health and Family Welfare (MoHFW) India. 2021. 'Liberalised Pricing and Accelerated National Covid-19 Vaccination Strategy'. New Delhi: Government of India. mohfw.gov.in/pdf/LiberalisedPricingandAcceleratedNationalCovid19VaccinationStrategy2042021.pdf.

Muanya, C. 2021. 'Over 40m Nigerians Infected with COVID-19, Survey Shows'. *The Guardian*, 26 February. guardian.ng/features/health/over-40m-nigerians-infected-with-covid-19-survey-shows/.

Nakkazi, E. 2021. 'Uganda Defends Price Paid for AstraZeneca COVID19 Vaccine'. *Health Policy Watch*, 2 March. healthpolicy-watch.news/uganda-defends-astrazeneca-price-says-its-not-higher-than-other-countries.

Our World in Data. 2021. 'OWID Covid Data'. Global Change Data Lab, Oxford. covid.ourworldindata.org/data/owid-covid-data.csv.

Owens, C. 2021. 'Republicans Are Least Likely to Want the Coronavirus Vaccine'. *Axios*, 25 February. axios.com/republicans-coronavirus-vaccine-hesitancy-023bf32f-3d68-4206-b906-4f701b87c39f.html.

Paget, J., Spreeuwenberg, P., Charu, V., Taylor, R. J., Iuliano, A. D., Bresee, J., Simonsen, L., Viboud, C. and Global Seasonal Influenza-associated Mortality Collaborator Network and GLaMOR Collaborating Teams. 2019. 'Global Mortality Associated with Seasonal Influenza Epidemics: New Burden Estimates and Predictors from the GLaMOR Project'. *Journal of Global Health* 92(020421). doi.org/10.7189/jogh.09.020421.

Paterson. P., Meurice, F., Stanberry, L. R., Glismann, S., Rosenthal, S. L., and Larson, H. J. 2016. 'Vaccine Hesitancy and Healthcare Providers'. *Vaccine* 34(52), 6700–6706. doi.org/10.1016/j.vaccine.2016.10.042.

Peel, M., Fleming, S., Mancini, D. P. and Kuchler, H. 2021. 'EU's AstraZeneca Vaccine Problems Linked to Mystery Factory Delay'. *Financial Times*, 13 March. ft.com/content/8e2e994e-9750-4de1-9cbc-31becd2ae0a8.

Pfizer Inc. and BioNtech. 2021. 'Pfizer-BioNTech COVID-19 Vaccine'. Pfizer Inc., New York. cvdvaccine-us.com/dosing-and-administration.

Phillips, N. 2021. 'The Coronavirus Is Here to Stay – Here's What That Means'. *Nature* 590, 382–384. doi.org/10.1038/d41586-021-00396-2.

Plotkin, S. A. and Halsey, N. 2021. 'Accelerate Coronavirus Disease 2019 COVID-19 Vaccine Rollout by Delaying the Second Dose of mRNA Vaccines'. *Clinical Infectious Diseases* 73(7), 1320–1321. doi.org/10.1093/cid/ciab068.

Polack, F. P., Thomas, S. J., Kitchen, N., Absolan, J. 2020. 'Safety and Efficacy of the BNT162b2 mRNA Covid-19 Vaccine'. *New England Journal of Medicine* 383, 2603–2615. nejm.org/doi/full/10.1056/NEJMoa2034577.

Press Information Bureau (PIB) Mumbai. 2021. 'All Preparations Are on Track for COVID-19 Vaccine Roll-Out from 16th January 2021: Health Secretary'. Ministry of Health and Family Welfare, New Delhi. pib.gov.in/PressReleaseIframePage.aspx?PRID=1688036.

Prime Minister's Office. 2021. 'Govt. of United Kingdom 2021 G7 Leaders' Statement: 19 February 2021'. Government of United Kingdom, London. gov.uk/government/news/g7-leaders-statement-19-february-2021.

Quinn, C. 2021. 'Rich vs. Poor Again at WTO'. *Foreign Policy*, 10 March. foreignpolicy.com/2021/03/10/wto-intellectual-propert-waiver-india-south-africa/.

Quinn, K. 2021. 'Is It the Adenovirus Vaccine Technology, Used by AstraZeneca and Johnson & Johnson, Causing Blood Clots? There's No Evidence Yet'. *The Conversation*, 14 April. theconversation.com/is-it-the-adenovirus-vaccine-technology-used-by-astrazeneca-and-johnson-and-johnson-causing-blood-clots-theres-no-evidence-yet-158944.

Raghavan, P. and Mukul, P. 2021. 'Third Dose of Covaxin Gets Nod for Trials, Six Months after 2nd Shot'. *Indian Express*, 2 April. indianexpress.com/article/india/third-dose-of-covaxin-gets-nod-for-trials-six-months-after-2nd-shot-7255088/.

Reuters. 2021a. 'Indonesia Orders 20 Million COVID-19 Vaccine Doses for Private Inoculations'. 15 March. reuters.com/article/us-health-coronavirus-indonesia-vaccine-idUSKBN2B70LV.

———. 2021b. 'A Slice and a Shot: Tel Aviv Pushes COVID-19 Vaccine with Free Food'. 16 February. reuters.com/article/us-health-coronavirus-israel-vaccination-idUSKBN2AG21N.

Robbins, R. and Stolberg, S. G. 2021. 'Helping People Find Covid-19 Vaccines Is Aim of C.D.C.-Backed Site'. *New York Times*, 24 February. nytimes.com/2021/02/24/business/vaccine-finder-org.html.

Roser, M. 2021. *Global Income Distribution in 2003 and 2013*. Oxford: Global Change Data Lab. ourworldindata.org.

Sagonowsky, E. 2021a. 'After Pfizer Deal, Sanofi Offers a Hand to Johnson & Johnson for COVID-19 Vaccine Production'. *Fierce Pharma*, 22 February. fiercepharma.com/pharma/after-pfizer-deal-sanofi-offers-a-hand-to-johnson-johnson-for-covid-19-vaccine-production.

———, E. 2021b. 'Pfizer Eyes Higher Prices for COVID-19 Vaccine after the Pandemic Wanes: Exec. Analyst'. *Fierce Pharma*, 23 February. fiercepharma.com/pharma/pfizer-eyes-higher-covid-19-vaccine-prices-after-pandemic-exec-analyst.

Sandel, M. J. 2012. 'What Isn't for Sale'. *The Atlantic* 309(3), 62–66. theatlantic.com/magazine/archive/2012/04/what-isnt-for-sale/308902/.

Sanofi. 2021. 'Sanofi to Provide Support to BioNTech in Manufacturing Their COVID-19 Vaccine to Help Address Public Health Needs'. Paris. sanofi.com/en/media-room/press-releases/2021/2021-01-27-07-30-00.

Setboonsarng, C. 2021. 'Thai Private Hospitals Reserve COVID-19 Vaccines ahead of Approval'. Reuters, 18 January. reuters.com/article/us-health-coronavirus-thailand-idUSKBN29N0XK.

Sette, A. and Crotty, S. 2021. 'Adaptive Immunity to SARS-CoV-2 and COVID-19'. *Cell*, 7 January. doi.org/10.1016/ j.cell.2021.01.007.

Sheriff, K. M. 2021. 'Centre Specifies Comorbidities for Vaccine Eligibility, Cap on Charge at Rs 250 per Dose'. *Indian Express*, 28 February. indianexpress.com/article/india/centre-specifies-comorbidities-for-vaccine-eligibility-cap-on-charge-at-rs-250-per-dose-7207792/.

Singanayagam, A., Hakki, S., Dunning, J., Madon, K.J., Crone, M.A., Koycheva, A., Derqui-Fernandez, N., Barnett, J. L., Whitfield, M.G., Varro, R. and Charlett, A., 2021. 'Community Transmission and Viral Load Kinetics of the SARS-CoV-2 Delta (B. 1.617. 2) Variant in Vaccinated and Unvaccinated Individuals in the UK: A Prospective, Longitudinal, Cohort Study'. *Lancet Infectious Diseases*, 29 October. thelancet.com/journals/laninf/article/PIIS1473-3099(21)00648-4/fulltext.

Stacey, K. and Burn-Murdoch, J. 2021 'Huge, Fast and Haphazard: Inside the US Vaccine Rollout'. *Financial Times*, 13 March. ft.com/content/a256b257-1e51-48ee-a63e-0b2def61934f.

Standaert, M. 2021. 'China Risks COVID "immunity gap" amid Slow Vaccine Uptake'. *Aljazeera*, 11 March. aljazeera.com/news/2021/3/11/china-risks-covid-immunity-gap-amid-slow-vaccine-uptake.

Steinhauer, J. 2021. 'Younger Military Personnel Reject Vaccine, in Warning for Commanders and the Nation'. *New York Times*, 27 February. nytimes.com/2021/02/27/us/politics/coronavirus-vaccine-refusal-military.html.

The Guardian. 2020. 'Belgian Minister Tweets EU's Covid Vaccine Price List to Anger of Manufacturers'. 18 December. theguardian.com/world/2020/dec/18/belgian-minister-accidentally-tweets-eus-covid-vaccine-price-list.

———. 2021. 'Israeli Real-World Data on Pfizer Vaccine Shows High Covid Protection'. 11 March. theguardian.com/world/2021/mar/11/israeli-real-world-data-on-pfizer-vaccine-shows-high-covid-protection.

The Wire. 2020. 'Nearly Half the People Who Have Died of COVID-19 in India Are Younger than 60'. 14 October. science.thewire.in/health/india-covid-19-mortality-comorbidities-age-health-ministry/.

———. 2021. 'Covaxin Exits "Clinical Trial Mode", Centre Says'. 12 March. science.thewire.in/health/covaxin-exits-clinical-trial-mode-centre-says/.

Thukwana, N. 2021. 'SA's Biovac Says It Can Make 30 Million Doses of CoVID Vaccine'. *Business Insider SA*, 11 February. businessinsider.co.za/sas-biovac-says-it-can-make-30-million-doses-of-covid-vaccine-heres-why-it-hasnt-started-2021-2.

Undurraga, E. A., Chowell, G. and Mizumoto, K. 2021. 'COVID-19 Case Fatality Risk by Age and Gender in a High Testing Setting in Latin America: Chile. March–August 2020'. *Infectious Disease of Poverty* 10(11). doi.org/10.1186/s40249-020-00785-1.

United Nations Children's Fund (UNICEF). 2021. 'COVAX Publishes First Round of Allocations'. United Nations Children's Fund, New York. unicef.org/supply/press-releases/covax-publishes-first-round-allocations.

United States International Development Finance Corporation (DFC). 2021. 'DFC Announces Support for Manufacturing of Vaccines during Quad Summit'. US International Development Finance Corporation, Washington, DC. dfc.gov/media/press-releases/dfc-announces-support-manufacturing-vaccines-during-quad-summit.

Van Gogh, M., Hausmann, L., Mohr, D. and Wolff, C. 2021. 'Is the World up to the Challenge of Mass COVID-19 Vaccination?' McKinsey & Company, Chicago, IL. mckinsey.com/industries/travel-logistics-and-infrastructure/our-insights/is-the-world-up-to-the-challenge-of-mass-covid-19-vaccination.

Vaski, T. 2021. 'Gov't Publishes Eastern Vaccine Contracts, Price of Sinopharm and Sputnik V'. *Hungary Today*, 12 March. hungarytoday.hu/hungary-vaccine-contracts-procurement-sinopharm-sputnik-v-price/.

Verma, R., Barthwal, A. and Najah, A. 2021. 'Most BJP Supporters Want to Take Vaccines Congress Supporters Not Far Behind'. *LiveMint*, 11 January. livemint.com/politics/news/most-bjp-supporters-want-to-take-vaccines-congress-supporters-not-far-behind-11610115072702.html.

Vecchiatto, P. and Sguazzin, A. 2021. 'South Africa to Take Months to Register Vaccine after AstraZeneca Setback'. *Bloomberg*, 25 February. bloomberg.com/news/articles/2021-02-25/s-africa-to-take-months-to-register-vaccine-after-astra-setback.

Vignaud, L.-H. 2021. 'If the French Distrust Vaccines, It's because They Distrust Their Politicians'. *The Guardian*, 15 February. theguardian.com/commentisfree/2021/feb/15/french-distrust-vaccines-politicians.

Voysey, M., Clemens, S. A. C., Madhi, S. A., Weckx, L. Y., Folegatti, P. M., Aley, P. K., Angus, B. 2021. 'Single-Dose Administration and the Influence of the Timing of the Booster Dose on Immunogenicity and Efficacy of ChAdOx1 nCoV-19 AZD1222 vaccine: A Pooled Analysis of Four Randomised Trials'. *The Lancet*, 19 February. thelancet.com/journals/lancet/article/PIIS0140-67362100432-3/fulltext.

Wadman, M. 2021. 'California Coronavirus Strain May Be More Infectious – and Lethal'. *Science*, 23 February. sciencemag.org/news/2021/02/coronavirus-strain-first-identified-california-may-be-more-infectious-and-cause-more.

Wei, L. 2021. 'Annual Production of Chinese Single-Shot COVID-19 Vaccine Can Reach 500m'. CGTN, 27 February. news.cgtn.com/news/2021-02-27/Production-of-Chinese-single-shot-COVID-19-vaccine-can-reach-500m-YdtcDBrWZW/index.html.

Wills, K. 2021. 'Meet the Super-Rich Skipping the Queue for a Vaccine Vacation'. *Evening Standard*, 25 February. standard.co.uk/insider/are-the-superrich-skipping-the-vaccine-queue-b921226.html.

Wingrove, J. and Ring, S. 2021. 'Biden Rebuffs EU, AstraZeneca and Says U.S. Will Keep Its Doses'. *Bloomberg*, 12 March. bloomberg.com/news/articles/2021-03-12/astrazeneca-asks-biden-to-consider-shipping-u-s-doses-to-eu.

Wintour, P. 2021. 'Boris Johnson to Pledge Surplus Covid Vaccine to Poorer Countries at G7'. *The Guardian*, 18 February. theguardian.com/world/2021/feb/18/boris-johnson-to-pledge-surplus-covid-vaccine-to-poorer-countries-at-g7.

Wise, J. 2021. 'Covid-19: Pfizer BioNTech Vaccine Reduced Cases by 94% in Israel Shows Peer Reviewed Study'. *The BMJ*, 25 February. bmj.com/content/372/bmj.n567.

World Bank. 2019. 'Populations Ages 65 and Above, Total'. The World Bank Group, Washington, DC. data.worldbank.org/indicator/SP.POP.65UP.TO.

World Bank, World Development Indicators (WDI). 2021. 'Data Bank: World Development Indicators'. The World Bank Group, Washington, DC. databank.worldbank.org/source/world-development-indicators.

World Health Organization (WHO). 2020. 'Tuberculosis'. World Health Organization, Geneva. who.int/news-room/fact-sheets/detail/tuberculosis.

———. 2021a. 'Status of COVID-19 Vaccines within WHO EUL/PQ Evaluation Process'. World Health Organization, Geneva. extranet.who.int/pqweb/sites/default/files/documents/Status_COVID_VAX_10March2021.pdf.

———. 2021b. 'Draft Landscape and Tracker of COVID-19 Candidate Vaccines'. World Health Organization, Geneva. who.int/publications/m/item/draft-landscape-of-covid-19-candidate-vaccines.

———. 2021c. 'COVAX Announces Additional Deals to Access Promising COVID-19 Vaccine Candidates; Plans Global Rollout Starting Q1 2021'. World Health Organization, Geneva. who.int/news/item/18-12-2020-covax-announces-additional-deals-to-access-promising-covid-19-vaccine-candidates-plans-global-rollout-starting-q1-2021.

———. 2021d. 'WHO Coronavirus (COVID-19) Dashboard'. World Health Organization, Geneva. covid19.who.int/.

———. 2021e. 'WHO Lists Two Additional COVID-19 Vaccines for Emergency Use and COVAX Roll-out'. World Health Organization, Geneva. who.int/news/item/15-02-2021-who-lists-two-additional-covid-19-vaccines-for-emergency-use-and-covax-roll-out.

————. 2021f. 'COVAX Updates Participants on Delivery Delays for Vaccines from Serum Institute of India (SII) and AstraZeneca'. World Health Organization, Geneva. who.int/news/item/25-03-2021-covax-updates-participants-on-delivery-delays-for-vaccines-from-serum-institute-of-india-(sii)-and-astrazeneca.

————. 2021g. 'COVID-19 Weekly Epidemiological Update'. World Health Organization, Geneva.   who.int/docs/default-source/coronaviruse/situation-reports/20210427_weekly_epi_update_37.pdf.

Yadav, P. D., Sapkal, G. N., Abraham, P., Raches, E., Gururaj, D., Patil, D. Y., Nyayanit, D. A., Gupta, N., Sahay, R. R., Shete, A. M., Panda, S., Bhargava, B. and Mohan, V. K. 2021. 'Neutralization of Variant under Investigation B.1.617 with Sera of BBV152 Vaccines'. *bioRxiv*, 23 April. doi.org/10.1101/2021.04.23.441101

Yan, R., Zhang, Y., Li, Y., Xia, L., Guo, Y. and Zhou, Q. 2020. 'Structural Basis for the Recognition of SARS-CoV-2 by Full-Length Human ACE2'. *Science* 367(6485), 1444–1448. science.sciencemag.org/content/367/6485/1444.

Yoon, D. 2021. 'Declining a Covid-19 Vaccine Risks Penalties in Some Countries'. *Wall Street Journal*, 22 February. wsj.com/articles/declining-a-covid-19-vaccine-risks-penalties-in-some-countries-11613998997.

10 | Enhancing the Provision of Global Public Goods

Ready for More Realism?

Inge Kaul

INTRODUCTION

Global challenges figure ever more prominently and in ever greater numbers on national and international policy agendas. They range from communicable disease control to climate change mitigation and from financial stability to the universalization of norms such as basic human rights. Old and new security challenges have also come up for consideration, including cybersecurity; the safe use of new technologies such as artificial intelligence; nuclear non-proliferation; terrorism control; and the prevention or cessation of war. As the recent coronavirus (COVID-19) pandemic taught us once again – and perhaps more directly than ever before – many global challenges may, for better or for worse, affect all countries and all people, irrespective of whether we are rich or poor, living in the Global North or in the Global South. Challenges of this type are referred to as global public goods (GPGs).[1] GPGs not only affect all of us directly or indirectly, but also require all of us to contribute to their adequate provision. In other words, they call for international cooperation (IC), often even universal multilateralism.

While state and nonstate actors worldwide are active contributors to GPG provision, experience shows that the sum of these contributions in many cases falls short of requirements. As a result, GPG-related problems often remain unresolved, even though their scientific and technical dimensions are well-understood, and the resources needed to resolve them are also within the bounds of what is feasible.

The question thus arises: Is the present system of multilateral cooperation not well equipped to tackle GPG-type challenges? This question has attracted the attention of world leaders. For example, in their Declaration on the Commemoration of the Seventy-Fifth Anniversary of the United Nations, the heads of state and government of United Nations (UN) member states emphasize that the global challenges confronting us "can only be addressed through reinvigorated multilateralism" (United Nations, 2020: para. 5). However, the Declaration does not specify how this reinvigorated multilateralism would need to differ from today's multilateral governance practices and, importantly, how it could come about. These issues will become the subject of future consultations and debates.

Accordingly, this chapter explores these two unaddressed points of the Declaration. More specifically, it aims, first, to better understand what type of reinvigorated multilateralism would be fit for purpose, that is, fostering more adequate GPG provision given the present policymaking realities, and second, to explore whether there already exists a momentum for such change on which further progress can potentially be based.

The discussion of these points is structured as follows. The first section analyses the key characteristics of GPGs from the special viewpoint of their governance requirements. Against this background, the second section examines the factors and forces that explain why these requirements are not adequately met today. The third and fourth sections explain how to do better in the future, assuming that the ultimate goal is to foster global sustainable growth and development, as stipulated in the United Nations 2030 Agenda (United Nations, 2015). The fifth section offers suggestions on the next steps that select actor groups could consider in order to help promote the needed governance reforms. The concluding section argues that fostering reinvigorated multilateralism and achieving enhanced GPG provision require a massive rethinking at the theoretical and practical policy level; and that now seems to be the right time for it, considering the broad-based and strong ambition among policymakers and the global public alike to do better in a post-COVID-19 era.

GPGs: Key Properties and Governance Requirements

This section identifies the distinguishing properties of a GPG and then presents a brief overview of the myriad inputs that, in many cases, must come together in order for the good to emerge. The discussion summary shows that GPGs constitute a new, additional type of public-policy challenge that does not fit easily into any of the conventional governance moulds.[2]

Key properties

The generic definition of a pure public good (PG) is that it is non-rival and non-excludable and, because of the latter property, public in consumption. Depending on the geographic reach of a good's public effects, it is said to be a local, national, regional or global PG. This may sound rather straightforward. In reality, however, matters are more complicated.

For example, some goods may be non-rival only up to certain points, after which their availability declines due to over-exploitation. An example of a GPG that is subject to over-exploitation is the atmosphere, which, if overloaded with greenhouse gas emissions, causes global warming. Consequently, if global warming is to be limited, the human impact on the atmosphere also needs to be limited by making the good in questions less global and public in consumption through deliberate policy choice. Or consider knowledge – a non-rival good par excellence. However, it can, for example, be patented and thereby taken out of the public domain, in many cases, even the global public domain; it thus becomes privatized as the property of the patent holder.

Therefore, thinking in terms of a public-private continuum can help us conceptualise PGs. The outer poles of the continuum comprise, at one end, purely private (rival and excludable) goods and, at the other end, purely public (non-rival and non-excludable) goods. Many other goods might fall somewhere between the two ends, based on various sociocultural, moral, ethical, environmental or economic/financial considerations. The 'globalness'[3] of GPGs is often not an innate property but reflects a policy choice, most notably, the choice to promote economic openness and, in support thereof, cross-border market integration and interoperable transportation and communication systems. Therefore, it is also useful to distinguish between, on the one hand, natural GPGs, such as the already mentioned atmosphere, or the moonlight and the high seas, the existence of which predates the existence of humans, and, on the other hand, human-made GPGs. The latter, for the most part, have arisen from deliberate human choices, such as the global institutional and physical communications and transport systems, or else global norms, such as national sovereignty or basic human rights that aim for global public acceptance: in other words, globally public consumption. In several cases, these deliberate policy choices have led to the (often unintended) globalization of essentially national (including local) PGs, such as financial contagion effects, crime and violence, and information and news.

In this connection, one might also point to the difference between making a non-rival good, such as knowledge, excludable and making a rival good, such as a vaccine, available for all. The latter proposal has emerged as a possible way to end the COVID-19 pandemic, with its advocates frequently calling for making the vaccine a global public good. However, due to its innate property of being rival in consumption, technically speaking, a vaccine cannot be turned into a GPG. All one can do is produce it in quantities sufficient to make it available to all who want it, at an affordable price or even free of charge, thus rendering the rival property moot. However, someone would still have to pay – perhaps several billion times or so – the price that producers charge per single dose of the vaccine, not counting other transaction costs involved in its safe transportation and administration.

On the other hand, if one were to ask inventors of, for example, a critical vaccine or green technology to allow the global and public use of the technology for which they hold the patents, one would perhaps have to reimburse them for the research costs they incurred. However, the invention would not need repeating millions or billions of times. This difference between a vaccine and a knowledge or technology product shows the importance of clarifying the consumption properties of a PG.[4]

A proper understanding of GPGs also requires us to clarify the meaning of the terms 'global' and 'good' as used in this context. Global means that the goods have worldwide effects, spanning countries in different parts of the world, areas beyond national jurisdiction (ABNJs) and, perhaps, multiple generations. Importantly, they tend to penetrate countries and ABNJs without asking for permission or a visa. Thus, considering that we live in a world of manifold differences, disparities and varying preferences among countries and population groups, the border-crossing penetration effects of a GPG may create conflict or contestation. This occurs because of their perceived negative impact on the welfare of the affected countries and because they run counter to the core principles of the present world order – non-violability of national borders and national policymaking sovereignty. In other words, the goods' global 'publicness'[5] in consumption entails policy interdependence among countries, which may or may not be welcomed by certain countries and population groups; and, therefore, when used in reference to a PG, the term 'good' is value neutral. It denotes a thing, product, service or condition, just as it does when used in reference to a private good, such as a cigarette or car.

Governance requirements

Just like most private goods, most PGs, including GPGs, are composed of various building blocks that need to be assembled in order for the desired final good to emerge. Similarly, once they exist, they need maintenance and care lest they stop generating their expected benefits.

The public goods literature has distinguished three main types of assembly processes: summation, summation with a weak link, and best shot (Cornes and Sandler, 1996). Figure 10.1 illustrates, in a highly stylized and simplified form, the provision path of a good following a summation-type provision process, as do many GPGs. Clearly, GPGs are not provided in a lump sum at the international level, by one or another global actor, such as the United Nations or the World Bank. This holds even for goods that follow a best shot provision path, such as the invention of a new vaccine.[6] GPG provision is a highly complex process. In order for the final product to emerge, many hands have to come on deck, including multiple state and nonstate actors, who can generate the required inputs at different levels of policymaking and, most likely, also in a wide range of economic sectors.

Thus, when considering how best to provide a GPG most efficiently and effectively, policymakers need to consider several aspects and make a number of choices. Crucially important is to determine whether the good in question has specific "systemic integrity requirements" that must be met for it to emerge and generate the expected benefits, or whether it can be improved incrementally (Costanza, 2015). If it is the former, then it is important to accept that in determining

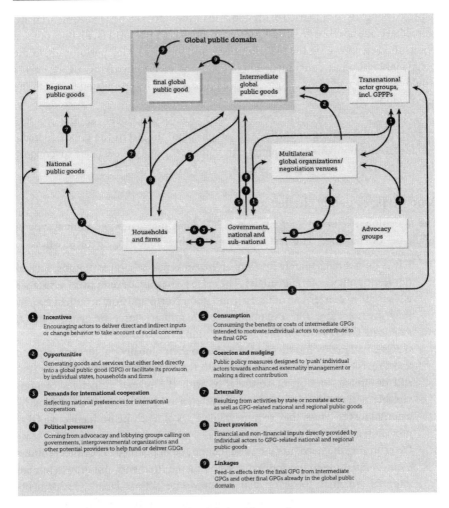

Figure 10.1   The provision path of a global public good
Source: Kaul et al. (2016: xxxix).

adequate provision, not only human interests count but also the interests, the systemic
integrity requirements of the good itself, a requirement of special importance now in
the Anthropocene.

Other provision aspects to consider would include, for example, the balances to
strike between horizontal and vertical decentralization; the willingness to cooperate
among essential input providers and the incentives they would eventually need; the
views and expectations of concerned stakeholders; the necessary types of financing
and how to mobilize them; and last but not least, how to share the costs and

expected benefits. Ideally, each of the goods to be provided, such as maritime security, would have one or more provision platforms, along with platform facilitators or focal points to keep an eye on the overall process and to report back periodically to the policymaking bodies concerned. The creation of such networking arrangements would make it possible for the governance processes of GPG provision to match the goods' global character.

Thus, GPG provision, too, involves interdependence, adding to the interdependence among countries and people stemming from the goods' globally public consumption; this consequently strengthens the sense of curtailed sovereignty that policymakers and the public often associate with GPGs.

A new type of policy challenge

The foregoing discussion suggests that GPGs constitute a new, additional type of public-policy challenge. This rests mainly on the three following characteristics:

1. GPGs do not fall squarely into any of the conventional policy moulds, such as domestic policy or foreign affairs. They also go beyond development assistance because they concern all of us, rich and poor, North and South, and, of course, they do not allow for resolution through military force or geoeconomics. Adequate GPG provision calls for institutional innovation.
2. GPGs entail policy interdependence due to their globally public consumption and provision. They therefore clash with the conventional 19th century (but still dominant) notion of sovereignty, with the related principles of non-violable national borders and non-interference in national policymaking by external forces. Thus, they require viable ways of reaching both effective GPG provision and policymaking sovereignty.
3. Determining the need, urgency and magnitude of planned GPG interventions requires attention to the goods' provisioning requirements, not only to human interests, whether those of state or non-state actors. Hence, investment-thinking rather than donor-thinking needs to underpin GPG financing.

Judging from recent reports on global crisis and gaps in GPG provision, it appears that the needed innovations have, to date, only happened in part if at all (WEF, 2021; WMO, 2021). The next section offers some explanations for this current state of GPG provision.

EXPLAINING TODAY'S UNDER-PROVISION OF GLOBAL PUBLIC GOODS

Psychological and behavioural factors receive the most frequent mention in the social-sciences literature as contributors to GPG under-provision. The most frequently assumed impediment is free riding on the part of individual actors in the presence of public goods. By now, however, evidence has mounted that this type of behaviour does not occur as generally as analysts assume. Many individual actors, whether organizational entities, such as state, business and civil-society groups, or human individuals, act out of mixed motives, or perhaps even out of pure altruism. Often, hesitation to cooperate arises from aversion to change or uncertainty stemming from lack of information or inability fully to grasp complex events.

No doubt such psychological and behavioural factors also contribute to GPG under-provision today. However, many seem to have deeper roots and serve as symptoms of more basic systemic and structural problems. Therefore, the following analysis focuses on systemic factors, notably lagging adjustment to today's policymaking realities within the operational system of multilateral cooperation and structural factors, especially as-yet-unsettled and intensifying global power shifts. The summary notes that concern about their national policymaking sovereignty makes countries reluctant to cooperate today.

Systemic factors

Global governance, or the system of IC, consists of two main interrelated processes: policy-setting or negotiations and operations or implementation. With the rising number of GPG-type challenges confronting us, the policy-setting part has become more and more global issue-focused. Special issue-focused multilateral, even universal multilateral negotiation processes now exist for older and newer GPGs, ranging from climate change to the United Nations Convention on the Law of the Sea (UNCLOS), cybersecurity and the combined global public spillover effects of GPG under-provision, such as swelling movements of forced international refugee and migration streams. In these forums, countries forge agreements on global goals, principles, norms and standards.

However, on the operational side, governance arrangements have largely remained unchanged. For the most part, the operational multilateral system still functions as a development assistance or aid system: much the same holds for the bilateral aid system. Most of its increasingly numerous agencies, funds and programmes, including the multilateral development banks (MDBs), have a country-focused business model and corresponding instruments, and, in the case of the MDBs, for example, sovereign loans. Of course, developing countries – like many industrialized countries – have a genuine interest in undertaking projects (even loan-financed ones) in GPG-related policy fields, projects that can generate national benefits and global co-benefits. This becomes evident from their voluntary nationally determined commitments (NDCs) to reduce greenhouse gases.

However, the experience in the Global South and Global North has also made it evident that the non-recognition of GPGs as policy concerns sui generis also creates many challenges. While countries, state and non-state actors contribute in myriad ways to numerous GPGs, the sum of all these individual efforts often does not meet requirements for adequate provision levels. Individual and global interests overlap only partially, and the present system has no effective pull mechanisms in place. As a result, especially in the case of binary goods, such as climate change mitigation, under-provision problems remain unresolved, and may even worsen and assume ever more serious, costly and potentially catastrophic proportions. The next section suggests that the ongoing global power shifts play a major role in this institutional lock-in and path dependency.

Structural factors

As more developing states have moved up the development ladder, some have become global powerhouses and have begun to play a more proactive role in multilateral forums, regionally and globally (Kaul, 2020; Lopes and Kararach, 2019). The world has begun a gradual move away from the conventional constellation of a small group of powerful states acting as global policy-setters, often under the leadership of one of the superpowers, with the rest of the countries largely relegated to policy-taker status.

In the wake of these shifts, top-down power politics have increasingly lost effectiveness as multilateralism's main operating principle. The industrialized countries have confronted ever more frequently what their developing counterparts have long known: namely that IC and sovereignty do not necessarily fit together quasi-automatically. Especially under the present conditions of increasing multipolarity, any such fit calls for compromises, acknowledging and respecting varying preferences and priorities, and striking win–win bargains to bring all on board.

However, rather than accepting that conditions have changed, industrialized countries began partially to retreat from universal multilateralism, negotiating select issues in mini-lateral forums and promoting club-based governance, for example by institutionalizing regular meetings of the Group of Seven (G7). The developing countries followed suit and set up their own mini-lateral initiatives, such as the BRICS Forum and other new mechanisms, including the Asian Infrastructure Investment Bank or the New Development Bank. Moreover, official development assistance (ODA) flows became more targeted to issues of special concern for donor countries. In fact, the principal change has come in greater reliance on private finance for development.

Unsurprisingly, under these circumstances very few if any countries have had a strong appetite for change. Universal multilateralism and perhaps even multilateralism in general became shallow. More omnibus agreements were adopted, such as the 2030 Agenda, which covers so wide a range of goals and sub-goals (many already approved in earlier UN resolutions) that adopting it did not require any too-difficult compromise. Similarly, the Paris Agreement on climate change could pass because, among other things, it emphasized voluntary nationally determined commitments to carbon-dioxide emissions reductions. To complicate matters further, rather than seeking new cooperation strategies, rivalry emerged between the major powers, notably between China and the United States. This left the world adrift without any clear vision of how to cooperate on GPG-type issues that, as both sides would perhaps readily admit, no one country, however powerful, can resolve unilaterally and alone.[7]

A lack of realism and vision holds back needed change

Thus, it appears that the under-provision of GPGs today stems from two main factors: institutional lock-in, notably the lagging adjustment of the operational system of IC to both the growing importance of GPGs and increasing multipolarity; and the ongoing global power shifts, which make both developed and developing countries follow a "logic of hedging" (Matthews, 2021: 12). This is a course of shallow, non-committal IC because, for quite different reasons, both groups of countries are concerned about lacking compatibility between IC and national policymaking sovereignty. Therefore, how could the world escape from this policy trap? The next section offers an initial set of reform ideas, while the fourth section explores whether there already exist change processes that appear to head in the direction of the changes suggested.

DOING BETTER IN THE FUTURE I: MAKING MULTILATERALISM FIT FOR PURPOSE

When taking the previous findings together, it seems that making multilateralism fit for purpose will at least need the following three reforms: first and foremost, to forge consensus on a new principle of mutual compatibility between IC and sovereignty as a new operating principle of multilateralism and, in support thereof, to recognize GPGs as a new, additional type of public policy issue; and to adopt a platform or 'mission-oriented approach' to GPG provision that is focused on actually achieving the resolution of existing under-provision problems (Mazzucato, 2017, 2021). We will discuss each of these three reforms in turn. As the search for doing better continues in the next section, we integrate and sum up the analysis in the final sections.

Making multilateral cooperation and sovereignty mutually compatible

The conventional and, until now, dominant operating principle of IC has been power politics. However, considering that this principle is fast losing out in political acceptance and consequently, effectiveness, the question arises of what could take its place in the future. Given countries' concerns about how to ensure that IC does not undermine their sovereignty, Kaul (2020) argues for replacing power politics as the chief operating principle of IC by a principle of 'dual compatibility,' referring to the mutual compatibility between IC and sovereignty. To foster such compatibility, the principle would require states to aim for two objectives:

1. Constructing IC bargains that all the concerned parties view as sovereignty-compatible, that is, enhancing their national welfare and well-being.
2. Making every effort possible to exercise their national policymaking sovereignty in a way that is compatible with the global.

To elaborate on the second objective, the respectful exercise of national policymaking sovereignty might imply, among other things, respect for other nations' sovereignty and to this end, willingness to internalize negative cross-border spillovers wherever possible and in line with established global goals and norms of fairness and justice. It would also include respect for the adequate-provision requirements of GPGs and hence, willingness to contribute a fair share of the inputs required, individually and collectively.

Clearly, reaching consensus on any one side of this notion of dual compatibility will depend on consensus on the other side. It may also depend on related processes of consultation and decision-making being fully participatory and transparent. Discussing and agreeing on a notion of dual compatibility could have the positive effect of changing the language and perception of IC, such that in the minds of many policymakers and the public, it loses its equation with giving up or losing national policymaking sovereignty. However, applying the new operating principle and enabling all concerned parties to judge for themselves whether a particular IC initiative meets the criterion of dual compatibility would critically depend on states' concurrent agreement to the reforms discussed next.

Recognizing a GPG

Given the intention stated in several recent global agreements to promote sustainable global growth and development, the resolution of the most pressing cases of GPG under-provision ought to be a top priority, not only at the level of rhetoric but also at the practical political level. It is difficult to imagine how an effective and efficient resolution of related problems could be achieved without granting GPGs their long overdue recognition as a policy type sui generis. To do so would imply accepting both that these goods differ in significant ways from other types of IC challenges, such as development assistance and financing for a global crisis response and stabilization facility and that there also exist numerous interlinkages and synergies between these different IC strands, as shown in Figure 10.2, which illustrates the resultant tripod-shaped architecture of IC finance.

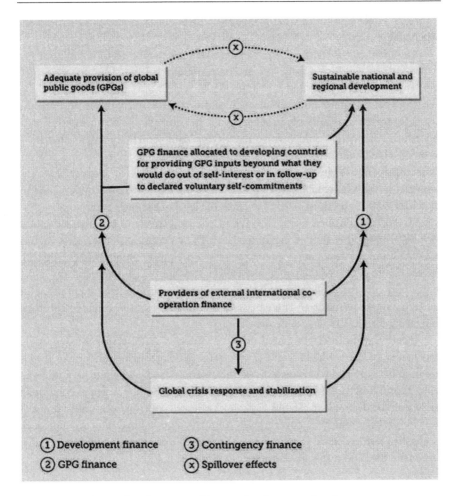

Figure 10.2   A tripod architecture of international cooperation finance
Source: Kaul (2020d: 154).

Adopting a mission-oriented approach to GPG provision

As discussed earlier, GPGs tend to be highly complex issues. On the political or negotiations side of IC, they tend to call for universal multilateralism for the simple fact that they often affect and concern all or at least many of us across the world. On the operational side, they call for extensive, often world-wide, multi-level, multi-sector and, therefore, also quasi-universal multilateral networking arrangements with decision makers, input providers and stakeholders. Therefore, they would best be tackled by setting up GPG-specific global platforms, along with platform facilitators and focal points, mandated to facilitate a comprehensive, integrated and result-oriented approach to the management of their provision. Such a platform approach would be akin to what Mazzucato (2017, 2021) describes as a "mission-oriented approach".

The main characteristic of such an approach is its ambition of not only to aim at but actually reach the goals, targets and timeframes decided by the concerned legislative bodies. To this end, it would also be a part of the mission not only to reach out to, exchange information with and provide a sense of direction to the myriad actors who voluntarily provide inputs. In addition, the platform or mission facilitators' mandate would involve identifying complementary inputs that need to be provided collectively at the international level and to mobilize the requisite financing for those. In this way, it could become possible to actually close the gaps that nowadays remain between the sum of the inputs voluntarily provided by individual actors and those needed to reach the level of adequate provision.

To illustrate, in the case of COVID-19, the collectively to-be-provided inputs include, among others, financing for the COVID-19 Vaccines Global Access Facility (COVAX) and the financing needed to support developing countries in coping with the economic effects of the pandemic. However, as the IC approach to COVID-19 is still of a conventional, fractured type, many of the additionally required inputs are seriously underfunded.[8] There exists no integrated mission-oriented approach to fighting the COVID-19 pandemic.

Clearly, key features of mission-oriented projects that deserve this name would systematically assess what it would cost to achieve their mission, undertake at least rough-and-ready but solid analyses of the financial and non-financial costs and benefits and mobilize the required funds. In cases that require urgent resolution, it could even be desirable to establish a scale of assessed contributions until a project's mission is accomplished, covering all countries and taking into account such established burden-sharing principles as the principle of common but differentiated responsibilities and respective capacities (UNFCCC, n.d.)

DOING BETTER IN THE FUTURE II: RECOGNIZING THE ROLE OF REGIONAL ORGANIZATIONS IN GPG PROVISION

A central thesis developed in economist Albert O. Hirschman's writings states that at any point in time, societal conditions are likely to contain both destructive and constructive forces (Adelman, 2013). So, can we discern these sorts of constructive forces at the present moment, ones that could help advance the change agenda discussed earlier. As the following discussion shows, the answer is 'Yes'.

Among the many ongoing global transformation processes, one that seems to qualify as constructive is the rising trend towards regionalism in the Global South. According to Acharya, "[r]egionalism – especially [...] 'open regionalism' that engages positively with outside actors – is key to the decentring and pluralisation of world politics. It allows different actors, regions and institutions to play a role in building global order" (Acharya, 2016: 3). Autochthonous regional organizations (ROs) have emerged as an important driving force behind the rise of regionalism in the developing world. These entities, for the most part created and governed by states of a particular geographic region, aim to enhance their member-states' welfare through various forms of cooperation and integration, including economic, sociocultural, environmental and political. These ROs differ from other regional entities, such as the UN's regional commissions, in that they are not arms of a conventional multilateral organization but rather associations rooted and headquartered in regions and subregions.

This section analyses the present role and functioning of ROs in the Global South in terms of their potential for enhancing GPG provision. It takes stock of current RO action in respect to GPGs and examines their models of multilateral cooperation.[9] It then assesses the role of ROs to date, suggesting that ROs already serve as pivotal meso-level intermediaries between the global and the individual in GPG provision. To date, this role of ROs has, however, received only limited attention, including from the international development assistance community.

ROs' present role in GPG provision

Most ROs were created with the overarching goal of improving the welfare and wellbeing of their member states through cooperative efforts aimed at fostering integration among them. The expectation, which, in large measure, has been realized, was that integration would give small- or middle-sized countries added economic and political visibility and strength and thus enhanced opportunities to pursue more self-determined development goals and to exercise more agency in international negotiations on global matters.

While some ROs, such as the South American trade bloc, MERCOSUR, have a main purpose, often economic cooperation and integration, most are multipurpose organizations that deal with economic, environmental and security challenges and sociocultural concerns, increasingly including human rights and gender equality issues. Importantly, considering the present context, ROs address a large number of GPG-type challenges. In fact, almost all GPGs, human-made or natural, long-standing or of recent origin, figure on some RO agenda, although with varying emphases depending on the RO's geographic location or its level of integration and institutional strength.

When one categorizes the GPG-related RO interventions according to their purpose, the typology shown in Box 10.1 emerges. It seems that in many cases, their activities are geared toward protecting their member states and the whole region against ill effects resulting from the under-provision of a wide range of GPGs, preventing problems in their neighbourhood from worsening, or supporting member states in individual and collective adaptation to climate change impacts, such as rising sea levels that result from melting polar ice.

Box 10.1   A typology of GPG-related functions performed by regional organizations

The GPG-related activities undertaken by ROs, often facilitated by their secretariat or other regional entities, fall into a number of different functional categories, including the following:

Protecting the region and individual countries in the region against negative 'spill-ins' from underprovided GPGs, such as climate change-related extreme weather events, health threats, excessive financial volatility, and international crime and violence.

Preventing simmering conflicts within the region from erupting, such as preventing the military skirmishes in the South China Sea or in the Indian Ocean from turning into war, or halting over-fishing before it reaches levels that threaten global food security.

Adapting to changed global conditions, such as melting ice caps, rising sea levels, and change in global production patterns and trade flows, through resilience-building and strengthening risk management at national and regional levels.

Facilitating member states' and the region's collective access to select GPGs, such as international markets, the Internet, outer space and new technologies and knowledge through national and regional-level capacity-building, thereby making the GPGs in question more de facto globally public in consumption.

Fostering the rollout of global norms, such as those concerning human rights, gender equality, democracy and the peaceful use of nuclear energy, in ways that fit the regional context and the preferences of individual member states, thereby contributing to the strengthening of the global normative framework.

Reinforcing rules-based global governance by making sure that regional initiatives are in line with existing international law, such as the UN Charter, UNCLOS, World Trade Organization agreements and international health regulations, and staying in touch with the concerned multilateral intergovernmental agencies.

Encouraging member states to avoid and, where they exist, internalize negative cross-border externalities through the establishment of regional research, education and training facilities as well as joint monitoring and review activities in such fields as climate-change mitigation, biodiversity preservation, communicable disease control and commitment to the safe use of nuclear materials.

Providing new and additional contributions to GPGs by enhancing member states' willingness to contribute to cooperative endeavours by creating problem and solution awareness, promoting a sense of community among member states and adopting an integrated public-policy approach to compensation for losses in one area of cooperation through benefits in another area, where and whenever possible.

Offering development assistance to weaker member states to foster regional fairness and create a basis for cooperation within the region and beyond.

Establishing upward linkages to relevant intergovernmental organizations with a worldwide mandate for GPGs of concern to the region.

Reaching out to various external partners to consult with them and seek their political, technical and financial support for planned or ongoing regional and global projects.

Another important function of ROs is to enable member states to access GPGs, such as international markets by, for example, fostering regional market integration and assisting members to strengthen their international competitiveness as buyers, sellers, investors and investment destinations. Many ROs wish to be seen not as stumbling blocks but rather as facilitators of globalization and enhanced GPG provision. To this end, they aim to operate within existing international laws. By doing so, they promote the rollout and upholding of global norms and standards as well as policy principles that range from free and fair trade to human rights, safe use of nuclear material and free passage for all through the high seas.

Yet another way in which ROs contribute to enhanced GPG provision is by supporting regional research and raining activities, as well as policy dialogue aimed at strengthening members awareness of existing challenges and new global opportunities and, thereby, their motivation to cooperate. This happens in areas such as climate change, biodiversity preservation, digitalization of the economy and the peaceful use of the outer space. In cases where member states require assistance in order to participate in a particular project, ROs offer them support, recognizing that contributing to GPGs often depends on the existence of requisite national capacity and resources.

Through these various activities aimed at enhancing member states' access to GPGs, ROs demonstrate that fairness can be granted, for example, by richer to poorer countries, but that it can – and, perhaps often, must – be self-made. Actors must acquire the capacity to benefit from available opportunities.

Given their emphasis on a comprehensive and integrated perspective on policymaking, ROs demonstrate an awareness of the multiplex nature of GPGs. This can be seen from the Indian Ocean Rim Association (IORA), which deals with the multi-dimensional GPG of maritime security. IORA not only adopts a multi-issue/sector/actor approach, but has membership comprising African and Asian countries. In this case, the GPG is the region or space that determines the organization's membership. A similar phenomenon can be observed in the Association of Southeast Asian Nations (ASEAN) region where the health and peacefulness of the South China Sea are important rallying points that make countries cooperate around issues of sustainable fisheries, illicit trade and free passage through the sea. The notion of integrated, continent-wide development obviously also underpins the work of the African Union (AU), as evident from its 2063 Agenda (African Union, n.d.a). Regional public goods (RPGs), such as the aforementioned, clearly show the significant global spillover effects that RPGs can have. They are dual-purpose RPGs, because they serve the region and the world, for example, by making it possible also for external actors to access and utilize these RPGs, be it in the form of natural-resource mining or enjoying a free and safe passage of their ships through the high seas.[10]

Many of the ROs' functions mentioned in Box 10.1 have become institutionalized in various forms, including regional crisis management mechanisms; research and training centres; centres for disease control; regimes harmonizing physical and institutional infrastructure; regular consultations, monitoring and review processes; and, in support of these and other functions, the establishment of RO secretariats.[11] These entities can be viewed as intermediate dual-purpose RPGs, serving the region and contributing to GPG provision by easing goods under-provision or enhancing their provision levels, thereby making globalization look better than it would without the corrective efforts of the ROs. The quantity and quality of RO-produced RPGs, in turn, depend on a critically important intangible RPG: the trust that exists among RO member states. Comparative analyses of South Asian Association for Regional Cooperation (SAARC), on the one hand, and for example, ASEAN and the Bay of Bengal Initiative for Multi-Sectoral Technical and Economic Cooperation (BIMSTEC), on the other hand, show that differences in the level of trust among RO member states helps explain the differences in these organizations' respective performance, including the internal and external legitimacy enjoyed by their representatives, notably their secretariats.[12]

Several ROs clearly recognize the limits of their regional interventions in dealing with GPGs and, therefore, they proactively seek and establish links with external, state and nonstate partners beyond their region. To do this effectively, their representatives must enjoy external agency; to enjoy external agency they need to be seen by their partners as enjoying internal agency and legitimacy, the trust of their member states. The issue of trust, legitimacy and partnering brings us straight to the next point: the ROs' models of multilateralism.

Regional models of multilateralism

Of course, different ROs function differently, mainly because they operate under varied regional conditions and external influences. However, assessments of RO effectiveness generally show that these organizations have generated positive results. For example, analysts recognize ASEAN's major achievement in terms of preventing conflicts relating to the South China Sea from exploding. The recently concluded Regional Comprehensive Economic Partnership (RCEP), which ASEAN facilitated over several years, marks yet another one of its achievements. Despite the tensions existing between SAARC's members, notably between India and Pakistan, it, too, has achieved important positive results. It has kept the communication channels among its members alive. In addition, as noted earlier, several regional centres were established and continue to function. Moreover, the COVID-19 pandemic appears to have engendered a new, strengthened willingness among SAARC members to engage in more active cooperation (PSRP, 2021a).

In fact, despite various external interferences and efforts to pull RO member states apart, most ROs have survived and are, to varying degrees, able to produce results (Chirathivat and Langhammer, 2020). This appears in large measure to be due to the basic type of multilateralism that more or less all ROs practice, whether located in Asia or other parts of the Global South, which has become known as the 'ASEAN way'. Its hallmarks include mutual respect among RO member states for each other's sovereignty, territorial integrity and independence; decision-making through consultation and by consensus; seeking unity in diversity; promoting a sense of community among member states; and practicing open multilateralism by reaching out to external partners while maintaining the RO's centrality (ASEAN, 2007). The last point, that of RO centrality, receives special emphasis in ASEAN's Charter (ASEAN, 2007: article 2.1[m]). But it also appears in African pronouncements that stress the importance of increased African agency and equality of partnership, including in global matters that also concern the continent. ROs are open to the views and preferences of others, respect them, but do not want to get instrumentalized by external partners for purposes that are not the RO's.

However, the ASEAN Charter's stipulation on centrality should be read together with its Article 2.1(n) calling on RO members' respect for and follow-up to the global commitments they have undertaken. This duality – the emphasis on one's sovereignty, on the one hand, and commitment to agreed-upon global goals, on the other hand – explains RO concern about implementing global goals in a region-specific manner while also reaching out to external partners and multilateral organizations in order for regional preferences and priorities to be better heard and taken into account in global negotiations and decision-making.

Thus, ROs act as meso-level intermediaries in the system of global governance, engage in linking and fostering compatibility between individual interests, whether local, national, regional or other, and the global interest. This intermediary role is, in many cases, an explicit part of ROs' identity. For example, according to its charter, ASEAN has the task of finding or, where it does not yet exist, promoting 'unity in diversity' (ASEAN, 2007: article 2.1[i]). It is barely imaginable how, in today's world, agreement on global goals and their implementation could be achieved without such a commitment to seeking unity in diversity, both among RO member states and between them and external interlocutors and partners.

Assessing current and potential future roles

As can be seen from the foregoing analysis and the regionalism literature, ROs are already playing an important role in both enhanced GPG provision and in making multilateralism function. In fact, some of the global challenges confronting the world could prove to be much more serious but for the activities undertaken by the ROs in Asia and elsewhere.

Moreover, the existence of ROs has meant that the stark contrast between a few major global policy-setters and many policy-takers, characteristic of earlier global governance eras, has begun to fade, gradually giving way to a more even global distribution of power among today's large countries, such as China, Japan, Russia and the United States, and the RO clusters of middle and smaller countries. In fact, in terms of joint economic strength, a few ROs have already moved up the development ranks closer to some of the top-ranking countries. For example, if the member states of ASEAN counted as one economy, in 2020 it was the fifth largest economy in the world, behind the United States, China, Japan and Germany (ASEAN, 2020). Certainly, the high-level attention that some ROs already enjoy depends not only on the critically important role they play in respect to GPG provision, but also on their growing importance as markets and natural-resource endowment.

Nevertheless, some ROs by now possess considerable internal and external 'actorness,'[13] including strong convening powers, as shown, for example, by the attendance at ASEAN and AU summit meetings (ASEAN, 1993; African Union, n.d.b). This strength equips them to play a role as intermediary between the global and the individual in both directions, downward and upward.

While some major powers seem well aware of them, links between ROs and the conventional entities of the IC system, notably the development assistance community, appear to be less well-developed. For the most part, development assistance agencies still view regions only as geographic spaces made up of individual countries and not as communities. Consequently, for them, integration means mainly furthering, country-by-country, interoperability of physical and institutional infrastructure and less so supporting the development of integrated communities capable of doing together what is best done together.[14] Of interest, however, is that a number of UN General Assembly resolutions recognized the role of ROs,[15] and several ROs have been granted consultative status to the United Nations. Moreover, ROs were sometimes invited to meet with the UN Secretary-General or attend a meeting of the UN Security Council. These and other signs suggest that the new reality of increasing regionalism is beginning to be recognized and appreciated as a force potentially to be relied on to foster more sustainable global growth and development and that it is time for IC agencies, including the UN regional commissions, to shift gears from doing development for individual countries in their respective region to enabling individual countries and ROs as regional communities to promote development that is done by and for themselves and the world, in line with the principle of mutual compatibility between IC and sovereignty.

Thus, regionalism will prove less a stumbling block and more a building block of a type that has been sorely lacking in global governance until now: agency at the meso-level. This is where ROs facilitate context-specific agreements with and among their member states to foster compatibility between IC and national policymaking sovereignty, a feat unlikely to be achieved as well, if at all, in any other international relations setting, including that of universal multilateralism. Certainly, at some future date, there may also arise a need for considering a multilateralization of regional developments, but for now the issue remains one of encouraging regionalism and multiple solutions. Barbieri (2019: 436) even argues that "[r]ather than regionalism being guided by globalization, the relationship between the two can be said to flow in both directions". And, in fact, it ought to flow in both directions, because, as discussed earlier, multilateralism – especially universal multilateralism at the global level – also needs a new operating principle, similar to that underpinning the RO model.

The four distinguishing features of a fit-for-purpose multilateralism

Clearly, the reforms discussed here require one another for each to work, and for all to achieve the goal: the grand mission of making multilateralism more fit for the purpose of enhanced GPG provision. Together, they constitute a four-point reform agenda that, once accomplished, would lead to a fit-for-purpose multilateralism with four distinguishing features. It would:

1. Operate on the principle of mutual compatibility between IC and sovereignty.
2. Recognize GPGs as a new, additional type of policy challenge and end their confounding with development assistance.
3. Adopt a mission-oriented approach to resolving GPG-related challenges.
4. Involve ROs as meso-level intermediaries between the global and the individual, including the specific interests of individual states, in matters of global governance.

As several analysts argue, among them Söderbaum (2016), regionalism is here to stay. Considering that several ROs are already actively interlinked with various external partners, including ROs outside their own geographic space, it seems reasonable to assume that over time regionalism and its model of multilateralism will increasingly flow upward into the global realm and help generate more understanding and support for applying the principle of mutual compatibility between IC and sovereignty, also in the context of universal multilateralism.

However, many of today's global challenges need to be addressed urgently and decisively. The next section offers recommendations on how to kickstart and accelerate the needed change processes.

MOVING FORWARD: CATCHING UP WITH REALITY

Clearly, enhancing the provision of GPGs, notably resolving the most pressing problems resulting from their under-provision, requires a major rethinking of current concepts, institutional arrangements and IC strategies. Isolated ad hoc changes and a bit more money here or there will not suffice, as the analysis in this chapter shows. Basic constraints require removal and new opportunities need tapping. However, mounting empirical evidence demonstrates that several of the present policy paths, notably the present way of addressing GPG-type challenges, are not only becoming increasingly costly but also posing global systemic risks. Hence, a continuation of business as usual seems to be highly undesirable, leading us not toward but away from the agreed goal of global sustainability.

But what would it take, then, to set the necessary rethinking in motion? Here are some suggestions on possible next steps.

Recommendation 1   Most important for policymakers and the global public at large is perhaps to bear in mind Mahbubani's (2013, p.87) words: "The world has changed. Our way of managing it has not." Therefore, most important would be for scholars and experts working in relevant policy fields to, first of all, take stock of, synthesize and communicate in an accessible form for further public debate what we know already about how concretely we could more fully and systematically adjust to today's policymaking realities. Additional policy research and development ought to be undertaken and well-documented proof that describes the conditions under which to implement reforms. Without such additional information about the how, when and why, many policymakers and their various constituencies would most likely hesitate to innovate unless a major global disaster would finally compel them to do so. Clearly, the better way is to rethink and act out of realism and enlightened self-interest.

Recommendation 2   As regards the suggested strengthening of the role of ROs in the Global South, it could be useful to take a clue from how the UN Economic Commission for Africa (UNECA) and the AU have decided to organize the relationship between them. Whereas other UN economic commissions still tend to do a lot of development for the region, the UNECA and AU have agreed on a partnership model of development with and by the AU, in line with the AU's basic principle that Africa's development ought to be driven by Africans. If similar agreements were reached in other parts of the world, ROs' capacities could receive a significant boost as could their contributions to GPG provision and global sustainable growth and development.[16]

Recommendation 3   Much could also be gained in terms of strengthening ROs and, beyond that, furthering the emergence of a more fit-for-purpose multilateralism if the conventional development assistance agencies, including the MDBs and Organisation for Economic Cooperation and Development/Development Assistance Committee, would undertake a review of their current activities to determine to what extent they have or have not yet adjusted their operational modalities to today's policymaking realities. More specifically, have they initiated reforms to help create the new tripod architecture of IC finance discussed earlier (Figure 10.2), which would be an essential step towards realizing a new multilateralism? What additional reforms are they intending to implement next? And what are the lessons they have learned that could be useful to share with the wider IC community?

Recommendation 4   In several respects, the reforms needed to realize the type of a new multilateralism suggested here go right to the core of today's world order by calling for a modernized interpretation of the notion of sovereignty. Therefore, it would only be fitting if the UN Secretary-General would seek member states' agreement on the establishment of a panel of renowned personalities to hold global consultations on this proposed agenda and offer their advice on how to proceed further.

Recommendation 5   Considering the urgency of several of the global challenges we confront, why would the UN member states not dare to be bold and decide to establish two mission-oriented pilots as soon as possible: one for climate change mitigation and adaptation and one for global health, including the fight against COVID-19 and strengthening global preparedness for the next health threats likely to attack the world, such as microbial resistance? Certainly, member states would find it easier to take this decision if there was strong support for it from civil society, the business community, think tanks and academia, that is, the global public.

Of course, the message here is not to halt current action to address global challenges. All of that can and should for now continue, even with incremental improvements, but always with the awareness that these measures will not suffice. More fundamental change is needed and hence the call here for a willingness to rethink and innovate so that, come 2030, we may not see ourselves fall too far short of the goal of global sustainable growth and development.

Conclusion

The analysis in the first two sections of this chapter shows that sovereignty is coming under pressure in IC contexts. This demotivates states from engaging in multilateral cooperation, notably the universal multilateralism that many GPGs require. So far, however, no clear vision exists of how to realize mutual compatibility between effective IC and national policymaking sovereignty. The third and fourth sections offer a possible vision of fit-for-purpose multilateralism. As the fifth section argues, translating this vision into policy practice requires a major rethinking and notably more realism: on the one hand, a willingness to accept that the world has changed and, on the other hand, acceptance of the fact that in GPG-related policy fields that entail interdependence among countries, effective cooperation tends to be the better way forward towards realizing national interests because it solves problems that cannot be resolved unilaterally. Are policymakers and the global public ready for that? The many calls and expressed commitments to doing better in the post-COVID-19 era suggest that now could be the right time to introduce some long-overdue corrective steps and facilitate faster and scaled-up progress towards global sustainable growth and development.

APPENDIX 10A.A METHODOLOGICAL NOTE ON THE SOURCES REVIEWED FOR THE FOURTH SECTION OF THIS CHAPTER

The discussion in the fourth section of this chapter is based on a comprehensive review of the literature on regionalism and the role of regional organizations in the Global South. Included in this review have been contributions from multiple disciplines, including economics, political science, international relations, and peace and security studies, as well as contributions focusing from a regional perspective on particular GPG-related aspects, including, among others, the following: Alisjahbana, 2020; Alston et al., 1996; Acharya, 2008a, 2008b, 2008c, 2015; Barbieri, 2019; Bergin et al., 2019; Berkofsky and Sciorati, 2021; Börzel and Risse, 2016; Börzel et al., 2016; Chirathivat et al., 2020; Chirathivat and Langhammer, 2020; Cohen and Fontaine, 2020; Cornell and Starr, 2018; Dembowski, 2018; Ergenç, 2021; Fawcett, 2019; Foot and Goh, 2019; Islam and Kieu, 2020; Jones et al., 2019; Kaul, 2020; Khor et al., 2020; Libman, 2019; Lissovolik, 2019; Lopes and Kararach, 2019; Mahbubani, 2013; Mahbubani, 2020; Meyer et al., 2019; Mirelli, 2018; Pelkmans, 2020; Pizarro, 1999; PSRP, 2021a, 2021b; Rivera, 2017; Söderbaum, 2016, 2018; Susantono and Park 2020; Wang and Song 2020. In addition to the aforementioned contributions, the websites of a select sample of ROs were consulted to see how different ROs describe the purpose, functioning and outcomes of their GPG-related interventions. Among the ROs selected for this purpose were the following: African Union (AU), Association of Southeast Asian Nations (ASEAN), Bay of Bengal Initiative for Multi-Sectoral Technical and Economic Cooperation (BIMSTEC), Central Asian Cooperation Organisation (CACO), Caribbean Community/Community of Latin American and Caribbean States (CARICOM/CELAC), Gulf Cooperation Council (GCC), Indian Ocean Rim Association (IORA), Mercado Común del Sur (MERCOSUR), Organization of American States (OAS), Pacific Islands Forum (PIF), South Asian Association for Regional Cooperation (SAARC), Shanghai Cooperation Organisation (SCO).

NOTES

1.   Drawing on Paul A. Samuelson (1954), standard economic theory distinguishes between two main categories of goods: private goods and public goods. This classification depends on two characteristics of goods: (1) their rivalry, that is, whether one's consumption of the good reduces another person's ability to consume the good, and (2) their excludability, or the ability of the owner of the good to prevent its use by another person. A good that is both rival, meaning one person's consumption prevents another person from consuming it, and excludable, meaning the owner can prevent someone from using the good, is a private good. Conversely, a good that is non-rival, meaning one person's consumption does not diminish another person's ability to consume it, and non-excludable, meaning the owner cannot easily prevent others from using the good,

is a public good. The public effects of a good can be local, national, regional, worldwide and cross-generational. Global public goods are goods of which benefits or costs are of nearly universal reach or potentially affect anyone anywhere (Kaul, 2015).

2. For a comprehensive overview of the evolution and the current state of the debate in the social-science, political-science and international relations literature on GPGs, see Kaul (2016) and Kaul et al. (2016)

3. The term 'globalness' originated in the field of marketing, where it describes how a brand is widely available and accepted across the world; see Liu et al. (2021).

4. For a more detailed discussion on making vaccines available for all, see Kaul (2020d) and Reddy and Acharya (2020).

5. On the concept of 'publicness' and global governance, see Koenig-Archibugi and Zürn (2006).

6. On the process of vaccine research and development, see Felter (2021) and WHO (2021).

7. On this point, also see the 2021 Earth Day Summit on Climate convened by the US President and attended by 40 heads of state or government (Neuberger, 2021).

8. On the COVAX funding gap, see Farge (2021) and, on financial support for developing countries, see Mazarei (2021).

9. The methodological note in the Appendix 10A.A explains the data collection for this section.

10. For more information, see Bergin et al. (2020) and Birdwell and Taherian (2020).

11. Examples of these dual-purpose RPGs are organizations such as the African Union's Centres for Disease Control and Prevention (africacdc.org/); the Chiang Mai Initiative, an emergency liquidity facility launched by ASEAN and China, Japan and the Republic of Korea (that is, ASEAN+3) (https://aric.adb.org/initiative/ chiang-mai-initiative); the Disaster Management Centre of the South Asian Association for Regional Cooperation (SAARC) (saarc-sdmc.org/); and the Caribbean Center for Renewable Energy and Energy Efficiency of the Caribbean Community (CARICOM) (caricom.org/institutions/caribbean-center-forrenewable-energy-and-energy-efficiency-ccreee/). Besides the aforementioned tangible dual-purpose RPGs, there also exist less tangible ones, such as the normative frameworks that ROs have created, including, for example, the agreements that they forged on economic cooperation and integration; the norms laid down in various charter documents and subsequent declarations calling for commitment to international cooperation within and beyond the region; the peaceful settlement of disputes; and, increasingly, promotion of environmental sustainability, respect for human rights and the strengthening of women's role in development

12. See, for example, the case studies presented in Bhattacharjee (2018), Meyer et al. (2019) and Zaum (2013).

13. On the concept of 'actorness' and interregional relations conceptualised in terms of institutions, recognition and identity, and as a relational concept dependent on context and perception, see Mattheis and Wunderlich (2017).

14. For examples of such so far rather rare activities of regional community-building or, perhaps better, region-building performed by development assistance agencies, see ADB (2016) and AfDB (2019).

15. See, for example, UN General Assembly Resolution 75/69 adopted 25 March 2021, concerning cooperation between the United Nations and the Shanghai Cooperation Organization (United Nations, 2021).
16. On the UNECA/AU relation, see African Union (2017).

REFERENCES

Acharya, A. 2008a. 'EU's Crisis: Lessons for Asia'. In *Asia Rising: Who Is Leading?* Singapore: World Scientific Publishing Co. Pte. Ltd., 187–191.

———. 2008b. 'Sovereignty: Asians Are Wary of Pushy Outsiders'. In *Asia Rising: Who Is Leading?* Singapore: World Scientific Publishing Co. Pte. Ltd., 173–175

———. 2008c. *Asia Rising: Who Is Leading?* Singapore: World Scientific Publishing Co. Pte. Ltd.

———. 2015. 'Will ASEAN Survive Great Power Rivalry in Asia?' *East Asia Forum Quarterly* 7(4), 17–20.

———. 2016. 'Interview – Amitav Acharya'. *E-International Relations*, 15 April. e-ir. info/2016/04/15/interview-amitav-acharya/.

Acharya, A. and Plesch, D. 2016. 'The United Nations: Managing and Reshaping a Changing World Order'. *Global Governance: A Review of Multilateralism and International Organizations* 26(2), 221–235.

Adelman, J., ed. 2013. *The Essential Hirschman.* Princeton: Princeton University Press.

African Development Bank (AfDB). 2019. *Regional Integration: Policy and Strategy (RIPoS) 2014–2023.* Abidjan: African Development Bank Group.

African Union. 2017. 'Concept Note'. The AU-RECs-UNECA-AFDB-NEPAD-ACBF Joint Expert Coordination Meeting, Nairobi, Kenya, 10–12 July 2017. The African Union Commission, Addis Ababa. au.int/sites/default/files/pages/32823-file-concept_note_au-recs-uneca-afdb-nepad-acbf_joint_expert_coordination_meeting_2017.pdf.

———. No date a. 'Agenda 2063: The Africa We Want'. The African Union Commission, Addis Ababa. au.int/en/agenda2063/overview.

———. No date b. 'AU Summits'. The African Union Commission, Addis Ababa. https:// au.int/en/summits/.

Alisjahbana, A. S. 2020. 'Harnessing Regional Cooperation for Building Back Better in Asia and the Pacific'. Dialogue of the Executive Secretaries of the Regional Commissions with the UN General Assembly Second Committee, 75th Session of the UNGA. United Nations Economic and Social Commission for Asia and the Pacific, Bangkok.

Asian Development Bank. 2016. *ASEAN–ADB Cooperation Toward the ASEAN Community; Advancing Integration and Sustainable Development in Southeast Asia.* Manila: Asian Development Bank.

Association of Southeast Asian Nations (ASEAN). 1993. 'ASEAN Regional Forum'. ASEAN Secretariat, Jakarta. aseanregionalforum.asean.org/about-arf/.

———. 2007. *Charter of the Association of South East Asian Nations.* Jakarta: The ASEAN Secretariat. asean.org/asean/asean-charter/charter-of-the-association-of-southeast-asian-nations/.

———. 2020. *ASEAN Key Figures 2020.* Jakarta: ASEAN Secretariat. aseanstats.org/wp-content/uploads/2020/11/ASEAN_Key_Figures_2020.pdf.

Barbieri, G. 2019. 'Regionalism, Globalism and Complexity: A Stimulus towards Global IR?' *Third World Thematics: A TWQ Journal* 4(6), 424–441.

Bergin, A., Brewster, D. and Bachhawat, A. 2019. *Ocean Horizons: Strengthening Maritime Security in Indo-Pacific Island States*. Canberra: Australian Strategic Policy Institute

Berkofsky, A. and Sciorati, G., eds. 2021. *Post-Pandemic Asia: A New Normal for Regional Security?* Milan: Ledizioni Ledi Publishing.

Bhattacharjee, J. 2018. 'SAARC vs BIMSTEC: The Search for the Ideal Platform for Regional Cooperation'. Observer Research Foundation Issue Brief, 2018(226). orfonline.org/wp-content/uploads/2018/01/ORF_Issue_Brief_226_BIMSTEC-SAARC.pdf/.

Birdwell, I. and Taherian, S. 2020. 'Expansionism, Projecting Power, and Territorial Disputes: The South China Sea'. ODU Issue Brief, Old Dominion University, Norfolk.

Börzel, T. A., Goltermann, L. and Striebinger, K. 2016. *Roads to Regionalism: Genesis, Design, and Effects of Regional Organizations*. London: Routledge.

Börzel, T. and Risse, T., eds. 2016. *Comparative Regionalism*. Oxford: Oxford University Press.

Chirathivat, S. and Langhammer, R. J. 2020. 'ASEAN and the EU Challenged by "Divide and Rule" Strategies of the US and China: Evidence and Possible Reactions'. *International Economics and Economic Policy* 17, 659–670.

Chirathivat, S., Kunnamas, N. and Welfens, P. J. 2020. 'Regional Integration in the EU and ASEAN in the Period of Declining Multilateralism and Corona Shocks'. *International Economics and Economic Policy* 17, 555–561.

Consuegra, L. J. 2020. *Democracy and Peacebuilding in the Framework of SDG 16+*. Stockholm: International Institute for Democracy and Electoral Assistance.

Cornes, R. and Sandler, T. 1996. *The Theory of Externalities, Public Goods, and Club Goods*. Cambridge: Cambridge University Press.

Costanza, R., Cumberland, J.H., Daly, H., Goodland, R. and Norgaard, R. B. 2015. *An Introduction to Ecological Economics*. New York: CRC Press.

Economic Commission for Latin America and the Caribbean. 2020. *Building a New Future: Transformative Recovery with Equality and Sustainability*. Santiago: Economic Commission for Latin America and the Caribbean. repositorio.cepal.org/bitstream/handle/11362/46228/4/S2000698_en.pdf.

Enderwick, P. and Buckley, P. 2020. 'Rising Regionalization: Will the Post-COVID-19 world See a Retreat from Globalization?' *Transnational Corporations* 27(2), 99–112.

Ergenç, C., ed. 2021. *ASEAN as a Method: Re-Centering Processes and Institutions in Contemporary Southeast Asian Regionalism*. New York: Routledge.

Farge, E. 2021. 'U.S. Alone Won't Fill COVAX Funding Gap, Lead Official Says'. Reuters, 22 January. reuters.com/article/us-health-coronavirus-who-covax-idUSKBN29R1Q3.

Fawcett, L. 2019. 'The Evolution of Competitive Latin-American Regionalism'. In T. Meyer, J. L. de S. Marques and M. Telò, eds., *Regionalism and Multilateralism: Politics, Economics, Culture*. London: Routledge, 108–126.

Felter. C. 2021. 'A Guide to Global COVID-19 Vaccine Efforts'. Council on Foreign Relations, New York. cfr.org/backgrounder/guide-global-covid-19-vaccine-efforts/.

Foot, R., and Goh, E. 2019. The International Relations of East Asia: A New Research Prospectus'. *International Studies Review* 21(3), 398–423.

Islam, M. S. and Kieu, E. 2020. 'Tackling Regional Climate Change Impacts and Food Security Issues: A Critical Analysis across ASEAN, PIF, and SAARC'. *Sustainability* 12(3), 1–21.

Jones, A., Tadesse, L. and Apiko, P. 2019. *Continental Drift in a Multipolar World*. Maastricht: European Centre for Development Policy Management.

Kaul, I. 2015. 'Global Public Policy'. In J. D. Wright, ed., *International Encyclopedia of the Social and Behavioral Sciences*. Amsterdam: Elsevier, 78–185.

———. 2019. 'The G20@10: Time to Shift Gears'. *South African Journal of International Affairs* 26(4), 563–582.

———. 2020a. 'Exit and Voice in Global Governance'. In L. Meldolesi and N. Stame, eds., *A Passion for the Possible; Excerpts from the Third Conference on Hirschman Legacy*. Rome: Italic Digital Editions, 313–332.

———. 2020b. 'Multilateralism 2.0: It Is Here – Are We Ready for It?' *Global Perspectives* 1(1), 17639. doi.org/10.1525/gp.2020.17639.

———. 2020c. 'Redesigning International Co-operation Finance for Global Resilience'. In *Development Co-operation Report 2020: Learning from Crises, Building Resilience*. Paris: Organisation for Economic Co-operation and Development Publishing. doi. org/10.1787/f6d42aa5-en.

———. 2020d. 'Want to Take the Africa–EU–partnership to the Next Level? Press the Reset Button'. *CESifo Forum* 212(2), 16–21.

———, ed. 2016. *Global Public Goods*. Cheltenham: Edward Elgar Publishing Ltd.

Kaul, I., Blondin, D. and Nahtigal, N. 2016. 'Introduction: Understanding Global Public Goods: Where We are and Where to Next'. In *Global Public Goods*. Cheltenham: Edward Elgar Publishing Ltd, xiii–xcii.

Khor, S. K., Lim, J., Hsu, L. Y. and Mahmood, J. 2020. 'Southeast Asia Needs Its Own CDC'. *Think Global Health*, 2 July, National University of Singapore, Singapore.

Koenig-Archibugi, M. and Zürn, M. 2006. *New Modes of Governance in the Global System; Exploring Publicness, Delegation and Inclusiveness*. London: Palgrave Macmillan.

Libman, A. 2019. 'Russia and Eurasian Regionalism: How Does It Fit into Comparative Regionalism Research?' In T. Meyer, J. L. de S. Marques and M. Telò, eds., *Regionalism and Multilateralism: Politics, Economics, Culture*. London: Routledge, 129–142.

Lissovolik, Y. 2019. *Regionalism in Global Governance: Exploring New Pathways*. Valdai Discussion Club Report. Moscow: Valdaiclub.

Liu, H., Schoefer, K., Fastoso, F. and Tzemou, E. 2021. 'Perceived Brand Globalness/Localness: A Systematic Review of the Literature and Directions for Further Research'. *Journal of International Marketing* 29(1). doi.org/10.1177/1069031X20973184.

Lopes, C. and Kararach, G. 2019. *Misperceptions, New Narratives and Development in the 21st Century*. Abingdon: Oxon and New York: Routledge.

Mahbubani, K. 2013. *The Great Convergence: Asia, the West, and the Logic of One World*. New York: Public Affairs Perseus Books Group.

———. 2020. *Has China Won? The Chinese Challenge to American Primacy*. New York: Public Affairs Hachette Book Group, Inc.

Mazarei, A. 2021. *Developing Countries Need Greater Financing and Debt Relief for COVID-19 and Future Pandemics*. Washington, DC: Peterson Institute for International Economics. piie.com/blogs/realtime-economic-issues-watch/developing-countries-need-greater-financing-and-debt-relief/.

Mazzucato, M. 2017. *Mission-Oriented Innovation Policy: Challenges and Opportunities*. London: University College.

———. 2021. *Mission Economy: A Moonshot Guide to Changing Capitalism*. New York: Penguin Random House.

Matthews, J. T. 2021. 'Present at the Re-creation? U.S. Foreign Policy Must Be Remade, Not Restored'. *Foreign Affairs* 100(2), 10–17.

Mattheis, F. and Wunderlich, U. 2017. 'Regional Actorness and Interregional Relations: ASEAN, the EU and Mercosur'. *Journal of European Integration* 39(6), 723–738. publications.aston.ac.uk/id/eprint/30834/.

Meyer, T., Marques, J. L. de S. and Telò, M., eds. 2019. *Regionalism and Multilateralism: Politics, Economics, Culture*. London: Routledge.

Mirelli, A. 2018. 'It's Not Just Trump. The US Has Always Broken Its Treaties, Pacts and Promises'. *Quartz Daily Brief*, 12 May. qz.com/1273510/all-the-international-agreements-the-us-has-broken-before-the-iran-deal/.

Neuberger, E. 2021. 'Here's What Countries Pledged on Climate Change at Biden's Global Summit'. CNBC, 22 April. cnbc.com/2021/04/22/biden-climate-summit-2021-what-brazil-japan-canada-others-pledged.html.

Neves, B. C. and Honório, K. 2019. 'Latin American Regionalism under the New Right'. *E-International Relations*, 27 September. e-ir.info/2019/09/27/latin-american-regionalism-under-the-new-right/.

Nordhaus, W. D. 2010. 'Some Foundational and Transformative Grand Challenges for the Social and Behavioral Sciences: The Problem of Global Public Goods'. American Economic Association, Ten Years and Beyond: Economists Answer NSF's Call for Long-Term Research Agendas. dx.doi.org/10.2139/ssrn.1889357.

Pelkmans, J. 2020. 'New Asia-Pacific Trade Deal: Implications for East Asia and Globalisation'. *CEPS Policy Insight* No. PI2020-30. Centre for European Policy Studies, Brussels.

Pizarro, R. 1999. *Comparative Analysis of Regionalism in Latin America and Asia-Pacific*. Santiago: Economic Commission for Latin America and the Caribbean.

Political Settlements Research Programme (PSRP). 2021a. *Responding to Covid-19: The Coming age of Regionalism in Asia?* Edinburgh: University of Edinburgh School of Law.

———. 2021b. *Cooperation in Latin America: Responses to COVID-19 Expose Existing Cracks in Regional Infrastructure*. Edinburgh: University of Edinburgh School of Law.

Radziyevska, S. and Us, I. 2020. 'Regionalization of the World as the Key to Sustainable Future'. *E3S Web of Conferences* 166(1306).

Reddy, S.G. and Acharya, A. 2020. 'The Economic Case for a People's Vaccine: Ensuring a COVID-19 Vaccine Is Available to All Makes Both Moral and Economic Sense'. *Boston Review*, 15 September. bostonreview.net/science-nature/sanjay-g-reddy-arnab-acharya-economic-case-peoples-vaccine.

Rivera, T. C. 2017. 'The ASEAN and the Politics of Major Powers: Impact on the Quest for a Regional Order'. In E. E. A. Co and C. C. Tabundi, Jr., eds., *The ASEAN Drama: Half a Century and Still Unfolding*. Quezon City: University of the Philippines Center for Integrative and Development Studies and Pasig City: Development Academy of the Philippines, 46–73.

Rodrik, D. 2019. Globalization's Wrong Turn and How It Hurt America'. *Foreign Affairs* 98(4), 25–33.

Samuelson, P. A. 1954. 'The Pure Theory of Public Expenditure'. *Review of Economics and Statistics* 36(4), 387–389. jstor.org/stable/1925895?seq=1.

Söderbaum, F. 2016. *Rethinking Regionalism*. London: Palgrave Macmillan.

————. 2018. 'Rethinking Regionalism in the 21st Century'. In A. Mania, M. Grabowski, and T. Pugacewicz, eds., *Global Politics in the 21st Century: Between Regional Cooperation and Conflict*. Berlin: Peter Lang Publishing, 25–40.

Susantono, B. and Park, C.-Y., eds. 2020. *Future of Regional Cooperation in Asia and the Pacific*. Manila: Asian Development Bank.

United Nations (UN). 2015. *Transforming our World: The 2030 Agenda for Sustainable Development*. New York: United Nations. documents-dds-ny.un.org/doc/UNDOC/GEN/N15/291/89/PDF/N1529189.pdf?OpenElement.

————. 2020. 'Declaration on the Commemoration of the Seventy-Fifth Anniversary of the United Nations'. United Nations, New York. un.org/pga/74/wp-content/uploads/sites/99/2020/07/UN75-FINAL-DRAFT-DECLARATION.pdf.

————. 2021. 'Resolutions of the 75th Session'. United Nations, New York. un.org/en/ga/75/resolutions.shtml.

————. No date. 'Intergovernmental and Other Organizations'. United Nations, New York. un.org/en/about-us/intergovernmental-and-other-organizations.

United Nations Framework Convention on Climate Change (UNFCCC). 'Introduction to Climate Finance'. United Nations Framework Convention on Climate Change, Bonn. unfccc.int/topics/climate-finance/the-big-picture/introduction-to-climate-finance.

Wang, J. and Song, W. 2019. 'Chinese Multilateralism in Central and Southeast Asia: A Relational Perspective'. In T. Meyer, J. L. de S. Marques and M. Telò, eds., *Regionalism and Multilateralism: Politics, Economics, Culture*. London: Routledge, 143–165.

World Economic Forum (WEF). 2021. *The Global Risks Report*. Geneva: World Economic Forum.

World Health Organization (WHO). 2021. 'Draft Landscape and Tracker of COVID-19 Candidate Vaccines'. World Health Organization, Geneva. who.int/publications/m/item/draft-landscape-of-covid-19-candidate-vaccines.

World Meteorological Organization (WMO). 2021. *State of the Global Climate 2020*. Geneva: World Meteorological Organization.

Zaum, D. 2013. *Legitimating International Organizations*. Oxford: Oxford University Press.

11 | Asian-Pacific Regional Cooperation in the Post-COVID-19 Era

Khalil Hamdani

INTRODUCTION

The international development agenda went on hold as countries responded to COVID-19 in 2020. The pandemic has not yet subsided as of this writing (Spring 2021), and the collateral damage may linger for years to come. Yet the COVID-19 crisis poses both a threat and an opportunity. Regional cooperation in the post-COVID-19 era should rise to that dual challenge, helping countries to seize opportunities to advance the United Nations Sustainable Development Goals (SDGs), and to devise new ways to respond to future threats.

Regionalism is a core strength of the Asia-Pacific Region (APR). Regional trade, investment and technology flows have spurred rapid economic growth and development for decades. Even in crisis, regionalism has helped shape recovery. For example, the Chiang Mai Initiative established currency swap arrangements among countries to balance payments difficulties in the 1997 Asian financial crisis. Additionally, the vulnerability of the APR to natural disasters prompted a regional response that led to a global framework for risk reduction (UN, 2015). Such examples show that regional cooperation can and should play a leading role in the post-COVID-19 era.

Moreover, the five pillars of the United Nations Framework for COVID Response envision a set of priorities requiring regional policy frameworks – one that dovetails with efforts to achieve the SDGs. Various mechanisms to achieve this already exist, as this chapter will describe, but some remain underutilized or will require the development of country- and region-level capabilities. As we will see, both pandemic response and robust, sustainable recovery require consensus about regional public goods, with health, social safety nets, financial support and digitalization informing pathways for collaboration and integration.

This chapter outlines the agenda for a post-COVID-19 regionalism. The first section recaps the initial country responses to contain the pandemic.

Their largely reactive character impeded regional cooperation and limited national implementation. These containment measures require a safe but speedy unwinding for a robust regionwide economic recovery. The second section reviews the regional effort to support recovery. The various subregional responses currently underway call for sharing, harmonization and scaling-up, with technical and financial support, into a larger policy framework. The third section identifies priorities for regional cooperation that can advance the SDGs. These should aim to turn a post-COVID-19 economic upturn into a robust recovery, one that is inclusive, resilient and sustainable. Tapping these possibilities requires multidimensional responses within the framework of the 2030 Agenda for Sustainable Development. The final section concludes with new forms of cooperation that may reduce vulnerabilities and build resilience. A shared engagement will require delineation of regional public goods, and entail deeper cooperation and integration, involving coordination and collaboration on regulatory standards in multiple areas across diverse national frameworks. Such engagement, underway in subregions, should extend across the APR.

Re-opening the Asia-Pacific Region Will Require a Collective Response

The COVID-19 pandemic is a shared crisis that calls for a collective response, but instead evoked defensive national actions around the world. Countries everywhere closed borders, suspended travel, restricted exports, and repatriated temporary workers. There was competition for medical supplies and protective equipment. Industrialized countries placed bids on first allotments of future vaccines. International forums devolved into recrimination rather than cooperation. Meanwhile, the pandemic spread and commenced a second wave, leaving governments less policy space to respond.

The failure to respond collectively enlarged a health crisis into an economic crisis. The closing of national borders and lockdown of domestic economies contracted the world economy by 4.4 per cent in 2020 (IMF, 2020; UNCTAD, 2020a). International trade declined by nearly 10 per cent (WTO, 2020a). Foreign direct investment flows fell by up to 40 per cent, and remittances dropped by almost 20 per cent (UNCTAD, 2020b; World Bank, 2020a). Income inequality worsened in developing countries, and overall welfare fell by 8 per cent (World Bank, 2020a). Poverty rose for the first time since 1988, leaving a projected 150 million more persons to struggle on less than US$1.90 a day by the end of 2021 (World Bank, 2020b). While COVID-19 vaccines have emerged, complex logistics limit their distribution. A 'people's vaccine' – affordable to produce and easy to dispense — may require further research and development (The People's Vaccine, 2021). With the pandemic not yet over, the global prospect warns of a protracted economic slowdown that may extend into 2022 and beyond.

The APR remains relatively better off. Its decline in trade was half as severe as elsewhere (WTO, 2020a). It saw an economic contraction in 2020 of less than 1 per cent overall, although declines varied across countries and sub-regions, from -4.8 per cent in South Asia, to -4.5 per cent in West Asia and -3.4 per cent in the Pacific (UNCTAD, 2020c). East Asia sustained a modest 1 per cent growth. However, 70 per cent of the world's job losses occurred in the APR (ADB, 2020a). These aggregates contain graver impacts at national and subnational levels, and particularly among the more vulnerable populations. Rising poverty, food insecurity, lost jobs and failed businesses can turn a contraction into an enduring loss of potential output. It seems likely that, even with a fast recovery in the overall region, differential and even divergent recovery trajectories will take place, between and within Asian-Pacific nations.[1]

Thus, regionalism faces the immediate challenge of initiating a robust economic recovery across the APR. It begins with helping countries to emerge from lockdown safely. Unilateral reopening may prove short-lived, as seen in Europe, or it can be sustained through collective action. A regional approach would harmonize and reinforce critical preventive measures while unwinding other containment measures, thereby restoring cross-border activity and boosting trade and financial flows across the APR.

OVERVIEW OF ASIAN-PACIFIC REGIONAL CRISIS-RESPONSE MECHANISMS

Country-level actions vary greatly but always have the potential to impact those outside their borders. Regional mechanisms help mitigate negative impacts and enhance the ability to respond individually and collectively. These include exchange of experiences, common policy frameworks and mutual policy support. The various mechanisms at the sub-regional level can complement and galvanize broader cooperation in the APR. This section provides an overview of some of these mechanisms and their potential applications during this critical period.

Exchange of experience

Countries stand to gain by sharing their diversity of experiences and capabilities in the context of handling the COVID-19 pandemic. All countries have taken steps to arrest the pandemic (UNESCAP, 2021). The measures range from containment, such as lockdowns and travel bans, to relief, such as income support and social protection (Huang and Saxena, 2020). The containment measures have slowed the spread of COVID-19, but they have also blocked economic activity. The relief measures have provided temporary support, but also drained public funds and accumulated debt. An exchange of experience helps identify the most critical measures and the most effective combination of policies. United Nations' entities have provided timely substantive and intergovernmental support. The knowledge tools include a COVID-19 Policy Tracker, a COVID-19 Policy Database, a COVID-19 Supply Portal, analytical reports, policy briefs, on-line forums and monitoring the impact in the 58 Asian-Pacific countries and territories (IMF, 2021; ADB, 2021; WHO, 2021).

Policy frameworks

While national measures should reflect country circumstances and needs, a common policy framework facilitates a collective response. On the health front, the regional shortage of medical supplies, facemasks and protective equipment has been largely overcome but delivery of health services remains uneven. The successful experience of the Republic of Korea and other countries in testing and contact tracing of COVID-19 could find wider application in the region. Cooperation on appropriate health protocols, including hygiene, protective gear and social distancing, and application of digital technological tools, such as the Indonesian PeduliLindungi app for contact tracing, can help countries finetune their containment measures with less dependence on blanket lockdowns.

Surprisingly, a number of Asian-Pacific countries took their time in joining the Gavi Vaccine Alliance/Coalition for Epidemic Preparedness Innovations/World Health Organization COVID-19 Vaccines Global Access (COVAX) initiative for rapid, equitable access to COVID-19 vaccines, even countries eligible for financial support under the COVAX Facility (GAVI, 2021). This may in part reflect the expectation of an expanded regional vaccination supply. Several countries, including China, India, Indonesia, Pakistan, Thailand and Viet Nam, have companies in the process of manufacturing vaccines. As vaccines become available, guidance on safe procedures for distribution and inoculation can help countries designate approved vaccinating centres, in compliance with World Health Organization (WHO) regulations for an International Certificate of Vaccination. Health officials plan to harmonize policies in an Association of Southeast Asian Nations (ASEAN) Comprehensive Recovery Framework. The Pacific Islands have operationalized their crisis-response framework (the Biketawa Declaration, 2000), by agreeing to establish a Pacific Humanitarian Pathway on COVID-19 to expedite delivery and customs clearance of medical supplies (UN, 2020a).

Concerning trade, nearly all countries have implemented transport health and safety measures and reopened border crossings for freight. In North and Central Asia, the Eurasian Economic Union introduced 'green corridors' with uniform sanitary requirements at border crossings (Vassilevskava, 2020: 84). The launching of the ASEAN Smart Logistics Network aims to strengthen supply chains and flow of goods. A number of countries have also rolled back some trade barriers applied at the onset of the outbreak. For example, Bangladesh removed a temporary export ban on surgical-mask disinfectants (WTO, 2020b). A further easing of restrictions on the export of medical supplies and equipment would facilitate diversification of supply chain production, as well as the manufacturing and distribution of vaccines within the region. The proposed Asia-Pacific Economic Cooperation (APEC) coordination mechanism should receive priority, thus allowing countries to collaborate on agreed criteria for reopening borders (UNESCAP 2020a).

Most countries have restricted travel, with damage to tourism, trade in services and, particularly, migrant workers. Tourism revenue plays a critical role in some 30 countries and territories, particularly Cambodia, Fiji, Georgia, Hong Kong SAR (China), China, Maldives, Palau, Thailand, Tonga, Samoa and Vanuatu (Helble and Fink, 2020). A collective policy framework could introduce coordinated precautions at borders, such as COVID-19 testing on embarkation, certification of negative test results or vaccination, enabling safe movements without long periods of quarantine. Such protocols have come into effect at travel hubs for some transcontinental routes and also bilaterally between countries, such as China–Republic of Korea, China–Singapore and Japan–Viet Nam. An ASEAN Travel Corridor Arrangement Framework was to have become operational for essential travel in early 2021. In the Pacific, a limited international travel zone, the 'Bula Bubble' involving Australia, Fiji and New Zealand, has been proposed (Helble and Fink, 2020: 9). Such measures offer short-term solutions that may need to remain in place for the medium term.

The use of digital technologies has already played a major role in pandemic response. It has helped ease the pandemic lockdown by allowing people to work at home, businesses to engage in e-commerce and governments to meet virtually. For example, consumers and merchants in India have embraced digital transactions and online payments. Mobile payment wallets (EziPei) were launched in the Solomon Islands (Schou-Zibell and Phair, 2020). India disbursed $3.9 billion in bank transfers to the accounts of 320 million persons in April 2020 (Lee and Chatterjee, 2020). Electronic transfers supplied cash grants in Pakistan, cash cards in the Philippines and digital payments to garment workers in Bangladesh. Kazakhstan automated a range of services, including remote processing of shipping documentation and digital payment of social benefits.

This surge in digitalization largely reflects necessity rather than policy, although it has also strengthened regional cooperation. The ASEAN Summit (9–15 November 2020) updated its Accelerating Inclusive Digital Transformation strategy to combat the impact of COVID-19. This included digitalization of trade processes for movement of 152 essential goods, and activation of the Go Digital initiative (in collaboration with Google and The Asia Foundation) to provide digital tools and skills to small enterprises and youth in severely impacted areas (TAF, 2020). Responses would also be aided by regional sharing of other initiatives, namely The Better Than Cash Alliance,[2] the Level One Project,[3] and the Mojaloop Foundation,[4] and country experiences, including India's Unified Payments Interface, Indonesia's standardization of digital quick response QR codes and Thailand's e-payment roadmap for 2020. The potential for cooperation on digitalization has only begun to be realized.

Policy and financial support

All countries have implemented measures to help households and businesses cope with income loss, unemployment and economic inactivity. However, in a prolonged contraction, these emergency safety nets strain public budgets, foreign exchange reserves, and debt servicing capacity. The Group of 20 and the Paris Club have advanced a Debt Service Suspension Initiative, and the International Monetary Fund, World Bank and Islamic Development Bank have pledged to enlarge borrowing facilities for vulnerable countries, including in the APR. The private sector has been urged to extend the debt moratorium to non-official liabilities. These commitments need implementation and continuance beyond the envisaged mid-2021 timeline.

The APR can also deploy ample financial resources and instruments to alleviate liquidity and fiscal constraints. The mechanisms include the Chiang Mai currency swap arrangements, the Asian Bond Market Initiative, the ASEAN+3 Bond Market Forum and the Asian Clearing Union. The currency swap arrangements primarily aim to provide supplemental liquidity support for balance of payment difficulties (AMRO, 2018). In practice, the ASEAN+3[5] implementation mechanism has prioritized policy surveillance over policy support, and its $240 billion financing facility remains unused due to high conditionality; its future role may depend on revisiting these constraints (Negus, 2020).

The spirit of regional cooperation should prompt reactivation of the swap arrangements and their extension to a larger group of countries in need of short-term financial support. The Asian Clearing Union (of Bangladesh, Bhutan, India, Iran, Maldives, Myanmar, Nepal, Pakistan and Sri Lanka) remains active but could also play a more significant role by allowing for local currency transactions (Asian Clearing Union, 2021). The initiatives to develop bond markets have borne fruit. The ASEAN+3 markets are the world's most active, with issuance of local currency bonds in excess of $16 trillion. But only a few countries participate. The Asian Bond Market Initiative should launch a second phase to develop capabilities in a broader group of countries. Some countries, including Armenia, Azerbaijan, Bhutan, Nepal, Pakistan and Sri Lanka, have established COVID-19 response funds that pool private donations, public resources and external finance (Rahim et al., 2020). These funds carry some risk but, when carefully designed and managed, offer potential for wider replication in the region.

The regional development banks have incorporated COVID-19 recovery components into their project activity. The European Bank for Reconstruction and Development has announced a EUR 1 billion solidarity package; the Asian Development Bank (ADB) allocated $20 billion, and the Asian Infrastructure Investment Bank committed $13 billion. The ADB has provided $2.5 billion in concessional resources, and also offers support to micro-, small- and medium-sized enterprises. The ADB Supply Chain Finance Program has provided trade finance, such as pre- and post-shipment loans to expedite transactions between manufacturers, suppliers and distributors of medicines, masks, gloves, ventilators, test kits and other critical items needed to combat COVID-19. All told, these banks facilitated approximately $2 billion worth of transactions in 2020 (Beck, 2020). They should also augment export credit facilities and tailor them for small and medium enterprises (Chatterjee et al., 2020).

Bilateral mechanisms include a $4.5 billion pledge by Japan for emergency loans and assistance from the China International Development Cooperation Agency. In the commercial sphere, the China Development Bank signed loan agreements, involving more than $700 million, with beneficiaries of the G20 Debt Service Suspension Initiative (CDB, 2020). The bank has also issued market-based 'fighting the COVID-19 epidemic' bonds. Chinese, Republic of Korea, Thai, Philippine and Indonesian companies have also issued corporate COVD-19 bonds. The proceeds commonly support the manufacture of medical supplies.

Two COVID-19 response funds have emerged at the subregional level. In South Asia, the South Asian Association for Regional Cooperation (SAARC) Development Fund has committed $7.7 million to assist regional health centres, and SAARC member-countries have pledged another $22 million of medical supplies and equipment to dispense bilaterally outside the formal structure of SAARC (UNESCAP, 2020a). In addition, an Information Exchange Platform for medical professionals was established in the SAARC Disaster Management Centre (Pattanaik, 2020). SAARC has also sponsored an effort to evolve common Pandemic Protocols, both for application within countries and for trade facilitation among them. Second, while ASEAN has largely emphasized information exchange, it also offers a dozen or so coordination mechanisms and a dedicated response fund, which has solicited pledges of $10 million in the first five months of its establishment (Djalante et al., 2020). The ASEAN fund has also received pledges from outside their membership, such as from Germany, the European Union, India and Japan. In Central Asia and the Pacific Islands, the COVID-19 response has received bilateral assistance, including pledges by Australia and the United States for the Pacific Islands. There is also the ASEAN–UN Comprehensive Partnership (UN, 2020b).

Overall, this affirmative response to COVID-19 has ranged widely, driven by necessity, experimentation and assorted mechanisms – the pragmatic Asian way. Its main features include arresting the pandemic, protecting vulnerable groups, reviving economic activity, and reopening borders for goods if not people. However, the response has remained more national than regional, leaving scope for greater collective action. Regional finance can boost fiscal stimulus and social protection measures. Regional protocols can speed reopening. Urgency should underpin agency, driven by the caution that "[t]he longer the containment period, the more difficult and prolonged the recovery will be" (ADB, 2020a: 1).

Moreover, a robust recovery must encompass all countries. The impact of COVID-19 — and of policy response – has proven uneven. The less capable have remained less resilient and more vulnerable (UNCTAD, 2020d). The least-developed countries (LDCs), such as Kiribati and Nepal, saw severe impacts from the decline in remittances and from the collapse of single-export-dependent markets in garments and tourism. Although the least-developed island countries, including Kiribati, the Solomon Islands, Tuvalu and Vanuatu, largely escaped COVID-19 infection, they were deeply impacted by the economic contraction and experienced the highest headcount increase in extreme poverty (UNCTAD, 2020d). The LDCs also proved unable to fund much policy support; for example, Bangladesh could earmark fiscal measures of not more than 1 per cent of its gross domestic product (GDP) (UNCTAD, 2020d). However, unequal access proved more of a hurdle than national income (UNESCAP, ADB and UNDP, 2020). The overriding challenge remains that of ensuring a robust recovery, one that encompasses all countries and peoples and provides renewed impetus towards the SDGs.

ASIAN-PACIFIC PANDEMIC COOPERATION INITIATIVES CAN ALSO ADVANCE THE SDGS

In crisis situations, countries respond more to emergency than opportunity. Regional cooperation can help ensure that the responses to COVID-19 do not overlook the opportunities in crisis to make emergency response inclusive, resilient and sustainable.

In particular, regional cooperation should align recovery measures with the United Nations 2030 Sustainable Development Agenda. The opportunities include a fortified health response, an enlarged safety net, a catalytic financial stimulus and a transformative role for digitalization. These efforts could soften the impact of COVID-19 by as much as 40 per cent (Villafuerte, 2020). A broader aim is to enable "a smooth transition from emergency response to resilience recovery and sustainable development" (UNESCAP, 2020b: 28). This section examines recovery response in light of these opportunities and the United Nation's frameworks for fighting COVID-19.

A fortified health response

The sudden and rapid spread of COVID-19 strained health facilities everywhere. The standard emergency response was to 'flatten the curve' with measures to suppress transmission — reduce the reproductive (R) number – so as to not overwhelm health services. The response is appropriate with adequate national capacity, but countries with weak facilities also need to 'raise the bar' with policies to strengthen health care systems. This holds especially for the APR, where over 40 per cent of the population lacks access to health care (UNESCAP, 2020c). Such situations supply both the need and opportunity to upgrade health services toward effective delivery of emergency medical supplies, protective equipment and eventual vaccines for the general population. In May 2020, the ADB launched a tool to unblock supply chains of health care products (ADB, 2020b). Sharing experience in extending health insurance to frontline workers in Bangladesh, India, Indonesia and Nepal could benefit other countries. In this way, regional mechanisms can support national efforts to strengthen access and availability of basic health services and advance progress towards universal primary health coverage. A comprehensive health response is the first of the five pillars of the UN framework to combat COVID-19 (UN, 2020c).

An enlarged safety net

The death toll of COVID-19 will continue to rise even after the disease has subsided. The collateral damage stems from disruption of social services, loss of livelihood and increased poverty.[6] Other proximate causes include hunger and malnutrition, as well as intergenerational effects of extreme poverty. The damage has the greatest impact on the most vulnerable, but it responds to prevention: Countries with social protection measures suffer less and recover faster. However, the APR is ill-prepared. Over 60 per cent of the population has no access to social services and many governments lack the capacity to provide it (UNESCAP, 2020b). All countries have implemented social protection measures as part of their pandemic response. These emergency measures require scaling-up and expansion to include the 'missing vulnerable' who slip past safety nets: self-employed workers and daily wage earners, the informal sector, rural poor, urban slum dwellers, internally displaced persons and migrant workers, and the women, children, people with disabilities and elderly among those groups.

The pandemic response also offers opportunities to empower the vulnerable with cash transfers and self-help schemes, and through community public work initiatives that build local infrastructure, such as basic health centres, schools, and sanitation facilities. Income transfers through remittances can be facilitated. Public–private partnerships can create jobs through massive public work programmes for rural development and urban clean-up (Sabu, 2020). The cumulative experience of the South-East Asian countries in disaster recovery has yielded the ASEAN Guidelines for Disaster Responsive Social Protection, which emphasize interrelated actions in social welfare, health and disaster risk management (UNESCAP, 2020b). The guidelines have contributed to country roadmaps for Cambodia, Myanmar, the Philippines and Viet Nam, but other subregions would benefit from sharing this experience. Thus, regional cooperation should encourage national efforts to protect and to empower those most affected by the pandemic. In this way, safety nets provide immediate social protection as well as enduring social welfare. Social protection and cohesion are the second and fifth pillars of the UN framework to combat COVID-19 (UN, 2020c).

A catalytic financial stimulus

Most countries provide support to business, in some cases giving this a higher priority than health and social protection. The fiscal stimulus – averaging 3 per cent of GDP – aims at emergency relief but also creates space for economic activity (Huang and Saxena, 2020). All countries could give greater support to small and medium enterprises – major employers that have few buffers for retaining workers, considering the collapse of the services sector, disruption of supply chains and closure of borders. The overall stimulus could also act in more catalytic manner, helping mobilize funds and spurring productive recovery. It offers scope to leverage public finance with private domestic finance and external funding. Financial packages can blend liquidity finance with concessional and long-term finance to build infrastructure. Complementary support could help firms tap trade finance and access capital markets. Certain instances of these enhanced financing possibilities could apply on a wider regional basis (ADB, 2020c). A scaled-up fiscal stimulus could encourage responsible investor behaviour and catalyse productive investment in order to diversity manufacturing, build resilience in supply chains, accelerate low-carbon transitions, and support climate change mitigation and adaptation. Attractive investment opportunities would stem capital outflows and steady debtor confidence. Intra-regional trade would accelerate recovery and development in the countries affected. However, regional financial mechanisms have an important role to play, both for mobilizing funds and for pre-empting a pandemic-induced debt crisis (Susantono, 2020). Economic policy response and recovery are the third and fourth pillars of the UN framework to combat COVID-19 (UN, 2020c).

A transformative role for digitalization

A common feature in all responses to COVID-19 is digitalization. Innovative electronic tools have helped mitigate the hardship of lockdown. The creative flood of applications and services, including telework, e-education, e-medicine, e-payment, e-commerce, e-finance and e-government, have empowered people while energizing enterprise and opening fresh pathways for inclusive, resilient and sustainable development. The transformative role of digitalization has proven particularly visible in digital finance, enabling increased savings and spending on health and education by households, income generation in the informal sectors, improved delivery of government welfare payments, and efficient money transfers across borders (UN, 2020d). The full potential of the Internet depends on physical infrastructure, consistent regulations and data transfer protocols for cross-border connectivity, and affordable digital devices and services. These are challenging but not insurmountable barriers, as evidenced in the rapid coverage in mobile connectivity. Satellite technology, such as Kacific's geostationary satellite, can provide fast, economical and accessible broadband Internet for Papua New Guinea other island nations.

Institutional response

Regional cooperation requires a complement in assertive global efforts and effective country support. At the global level, the United Nations issued an early call in March 2020 for emergency political leadership and cooperation to combat COVID-19 at a magnitude of 10 per cent of global GDP (UN, 2020e). Follow-up included a comprehensive plan, convening of the UN Security Council, and various multilateral summits (UN, 2020f). Despite a recognition of the need for action, with some governments providing significant stimulus to their own economies, the appeal for funding an international response has fallen short. In particular, the modest request of the UN Secretary-General for an additional $1 billion for socioeconomic response and recovery had raised only $58 million by mid-year (UN, 2020f).

At the country level, the United Nations organizations have repurposed a significant proportion of their combined $17.8 billion development budgets towards COVID-19 response. The initial plan, already underway, proposes a 12-to-18-month delivery – within the UN framework and through the existing 131 country teams – of enhanced socioeconomic support for national COVID-19 response and recovery efforts (UN, 2020c). The initiatives should form part of a longer duration strategy. The outcomes will largely depend on the commitment of counterpart governments.

Thus, at the regional level, the existing mechanisms for cooperation – exchange of experience, common policy frameworks and mutual policy support – can play a crucial role in reinforcing national commitments to advancing the SDGs and also demonstrate the value of multilateralism to the larger international community. The contribution of regional banks and financial facilities will prove critical. The United Nations should focus in particular on fostering collaboration with the several subregional intergovernmental organizations, including ASEAN, SAARC, the Pacific Island Forum and the Shanghai Cooperation Organization (UNESCAP, 2020b). Cooperation between these bodies should also receive every encouragement. They possess a wealth of knowledge, capabilities and finance that need sharing across the entire region.

REGIONAL COOPERATION INITIATIVES CAN INCREASE RESILIENCY AND REDUCE VULNERABILITIES

Governments respond to pandemics and other crises in different ways (Hamdani, 2014). They can reduce their exposure by closing borders to contain a pandemic. They can also lessen the impact on particularly vulnerable groups with safety nets. And, ideally, they can strengthen their capacity to anticipate and ride out potential crises with actions that reinforce resilience. The latter responses generally require a shared framework for collective action.

The APR does not lack mechanisms for regional crisis cooperation. The ASEAN health security framework dates back to 1980; it assisted with earlier pandemics, including severe acute respiratory syndrome (SARS), influenza H1N1 and Middle East respiratory syndrome (MERS-CoV), but national measures remained the main response to COVID-19 (Djalante et al., 2020). The South Asian countries were the first to establish a COVID-19 response fund, but they acted alongside the SAARC. Oddly, COVID-19 interrupted plans to launch the Pacific Resilience Facility (proposed in 2018, now deferred to 2022), when the pandemic ideally should have brought forward its implementation, not pushed it back (Pacific Islands Forum Secretariat, 2020). The priorities identified in the regional roadmap for implementing the SDGs – finance, technology, capacity-building and connectivity – remain valid (UNESCAP, 2017a). These and other mechanisms need strengthening, with greater collaboration and financial commitment.

The third Ministerial Conference on Regional Economic Cooperation and Integration in Asia and the Pacific, slated to take place in 2022, will offer an occasion for revitalizing commitments. The agenda, set in 2013 and renewed in 2017, could not be timelier. It proposes market integration by reducing trade and transit costs through trade facilitation, and addressing protectionism; seamless connectivity in transport, energy, and information and communications technology; regional financial cooperation; and cooperation to address shared vulnerabilities, risks and challenges (UNESCAP, 2018a). All items have continued relevance, and the fourth anticipated the needs that COVID-19 would amplify.

In particular, regional cooperation should accentuate collaboration on regional public goods, while regional integration should advance connectivity in ways that make countries more resilient to cross-border vulnerabilities.

Regional public goods

Vulnerability is a public concern best addressed as a public good. At the country level, governments have the responsibility for wholly or at least partially funding public goods, since the high outlays and subsequent lack of profitability will not attract the private sector. An analogous argument can be made for global public goods – like a 'people's vaccine' or actions against climate change – where delivery proceeds on international agreement. In cases where the regional level offers clearer identification of a given issue and relative ease in reaching agreement, one could potentially delineate policy frameworks for the provision of regional public goods (Susantono, Sawada and Park, 2020).

In the APR, notable examples of actions to address vulnerabilities include a long-standing water management effort in the Mekong Basin to preserve the rice bowl of Asia, which dates back to 1954; currency swap arrangements established in the 1997 Asian financial crisis; an early warning system set-up after the 2004 tsunami in the Indian Ocean; fisheries management efforts in the Pacific; and an immunization plan to eradicate polio in Asia, the only region where the disease has not yet been eliminated.

Other projects monitor specific risks. The Long-Range Transboundary Air Pollution programme in Northeast Asia and the Acid Deposition Monitoring Network in East Asia monitor dispersion of cross-border pollutants in the more industrial sub-regions. The Greater Mekong Subregion Health Security Project oversees threats of infectious disease. The Coral Triangle Initiative on Coral Reefs, Fisheries, and Food Security partnership protects the marine ecosystem. The Economic Review and Policy Dialogue and the ASEAN+3 Macroeconomic Research Office provide surveillance of banking and financial stability.

Dozens of other mechanisms exist at the subregional and lower levels, including, in fact, examples for all of the SDGs (ADB, 2018). This proliferation reflects strategic interests as well as shared perception of issues, benefits and costs. The usual worries around public goods – who pays, which weaker members need support and how to avoid hegemony and free riders – become easier to operationalize among smaller, like-minded groups. In classic Asian style, the regional approach has been to 'let many flowers bloom' at bilateral, subregional and plurilateral levels, and while fruitful, the activities still need cohesion. Their success suggests a more ambitious challenge: enhancing the complementarity of efforts to improve the multidimensionality of public goods (as demonstrated by supplementing water management with health security in the Mekong Basin), as well as enlarging their accessibility in other countries. The more durable efforts could, potentially, serve as building blocks for a more integrated APR.

The Asia-Pacific Information Superhighway Initiative offers one ambitious example. It advocates cost-effective 'broadband for all' by utilizing the 'rights of way' in existing and planned transport infrastructure, such as the Asian Highway and Trans-Asian Railway networks, to deploy optical fibre lines within and across countries (UNESCAP, 2016). While certain missing links still need filling, a regionwide, or possible even global, mapping appears feasible. The master plan envisages an affordable, reliant and seamless Internet ecosystem for the entire APR. The outcome could prove transformative: lessening the digital divide, empowering people as savers and consumers, equipping small- and medium-sized enterprises for e-commerce, and digitalizing government functions (UN, ADB and UNESCAP, 2021: 15–34).

Priority areas in reducing vulnerabilities include human development, such as health and education; sustainability, including food security, ecosystems and climate change; and connectivity through physical and digital infrastructure. These public goods will require creative partnerships and innovative financing (UNESCAP, 2017b). While the sums appear large, the marginal cost of addressing resilience or targeting aid to the vulnerable remains relatively small, particularly with the involvement of the private sector.

On resilience, for example, universal health coverage in the developing Asian-Pacific countries will require annual investments of $475 billion through 2030, but strengthening their health systems for emergency preparedness, risk management and response, will entail additional investments of only $880 million per year (Huang and Saxena, 2020). Similarly, current estimates put annual investment in infrastructure at $1.5 trillion, but ensuring its climate resilience requires an additional investment of only $200 billion per year (ADB, 2017).

As for infrastructure that can target the needs of the vulnerable: After excluding China and India, which have better capacity for raising the necessary funds, the cost estimates amount to only $383 billion per year for all other countries, or 22 per cent of the aggregate (ADB, 2017). The financial cost is small relative to the opportunity cost of weak links that threaten the integrity of the larger endeavour.

One strategy for engaging the private sector would be to design projects as quasi-public private goods. Economies of scale and possibilities for cost recovery can incentivize the private provision of affordable services. Telecommunications, for example, offer such attractive economies that governments auction lucrative licenses to competing companies, domestic and foreign. Cheap mobile devices and competitive, low monthly user charges have allowed private provision of near-universal telephone coverage in many countries and have allowed developing countries to leapfrog the era of landlines (GSMA, 2020).

In these various ways, enhanced collaboration on regional public goods can help reduce vulnerabilities in the APR. The priority areas remain human development, sustainability and connectivity. The design of relevant policy frameworks could move forward with the establishment of an Asia-Pacific Task Force on Regional Public Goods.[7]

Connectivity[8]

Building physical infrastructure, grids and networks for connectivity are classic public goods. Statistical estimates of the direct and indirect effects on economic output suggest that transport infrastructure, including roads and railways, and power projects, namely electricity generation, have positive direct benefits for participating countries; rail projects also show indirect or 'spillover' benefits for other countries (Kim et al., 2020). The direct effects of digital infrastructure, including mobile phones and broadband access, also appear positive, with broadband access to the Internet having spillover benefits for neighbouring countries, as well. The secondary direct effects of Internet access include raising the equity and quality of education through application of digital technologies in teaching and learning (ADB, 2017a).

The direct benefits accrue from improved productivity and competitiveness in source countries (Lee, Lee and Kim, 2020). The indirect benefits spill over to other countries via cheaper imports, which in turn stimulate growth in source countries. Cross-border exchange permits access to raw materials, technology and markets. It helps diversify exports, expand supply chains, and energize small- and medium-sized enterprises and the services sector. It is particularly important for the landlocked, least developed and small island economies. It also strengthens links of large countries with their neighbours. These wider economic and strategic benefits underpin the deep cooperation of the ASEAN countries, the ambition of the Belt and Road Initiative, which involves China and dozens of countries in the APR and other regions, and the emergence of the South Asia Growth Quadrangle Initiative between Bangladesh, Bhutan, India and Nepal. In the latter, the initiative's planned power corridor would regionalize bilateral links to enable transit transmission of surplus energy to deficit areas. Bangladesh has relatively large energy investments in Bhutan ($1 billion) and plans to invest in Nepal (approximately $2 billion). The corridor has facilitated graduation of these three LDCs.

However, the economic benefits of connectivity depend on productive capacity and the trade and investment linkages between countries (Kim and Khan, 2020). To meet such needs, the region still requires capacity-building, common protocols for seamless connectivity, financial cooperation, and inclusive trade.

Capacity building

Weak economic structure and low technological and human capabilities limit absorptive capacity. While global value chains should enable less-developed economies to participate in trade and international production, the main participants are still high- and middle-income economies (UNESCAP, 2018b). The gap in productive capacity has widened in the APR in recent decades, with India, China and other East Asian countries able to build their capacities while economies with lower capacities fell further behind (Freire, 2011). Moreover, the shock of COVID-19 affected the latter economies more significantly (UNCTAD, 2020e).

The challenge, therefore, lies in fostering productive capacities alongside connectivity, thereby helping countries become more resilient to cross-border vulnerabilities. Increased official development assistance and Aid for Trade would bolster this effort. The Asian Development Fund has enhanced its COVID-19 responsiveness to cover health emergencies, provide technical assistance for debt sustainability and support the private sector, for example, through women-led small- and medium-sized enterprises (ADB, 2020d).

Common protocols

Connectivity requires hard and soft infrastructure. Physical infrastructure is only one of the four pillars of the Asia-Pacific Information Superhighway Initiative: the others include regulation, management and policy support. Trade facilitation greatly enhances the benefits of the Belt and Road Initiative. This includes harmonization of border procedures, adoption of common standards and use of digital technology to simplify processes. Such soft measures can double the benefits of hard infrastructure (UNESCAP, 2017d). Digitalization of procedures can lower trade costs by an average of 16 per cent in the APR (ADB and UNESCAP, 2019). Trade costs vary significantly within the region – running lowest in East Asia, 50 per cent higher in South Asia, and even higher in the Pacific Island developing countries – suggesting considerable scope for regional cooperation within The United Nations Framework Agreement on Facilitation of Cross-Border Paperless Trade in Asia and the Pacific (ADB and UNESCAP, 2019). A common framework for e-transaction laws and enforcement infrastructure also plays a critical role in e-commerce which, in turn, requires logistics (ADB and UNESCAP, 2018).

The pandemic has underscored how trade barriers hamper economic resilience. Countries need to jointly reduce exchange barriers, not just tariffs but also non-tariff barriers and rules of origin (Montes and Waglé, 2006). They need to agree on common protocols for shipment of freight and for e-commerce, and common quality standards for food products. They could be flexible on energy transmission charges in the event of unexpected spikes or declines in electricity consumption. They could agree on temporary cross-border movement of workers. Importantly, they need to devise compatible technological options for digital networks, such as fibre optics, terrestrial wireless, geo-stationary and low earth orbit satellites (ITU, 2020). An open-access architecture would allow all to participate and benefit.

The several regional bodies should deepen collaboration. These include the South Asian Telecommunication Regulator Council, which brings together regulatory bodies of the nine member countries to harmonize telecommunication standards. Other institutions include the East Asia and Pacific Infrastructure Regulatory Forum, the South Asia Forum for Infrastructure Regulation, the Power Interconnection Framework for Turkmenistan, Uzbekistan, Tajikistan, Afghanistan and Pakistan, and the Cross-Border Transport Facilitation Agreement for the Greater Mekong.

The ASEAN Blueprint 2025 offers an exemplary framework for how collaboration in the APR should be conducted (ASEAN Secretariat, 2015). For example, the Master Plan on ASEAN Connectivity (MPAC) 2025, adopted by ASEAN Leaders at the 28th/29th ASEAN Summits in Vientiane, Lao PDR, in September 2016 aims to enhance the aggregate economic impact of physical connectivity through transport, energy and telecommunications; institutional connectivity through regulations and standards; and user connectivity, such as financial and digital access for enterprise, and movement of capital and people (ASEAN Secretariat, 2016).

Financial cooperation

Connectivity enables access to financial hubs. The APR comprises vibrant offshore and domestic capital markets that have flourished amidst the pandemic on electronic platforms with interoperable digital banking and financial services. The capital markets in East Asia hosted bonds in excess of $16 trillion 2020. Most were local-currency government issues, including green, social, sustainability and

COVID-19 bonds. Some were cross-border, and some had no sovereign rating. For example, Lao PDR has financed domestic infrastructure projects with issues in the local currency bond market of Thailand and has recently issued rated bonds (ADB, 2017b). The infrastructure bond scheme could extend to other ASEAN member and non-member countries. The benefits of entry would motivate the private sector to join public efforts to invest in the necessary physical infrastructure.

The Asian Bond Markets Initiative provided technical assistance to Cambodia, Indonesia, Lao PDR, Myanmar and Viet Nam, building capacity for participation in capital markets. Such assistance could also extend to other countries and, as noted earlier, such opportunities remain underutilized. Apart from technical capacity, governments would need to update national regulations and institutions – that is not easy, but digitalization could help them leapfrog the chore of modernizing their legacy financial systems (Claessens, Glaessner and Klingebiel, 2001). In addition, regional cooperation could devise, with the involvement of the private sector, a market-based framework for efficient and secure cross-border digital transactions. This would facilitate innovative private investment for development (UNESCAP, 2017b). It would also have wide benefits in stimulating e-commerce, facilitating remittance flows and mobilizing investment for advancing the SDGs and combating climate change.

A regional initiative on finance for digital technologies could build upon and enhance the benefits of the various connectivity efforts. Although the APR is a global leader in growth, trade and finance, it has lagged in digitalization. Fewer than five of the leading 50 countries in digital technology are in the APR (UN, 2020g). Yet the region has the potential to rise from follower to leader. It has large consumer and capital markets, attractive to innovative private enterprise. Public infrastructure and private capital can enable investment in digital technology. Regional cooperation can devise appropriate policy frameworks and financing modalities. If leading Asian countries share their experience, such as Japan, China and the Republic of Korea, this can facilitate the diffusion of technological capabilities among the followers. Capacity-building support can help latecomers and bystanders become participants in the technological revolution. The multinational private sector, mobilized within a regional initiative, can shoulder much of this effort. The initiative could become a regional contribution to the call for a "Global Commitment for Digital Cooperation" (UN, 2019: 5).

Inclusive trade

Connectivity does not end at borders. Trade and transport facilitation should include measures for building trade capacity within countries. Transport corridors and power grids can sprout economic clusters of enterprises – domestic and foreign, large and small – engaged in upstream and downstream activity. Add-ons to make large infrastructure accessible to small- and medium-sized enterprises are relatively inexpensive. The social benefits include worker mobility, empowerment of women and decent work conditions (ADB, 2013). Partnerships with the private sector can enable shared-use infrastructure, such as sharing rail transport and port facilities of extractive companies, or power and telecommunications facilities of industrial companies, for community and consumer use (Brauch et al., 2020). In these ways, transport corridors become development corridors (Prasad, 2017). A new trade credit and investment guarantee agency could support small- and medium-sized enterprise participation in the regional market. The case for the latter is strong: only 18 of the 45 ADB members have export credit facilities, leaving an overall gap of $600 billion in trade finance in the APR in 2019 (Chatterjee et al., 2020).

Finally, connectivity itself should be networked. The subregions have different paces and forms of connectivity, and some have interconnected more than others. Networking maintains individual regional structures while enhancing interchange between them. It bolsters investment, trade, finance, and information flows across the region. A distributed network of economic nodes will also prove more resilient than a single integrated system. If one part undergoes a shock, the others do not collapse. Supply chains can reroute if interrupted in one part by, for example, an earthquake or a political tremor from a great power rivalry. Networking requires subregional arrangements to have open architecture and governance. For example, fears that the Asian Infrastructure Investment Bank would exclude many participants were allayed by governance procedures that encouraged wide participation. Similarly, the new Regional Comprehensive Economic Partnership of 15 dynamic Asian economies should allow other Asian countries to participate in the enlarged trade, investment and finance that would flow to and from the world's largest market. To qualify as a regional public good, this economic partnership should not allow pre-emptive exclusions of any country in the region: The Regional Comprehensive Economic Partnership should be nonexcludable (Acharya, 2017).

CONCLUSION

Relief, recovery and resilience are the priorities for regionalism in 2021–2023. The pandemic has not yet dissipated, but economic recovery cannot wait. It begins with helping countries emerge from lockdown safely, and in ways that make them better prepared for the future.

Regional cooperation should shape a collective way forward, despite differential, even divergent, recovery trajectories between and within nations. But a more robust outcome becomes feasible if recovery measures align with the United Nations 2030 Development Agenda. The relative successes of South Asia in universal health care, of ASEAN on responsive social protection, of Central Asia in digitalizing regulatory procedures, and of the Pacific in expediting customs clearance, can shape wider actions and supply guidelines and roadmaps. The United Nations can facilitate a "shift from reactive response to proactive vulnerability reduction, bridging humanitarian assistance and development" (UNESCAP, 2020b: para. 40).

Even as governments assemble a collective response to this emergency, they should consider new forms of cooperation to respond to future threats. Regional cooperation should strengthen the multidimensional aspects of development activity. Programming multiple goals within projects – inclusion, resilience and sustainability – has proven cost-effective. Moreover, governments can share those costs with the private sector.

Overall, regional cooperation in the post-COVID-19 era demands an enhanced paradigm. The customary approach of 'cooperation and integration' needs focus and realism. Existing mechanisms require better utilization, lowered barriers, and development of local or subregional capacity. Future cooperation should emphasize collaboration. A public goods perspective would sharpen the focus on reducing vulnerabilities and building resilience across the APR, inclusive of all countries and peoples. Also, realism calls for grounding regional integration in pragmatic networking of the several subregional initiatives and orienting them towards greater collaborative interaction. Integration should foster an interactive, networked regionalization of sub-regional efforts.

The Asia-Pacific SDG Partnership exemplifies a unified mechanism for regional leadership. The ADB must catalyse finance and investment to overcome debt overhangs and jumpstart recovery with intra-regional trade and new sources of growth. The UNDP must work with country teams and issue-based coalitions to operationalize regional public goods. UNESCAP must catalyse intergovernmental discussions on pandemics and planetary boundaries; universal health care, social protection and a rights-based approach to inequality; and collective management of the regional commons, from deep oceans to the Himalayas. Promising examples from the region should be shared for the benefit of all countries.

Regionalist action that could 'build forward better' (to paraphrase the UNESCAP mission statement) would help countries meet four challenges. First, it should help them safely reopen their economies to one another, thereby restoring travel, trade, and supply-chain production. Second, it should help revive domestic economies through cross-border connectivity and access to regional finance and investment. Third, it should assist the least-developed, landlocked, and island developing economies in finding opportunities during the recovery to advance sustainability and address climate change. Fourth, it should devise new forms of cooperation to reduce vulnerabilities and build resilience to future shocks.

The upcoming third Ministerial Conference on Regional Economic Cooperation and Integration in Asia and the Pacific, currently scheduled to convene in 2022, should launch the next chapter of regionalism.

NOTES

1. For a discussion of possible divergent K-shaped recoveries, see UN, ADB and UNDP (2021: 1–14).
2. See Better Than Cash Alliance (2021).
3. See Level One Project (2021).
4. See Mojaloop Foundation (2021).
5. The ASEAN Plus Three (ASEAN+3) cooperation process began in December 1997 with an informal summit between ASEAN, China, Japan and Republic of Korea leaders. See https://aseanplusthree.asean.org.
6. As noted in a UN report, "[d]uring the Ebola outbreak in West Africa in 2014, more people died from the interruption of social services and economic breakdown than from the virus itself" (UN, 2020c: 1).
7. For a prototype, see The International Task Force on Global Public Goods (2006).
8. Connectivity is defined "as a network of regional infrastructure that facilitates the flow of goods, services, people and knowledge in a cost and time effective way" (UNESCAP, 2017c: 23).

REFERENCES

Acharya, A. 2017. 'Regionalism in the Evolving World Order: Power, Leadership, and the Provision of Public Goods'. In A. Estevadeordal and L. W. Goodman, eds., *21st Century Cooperation: Regional Public Goods, Global Governance, and Sustainable Development.* London: Routledge, 39–55.

ASEAN+3 Macroeconomic Research Office. 2018. 'Overview of the CMIM'. ASEAN Secretariat, Jakarta. amro-asia.org/about-amro/amro-and-the-cmim/.

Asian Clearing Union. 2021. 'ACU in Brief'. Asian Clearing Union, Tehran. asianclearingunion.org/.

Asian Development Bank (ADB). 2013. *Gender Tool Kit: Transport – Maximizing the Benefits of Improved Mobility for All.* Manila: Asian Development Bank. adb.org/sites/default/files/institutional-document/33901/files/gender-tool-kit-transport.pdf.

———. 2017a. *Meeting Asia's Infrastructure Needs.* Manila: Asian Development Bank. dx.doi.org/10.22617/FLS168388-2.

———. 2017b. *The Asian Bond Markets Initiative: Policy Maker Achievements and Challenges.* Manila: Asian Development Bank. dx.doi.org/10.22617/TCS178831-2.

———. 2018. *Asian Economic Integration Report 2018: Toward Optimal Provision of Regional Public Goods in Asia and the Pacific.* Manila: Asian Development Bank. dx.doi.org/10.22617/TCS189598-2.

———. 2020a. *An Updated Assessment of the Economic Impact of COVID-19.* Manila: Asian Development Bank.

———. 2020b. 'New ADB Tool Offers Road Map to Unblock Supplies of Life-Saving Products'. In B. Susantono, Y. Sawada and C.-Y. Park, eds., *Navigating COVID-19 in Asia and the Pacific.* Manila: Asian Development Bank, 163–166.

————. 2020c. 'ADB Supports Thailand's Green, Social, and Sustainability Bonds for COVID-19 Recovery'. Asian Development Bank, Manila. adb.org/news/adb-supports-thailand-green-social-and-sustainability-bonds-covid-19-recovery.

————. 2021d. *Asian Development Fund 13 Donors' Report: Tackling the Covid-19 Pandemic and Building a Sustainable and Inclusive Recovery in line with Strategy 2030*. Manila: Asian Development Bank. adb.org/documents/asian-development-fund-13-donors-report-tackling-covid-19-pandemic.

————. 2021. 'COVID-19 Policy'. Asian Development Bank, Manila. covid19policy.adb.org.

Asian Development Bank (ADB) and United Nations Economic and Social Commission for Asia and the Pacific (UNESCAP). 2018. *Embracing the E-Commerce Revolution in Asia and the Pacific*. Manila: Asian Development Bank. dx.doi.org/10.22617/TCS189409-2.

————. 2019. 'Asia–Pacific Trade Facilitation Report 2019: Bridging Trade Finance Gaps through Technology'. Asian Development Bank, Manila. adb.org/sites/default/files/publication/523896/asia-pacific-trade-facilitation-report-2019.pdf.

Association of Southeast Asian Nations (ASEAN). 2015. *ASEAN Economic Community Blueprint 2025*. Jakarta: ASEAN Secretariat. asean.org/storage/2016/03/AECBP_2025r_FINAL.pdf.

————. 2016. *Master Plan on ASEAN Connectivity 2025*. Jakarta: ASEAN Secretariat. https://asean.org/wp-content/uploads/2016/09/Master-Plan-on-ASEAN-Connectivity-20251.pdf.

Beck, S. 2020. 'Even with Borders Closing, We Need to Keep Trade Flowing'. In B. Susantono, Y. Sawada and C.-Y. Park, eds., *Navigating COVID-19 in Asia and the Pacific*. Manila: Asian Development Bank, 148–151.

Better Than Cash Alliance. 2021. 'Homepage'. Better Than Cash Alliance, New York. betterthancash.org/.

Brauch, M. D., Maennling, N., Toledano, P., Monteiro, E. S. and Tavares, F.B. 2020. 'Shared-Use Infrastructure along the World's Largest Iron Ore Operation: Lessons Learned from the Carajás Corridor'. Columbia Center on Sustainable Investment, New York.

Chatterjee, A. K., Goswami, A., Hugot, J. and Vital, M. 2020. 'The Case for Regional Cooperation in Trade and Investment Finance for Asia'. In B. Susantono, Y. Sawada and C.-Y. Park, eds., *Navigating COVID-19 in Asia and the Pacific*. Manila: Asian Development Bank, 152–158.

China Development Bank. 2020. 'CDB Signed Agreements with G20 DSSI Beneficiaries'. China Development Bank, Beijing. cdb.com.cn/English/xwzx_715/khdt/202011/t20201104_7894.html.

Claessens, S., Glaessner, T. and Klingebiel, D. 2001. 'E-Finance in Emerging Markets: Is Leapfrogging Possible?' Financial Sector Discussion Paper No. 7, The World Bank Group, Washington, DC.

Djalante, R., Nurhidayah, L., Van Minh, H., Phuong, N., Mahendradhata, Y., Trias, A., Lassa, J. and Miller, M. A. 2020. 'COVID-19 and ASEAN Responses: Comparative Policy Analysis'. *Progress in Disaster Science* 8(100129).

Freire, C. 2011. *Productive Capacities in Asia and the Pacific*. Bangkok: United Nations Economic and Social Commission for Asia and the Pacific.

Gavi. 2021. 'COVAX Facility'. Gavi, the Vaccine Alliance, Geneva. gavi.org/covax-facility.

GSM Association (GSMA). 2020. *The State of Mobile Internet Connectivity 2020*. London: GSM Association. gsma.com/r/wp-content/uploads/2020/09/GSMA-State-of-Mobile-Internet-Connectivity-Report-2020.pdf.

Hamdani, K. 2014. 'Trans-border Vulnerabilities'. In K. Malik, ed., *Safeguarding Human Progress: Reducing Vulnerabilities, Building Resilience*. New York: United Nations Development Programme, 451–485.

Helble, M. and Fink. A. 2020. *Reviving Tourism amid the COVID-19 Pandemic*. Manila: Asian Development Bank.

Huang, Z. and Saxena, S. C. 2020. *Combating COVID-19 in Asia and the Pacific: Measures, Lessons and the Way Forward*. Bangkok: United Nations Economic and Social Commission for Asia and the Pacific.

International Monetary Fund (IMF). 2020. *World Economic Outlook*. Washington, DC: International Monetary Fund. imf.org/en/Publications/WEO.

———. 2021. 'Policy Responses to COVID-19'. International Monetary Fund, Washington, DC. imf.org/en/Topics/imf-and-covid19/Policy-Responses-to-COVID-19.

International Telecommunication Union (ITU). 2020. *The Last-mile Internet Connectivity Solutions Guide: Sustainable Connectivity Options for Unconnected Sites*. Geneva: International Telecommunication Union. https://assets.foleon.com/eu-west-2/uploads-7e3kk3/16601/the_last-mile_Internet_connectivity_solutions_guide.3b7086016604.pdf.

Kim, K. and Khan, F. 2020. 'Trade Facilitation and Aid for Trade for Inclusive Trade in Asia and the Pacific'. In B. Susantono and C.-Y. Park, eds., *Future of Regional Cooperation in Asia and the Pacific*. Manila: Asian Development Bank, 146–179.

Kim, K., Lee, J., Albis, M. L. and Ang, R. 2020. 'Benefits and Spillover Effects of Infrastructure: A Spatial Econometric Approach'. In B. Susantono and C.-Y. Park, eds., *Future of Regional Cooperation in Asia and the Pacific*. Manila: Asian Development Bank, 62–94.

Lee, C-S., Lee, J. and Kim, K. 2020. 'Measuring the Economic Impacts of Cross-Border Infrastructure and Technology: CGE Analysis'. In B. Susantono and C.-Y. Park, eds., *Future of Regional Cooperation in Asia and the Pacific*. Manila: Asian Development Bank, 95–144.

Lee, J. and Chatterjee, A. 2020. 'The Informal Sector Needs Financial Support'. In B. Susantono, Y. Sawada and C.-Y. Park, eds., *Navigating COVID-19 in Asia and the Pacific*. Manila: Asian Development Bank, 117–119.

Level One Project. 2021. 'Level One Project'. Bill and Melinda Gates Foundation, Seattle, WA. leveloneproject.org.

Mojaloop Foundation. 2021. 'Mojaloop Foundation'. Mojaloop Foundation, Wakefield, MA. mojaloop.io.

Montes, M. F. and Waglé, S., 2006. 'Why Asia Needs to Trade Smarter'. *Far Eastern Economic Review* 169(5), 45–48.

Negus, O. 2020. 'The Chiang Mai Initiative Multilateralization (CMIM): If Not Now, then When?' Center for Strategic and International Studies, Washington, DC. csis.org/blogs/new-perspectives-asia/chiang-mai-initiative-multilateralization-cmim-if-not-now-then-when.

Pacific Islands Forum Secretariat. 2020. 'Pacific Resilience Facility'. Pacific Islands Forum Secretariat, Suva. forumsec.org/wp-content/uploads/2020/08/PIFS20FEMM.6-Pacific-Resilience-Facility_Final.pdf.

Pattanaik, S. S. 2020. 'SAARC COVID-19 Fund: Calibrating a Regional Response to the Pandemic'. *Strategic Analysis* 44(3), 241–252.

The People's Vaccine. 2021. 'Available to All, Everywhere, Free of Charge'. Oxfam, Oxford. peoplesvaccine.org.

Prasad, J. 2017. 'Connectivity and Infrastructure as 21st Century Regional Public Goods'. In A. Estevadeordal and L. W. Goodman, eds., *21st Century Cooperation: Regional Public Goods, Global Governance, and Sustainable Development*. London: Routledge, 137–157.

Rahim, F., Allen, R., Barroy, H., Gores, L. and Kutzin, J. 2020. 'COVID-19 Funds in Response to the Pandemic'. International Monetary Fund, Washington, DC.

Sabu, J. 2020. 'South Asia's Prospects of Achieving the SDGs in View of the COVID-19 Pandemic'. *Trade Insight* 16(3), 9–11.

Schou-Zibell, L. and Phair, N. 'COVID-19 Has Created Digital Opportunities in the Pacific'. In B. Susantono, Y. Sawada and C.-Y. Park, eds., *Navigating COVID-19 in Asia and the Pacific*. Manila: Asian Development Bank, 182–186.

Susantono, B. 2020. 'Pandemic Highlights the Need to Manage Asia's Debt Problem'. In B. Susantono, Y. Sawada and C.-Y. Park, eds., *Navigating COVID-19 in Asia and the Pacific*. Manila: Asian Development Bank, 63–66.

Susantono, B., Sawada, Y. and Park, C.-Y., eds. 2020. *Navigating COVID-19 in Asia and the Pacific*. Manila: Asian Development Bank. dx.doi.org/10.22617/TCS200247-2.

The Asia Foundation (TAF). 2020. 'Go Digital ASEAN Digital Skills to Unlock New Economic Opportunities'. The Asia Foundation, San Francisco. asiafoundation.org/wp-content/uploads/2020/04/Go-Digital-ASEAN_June-2020.pdf.

The International Task Force on Global Public Goods. 2006. *Meeting Global Challenges: International Cooperation in the National Interest*. Stockholm: The International Task Force on Global Public Goods.

United Nations (UN). 2015. *Sendai Framework for Disaster Risk Reduction 2015–2030*. New York: United Nations. undrr.org/publication/sendai-framework-disaster-risk-reduction-2015-2030.

———. 2019. *The Age of Digital Interdependence, Report of the UN Secretary General's High-level Panel on Digital Cooperation*. New York: United Nations. digitalcooperation.org/wp-content/uploads/2019/06/DigitalCooperation-report-web-FINAL-1.pdf.

———. 2020a. 'Pacific Islands Forum Agrees to Establish a Pacific Humanitarian Pathway on COVID-19'. United Nations, New York. www.un.int/tuvalu/fr/news/pacific-islands-forum-agrees-establish-pacific-humanitarian-pathway-covid-19.

———. 2020b. 'The Impact of Covid-19 on South-East Asia'. United Nations, New York. unsdg.un.org/resources/policy-brief-impact-covid-19-south-east-asia.

———. 2020c. *A UN Framework for the Immediate Socioeconomic Response to COVID-19*. New York: United Nations. unsdg.un.org/resources/un-framework-immediate-socio-economic-response-covid-19.

———. 2020d. *People's Money: Harnessing Digitalization to Finance a Sustainable Future*. New York: United Nations. unsdg.un.org/resources/peoples-money-harnessing-digitalization-finance-sustainable-future.

———. 2020e. *Shared Responsibility, Global Solidarity: Responding to the Socioeconomic Impacts of COVID-19*. New York: United Nations. unsdg.un.org/resources/shared-responsibility-global-solidarity-responding-socio-economic-impacts-covid-19.

————. 2020f. *United Nations Comprehensive Response to COVID-19 Saving Lives, Protecting Societies, Recovering Better*. New York: United Nations. unsdg.un.org/resources/united-nations-comprehensive-response-covid-19-saving-lives-protecting-societies-0.

————. 2020g. *Shaping the Trends of Our Time*. New York: United Nations. un.org/development/desa/publications/wp-content/uploads/sites/10/2020/09/20-124-UNEN-75Report-2-1.pdf.

United Nations Conference on Trade and Development (UNCTAD). 2020a. *Impact of the Pandemic on Trade and Development: Transitioning to a New Normal*. New York: United Nations Conference on Trade and Development. unctad.org/system/files/official-document/osg2020d1_en.pdf.

————. 2020b. *Transforming Trade and Development in a Fractured, Post-Pandemic World*. New York: United Nations Conference on Trade and Development.

————. 2020c. *Trade and Development Report – From Global Pandemic to Prosperity for All: Avoiding Another Lost Decade*. New York: United Nations Conference on Trade and Development. unctad.org/webflyer/trade-and-development-report-2020.

————. 2020d. *The Least Developed Countries Report 2020: Productive Capacities for the New Decade*. New York: United Nations Conference on Trade and Development. unctad.org/webflyer/least-developed-countries-report-2020.

————. 2020e. *UNCTAD Productive Capacities Index: Focus on Landlocked Developing Countries*. New York: United Nations Conference on Trade and Development. unctad.org/system/files/official-document/aldc2020d2_en.pdf.

United Nations Economic and Social Commission for Asia and the Pacific (UNESCAP). 2016. 'Master Plan for the Asia-Pacific Information Superhighway'. United Nations Economic and Social Commission for Asia and the Pacific, Bangkok. unescap.org/sites/default/files/Master_Plan_for_APIS_English_0.pdf.

————. 2017a. *Regional Road Map for Implementing the 2030 Agenda for Sustainable Development in Asia and the Pacific*. Bangkok: United Nations Economic and Social Commission for Asia and the Pacific. unescap.org/sites/default/files/publications/SDGs-Regional-Roadmap.pdf.

————. 2017b. *Innovative Financing for Development in Asia and the Pacific: Government Policies on Impact Investment and Public Finance for Innovation*. Bangkok: United Nations Economic and Social Commission for Asia and the Pacific. unescap.org/sites/default/files/%2B%2BFinal_IFfSD.pdf.

————. 2017c. *Enhancing Regional Economic Cooperation and Integration in Asia and the Pacific*. Bangkok: United Nations Economic and Social Commission for Asia and the Pacific. unescap.org/publications/enhancing-regional-economic-cooperation-and-integration-asia-and-pacific.

————. 2017d. *Belt and Road Initiative and the Role of ESCAP*. Bangkok: United Nations Economic and Social Commission for Asia and the Pacific.

————. 2018a. 'Ministerial Declaration on Enhancing Regional Economic Cooperation and Integration to Support the Implementation of the 2030 Agenda in Asia and the Pacific'. United Nations Economic and Social Commission for Asia and the Pacific, Bangkok. unescap.org/sites/default/d8files/event-documents/E74_33A1E.pdf.

———. 2018b. *The Role of Asia and the Pacific in Global Governance and Multilateralism*. Bangkok: United Nations Economic and Social Commission for Asia and the Pacific. unescap.org/publications/role-asia-and-pacific-global-governance-and-multilateralism.

———. 2020a. *The Role of South–South Cooperation in Building Back Better from COVID-19 Pandemic in Asia and the Pacific*. Bangkok: United Nations Economic and Social Commission for Asia and the Pacific.

———. 2020b. 'Highlights of System-wide Contributions of the United Nations at the Regional Level in Support of the 2030 Agenda'. United Nations Economic and Social Commission for Asia and the Pacific, Bangkok. digitallibrary.un.org/record/3881846.

———. 2020c. 'Socio-Economic Response to COVID-19: ESCAP Framework'. United Nations Economic and Social Commission for Asia and the Pacific, Bangkok. unescap. org/resources/socio-economic-response-covid-19-escap-framework.

———. 2021. 'Policy Responses to COVID-19 in Asia and the Pacific'. United Nations Economic and Social Commission for Asia and the Pacific, Bangkok. unescap.org/ covid19/policy-responses.

United Nations Economic and Social Commission for Asia and the Pacific (UNESCAP), Asian Development Bank and United Nations Development Programme. 2020. *Fast-Tracking the SDGS: Driving Asia-Pacific Transformations*. Bangkok: United Nations Economic and Social Commission for Asia and the Pacific. dx.doi.org/10.22617/ SPR200149-2.

Vassilevskaya, Y. 2020. *Trade Facilitation in Times of Pandemic: Practices from North and Central Asia*. Bangkok: United Nations Economic and Social Commission for Asia and the Pacific.

Villafuerte, J. 2020. 'The COVID-19 Economic Impact'. In B. Susantono, Y. Sawada and C.-Y. Park, eds., *Navigating COVID-19 in Asia and the Pacific*. Manila: Asian Development Bank, 19–20.

World Bank. 2020a. 'World Bank Predicts Sharpest Decline of Remittances in Recent History'. The World Bank Group, Washington, DC. worldbank.org/en/news/press-release/2020/04/22/world-bank-predicts-sharpest-decline-of-remittances-in-recent-history.

———. 2020b. *Poverty and Shared Prosperity 2020: Reversals of Fortune*. Washington, DC: The World Bank Group. worldbank.org/en/publication/poverty-and-shared-prosperity.

World Trade Organization (WTO). 2020a. 'Trade Outlook'. World Trade Organization, Geneva. wto.org/english/news_e/pres20_e/pr855_e.htm.

———. 2020b. 'Notification Pursuant to the Decision on Notification Procedures for Quantitative Restrictions' (G/L/59/REV.1). World Trade Organization, Geneva. docs.wto.org/dol2fe/Pages/SS/directdoc.aspx?filename=q:/G/MAQRN/BHR1R1A2. pdf&Open=True.

12 | Pandemic Governance and Human Development

Early Lessons from Asia

Sakiko Fukuda-Parr

INTRODUCTION

As the pandemic continues course into the second year, it is now widely recognized that it has worsened inequalities and exposed the longstanding fragilities and fractures in national and global governance (The Independent Panel, 2021; IMF, 2020; Oxfam, 2020b). The inequities in access to healthcare, the toll of job losses falling on low-wage workers, the burden of unpaid care work falling on women and escalating gender violence have magnified already existing vulnerabilities and powerlessness among marginalized groups. Vaccine nationalism and the weakness of multilateral cooperation in arranging universal access to COVID-19 vaccinations expose the economic and political fault lines of the 21st Century global order.

As Patel and Sridhar (2020) comment in the *Lancet Regional Health*, "the relative global success to control the COVID-19 pandemic, keep their economies afloat and avoid longer, harsh lockdown measures are markedly skewed towards the Asia-Pacific region". This success has depended largely on the effective implementation of non-pharmaceutical interventions (NPIs), combined with strong institutional capacity: primary health systems, effective leadership and active public engagement. This chapter further highlights how these successes reflect the importance of institutional capacity. The aim of this chapter is to review the consequences of the pandemic and the national responses to the public health and socioeconomic crises in order to learn lessons for governing pandemics, now and in the future. The analysis uses the framework of human development and capability approach and considers the objectives of pandemic governance to extend beyond stopping the spread of the virus and addresses broader socioeconomic and human consequences (Sen, 1999).[1]

Our analysis finds that, while many countries of the regions have had relative success in containing the epidemic outbreak so far, their strategies raise questions about equity, participation and human rights issues. Moreover, many of the low- and middle-income countries in the region have felt some of the strongest effects from the global recession. These complex challenges expose some key gaps in national and global institutions that require priority policy attention. The chapter highlights three of them: the underfunding of public health infrastructure; global norms for the provision of global public goods, notably vaccines; and the protection of low-wage workers in the global economy. The first section reviews the impact and response of countries in responding to the public health emergency and the global recession. The second section discusses selected policy priorities for governance, focusing on national public health capacity, access to global public goods and protection of workers' rights. As of writing this chapter (Spring 2021), the pandemic and the global recession continue their uncertain paths, creating new threats. The chapter represents reflections on the year 2020 at this particular point of time, based on the literature that has emerged in academic publications, media and reports from civil society and international organizations.

THE PANDEMIC SPREAD AND RESPONSE VARIED GREATLY

Pandemic's toll on human lives

Epidemics and economic shocks inevitably place a disproportionate toll on poor and vulnerable people and countries (Farmer, 1996). The COVID-19 pandemic has had a particularly devastating combination of effects, cumulating through three pathways: the spread of COVID-19; the lockdown and other measures to contain the virus; and the economic recession it has engendered. These have different effects on people, and each tends to widen inequalities.

First, the epidemic has a direct effect on people's health, but this does not depend on biology alone but on the conditions of life and work – that is, on the social determinants of health. Inadequate access to healthcare can lead to comorbidities that contribute to severe illness or death from COVID-19. Cramped and poorly ventilated living and workspaces, as well as occupational patterns, disproportionately expose low-wage workers, migrants and informal sector workers to workplace contagion. Additionally, the less bargaining power workers have, the less their capacity to demand appropriate safety measures, such as spaced workstations, personal protective equipment, or sanitary facilities. Evidence from across the world shows disproportionate numbers of low-income and minority groups dying and suffering from the pandemic (Pires, Carvalho and Rawet, 2020; Pires et al., 2020).

Second, the measures adopted to contain the virus have complex socioeconomic consequences. Workplace lockdowns and school closures in particular impact households differently and prove easier to manage for people in white-collar occupations, spacious living conditions and access to services. There are knock-on effects for poor households, such as the loss of access to school meals for children, estimated to put 300 million children at risk (Cash and Patel, 2020). School closures and other measures have undermined children's education and have led to huge increases in unpaid domestic and other care work (UN Women, 2021).

These socioeconomic effects are highly gendered. The burden of care work falls disproportionately on women, leading to reduction in female labour force participation and further widening gender inequalities. The lockdown has also further restricted the mobility of women and has often left them locked in with abusive partners. Strikingly, the pandemic has witnessed both an exponential rise in domestic violence and a marked deterioration of women's mental and physical health (UN Women, 2020).

Third, economic recessions lead to widespread unemployment, loss of income and loss of livelihoods. The pandemic has induced a global demand contraction, affecting a broad range of sectors and projected to shrink global trade and investment flows (UNCTAD, 2020). Analyses to date project that these effects will prove more severe for low-income households and for low- and middle-income countries (UNCTAD, 2020). The latter, particularly least-developed countries (LDCs), will likely find recovery more difficult (UNCTAD, 2020). The global recession is projected to push 88 to 115 million people into extreme poverty (World Bank, 2020a). This recession also has the potential to induce a longer-term restructuring of businesses, industries and the global economy (UNCTAD, 2020). Restructuring, too, has also historically tended to put stress on low-wage workers and on low-income countries without the ability to adapt to new opportunities (Stiglitz, 2020).

Containing the outbreak

Although the outbreak of COVID-19 first emerged in the Asia-Pacific Region (APR), many of its countries successfully stemmed outbreaks and kept cases at low levels, notwithstanding surges of third waves now underway and the continued threat of more outbreaks to come (Figure 12.1). Over the course of 2020, restrictions gradually lifted, and more normal life has resumed in many countries (OxCGRT, 2020). Although COVID-19 has become the worst epidemic ever experienced in any of the region's countries, morbidity and mortality rates have remained relatively low in comparison with international trends. Among these countries – 36 United Nations Development Programme (UNDP) Regional Bureau for Asia and the Pacific (RBAP) countries plus Japan, the Republic of Korea (South Korea), Singapore and Taiwan (Province of China) – data, as of 10 January 2021, show only one country (Iran) with a mortality rate higher than the world average (248.2 per million) or the rate in the United States (1,130.9 per million). Apart from Iran, eight countries have mortality rates above 50 per million, four between 10 and 49 per million, and 24 below 9 per million, including several with no deaths reported. India has the highest mortality rate at 110 per million, in the same range as the countries with the lowest mortality rates in Europe, namely Finland (105 per million) and Norway (87 per million) (Table 12.1 and Appendix 12A.1).

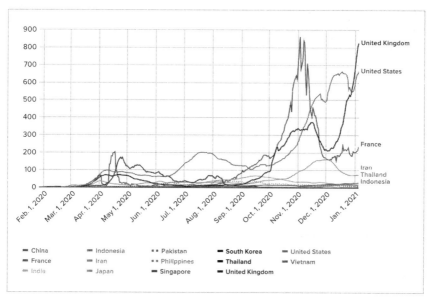

Figure 12.1 Evolution of COVID-19 cases in selected countries of Asia and the Pacific, February 2020–January 2021
New daily cases per million (smoothed)
Source: Roser et al. (2021).

What explains the relative success of countries in this region? It is not their technological prowess and financial resources. The geography of this pandemic, with epicentres located in Europe and North America, challenges the commonly held assumption that epidemic diseases flourish in low-income countries that do not have the capacity to control them. Global media have singled out several Asian countries, such as the Republic of Korea, Taiwan (Province of China), Viet Nam and Singapore, as 'exemplars' (along with countries in other regions, such as New Zealand, Australia and Finland) in having limited the outbreak. But many other countries in the region, including LDCs, such as Bhutan, Lao People's Democratic Republic (PDR) and Cambodia, have also managed to keep incidence low; Table 12.1 shows the list of 12 countries with the lowest case and death rates, while the full list of 36 countries appears in Appendix 12A.1. Global discussions often refer to culture and political regimes as important factors behind the success of countries in the region. However, these countries do not share the same characteristics in terms of history, culture, political regimes or economic models. They include small (Timor-Leste) and large countries (China, India) and a variety of citizen–state relationships in different types of political configurations. They also include countries with a wide range of financial means and technological capacities, from LDCs such as Bhutan,

Table 12.1   Mortality and morbidity rates in selected jurisdictions of the Asia-Pacific Region, as of 10 January 2021

Country	Deaths / million	Cases / million
United Kingdom	1,202	45,390
United States	1,131	67,701
World average	248	11,582
Highest mortality in region		
Iran	669	15,316
India	110	7,584
Indonesia	88	3,027
Nepal	65	9,088
Lowest mortality in region		
Japan	30	2,284
Korea, Rep. of	22	1,348
Singapore	5	10,069
China	3	67
Bhutan	1	1,054
Thailand	1	148
Viet Nam	0.4	16
Mongolia	0.3	440
Taiwan (Prov. of China)	0.3	35
Timor-Leste	0.00	37
Cambodia	0.00	23
Lao PDR	0.00	6

Source: Roser et al. (2021).

Timor-Leste, Lao PDR and Cambodia, to middle-income Thailand, to high-income Singapore, Republic of Korea and Japan. They include countries with a range of health systems, infrastructure and access to universal health coverage (Appendix 12A.3).

Accounts of the measures taken in these countries – especially reports from the ground up – provide interesting analyses and insights. They reflect some common elements in the responses by governments and societies, many of which differ from the approaches taken in Europe and North America.

Public health approach

Governments in these countries all implemented the conventional public health measures for infectious disease control, known as non-pharmaceutical interventions (NPIs): social distancing; testing, tracing and isolating; travel restrictions and border controls; mask-wearing and handwashing; and investment in public communications. These governments proactively initiated testing, tracing and isolating – what Dr Tedros Ghebreyesus, the World Health Organization (WHO) Director-General, calls the 'backbone' of infectious disease control – to contain the outbreak at an early stage, before mass community spread could take place. This stands in contrast to the priorities that countries in Europe and North America placed on treatment infrastructure, such as ventilators and intensive care unit (ICU) beds, strict lockdowns of social and economic activities, and investments in vaccines.

However, there is no single playbook, and country strategies differ considerably. Comprehensive lockdown measures were imposed in China, but not in Singapore, the Republic of Korea or Japan. Enforcement of NPIs entailed different measures, such as the use of technology, and methods, ranging from persuasion to fines or imprisonment. Massive expansion of testing has been identified as a key to success in Cambodia and the Republic of Korea, but had limited use elsewhere, as in Japan, Thailand and Viet Nam (Nit et al., 2021; Kim, 2020). Most began vigorous contact tracing with the first identified cases, but with substantial variation in methods: China, Singapore and the Republic of Korea made extensive use of mobile phone apps, while Japan and Viet Nam relied on manual means. Finally, one other feature distinguished a strategy common to many Asian countries but less used in Europe and North America: a more proactive approach to quarantine support, isolating asymptomatic or mild positive cases in dedicated treatment facilities, rather than leaving all to quarantine at home without supervision or treatment (Erkhembayar et al., 2020; Kim, 2020).

Rapid, early, and pre-emptive action

In many countries, health authorities began to prepare for an eventual contagion upon learning about the appearance of a novel coronavirus in Wuhan in December 2020. For example, Mongolia initiated measures, such as travel restrictions, school closures and an aggressive public awareness campaign, in early January, before WHO declared the outbreak a Public Health Emergency of International Concern on 30 January 2021 (Erkhembayar et al., 2020). In the Republic of Korea, only nine days after identifying its first case in late January, the Korean Centres for Disease Control (KDCC) set up 1,339 call centres to provide public information and to collect case data; the KDCC also coordinated with executives of pharmaceutical companies to scale up production of diagnostic test kits (Kim, 2020). According to public administration scholar Pan Suk Kim (2020: 1), "even after its early start in addressing the pandemic, the country placed a premium on working quickly". Governments in Cambodia, Hong Kong SAR (China), Singapore, Taiwan (Province of China), the Republic of Korea, Viet Nam and elsewhere also took prompt action, introducing measures in late January or February. Most opted to mobilize an emergency response – setting up response committees at the highest political levels, adopting a 'whole of government' approach and including relevant private-sector actors and scientific experts (Erkhembayar et al., 2020). In contrast, most European and North American countries responded to the outbreak once it happened, rather than intervening pre-emptively (Erkhembayar et al., 2020; An and Tang, 2020; Han, et al. 2020).

These prompt responses reflect the capacity of governments to make decisive choices, particularly ones involving the coordination of multiple governmental sectors and informed by expert scientific advice. Experience with severe acute respiratory syndrome (SARS) in China, Hong Kong SAR (China), Singapore, Taiwan (Province of China) and Viet Nam, and with Middle East respiratory syndrome (MERS) in Malaysia and the Republic of Korea, no doubt enhanced pandemic preparedness in these countries (Han, et al. 2020; An and Tang, 2020; Erkhembayer, et al., 2020). However, other countries hit by SARS, MERS or influenza A H1N1 did not respond so promptly. The significant difference is that the prepared countries had listened to repeated alerts in recent decades from the WHO and others about the potential threat of a novel disease that would spiral into a pandemic. They had the institutional arrangements and the political leadership necessary for a rapid response to the initial reports coming from Wuhan in the first days of January 2020.

Social norms, community engagement, and trust

Social norms play an essential role in implementing NPIs that involve change in the daily habits and behaviour of people. Compliance cannot depend entirely on punitive enforcement, but calls for a public buy-in about the need to address the public health crisis, and about the effectiveness of social distancing, mask wearing, personal hygiene, and compliance with testing, tracing and isolation.

Widespread and consistent mask wearing – evident to casual observers and shown in global surveys – has marked the response of many countries in Asia-Pacific (Chang et al., 2020). Observers often attribute this to culture, as the practice had met some resistance in other parts of the world. Indeed, this is a longstanding practice in parts of the region, but the cultural explanation detracts from a recognition of other key factors: the importance of public information, messaging from community and political leaders, and public education in creating new norms and reinforcing old ones for public health. Cultural practices shift. For example, Mongolia had no history of wearing masks, but adopted them without public resistance as a result of vigorous public information campaigns (Erkhembayar et al., 2020). In both the Ebola and HIV/AIDS crises, public information and messaging from community and political leaders and public health experts played a major role in shifting entrenched cultural practices and underscored the importance of public information.

Commentators have identified trust – in government, scientists, institutions and communities – as a critical factor in the pandemic response; the Independent Panel for Pandemic Preparedness and Response (2021: 24) concludes that a "trust deficit also fuelled the infodemic and set up a vicious cycle of disinformation and inadequate response". Community engagement, however, does not only rely on compliance with government policy, or trust in government; it also depends on the agency of people and the social norms that give value to individuals taking action for public health. These norms may well derive from an education in history and from public debate on the importance of personal hygiene as an essential element of public health (Watanabe, 2021).

These common elements of response combine a reliance on the traditional methods of infectious-disease control with institutional strengths. Here the term 'institutions' is defined as "humanly devised constraints that structure political, economic interactions", encompassing organizational structures and rules of behaviour, both formal and informal (North, 1990). Implementing these measures costs little and does not require massive investment in material resources or new technologies. But doing so requires two types of institutional strengths: state capacity in the social infrastructure of public health, including leadership, know-how, human resources, organization, and capacity in society, including values regarding the importance of public health, social norms of behaviour, and the ability to mobilize collective action for a shared goal, what Ibrahim (2011) refers to as "collective capabilities" and Stewart (2013) terms "social competencies".

However, as noted earlier, the objective of pandemic governance in the human development perspective goes beyond simply containing the virus. The past year has seen less evidence of policy attention given to equity as a priority objective, or attention to the social determinants of health. Containing the spread requires special attention to marginalized populations with particular exposure to risks. For example, in Singapore, the vast majority of positive cases (54,000 out of 58,000) have taken place in the migrant community, revealing stark inequalities and the poor conditions of their housing. When an outbreak occurred in dormitories for migrant workers, 47 per cent tested positive (Ministry of Health, 2020). Despite a prompt government response, little policy attention seems to have gone into the disproportional risk of COVID-19 among vulnerable population groups in Singapore. As pandemic governance seeks to go beyond containment, it will need to broaden and add to these capacities, the better to ensure equity and respect for human rights.

Uneven consequences of lockdowns and other measures

While containment measures, such as lockdowns, stem the spread of the virus, they come with a multitude of socioeconomic costs and raise concerns about equity, gender disparities and human rights. These costs will likely weigh most heavily on low- and middle-income countries with widespread poverty, weak social safety nets and large informal sectors. In the APR as elsewhere, emerging evidence from rapid surveys, civil society accounts and the media indicate the huge consequences of containment measures for marginalized people. Low-income households, migrants and women have felt the brunt of layoffs and job losses, increases in the gendered burden of care work, and rising stress and gender violence (UN Women, 2020; Tejani and Fukuda-Parr, 2021; UN Women, 2021).

Disproportionate income effects of lockdowns on the marginalized

Lockdown-induced job and livelihood losses disproportionately affect those whose work cannot move online. For people living at the edge of subsistence on daily wages, this becomes nothing short of catastrophic. Food insecurity and homelessness are on the rise. Migrant workers and women, as well as workers with precarious employment arrangements and informal sector subcontractors, are particularly vulnerable to layoffs. In India, the lockdown that shut down transport systems and overnight workplaces led to a veritable humanitarian crisis, where millions of migrant workers lost their jobs and had to walk home to their villages. Border closures in Myanmar, Nepal, Singapore and elsewhere stranded migrants, unable to repatriate (IHRB, 2020; Narayan, 2020).

State–citizen relations and human rights issues in implementation and enforcement

The implementation and enforcement of social distancing rules requires a social contract between the citizen and state based on human rights principles. Countries in the APR have a wide-ranging experience to date in this respect. Some have taken a proactively participatory approach, actively communicating government policy through information meetings and parliamentary debate, ensuring transparency. As noted earlier, this has worked well in achieving high levels of compliance on a voluntary basis without introducing punitive measures. Several countries have released thousands of prisoners in a public health and humanitarian move. On the other hand, other countries have used heavy-handed and inhumane methods for enforcement, such as mass beatings, huge fines, or imprisonment, raising widespread concern (Narayan, 2020; ICNL, n.d.). Many countries have declared a state of emergency that gives governments new powers to restrict movements and gatherings for public health. But these powers also open the way for the state to exercise greater restrictions for political purposes, for example, to detain political opponents on the pretext of quarantine, crack down on journalists on the grounds of misinformation about COVID-19 and broaden surveillance of citizens through smartphone apps (ICNL, n.d.).

Gender inequality

UN Women's rapid assessment surveys in Bangladesh, Cambodia, Maldives, Nepal, Pakistan, Philippines, Samoa and Thailand document a general increase in unpaid domestic and care work, although gender norms seem to have changed somewhat since the pandemic began and men have become more likely to share in the domestic work. Combined with the impact of the global recession, this has led to a disproportionate decline in global female employment (5 per cent) compared with male employment (3.9 per cent) (ILO, 2021).

Undermining other health priorities

The pandemic is not the only public health crisis. While COVID-19 has become a leading cause of death in countries with high mortality rates, WHO estimates that for 2020, COVID-19 would stand in sixth place globally among all causes. In low- and middle-income countries, it would rank further down the list. The lockdown severely restricted access to healthcare for non-COVID conditions and primary care. In India, data for March 2020 compared to March 2019 show a drastic reduction in the use of health services because of the closing of public transport; usage declines include sharp falls in childhood vaccination (69 per cent), institutionalized births (21 per cent) and clinical attendance for acute cardiac events (50 per cent) (Cash and Patel, 2020). The pandemic has also had a significant impact in reprioritizing health system resources, including personnel, supplies, efforts and finance. Multiple reports from the ground attest to patients postponing non-COVID healthcare and health providers prioritizing COVID care; physicians have expressed concern about weakening primary-care delivery (Rawal et al., 2020). One abiding lesson from the Ebola crisis is that "the indirect effects of the outbreak were more severe than the outbreak itself" (Roberton et al., 2020).

Health systems struggle to maintain services, particularly difficult in under-resourced settings and disproportionately likely to affect vulnerable populations. A study of the pandemic's indirect impact on maternal and child health estimates the potential impact of COVID-19 at 253,000 additional child deaths and 12,200 additional maternal deaths, or an increase of 9.8 per cent and 8.3 per cent, respectively, across 118 countries. This is the most conservative estimate. A higher estimate rises to as much as a 44.7 per cent increase in child deaths and a 38.6 per cent increase in maternal mortality (Roberton et al., 2020).

Global economic recession

The global economic downturn will have a wider impact than the Great Recession that followed the 2008–2009 financial crisis, shrinking global gross domestic product (GDP) in 2020 by an estimated 4.4 per cent and global trade by 10.4 per cent. For low- and middle-income countries (LMICs) of the APR, the International Monetary Fund (IMF) projects output growth in 2020 for emerging and developing Asia at -1.7 per cent. However, the rate varies greatly by country, with China estimated to show positive growth of 1.9 per cent and India to contract by -10.3 per cent while the five largest Southeast Asian economies (Indonesia, Malaysia, the Philippines, Singapore and Thailand) contract by -3.4 per cent (IMF, 2021). Although the high-income Organisation for Economic Cooperation and Development (OECD) countries have seen less severe contractions in terms of aggregate GDP, as noted here, LMICs and, particularly, LDCs will find it more difficult to recover from the recession and protect the vulnerable. Moreover, in the longer term, the recession exposes the vulnerability of countries in their dependence on the global economy. However well a country controls COVID-19 within its borders, it will struggle with the recession induced by demand contraction in large economies. This will prove a particular challenge for Asian-Pacific LMICs and exposes them to the risks of a development strategy dependent on low-wage labour in global value chains (GVCs).

As elsewhere, within-country inequalities are expected to worsen in the region, reflecting existing structures of employment, conditions of life, access to resources and opportunities as documented in multiple reports (IMF, 2021; ASEAN, 2020; Oxfam, 2020b; Oxfam India, 2021). In 2020, poverty increased by an estimated 4.41 million people in East Asia and 23.28 million in South Asia – reversing gains made in the past three decades (UNCTAD, 2020).

LMICs in the region adopted fiscal stimulus packages, totalling US$1.8 trillion or 7 per cent of GDP between March and September 2020; many of these include unprecedented social protection measures that have introduced systemic changes to existing arrangements (UNESCAP, 2020; ASEAN, 2020). However, this stimulus pales in comparison to the size of the response in high-income countries, estimated at 20 per cent of GDP. In LMICs, the scale and composition vary by country – for example, from 13 per cent of GDP in Thailand to 10 per cent of GDP in Mongolia and 1 per cent or less in Bangladesh, Cambodia and Lao PDR, averaging only 1.4 per cent of GDP for the region's LDCs (UNESCAP, 2020). Critics have raised concerns about the inadequate size of these packages and their lack of attention to human development priorities, such as the expansion of cash transfers, wage subsidies, unemployment benefits, health and care services, small-enterprise and informal sector support and environmental impact controls (Oxfam, 2020a). Here yet again, these responses expose the existing gaps. Countries with least means will likely find economic recovery more challenging; countries with high debt burdens may have limited scope for financing and could well face fiscal and debt crises. Loans from the IMF and multilateral development banks have played a major role in financing the packages, but overall bilateral official development assistance (ODA) declined in 2020 (UNESCAP, 2020). The most powerless and vulnerable face the highest risk of devastation; for example, worker support benefits omit low-wage, informal sector and home-based workers, along with migrants (UNESCAP, 2020).

The pandemic has set off a massive demand contraction and reduction in tourism and in trade. For LMICs, this poses a challenge for longer term development as well as in the present. Integrating into the world economy through the low-skill manufacturing end of GVCs has strategically served as a springboard for structural change. Yet COVID-19 highlights and amplifies the risks of dependence on GVCs, both for economies and peoples. Industries such as automotive, electronics and garment manufacturing have taken particularly hard hits, leading to major falls in exports and mass furloughs, layoffs and business closures (Tejani and Fukuda-Parr, 2021).

The human consequences of this global demand contraction have been severe for workers, particularly women (as noted earlier), migrants, home-based and informal-sector workers, and others contractually contingent workers. This starkly exposes the long-existing asymmetries of power and profit along GVCs, where lead firms capture most of the financial gains and wield market power, while manufacturers operate under highly competitive and low-margin environments. Workers have not only remained poorly paid but subjected to exploitative conditions that seem immune to reform. In the garment sector, for example, wages have seen a secular decline over recent years, even as the Rana Plaza disaster in 2013 set off significant efforts in the industry to provide better protections for workers (ILO, 2018). Once the pandemic hit Europe and North America, demand shrank and global brands promptly cancelled orders. Most declined to pay for these cancellations, leaving local suppliers in Bangladesh, India, Indonesia and elsewhere to bear the costs (Anner, 2020). Workers at the end of the supply chain have little or no bargaining power, and the widespread unpaid furloughs, layoffs and factory closures meant losing an already precarious livelihood. On-the-ground accounts from civil society and media give little sign of any compensation or other payments for these layoffs. On the contrary, reports highlight cases where the crisis opened up new opportunities for violating the human rights of workers, such as through wage cuts, suspension of collective bargaining and disregard for COVID-related workplace safety demands (Weber, 2020).

The pandemic also exposes the structural vulnerabilities of workers in the longer term. For firms and investors, it highlights the risks of labour-intensive production and may accelerate the trend towards automation already under way. Economists, such as Joseph Stiglitz (2020), have contemplated the potential for a major structural change in the economy, in patterns of production and consumption and in the organization of production, predicting that this would lead to a reduction in unskilled labour. The speed and scope will vary by industry, but across sectors, more repetitive and non-cognitive tasks will likely become candidates for automation. New jobs may be created, but access to them will require training and educational preparedness. Historically, defeminization of employment has accompanied technological upgrading in manufacturing because social norms favour men for higher-skill positions, as well as for the educational, vocational and sciences training that lays the groundwork for working with more advanced technology (Kucera and Tejani, 2014).

PRIORITIES MOVING FORWARD FROM HERE

While many countries of the APR showed institutional strengths in containing the outbreak as it emerged in 2020, this will not suffice for ending the pandemic as the global contagion continues into 2021. Social distancing will prove increasingly difficult for people and economies to maintain over the long term. While the vaccine is a game changer, its slow rollout across the world and the virtual absence of access for most low- and middle-income countries will facilitate the emergence of variants and hamper the resumption of economic activities. At the same time, the socioeconomic consequences of the pandemic-induced recession have exposed the vulnerability of economic strategies dependent on low-skilled and low-wage labour, as noted earlier.

Pandemic preparedness and containment

The experiences of countries in the region described in the preceding section show that it is possible to stem the tide of the pandemic without a high level of financial or other resources, using basic public health measures or NPIs. Low-income countries and LDCs, such as Bhutan, Lao PDR and Viet Nam, have succeeded in keeping down the spread and suppressing outbreaks, while high-income countries have the highest morbidity and mortality rates. It is also evident that no single one-size-fits-all recipe will succeed across the board; different countries had different strategies and strengths, set diverse objectives and used different methods of implementation in areas such as testing, tracing, isolation and lockdowns. Pandemic control does not simply aim to contain the disease; its public policy objectives also include managing the socioeconomic crisis and rising inequality. Designing pandemic control strategies that address the social determinants of health and build in greater equity will require greater attention. In particular, stringent lockdowns are a blunt and regressive instrument that call for rethinking and better understanding of consequences. Countries of the region have varied their approaches; even in China, testing, tracing and isolation proved more important than lockdown (Jomo, 2021). The disease itself, the containment measures and the recession have had huge and highly inequitable human consequences, exposing many existing gaps and posing major challenges for the future. Here we discuss three key priorities: public health capacity, access to vaccines and other medicines, and protecting workers in GVCs.

Public health capacity

The experience in the APR to date highlights the central role of basic public health measures for infectious disease control and the importance of robust public health infrastructure. Yet public health infrastructure has remained chronically underfunded and, in recent years, has deteriorated further. Public funding of health as a percentage of total government expenditures in 2018 ranged from 15 per cent in Thailand to

3 per cent in Bangladesh, and averaged 8.5 per cent for the region, compared with the OECD average of 15 per cent (OECD, 2020) (Figure 12.2). With dramatically rising costs, the share of household expenditures on health has also risen. While WHO estimates that countries require at least 2.5 medical staff (physicians, nurses and midwives) per 1,000 population to provide adequate coverage for primary care, several countries in the region fall below that norm. For example, Bangladesh has 1 staff per 1,000, Cambodia 1.2 (see Appendix 12A.2 for complete national data.)

The priorities of development cooperation have not focused on public health infrastructure, but rather on treatments and vaccines. For example, the $38.1 billion multilateral initiative, ACT-Accelerator, includes four so-called pillars: diagnostics, treatment, vaccines and health system strengthening. This last pillar has received the least funding so far, meeting only $0.3 billion out of the budget target of $9.5 billion (ACTaccelerator, 2020). Investment in public health, with priority to primary healthcare and expanded universal health coverage (UHC), offers a key instrument for addressing inequalities. Countries of the region have made progress, but still have a long way to go; for the 10 countries with data, the overall regional average for UHC is 61 per cent (2019), up from 46 per cent in 2010.

Global public goods: Vaccines and other diagnostics and treatments

While NPIs can go a long way in keeping outbreaks in check, they will not suffice to bring an end to the global spread of the disease in the way that vaccines can.

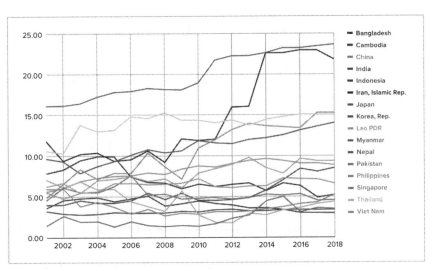

Figure 12.2   Government expenditure on health as a percentage of total government expenditure, 2002–2018
Source: WHO (2021a).

The failure to arrange for universal access to vaccines and make global immunization possible reveals a massive gap in global governance. Not only does this present an ethical issue, but it lengthens the pandemic and stymies recovery from the global recession; a recent study estimates the cost of not vaccinating the entire world at $4 trillion (Çakmaklı et al., 2021). Without global immunization, the pandemic cannot come fully under control, and economic recovery cannot take hold. Vaccine distribution remains highly skewed, advancing in high-income countries while most of the Global South has little to no access. As of January 2021, some 39 million vaccine doses had been administered globally, virtually all in the highest-income countries; by contrast, one lowest-income country had seen only 25 doses administered (Ghebreyesus, 2021a).[2] Under current agreements, and taking account of population size and vaccine supply deals, production constraints and adoption, estimates give high-income countries widespread coverage by late 2021 and middle-income countries by the end of 2022, while low-income countries would wait until 2023, if they ever receive vaccine access at all (Economist Intelligence Unit, 2021).

The multilateral system put in place to avoid this situation and achieve an objective of 'equitable access' – COVID-19 Vaccines Global Access (COVAX) – only secured 2 billion doses from five producers, with options on more than 1 billion more doses, only a fraction of those purchased through bilateral deals (Ghebreyesus, 2021a). Supply falls far short of global demand. COVAX arrangements do not yet facilitate mobilizing global manufacturing to take production to scale. Governments funded vaccine research, development and manufacturing, but kept ownership and decisions about production and allocation in the hands of companies. Production remains limited to the handful of companies that own the patents and a select few licensed to manufacture vaccines, such as the Serum Institute of India; these producers retain control over distribution.

Sharing technology, knowledge and know-how with pharmaceutical manufacturers across the world, especially in developing countries that have hubs of pharmaceutical production, would scale up vaccine production to the levels necessary for global immunization. Although 41 countries have pledged to support the COVID-19 Technology Access Pool (C-TAP) set up by WHO, it has not received funding. Another initiative currently under discussion is a proposal tabled by South Africa and India at the World Trade Organization (WTO) that would waive a number of provisions in the Agreement on Trade-Related Aspects of Intellectual Property Rights, specifically those related to COVID-19 prevention, containment and treatment, until the pandemic comes under control. The proposal has gained support from a number of developing countries.

As United Nations Secretary General António Guterres has repeatedly urged the international community, "we must ensure that vaccines are seen as a global public good – people's vaccines – accessible and affordable to all". The European Union and many governments have endorsed this as a principle, yet they have not voted for or funded removal of intellectual property obstacles to scaling up production. As efficacious and safe vaccines begin to rollout, they remain private goods supplied by a handful of corporations, for which national governments compete to negotiate bilateral purchases.

The APR includes countries having their own pharmaceutical research and development capacity to create vaccines and treatment (China, India) as well as those with massive generic manufacturing capacity (Bangladesh, India, Indonesia, Pakistan, Thailand and others). While each country must necessarily develop its own strategy for internal vaccination campaigns, countries of Asia and the Pacific can also contribute to promoting multilateral arrangements or consider developing regional approaches, as countries in Africa have done.

Workers

The pandemic has highlighted the importance of capacity to protect workers from the effects of global crises. For LMICs in the region, the vulnerability of workers, particularly those working in GVCs, poses a priority challenge given the strategic importance of these industries in long-term development. National governments undertook a number of initiatives to support workers through employment and sickness protection, cash and in-kind transfers, family leave and childcare support. For example, China issued a directive, Notice Number 5 of January 2020, that prohibited the dismissal of workers absent due to illness or emergencies and required employers to continue payments. The Republic of Korea provided a subsidy equal to 90 per cent of wages for all firms for a period of three months. Bangladesh offered low-interest loans to firms in the export sector to pay salaries for a period of three months (IMF, 2021). And as already noted earlier, countries have instituted major stimulus packages.

Nonetheless, the measures remain far from adequate for protecting livelihoods, with millions pushed into poverty and food insecurity. Considering the structural causes of the insecurity – the asymmetries of power in the structure of value chains that inevitably make both low-income countries and low-skilled workers vulnerable – a structural response will be required. This underscores the need for robust legal protection for labour rights, including collective bargaining. At the global level, the United Nations' guiding principles on business and human rights, endorsed by UN member states, should proactively hold national and foreign firms to basic human rights standards.

At the same time, the pandemic also serves as another reminder for the future of global industries and the growing demand for Industry 4.0 skills. This underscores the need for investment in education and training, and ensuring inclusion of women and other groups vulnerable to being left behind.

The vulnerabilities of workers in precarious forms of employment vividly highlight key institutional worker-empowerment and worker-protection gaps:

legal regulations and enforcement of worker rights, including collective bargaining, adequate social safety nets, and a pursuit of economic models that do not rely on exports built on low-wage labour.

CONCLUSION

What kind of institutional capacity – organizational structures and formal and informal norms – do countries need in governing the pandemic as it proceeds and in anticipation of the future emergence of new epidemic diseases?

A wide range of countries in the APR – from LDCs to the world's leading economies – highlight the critical importance of institutional capacity in government in mounting an effective response to the pandemic. Even low-income countries with limited technological and financial resources can successfully contain outbreaks, using time-tested and low-cost NPIs, but only if they have the knowledge, human resources, public health infrastructure, leadership and social norms to implement them. This should not come as a surprise. Technology and resources can only go so far in the absence of vaccines and known treatment protocols. On the other hand, a public-health emergency requires political leadership in crafting a policy response and public-health infrastructure to implement public interventions. It also needs social consensus and norms, including informal standards of individual behaviour. Curbing the spread of disease depends critically on NPIs – testing, contact tracing, quarantining, isolation, physical distancing, limiting travel and gatherings, handwashing and mask wearing – that entail changes in the daily habits of individuals. Often, government regulation alone will not suffice to ensure such changes. They call for consensus about accepting such behaviours as necessary to curb the pandemic, for collective and not only individual benefit, and compliance with those standards. Containment requires buy-in and engagement from the community and empowered citizens to act for the community. Norms and values regarding health as public health, the shared value of health as a priority, the understanding of individual behaviour as affecting others and having an impact on the community – all will prove essential in achieving a degree of compliance with NPIs. This requires capacity for action in organizational structures in the state and civil society and the capacity of communities to coalesce around shared norms.

Such factors have been underplayed in global policy debates and neglected by many governments and organizations. The global response has focused on investing in vaccines and other technologies, rather than on strengthening public health infrastructure. Clearly, these material tools will prove essential to combat, and ultimately end, the pandemic. But the reliance on technology and the neglect of institutions reflects a strategic choice, one favouring a vertical approach to addressing global health challenges to the detriment of building horizontal health systems.

The experience of countries with rampant community spread may well expose the high cost of neglecting institutional capacity. The United Kingdom, United States and other high-income countries invested heavily in vaccine development, a critical step for ending the pandemic; yet their difficulties in implementing NPIs cost a year of lost lives and health for hundreds of thousands of people. This approach is captured in a comment by the UK Health Secretary Jeremy Hunt in a recent interview:

> We did exhaustive pandemic preparations: we were lauded by the Johns Hopkins University as being the second-best prepared country in the world. But we were also part of a groupthink that said that the primary way that you respond to a pandemic is the flu pandemic playbook (with a focus on areas like vaccination and boosting hospital capacity), rather than the methods that you would use for SARS and MERS (surveillance and containment, community testing, contact tracing and isolation, and stockpiling personal protective equipment, and ventilators). (Dalton, 2021)

Even the development of vaccines emphasizes the need for institutional capacity: the ability to get the vaccines into the arms of people, particularly the most vulnerable. As technology writer Yong wrote in a recent article – using the term 'capacities' to refer to physical infrastructure – "in retrospect, many Western health experts were too focused on capacities, *such as equipment and resources*, and not on [...] *how you apply those in times of crisis*" (Yong, 2020, emphases added).

The pandemic also highlights other major gaps in national and global institutions. Pandemic governance aims not only to reduce prevalence and mortality, but to promote broader human development priorities of equity within a participatory process that addresses the socioeconomic consequences of a pandemic-induced recession. At the national level, this calls for more debate on the design of policies and processes in order to ensure equity and respect for human rights.

The pandemic has exposed the most glaring gap in global governance. As WHO Director-General Tedros Ghebreyesus stated at the opening of the WHO Executive Board meeting on 18 January 2021, "[t]he world is on the brink of *a catastrophic moral failure*". He went on to say that "the international community cannot allow a handful of companies to dictate the terms or the timeframe with *a restrictive approach to vaccine production* [that] is in fact more likely to prolong the pandemic [...] and is tantamount to *medical malpractice on a global scale*" (Ghebreyesus, 2021a, emphases added). In fact, this represents not only a moral failure but a failure of policymaking for public health and economic stability, for the restricted flow and delays in vaccination will merely prolong the pandemic and trigger further economic losses.

The pandemic has highlighted some of the defining stories of global inequality in the contemporary world. Progress in finding institutional arrangements for greater cooperation will, in turn, become the defining challenge for all countries and people.

Appendix 12A.1 Vital COVID-19 Statistics for Countries of Asia and the Pacific

Table 12A.1 Mortality, morbidity and test rates in countries of Asia and the Pacific, as of 10 January 2021

Country	Deaths / million	Cumulative deaths	Cases / million	Cumulative Cases	Tests / thousand	Cumulative tests
Afghanistan	58.49	2,277.00	1,374.04	53,489.00	5.86**	228,105**
Bangladesh	47.25	7,781.00	3,172.35	522,453.00	20.37	3,354,659.00
Bhutan	1.30	1.00	1,053.64	813.00	Not available	Not available
Cambodia	0.00	0.00	23.39	391.00	Not available	Not available
China	3.33	4,792.00	67.27	96,824.00	111.16[a]	160,000,000[a]
Cook Islands*	0.00	0.00	0.00	0.00	Not available	Not available
Fiji	2.23	2.00	59.12	53.00	25.41	22,774
India	109.54	151,160.00	7,584.47	10,466,595.00	131.23	181,096,622.00
Indonesia	88.22	24,129.00	3,027.26	828,026.00	19.25	5,264,664.00
Iran	668.76	56,171.00	15,315.64	1,286,406.00	95.17[b]	7,993,502[b]
Japan	30.44	3,850.00	2,283.57	288,818.00	39.47	4,992,128.00
Kiribati	0.00	0.00	0.00	0.00	Not available	Not available
Korea, DPR	0.00	0.00	0.00	0.00	Not available	Not available
Korea, Rep.	22.24	1,140.00	1,348.06	69,114.00	88.40	4,532,010.00
Lao PDR	0.00	0.00	5.64	41.00	Not available	Not available
Malaysia	17.02	551.00	4,201.69	135,992.00	112.06	3,626,785.00
Maldives	90.65	49.00	26,101.58	14,109.00	622.82[c]	33,6662[c]

Marshall Islands	0.00	0.00	67.57	4.00	Not available	Not available
Micronesia*	0.00	0.00	0.00	0.00	Not available	Not available
Mongolia*	0.31	1.00	439.86	1,442.00	225.87	740,477.00
Myanmar	52.31	2,846.00	2,400.38	130,604.00	36.401[c]	1,980,591[c]
Nauru*	0.00	0.00	0.00	0.00	Not available	Not available
Nepal	65.79	1,917.00	9,087.48	264,780.00	67.92[c]	1,978,847[c]
Niue*	0.00	0.00	0.00	0.00	Not available	Not available
Pakistan	48.33	10,676.00	2,282.98	504,293.00	32.09	7,088,014.00
Palau	0.00	0.00	0.00	0.00	Not available	Not available
Papua New Guinea	1.01	9.00	90.65	811.00	Not available	Not available
Philippines	85.83	9,405.00	4,450.49	487,690.00	60.83	6,665,240.00
Samoa	0.00	0.00	10.08	2.00	Not available	Not available
Singapore	4.96	29.00	10,068.98	58,907.00	960.27[d]	5,617,894[d]
Solomon Islands	0.00	0.00	24.75	17.00	Not available	Not available
Sri Lanka	10.83	232.00	2,259.35	48,380.00	64.91	1,389,831.00
Taiwan, Prov. of China	0.29	7.00	34.77	828.00	5.54	132,017.00
Thailand	0.96	67.00	147.54	10,298.00	23.29[e]	1,625,271[e]
Timor-Leste	0.00	0.00	37.17	49.00	Not available	Not available
Tokelau*	0.00	0.00	0.00	0.00	Not available	Not available
Tonga*	0.00	0.00	0.00	0.00	Not available	Not available

(Continued)

Table 12A.1 (Continued)

Country	Deaths / million	Cumulative deaths	Cases / million	Cumulative Cases	Tests / thousand	Cumulative tests
Tuvalu*	0.00	0.00	0.00	0.00	Not available	Not available
Vanuatu	0.00	0.00	3.26	1.00	Not available	Not available
Viet Nam	0.36	35.00	15.55	1,514.00	15.10[f]	1469955[f]

Sources: Roser et al. (2021a); Hasell et al. (2021).

Note: * WHO (2021b).

** WHO (2021b). Data point: 18 January 2021

[a] Last available data for China. Data point: 6 August 2020

[b] Last available data for Iran. Data point: 7 January 2021

[c] Last available data for Maldives, Myanmar, Nepal. Data point: 9 January 2021

[d] Last available data for Singapore. Data point: 4 January 2021

[e] Last available data for Thailand. Data point: 1 January 2021

[f] Last available data for Viet Nam. Data point: 19 December 2020

APPENDIX 12A.2   FUNDING FOR HEALTH IN COUNTRIES OF ASIA AND THE PACIFIC

Table 12A.2.1   Level of current health expenditure expressed as a percentage of GDP, Asia-Pacific countries, 2009–2018

Country Name/ Year	2009	2010	2011	2012	2013	2014	2015	2016	2017	2018
Afghanistan	9.82	8.57	8.56	7.90	8.81	9.53	10.11	10.96	11.78	9.40
Bangladesh	2.40	2.50	2.57	2.57	2.50	2.50	2.46	2.31	2.28	2.34
Bhutan	3.46	3.47	3.27	3.53	3.62	3.47	3.66	3.48	3.24	3.06
Cambodia	7.58	6.91	7.50	7.26	7.10	6.70	6.19	6.12	5.93	6.03
China	4.32	4.21	4.33	4.55	4.71	4.77	4.89	4.98	5.15	5.35
Cook Islands	N/A	N/A	N/A	N/A	N/A	N/A	N/A	N/A	N/A	N/A
Fiji	3.54	3.42	3.14	3.27	3.20	3.37	3.32	3.28	3.19	3.42
India	3.49	3.27	3.25	3.33	3.75	3.62	3.60	3.51	3.54	3.54
Indonesia	2.68	2.96	2.96	2.90	2.96	3.12	2.99	3.09	2.87	2.87
Iran	6.56	6.75	6.61	6.64	5.99	6.91	7.76	8.86	8.66	8.66
Japan	9.06	9.16	10.62	10.79	10.79	10.83	10.89	10.83	10.80	10.95
Kiribati	13.44	9.21	8.58	8.60	9.46	9.94	7.99	9.32	10.78	12.11
Korea, DPR	N/A	N/A	N/A	N/A	N/A	N/A	N/A	N/A	N/A	N/A
Korea, Rep.	5.78	5.92	6.01	6.13	6.25	6.47	6.65	6.91	7.11	7.56
Lao PDR	3.46	2.91	1.94	2.08	2.40	2.30	2.45	2.36	2.53	2.25
Malaysia	3.28	3.18	3.34	3.49	3.52	3.73	3.82	3.69	3.71	3.76
Maldives	10.09	8.49	7.92	8.67	8.14	7.91	8.69	10.20	9.03	9.41
Marshall Islands	15.88	15.08	14.57	14.31	14.62	14.72	17.36	17.65	16.40	17.55
Micronesia	12.55	13.11	13.10	12.31	12.18	11.77	12.50	13.18	12.32	12.59
Mongolia	4.46	3.74	3.59	3.85	4.07	4.19	4.24	4.42	4.01	3.79
Myanmar	2.10	1.87	1.92	2.44	3.24	4.39	5.48	5.11	5.09	4.79
Nauru	12.03	13.16	10.17	9.23	9.24	10.09	15.19	14.09	11.58	9.58
Nepal	4.45	4.97	5.08	5.17	5.32	5.77	6.22	6.28	5.49	5.84

(Continued)

Table 12A.2.1   *(Continued)*

Country Name/ Year	2009	2010	2011	2012	2013	2014	2015	2016	2017	2018
Niue	N/A	N/A	N/A	N/A	N/A	N/A	N/A	N/A	N/A	N/A
Pakistan	2.61	2.60	2.34	2.36	2.60	2.72	2.69	2.86	2.90	3.20
Palau	10.36	11.61	10.82	11.64	12.12	12.17	11.39	12.00	12.13	10.87
Papua New Guinea	2.33	2.11	2.29	2.67	3.00	3.27	1.82	2.33	2.27	2.37
Philippines	4.35	4.31	4.21	4.37	4.46	4.13	4.32	4.41	4.45	4.40
Samoa	5.41	5.49	5.42	4.82	6.17	6.23	5.67	5.51	5.51	5.21
Singapore	3.40	3.20	3.16	3.33	3.69	3.87	4.18	4.40	4.42	4.46
Solomon Islands	8.61	10.33	6.71	5.55	5.38	5.73	5.19	5.00	4.74	4.47
Sri Lanka	4.19	3.87	3.72	3.40	3.83	3.61	3.89	3.86	3.81	3.76
Thailand	3.62	3.39	3.57	3.52	3.45	3.68	3.67	3.76	3.83	3.79
Timor-Leste	1.66	1.43	1.26	1.22	2.11	2.72	3.95	4.55	4.34	4.33
Tokelau	N/A	N/A	N/A	N/A	N/A	N/A	N/A	N/A	N/A	N/A
Tonga	3.88	4.74	3.86	5.06	4.17	5.13	4.58	5.06	5.06	5.10
Tuvalu	14.36	16.40	15.39	15.33	18.13	16.86	16.70	16.88	17.73	19.05
Vanuatu	3.16	3.38	3.50	3.77	4.15	3.46	4.16	2.85	2.76	3.37
Viet Nam	5.29	5.97	5.87	6.28	6.34	5.78	5.65	5.66	5.93	5.92

Source: WHO (2021a).

Note: Estimates of current health expenditures include healthcare goods and services consumed during each year. This indicator does not include capital health expenditures such as buildings, machinery, information technology and stocks of vaccines for emergencies or outbreaks.

Table 12A.2.2 Public, private, and external health expenditures expressed as a percentage of current health expenditures, Asia-Pacific countries, 2016-2018 (% CHE)

Year	2016			2017			2018		
Country Name / Indicator	Government health expenditure (%CHE)	Private health expenditure (%CHE)	External health expenditure (%CHE)	Government health expenditure (%CHE)	Private health expenditure (%CHE)	External health expenditure (%CHE)	Government health expenditure (%CHE)	Private health expenditure (%CHE)	External health expenditure (%CHE)
Afghanistan	5.08	75.97	18.95	5.10	75.48	19.42	5.17	78.38	16.44
Bangladesh	16.42	75.77	7.82	16.69	76.56	6.75	16.98	76.50	6.52
Bhutan	73.95	21.29	4.76	74.52	14.31	11.17	79.55	14.40	6.05
Cambodia	21.81	59.24	18.95	18.40	61.13	20.47	21.27	58.19	20.54
China	58.10	41.90	0.00	56.67	43.33	0.00	56.42	43.58	0.00
Cook Is.	N/A	N/A	N/A	N/A	N/A	N/A	N/A	N/A	N/A
Fiji	63.90	33.01	3.09	66.23	31.44	2.33	68.31	29.49	2.20
India	26.84	72.52	0.64	27.13	72.06	0.81	26.95	72.35	0.70
Indonesia	45.84	53.74	0.42	46.51	52.95	0.54	49.33	50.29	0.38
Iran	50.61	49.36	0.03	51.25	48.73	0.02	45.93	54.05	0.02
Japan	84.04	15.96	0.0.00	84.21	15.79	00.00	84.09	15.91	0.0.00
Kiribati	79.54	3.43	17.03	75.67	3.11	21.22	76.40	0.10	23.50
Korea, DPR	N/A	N/A	N/A	N/A	N/A	N/A	N/A	N/A	N/A

(Continued)

Table 12A.2.2   (Continued)

Year	2016			2017			2018		
Country Name / Indicator	Government health expenditure (%CHE)	Private health expenditure (%CHE)	External health expenditure (%CHE)	Government health expenditure (%CHE)	Private health expenditure (%CHE)	External health expenditure (%CHE)	Government health expenditure (%CHE)	Private health expenditure (%CHE)	External health expenditure (%CHE)
Korea, Rep.	57.52	42.48	0.00	57.91	42.09	0.00	58.46	41.54	0.00
Lao PDR	32.40	49.48	18.12	35.19	48.14	16.67	38.70	48.85	12.45
Malaysia	51.24	48.74	0.02	51.86	48.12	0.02	51.18	48.81	0.01
Maldives	72.23	27.54	0.23	71.46	28.46	0.08	70.62	28.45	0.93
Marshall Is.	40.01	14.21	45.78	38.59	15.73	45.68	43.46	14.58	41.96
Micronesia	26.49	2.45	71.06	25.88	2.41	71.71	26.32	2.36	71.32
Mongolia	59.34	35.00	5.67	61.69	35.48	2.84	58.68	35.81	5.51
Myanmar	13.99	76.67	9.34	14.79	75.69	9.52	14.83	76.45	8.72
Nauru	68.54	3.83	27.63	72.77	4.33	22.90	82.76	5.08	12.16
Nepal	18.58	69.71	11.71	22.34	62.39	15.27	25.05	65.86	9.09
Niue	N/A	N/A	N/A	N/A	N/A	N/A	N/A	N/A	N/A
Pakistan	28.74	69.43	1.83	31.59	66.67	1.74	35.54	63.87	0.60
Palau	52.28	32.37	15.35	50.62	34.97	14.40	58.91	38.45	2.64

Papua New Guinea	72.00	10.14	17.86	75.41	9.00	15.59	70.04	9.74	20.21
Philippines	31.71	65.97	2.32	31.91	65.50	2.59	32.65	66.59	0.76
Samoa	76.64	12.49	10.87	74.93	12.07	13.00	72.20	12.60	15.20
Singapore	47.34	52.66	0. 0.00	48.20	51.80	0. 0.00	50.35	49.65	00.00
Solomon Is.	70.99	1.88	27.13	74.61	1.93	23.46	79.06	2.15	18.80
Sri Lanka	43.12	56.01	0.87	42.46	56.02	1.52	41.09	56.67	2.24
Thailand	75.95	23.95	0.09	76.58	23.19	0.22	76.27	23.39	0.33
Timor-Leste	49.64	11.21	39.15	65.99	11.62	22.39	60.64	11.36	28.00
Tokelau	N/A	N/A	N/A	N/A	N/A	N/A	N/A	N/A	N/A
Tonga	58.66	13.11	28.24	56.67	13.39	29.94	63.25	14.02	22.73
Tuvalu	77.36	3.27	19.38	70.24	3.81	25.95	79.87	3.87	16.26
Vanuatu	45.50	15.09	39.41	52.31	14.72	32.96	63.47	13.15	23.38
Viet Nam	47.43	50.27	2.30	46.11	52.81	1.09	45.56	52.59	1.85

Source: WHO (2021a).

Table 12A.2.3 Domestic general government health expenditures expressed as a percentage of total government expenditures, Asia-Pacific countries, 2009–2018

Country Name / Year	2009	2010	2011	2012	2013	2014	2015	2016	2017	2018
Afghanistan	2.51	2.26	2.19	1.37	1.78	1.86	2.01	2.14	2.32	1.80
Bangladesh	4.12	4.44	4.14	3.96	3.58	3.61	3.38	3.02	2.99	2.98
Bhutan	6.63	5.60	6.33	6.66	7.25	8.03	9.95	8.30	7.90	7.61
Cambodia	5.97	6.52	6.21	6.49	6.64	5.71	6.63	6.32	4.87	5.21
China	8.38	8.75	8.60	9.04	9.42	9.63	9.39	9.06	9.07	8.85
Cook Islands	N/A	N/A	N/A	N/A	N/A	N/A	N/A	N/A	N/A	N/A
Fiji	8.37	8.79	7.47	7.51	7.47	7.10	7.04	7.66	7.18	7.17
India	3.19	3.11	3.38	3.44	3.24	3.25	3.38	3.39	3.38	3.39
Indonesia	5.41	4.51	4.52	4.63	4.85	5.78	7.03	8.41	8.05	8.51
Iran	12.09	11.89	12.04	15.96	16.05	22.60	22.60	22.94	22.94	21.81
Japan	18.08	18.94	21.73	22.26	22.27	22.62	23.21	23.21	23.44	23.65
Kiribati	10.90	10.45	9.29	8.31	9.10	7.28	6.69	6.47	7.36	5.99
Korea, DPR	0.00	0.00	0.00	0.00	0.00	0.00	0.00	0.00	0.00	0.00
Korea, Rep.	10.60	11.86	11.58	11.48	11.99	12.20	12.55	13.13	13.60	14.04
Lao PDR	5.70	2.69	1.82	1.77	2.94	2.74	3.35	3.63	4.12	4.37
Malaysia	5.86	6.31	6.51	6.54	6.81	7.82	8.23	8.33	8.92	8.47
Maldives	15.76	13.60	12.28	14.36	15.74	14.62	18.50	20.43	21.44	21.44
Marshall Islands	8.69	7.67	10.53	11.40	11.92	11.64	11.57	12.15	9.67	12.08
Micronesia	3.44	3.40	4.65	3.95	4.64	6.16	5.77	5.64	4.95	4.80
Mongolia	8.75	7.74	5.62	6.49	7.03	7.38	7.75	6.62	7.64	7.73
Myanmar	1.44	1.35	1.65	2.32	2.71	4.47	4.98	3.10	3.61	3.49
Nauru	9.25	10.25	12.48	8.05	7.46	8.12	8.35	10.33	8.37	7.36
Nepal	4.69	4.81	4.87	4.69	4.88	5.27	5.15	5.31	4.51	4.58
Niue	N/A	N/A	N/A	N/A	N/A	N/A	N/A	N/A	N/A	N/A
Pakistan	2.95	2.81	3.16	3.13	3.22	3.48	3.74	4.12	4.30	5.26
Palau	9.43	8.54	9.20	9.80	11.55	11.03	10.99	16.51	17.39	16.83
Papua New Guinea	6.32	7.07	7.60	8.13	7.19	7.47	6.02	8.04	9.15	7.39

(Continued)

Table 12A.2.3 *(Continued)*

Country Name / Year	2009	2010	2011	2012	2013	2014	2015	2016	2017	2018
Philippines	6.64	7.18	6.19	6.08	6.27	6.29	7.25	7.17	7.11	6.60
Samoa	12.67	10.38	10.24	10.12	10.62	10.12	11.53	11.58	11.69	11.00
Singapore	7.15	10.94	11.97	13.21	13.96	13.66	13.54	13.40	15.28	15.28
Solomon Islands	6.90	6.75	6.96	7.11	6.74	7.49	7.57	7.53	7.44	7.88
Sri Lanka	7.84	7.83	7.97	8.06	10.10	9.03	8.40	8.56	8.43	8.29
Thailand	14.38	14.36	14.04	14.39	13.74	14.45	14.79	15.06	15.03	15.03
Timor-Leste	2.66	2.71	2.68	3.21	4.62	3.72	4.51	3.12	5.19	5.36
Tokelau	N/A	N/A	N/A	N/A	N/A	N/A	N/A	N/A	N/A	N/A
Tonga	11.15	9.03	8.68	8.06	8.36	8.08	6.84	7.33	7.15	7.47
Tuvalu	11.72	14.79	16.70	16.72	16.03	12.87	10.86	9.55	9.85	13.74
Vanuatu	7.27	6.85	9.39	9.40	9.80	2.06	5.14	3.73	4.04	6.97
Viet Nam	6.07	7.88	8.41	8.93	9.78	8.51	7.83	9.64	9.35	9.35

Source: WHO (2021a).

Appendix 12A.3　Public Health Infrastructure

Table 12A.3.1　Hospital beds per thousand people, Asia-Pacific countries, most recent year available

Country Name	Most recent year available	Hospital beds / 1,000 people
Afghanistan	2017	0.39
Bangladesh	2016	0.79
Bhutan	2012	1.74
Cambodia	2016	0.9
China	2017	4.31
Cook Islands		N/A
Fiji	2016	2
India	2017	0.53
Indonesia	2017	1.04
Iran	2017	1.56

(Continued)

Table 12A.3.1 *(Continued)*

Country Name	Most recent year available	Hospital beds / 1,000 people
Japan	2018	12.98
Kiribati	2016	1.86
Korea, DPR	2012	13.2
Korea, Rep.	2018	12.43
Lao PDR	2012	1.5
Malaysia	2017	1.88
Maldives	2009	4.3
Marshall Islands	2010	2.7
Micronesia	2009	3.2
Mongolia	2017	8
Myanmar	2017	1.04
Nauru	2010	5
Nepal	2012	0.3
Niue		N/A
Pakistan	2017	0.63
Palau	2010	4.8
Papua New Guinea	1990	4.024
Philippines	2014	0.99
Samoa	2007	1
Singapore	2017	2.49
Solomon Islands	2012	1.4
Sri Lanka	2017	4.15
Thailand	2010	2.1
Timor-Leste	2010	5.9
Tokelau		N/A
Tonga	2010	2.6
Tuvalu	2001	5.6
Vanuatu	2008	1.7
Viet Nam	2014	2.6

Source: WHO (2021a).

Table 12A.3.2 Physicians, nurses, and midwives per thousand people, Asia-Pacific countries, most recent year available

Country Name	Physicians / 1,000 people		Nurses and midwives / 1,000 people	
	Most recent year available	Indicator	Most recent year available	Indicator
Afghanistan	2016	0.2782	2017	0.1755
Bangladesh	2018	0.5809	2018	0.4124
Bhutan	2018	0.4242	2018	1.8518
Cambodia	2014	0.1927	2018	0.6855
China	2017	1.9798	2017	2.6621
Cook Islands	N/A	N/A	N/A	N/A
Fiji	2015	0.86	2018	3.3752
India	2018	0.8571	2018	1.7271
Indonesia	2018	0.4269	2018	2.4149
Iran	2018	1.5844	2017	2.6286
Japan	2016	2.4115	2018	12.1531
Kiribati	2013	0.2039	2018	3.8342
Korea, DPR	2017	3.6834	2017	4.4489
Korea, Rep.	2017	2.3608	2018	7.3009
Lao PDR	2017	0.3726	2018	0.9522
Malaysia	2015	1.5358	2017	3.4676
Maldives	2018	4.5627	2018	6.4282
Marshall Islands	2012	0.4233	2018	3.339
Micronesia	2010	0.177	2018	2.0426
Mongolia	2016	2.8592	2018	3.8938
Myanmar	2018	0.677	2018	0.9993
Nauru	2015	1.3462	2018	7.6636
Nepal	2018	0.7486	2018	3.1084
Niue	N/A	N/A	N/A	N/A
Pakistan	2018	0.9801	2018	0.6683
Palau	2014	1.4205	2018	7.2626
Papua New Guinea	2018	0.0699	2018	0.4548

(Continued)

Table 12A.3.2   *(Continued)*

Country Name	Physicians / 1,000 people		Nurses and midwives / 1,000 people	
	Most recent year available	Indicator	Most recent year available	Indicator
Philippines	2017	0.6004	2018	4.9351
Samoa	2016	0.3445	2018	2.4885
Singapore	2016	2.2936	2017	6.2432
Solomon Islands	2016	0.1937	2018	2.1642
Sri Lanka	2018	1.0041	2018	2.1803
Thailand	2018	0.805	2018	2.7593
Timor-Leste	2018	0.7224	2018	1.668
Tokelau	N/A	N/A	N/A	N/A
Tonga	2013	0.5403	2018	4.157
Tuvalu	2014	0.9174	2018	4.2609
Vanuatu	2016	0.1653	2018	1.4247
Viet Nam	2016	0.8281	2016	1.4463

Source: WHO (2021a).

Table 12A.3.3   Share of the population with basic handwashing facilities on premises, Asia-Pacific countries, most recent year available

Country Name	% Population with basic handwashing facilities
Afghanistan (2017)	37.75
Bangladesh (2017)	34.81
Bhutan (2014)	79.81
Cambodia (2017)	66.23
China	N/A
Cook Islands	N/A
Fiji	N/A
India (2017)	59.55
Indonesia (2017)	64.20

(Continued)

Table 12A.3.3 *(Continued)*

Country Name	% Population with basic handwashing facilities
Iran	N/A
Japan	N/A
Kiribati	N/A
Korea, DPR	N/A
Korea, Rep.	N/A
Lao PDR (2017)	49.84
Malaysia	N/A
Maldives (2017)	95.80
Marshall Islands (2017)	82.50
Micronesia	N/A
Mongolia (2017)	71.18
Myanmar (2017)	79.29
Nauru	N/A
Nepal (2017)	47.78
Niue	N/A
Pakistan (2017)	59.61
Palau	N/A
Papua New Guinea	N/A
Philippines (2017)	78.46
Samoa	N/A
Singapore	N/A
Solomon Islands (2017)	35.89
Sri Lanka	N/A
Thailand (2017)	83.92
Timor-Leste (2017)	28.18
Tokelau	N/A
Tonga	N/A
Tuvalu	N/A
Vanuatu (2017)	25.21
Viet Nam (2017)	85.85

Source: WHO (2021a).

Acknowledgements

I gratefully acknowledge the very able research assistance of Angelia Rengifo Gomez and Natalia Vega Varela.

Notes

1. Following Amartya Sen (1999), 'capabilities' here means the ability of individuals to be and do in life according to their aspirations. This is a very different meaning of the term than, for example, Ed Yong (2020) and others who refer to capability as the ability to make use of capacity, including physical infrastructure or financial capital.
2. At the end of April 2021, the director of the WHO noted that nearly 1 billion doses had been administered: 81 per cent in high- and upper-middle-income countries and only 0.3 per cent in low-income countries (Ghebreyesus, 2021b).

References

ACTaccelerator. 2020. *Urgent Priorities and Financing Requirements at 10 November 2020.* Geneva: World Health Organization. cdn.who.int/media/docs/default-source/a-future-for-children/act-accelerator-urgent-priorities-financing-requirements-23_nov-single-page.pdf.

An, B. Y. and Tang, S.-Y. 2020. 'Lessons from Covid-19 Responses in East Asia: Institutional Infrastructure and Enduring Policy Instruments'. *American Review of Public Administration* 50(6–7), 790–800.

Anner, M. 2021. *Leveraging Desperation: Apparel Brands' Purchasing Practices during COVID-19.* University Park, PA: Center for Global Workers' Rights, Pennsylvania State University.

Association of Southeast Asian Nations (ASEAN). 2020. *Social Protection Responses to COVID-19 in Asia and the Pacific.* Jakarta: The ASEAN Secretariat.

Belluz, J. 2020. 'China's Cases of Covid-19 Are Finally Declining. A WHO Expert Explains Why'. *Vox*, 3 March. vox.com/2020/3/2/21161067/coronavirus-covid19-china.

Bottan, N., Hoffman, B. and Vera-Cossio, D. 2020. 'The Unequal Impact of the Coronavirus Pandemic: Evidence from Seventeen Developing Countries'. *PLOS One*, 7 October. journals.plos.org/plosone/article?id=10.1371/journal.pone.0239797.

Çakmaklı, S., Demiralp, S., Kalemli-Özcan, S., Yesiltas, S. and Yildirim, M. 2021. 'The Economic Case for Global Vaccinations: An Epidemiological Model with International Production Networks'. National Bureau of Economic Research, Cambridge, MA. nber.org/system/files/working_papers/w28395/w28395.pdf.

Cash, R. and Patel, V. 2020. 'Has COVID-19 Subverted Global Health?' *The Lancet* 395(10238), 1687–1688.

Chang, T.-H., Goicoechea, E. B., Stuart, E., Kim, E., Morris, K., LaRocca, S. Cobb, C. Deng, X. Chiu, S. Bradford and A. Kreuter, F. 2020. 'Global Trends of Mask Usage in 19 Million Adults'. Social Data Science Center, 12 October. socialdatascience.umd.edu/global-trends-of-mask-usage-in-19-million-adults/.

Dalton, J. 2021. 'We Prepared for the Wrong Pandemic, Admits Former Health Secretary Jeremy Hunt'. *Independent*, 8 February.

Economist Intelligence Unit. 2021. 'Coronavirus Vaccines: Expect Delays. Q1 Global Forecast 2021'. Economist Group, London.

Erkhembayar, R., Dickson, E., Badarch, D., Narula, I., Warburton, D., Neil Thomas, G. and Manaseki-Holland, S. 2020. 'Early Policy Actions and Emergency Responses to the COVID-19 Pandemic in Mongolia: Experiences and Challenges'. *The Lancet* 8(9), E1234–E1241. thelancet.com/journals/langlo/article/PIIS2214-109X(20)30295-3/fulltext#.

Farmer, P. 1996. *Social Inequalities and Emerging Infectious Diseases.* Berkeley, CA: University of California Press.

Ghebreyesus, T. A. 2021a. 'Opening Remarks at 148th Session of the Executive Board'. World Health Organization, Geneva. who.int/director-general/speeches/detail/who-director-general-s-opening-remarks-at-148th-session-of-the-executive-board.

Ghebreyesus, T. A. 2021b. 'I Run the WHO and I Know Rich Countries Must Make a Choice'. *New York Times,* 22 April. nytimes.com/2021/04/22/opinion/who-covid-vaccines.html.

Han, E., Tan, M. M. J., Turk, E., Sridhar, D., Leung, G. M., Shibuya, K., Asgari, N., Oh, J., García-Basteiro, A. L., Hanefeld, J., Cook, A. R., Hsu, L. Y., Teo, Y. Y., Heymann, D., Clark, H., McKee, M. and Legido-Quigley, H. 2020. 'Lessons Learnt from Easing COVID-19 Restrictions: An Analysis of Countries and Regions in Asia Pacific and Europe'. *The Lancet* 396(10261),1524–1534. doi.org/10.1016/S0140-6736(20)32007-9.

Hasell, J., Mathieu, E., Beltekian, D., Macdonald, B., Giattino, C., Ortiz-Ospina, E., Roser, M. and Ritchie, H. 2021. 'A Cross-Country Database of COVID-19 Testing'. *Scientific Data* 7(345).

Ibrahim, S. 2011. 'From Individual to Collective Capabilities: The Capability Approach as a Conceptual Framework for Self-Help'. *Journal of Human Development and Capabilities* 7(3), 397–416.

Institute for Human Rights and Business (IHRB). 2020. 'The Compounding Impacts of Covid-19 on Migrant Workers across Asia'. Institute for Human Rights and Business Copyright, East Sussex. ihrb.org/focus-areas/covid-19/covid19-migrant-workers-overview.

International Center for Not-for-Profit Law (ICNL). No date. 'Covid-19 Civic Freedom Tracker'. International Center For Not- For- Profit Law, Washington, DC. icnl. org/covid19tracker/?location=9,21,24,53,56,57,195,63,78,86,88,94,99,111,116,122, 137&issue=&date=&type=.

International Labour Organization (ILO). 2018. 'The Rana Plaza Accident and Its Aftermath'. International Labour Organization, Geneva. ilo.org/global/topics/geip/ WCMS_614394/lang--en/index.htm.

———. 2021. 'ILO Monitor: COVID-19 and the World of Work', Seventh Edition. International Labour Organization, Geneva. ilo.org/wcmsp5/groups/public/---dgreports/--dcomm/documents/briefingnote/wcms_767028.pdf.

International Monetary Fund (IMF). 2020. *World Economic Outlook.* Washington, DC: International Monetary Fund. imf.org/en/Publications/WEO.

———. 2021. 'Policy Responses to COVID-19'. International Monetary Fund, Washington, DC. imf.org/en/Topics/imf-and-covid19/Policy-Responses-to-COVID-19.

Jomo, K. S. 2021. 'Nothing to Learn from East Asia?' KS Jomo, Kuala Lumpur. ksjomo.org/ post/nothing-to-learn-from-east-asia.

Kim, P. S. 2020. 'South Korea's Fast Response to Coronavirus Disease: Implications on public Policy and Public Management Theory'. *Public Management Review* 23(12), 1736–1747. tandfonline.com/doi/full/10.1080/14719037.2020.1766266.

Kucera, D. and Tejani, S. 2014. 'Feminization, Defeminization, and Structural Change in Manufacturing'. *World Development* 64(12), 569–582.

Ministry of Health. 2020. 'Measures to Contain the Covid-19 Outbreak in Migrant Worker Dormitories'. Government of Singapore, Singapore. moh.gov.sg/news-highlights/details/measures-to-contain-the-covid-19-outbreak-in-migrant-worker-dormitories.

Narayan, R. 2020. 'How Covid-19 Has Been Battering Human Rights: An Asia-Pacific Perspective'. *Global Asia* 15(2). globalasia.org/v15no2/focus/how-covid-19-has-been-battering-human-rights-an-asia-pacific-perspective_rajiv-narayan.

Nit, B., Samy, A. L., Tan, S. L. and Ahmadi, A. 2021. 'Understanding the Slow COVID-19 Trajectory of Cambodia'. *Public Health in Practice* 2(100132). doi.org/10.1016/j.puhip.2021.100132.

North, D. 1990. *Institutions, Institutional Change and Economic Performance*. Cambridge: Cambridge University Press.

Organisation for Economic Cooperation and Development (OECD). 2020. 'Public Funding of Healthcare'. Organisation for Economic Cooperation and Development, Paris.

Oxfam. 2020a. 'From Catastrophe to Catalyst: Can the World Bank Make COVID-19 a Turning Point for Building Universal and Fair Public Healthcare Systems?' Oxfam, Oxford.

———. 2020b. 'The Inequality Virus'. Oxfam, Oxford.

Oxfam India. 2021. 'The Inequality Virus: Davos India Supplement'. Oxfam India, New Delhi.

Oxford COVID-19 Government Response Tracker (OxCGRT). 2020. 'Oxford COVID-19 Government Response Tracker Regional Report – East Asia-Pacific'. Blavatnik School of Government, University of Oxford, Oxford. github.com/OxCGRT/covid-policy-scratchpad/blob/master/regional_reports/LatestEastAsiaPacificRegionalSummary.pdf.

Patel, J. and Sridhar, D. 2020. 'We Should Learn from the Asia-Pacific Responses to COVID-19'. *The Lancet Regional Health* 5(100062). doi.org/10.1016/j.lanwpc.2020.100062.

Pires, L. N., Carvalho, L. and Rawet, E. 2020. 'Multidimensional Inequality and COVID-19 in Brazil'. Public Policy Brief No.153. Levy Economics Institute of Bard College, Annandale, NY.

Pires, L. N., de Lima Xavier, L., Masterson, T., Nikiforos, M. and Rios-Avila, F. 2020. 'Pandemic of Inequality'. Public Policy Brief No.149. Levy Economics Institute of Bard College, Annandale, NY.

Putnam, R. 2000. *Bowling Alone: The Collapse and Revival of American Community*. New York: Simon and Schuster.

Rawal, S., Allen, L., Stigler, F., Kringos, D., Yamamoto, H. and van Weel, C. 2020. 'Lessons on the COVID-19 Pandemic for and by Primary Care Professionals Worldwide'. *European Journal of General Practice* 26(1), 129–133. doi.org/10.1080/13814788.2020.1820479.

Roberton, T., Carter, E., Chou, V., Stegmuller, A., Jackson, B., Tam, Y. and Walker, N. 2020. 'Early Estimates of the Indirect Effects of the COVID-19 Pandemic on Maternal and Child Mortality in Low-Income and Middle-Income Countries: A Modelling Study'. *Lancet Global Health* 8(7), E901–E908. doi.org/10.1016/S2214-109X(20)30229-1.

Roser, M., Ritchie, H., Ortiz-Ospina, E. and Hasell, J. 2021. 'Coronavirus Pandemic COVID-19'. Global Change Data Lab, Oxford. ourworldindata.org/coronavirus.

Sen, A. 1999. *Development as Freedom*. New York: Alfred Knopf.

Stewart, F. 2013. 'Capabilities and Human Development: Beyond the Individual-the Critical Role of Social Institutions and Social Competencies'. United Nations Development Programme, New York. hdr.undp.org/sites/default/files/hdro_1303_stewart.pdf.

Stiglitz, J. E. 2020. 'Recovering from the Pandemic: An Appraisal of Lessons Learned'. FEPS Covid Response Paper, Foundation for European Progressive Studies, Brussels.

Tejani, S. and Fukuda-Parr, S. 2021. 'Gender and Covid-19: Workers in Global Value Chains'. New School for Social Research, Department of Economics, New York. ideas. repec.org/s/new/wpaper.html.

The Independent Panel for Pandemic Preparedness and Response. 2021. *Second Report on Progress*. Geneva: The Independent Panel for Pandemic Preparedness and Response. theindependentpanel.org/wp-content/uploads/2021/01/Independent-Panel_Second-Report-on-Progress_Final-15-Jan-2021.pdf.

UN Women. 2020. 'The Impact of COVID-19 on Women'. UN Women, New York.

———. 2021. 'Whose Time to Care? Unpaid Care and Domestic Work During COVID-19'. UN Women, New York.

United Nations Conference on Trade and Development (UNCTAD). 2020. *Transforming Trade and Development in a Fractured, Post-Pandemic World*. New York: United Nations Conference on Trade and Development.

United Nations Economic and Social Commission for Asia and the Pacific (UNESCAP). 2020. 'An Assessment of Fiscal Space for COVID-19 Response and Recovery in Asia-Pacific Developing Countries'. United Nations Economic and Social Commission for Asia and the Pacific, Bangkok.

Watanabe, E. 2021. 'Nagayo Sensai, Father of Public Health in Japan: Some Lessons for Managing COVID-19'. India China Institute, New York. indiachinainstitute.org/research/pandemic-discourses/.

Weber, F. 2020. 'With Labour Exploitation Worsening during Covid, Tech Giants Must Allow Workers to Join Unions'. Reuters, 22 June. ethicalcorp.com/labour-exploitation-worsening-during-covid-tech-giants-must-allow-workers-join-unions.

World Bank. 2020. *Poverty and Shared Prosperity 2020: Reversals of Fortune*. Washington, DC: The World Bank Group. worldbank.org/en/publication/poverty-and-shared-prosperity.

World Health Organization (WHO). 2021a. 'Health, Nutrition and Population Statistics, World Bank – Metadata'. World Health Organization, Geneva. apps.who.int/nha/database.

———. 2021b. 'WHO Health Emergency Dashboard'. World Health Organization, Geneva. https://extranet.who.int/publicemergency

Yong, E. 2020. 'Where Year Two of the Pandemic Will Take Us'. *The Atlantic*, 29 December. theatlantic.com/health/archive/2020/12/pandemic-year-two/617528/.

13 | Seven Lessons for Development Policy from the COVID-19 Pandemic

Sanjay G. Reddy

INTRODUCTION

Does the experience of the COVID-19 pandemic provide lessons for furthering sustainable human development? Do any of these lessons derive from or apply in particular to the Asia-Pacific Region (APR)?[1] Some initial reflections on these questions may now be possible,[2] recognizing that, as Zhou Enlai is famously rumoured to have said about the French Revolution more than 150 years later, "it is too early to tell" (*SCMP*, n.d.). In this chapter, we make some observations about the national, regional and international responses during the crisis, critically evaluate these efforts, and identify institutional gaps and weaknesses that should be remedied to increase preparedness and improve responses to future pandemics and crises. We also use a lens borrowed from English art critic John Berger (1972) to focus on 'ways of seeing' policy rather than on identifying specific policy lessons.

LESSON 1: ACT STRATEGICALLY BY ACTING SPECIFICALLY

One of the most elementary but also consequential observations about the pandemic is that its effects have varied enormously across countries. This observation applies not only to how successfully countries have contained COVID-19 itself, but to how well they have avoided its damaging economic and social consequences. The measures governments have taken differ widely, as have the speed, effectiveness, and consequences of their implementation. The weight placed on distinct policy objectives, such as avoidance of COVID-19 deaths versus avoidance of economic contraction, has also varied across countries. Several countries have clearly done better in terms of some, perhaps all, major objectives, and this seems to be due to the specifics of their actions: not merely whether they took early, decisive or substantial action, but where and how they focused interventions. The best performing countries did better in terms of both health and economic outcomes and did not rely on untargeted, generalized lockdowns alone (Box 13.1). Of course, it is not possible to be certain that differences in outcomes have only to do with policies, since biological and epidemiological features, such as the strains of the virus affecting a country, would also have been relevant.

Box 13.1   The relationship between COVID-19 cases or deaths and economic performance

Figures 13.1 and 13.2 show the relationship between COVID-19 cases or deaths and economic performance in 185 countries, as judged by the estimated 2020 gross domestic product (GDP) growth rate (or rate of contraction, in the case of most countries), using data available as of January 2021. The data illustrate the range of trade-offs between these goals across countries. The figures show a wide range of experiences: Countries have had very different GDP growth rates at the same level of COVID-19 confirmed cases or deaths and, correspondingly, very different case and death levels for the same GDP growth rates.

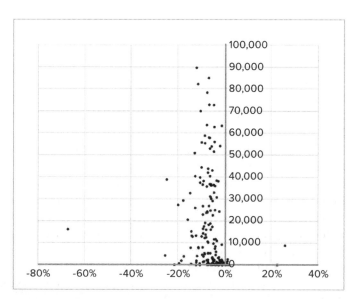

Figure 13.1   Worldwide cumulative COVID-19 cases per million versus per capita GDP growth rate, 2020
Sources: GDP growth rates are estimations from IMF (2020); confirmed cases and deaths from WHO (2021).

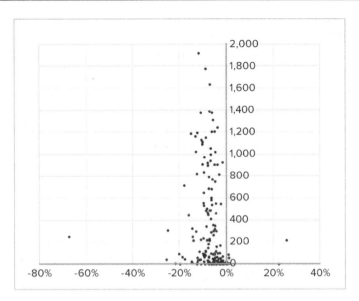

Figure 13.2 Worldwide cumulative cases of COVID-19 deaths per million versus per capita GDP growth rate, 2020
Sources: GDP growth rates are estimations from IMF (2020); confirmed cases and deaths from WHO (2021).

The R-squared of the fitted (ordinary least squares) relationship between COVID-19 incidence (cases or deaths) and per capita GDP growth also tells us that the former provides very limited information about the latter (Tables 13A.1 and 13A.2). The estimated regression coefficient is negative for both cases and deaths (although not always statistically significant), suggesting that, on average, greater disease incidence corresponded with greater economic contraction. But the extent of the variation explained by the bivariate relationship was low. The adjusted-R-squared tells us that most of the variation in estimated growth does not reflect variation in confirmed cases (85 per cent unexplained) or in deaths (88 per cent unexplained).

There does not appear to have been a necessary economy-health trade-off. The average relationship tells us that countries that better safeguarded health, as judged by confirmed COVID-19 cases and mortality, also generally experienced smaller economic contractions. The estimated coefficient suggests that, on average, for each additional 10,000 cumulative cases per million, a bit more than half a percentage point of growth was given up. Similarly, for each additional 100 cumulative deaths per million, around 2 percentage points of growth was given up on average. No trade-off appeared in the average relationship between economic contraction and COVID-19 incidence (cases and deaths), since both tended to worsen together, to the extent that a relationship can be found at all. But these average relationships also mask the large variation around the average. The low proportion of the variation explained by the bivariate relationship (the correlation between the two variables is only 0.14) tells us that the more important factor was the variation in the extent of economic contraction among countries that experienced similar health consequences of the pandemic.

A more complete model, capable of explaining a larger portion of the observed variation in economic outcomes, would have to introduce additional explanatory variables. These might include, for instance, the specific form of the policies adopted, such as general lockdowns versus more targeted approaches or the extent of testing and contact tracing. One might also argue that alternative indicators could provide a more accurate picture of the health or economic consequences experienced. For instance, to provide a more precise indicator of the economic impact of the COVID-19 crisis in most countries, one might use the shortfall of the per capita income growth rate from trend growth rather than the unadjusted growth rate, that is, the extent of economic contraction. It seems unlikely, however, that introducing such nuances will overturn the overall conclusion that much of the variation remains unexplained.

As the regression results and Figures 13.3 and 13.4 show, a weak or non-existent relationship between COVID-19 cases or deaths and contraction in national income due to policies to address the pandemic appears in every region during 2020, with some evidence of a stronger relationship, that is, a greater economic contraction associated with more cases or deaths, in the APR than elsewhere. In other words, the magnitude of the regression coefficients describing this bivariate relationship and the proportion of the variation explained by the relationship appear slightly higher in the APR.

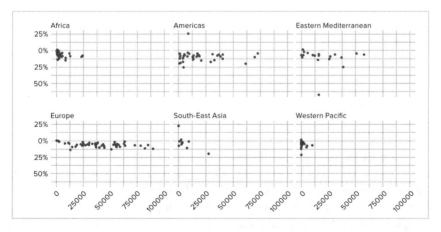

Figure 13.3   Regional cumulative COVID-19 cases per million versus per capita GDP growth, 2020
Source: Author calculations based on WHO (2021); IMF (2020).

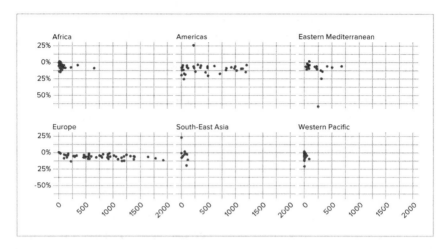

Figure 13.4   Regional cumulative COVID-19 deaths per million versus per capita GDP growth, 2020
Source: Author calculations based on WHO (2021); IMF (2020).

Table 13.1   Regional cumulative COVID-19 cases and deaths per million and per capita GDP growth, 2020

WHO Region	Cumulative cases per million	Cumulative deaths per million	Per capita GDP growth (%)
Americas	42,045.65	966.16	−6.3
Europe	32,032.17	683.74	−6.9
Eastern Mediterranean	7,686.90	185.53	−6.8
South-East Asia	6,295.97	96.63	−8.2
Africa	2,154.92	50.86	−5.7
Western Pacific	673.68	11.71	−0.7

Sources: IMF (2020); WHO (2021).

There are marked regional differences in the impact of COVID-19 on morbidity and mortality, with very low rates of cases and deaths in East Asia compared with Europe and the Americas (Figures 13.3 and 13.4). Table 13.1 summarizes the difference in case and mortality incidence by region, describing cases and deaths per million by region, using WHO's regional classifications. Figure 13.5 shows cumulative total deaths using a more generally familiar classification of regions (Our World in Data, 2021). Asia had only 366,000 deaths out of 2.13 million worldwide, or 17.2 per cent of the world total, as of 28 January 2021, despite the region having nearly 60 per cent of the world's population. Similarly, large variations appear in both confirmed cases and deaths per million among countries at similar income levels (Figure 13.6). Although inter-regional differences account for some of these differences, one can observe that they are sizable among countries within the same region as well.

Differences in age structure between regions – potentially consequential due to the higher COVID-19 mortality risks faced by older people – appear to explain only

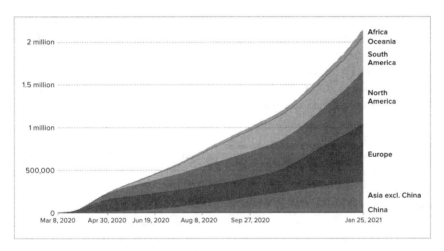

Figure 13.5   Total confirmed COVID-19 deaths by region, 8 March 2020 to 25 January 2021
Source: Johns Hopkins Coronavirus Resource Center (2021a).

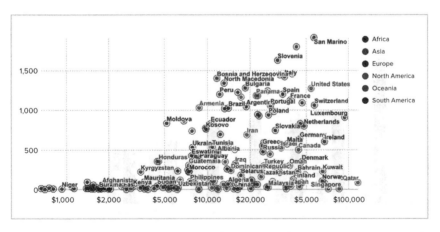

Figure 13.6   Total confirmed COVID-19 deaths per million versus per capita GDP by region and by country, 8 March 2020 to 25 January 2021
Source: Johns Hopkins Coronavirus Resource Center (2021a).

partially the observed inter-country variations in deaths (Figure 13.7). In particular, they do not seem to fully explain the relatively favourable performance of Asia. It is also not obvious how these differences would explain the variation in confirmed cases, although some correlation between an older population and confirmed cases may arise if older people tend to have more serious symptoms and therefore undergo testing. While the proportion of the population over the age of 65 in Asia is about half of what it is in Europe and North America (9 per cent compared to 17 and 19 per cent, respectively), the ratio of COVID-19 cases and deaths per million in Asia appears much lower than this difference would explain: as of late January 2021, Asia had around 370,000 deaths while Europe and North America combined accounted for 1.3 million deaths out of 2.2 million worldwide. Notably, Japan, with 28 per cent of its population aged over 65 (a much higher percentage than the average in Europe, Asia and North America), had only 76 deaths per million whereas the United States, with 15 per cent of its population over 65, experienced 1,721 deaths per million (*Statista*, 2021a).

The main difference between those countries with clear successes and those without appears to be the quality, as distinguished from the quantity, of government interventions.[3] A comparison of national-level actions in the crisis highlights this finding. Quick and decisive actions were critical but not sufficient if they gave less attention to crucial measures or implemented them poorly. This is clear even if we focus narrowly on the impact of COVID-19. Taking a broader range of concerns into account further underscores the importance of policy design, as we shall discuss later.

India offers an example from the APR. The argument for the early lockdown introduced in the country on 25 March 2020 – a lockdown identified by some as one of the most stringent in the world – posited that it would decisively arrest the progress

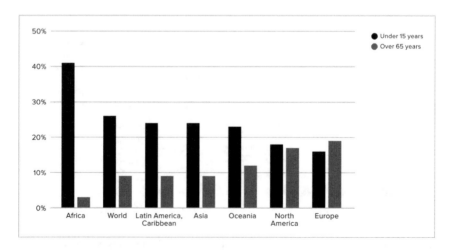

Figure 13.7   World population under age 15 and over age 65 by region, 2020
Source: *Statista* (2021b).

of the disease, giving rise to substantial long-term gains in comparison with inaction (OxCGRT, 2020). But buying time matters little if use is not made of it. China, despite earlier occurrence of the disease, used its period of stringent national lockdown to good effect, isolating the disease to pockets of outbreaks or eliminating it altogether. China implemented widespread testing, effective contact tracing and other measures to avoid and suppress subsequent outbreaks; it also enhanced treatment capacity (Xu et al., 2020). In contrast, the time gained by India does not appear to have been put to good use. When India relaxed its lockdowns, the trajectory of the disease returned to what might have been its expected pattern without such drastic action. COVID-19 eventually spread extensively in the country (Figure 13.8) in the second half of 2020, even prior to a second wave of the disease in 2021.

In some APR countries, such as India, the early pandemic response attached disproportionate weight to one policy instrument: the on-and-off application of generalized lockdowns. Other countries placed greater emphasis on more specific policy instruments, such as stringent testing, contact tracing, quarantining and universal mask wearing, as in Taiwan (Province of China),[4] Viet Nam[5] and China, or intensive measures to protect the elderly, as in Japan.[6] Many made efforts to develop capacities rapidly where these did not already exist. Countries that used a broader range of policy instruments – some highly specialized and often deployed in a selective and targeted way – to achieve specific goals appeared to do better in managing the spread of the disease than those that applied a narrow range of instruments in a very diffuse, untargeted, and nonstrategic way, specifically, society-wide lockdowns. However, no sure-fire solution emerged for containing the virus, as demonstrated by subsequent outbreaks in relatively successful jurisdictions, such as

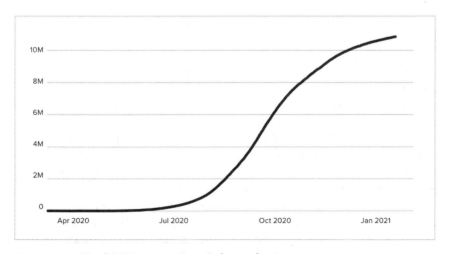

Figure 13.8   Total COVID-19 cases in India as of 25 January 2021
Source: Johns Hopkins Coronavirus Resource Center (2021b).

China, Taiwan (Province of China)[7] and Australia,[8] even before the worldwide spread of new, more transmissible SARS-CoV-2 virus variants in the first months of 2021.

As scientific knowledge of the virus has expanded during the world's collective crash course in COVID-19, it has considerably altered initial understandings of effective policies, causing a movement away from, for example, cleaning surfaces and toward minimizing prolonged respiratory contact (*Nature*, 2021). In addition, there has been growing recognition that specific environments, such as poorly ventilated indoor spaces, favour viral transmission and a recognition that children and asymptomatic persons are likely to transmit the disease less (Bulfone et al., 2020; Zhu et al., 2020). Some countries that have performed well may simply have been lucky, but they may have also learned more quickly – a point to which we return later.

Lesson 2: Take an Integrated View and Anticipate Possible Spillovers

The crisis has underlined potential trade-offs. As noted earlier, the cross-country data on national performance show that some have handled the pandemic with relative success at less economic cost. The data show that the goal of limiting the impact of the disease need not come at a severe cost to economic prosperity. Where trade-offs do exist, they call for a policy framework that can identify and balance goals, keeping uncertainties in mind. Even where trade-offs are not necessary, the situation requires careful steering to avoid falling into or creating trade-offs, in other words, implementing policies in the combination and sequence that best secures diverse goals.

The theory of economic policy outlined decades ago by Jan Tinbergen, an economist closely associated with the United Nations, emphasized the need for a decision-making and institutional framework capable of identifying the linkages and trade-offs that are ever-present in national and global policymaking. Even in cases of pervasive uncertainty, rational planning requires taking note of the possible connections, however tentatively. Sound policymaking requires anticipating causal spillovers that affect the ability to achieve different goals.

Some countries had prepared for the possibility of a pandemic by making plans and undertaking scenario-planning exercises. But one would be hard put to identify a single country in the world that had an integrated policymaking framework in place to respond to the pandemic, one that estimated the diverse benefits and costs of policies as an input to decision-making. For instance, scant attention went to the potential trade-off between preventing deaths arising from COVID-19 and increased deaths from other sources, such as under-nutrition, lack of access to health services, loss of employment and income and resulting distress, and other consequences. Such trade-offs do not appear to have informed emergency decision-making in the early months of the pandemic, and it is not clear that previous preparedness plans had considered these connections either.[9]

In many cases, the knock-on effects of COVID-19 policies, which proved significant, appeared to receive little or no attention in policymaking. Once again, India offers a useful cautionary tale, with a massive portion of the population returning to their natal homes due to a prospective loss of income caused by a national lockdown announced in early 2020 with only a few hours of notice.[10] In other countries, national expert advisory panels formed in response to the crisis showed a narrow focus on COVID-19-related consequences, with few social or even medical scientists having relevant broader expertise involved. The United Kingdom offers one such case. Its widely publicized Scientific Advisory Group for Emergencies (SAGE) appears to have disproportionately favoured specialists in a few narrow scientific areas immediately relevant to COVID-19 containment (SAGE, 2021). As noted by Van Rens and Oswald (2020), "It may not be widely realized, for example, that SAGE [...] had from the start, and apparently still has, no economists on it." This is merely one indication of a probable larger failure to integrate all relevant expertise.

Even if experts can offer insights on trade-offs, societal decision-making remains outside their remit, since it requires judgments based on ethical values, attitudes to risk and other broader concerns. All interested persons should have the chance to participate, with elected representatives ultimately taking due responsibility for the choices made. Politicians in various countries have instead emphasized that they would listen to the scientists, not recognizing that experts focused on a narrow domain could not offer insights into the broader societal questions involved. There is considerable ambiguity as to whether the phrase "listen to the scientists" refers to taking science into account, which is necessary, or if it means putting scientists in charge of policy, for which science alone does not provide adequate training or conceptual resources. Scientists themselves have shown understandable resistance to this latter idea (Ramakrishnan, 2020).

The lack of an adequate integrated framework for policymaking, even within the health domain, has strikingly emerged as a result of unanticipated, and in many cases still unaddressed, adverse health effects of COVID-19 policies. The national and global health consequences of phenomena, such as missed screenings for health risks and other forms of health surveillance, interruptions to immunization and other preventative health campaigns, lack of timely curative interventions, and the physical and mental health consequences of economic and social disruptions, all require consideration in policymaking. There is, however, little evidence that policymakers have addressed such considerations, even at later stages of the crisis (Reddy, 2020a).

Quite apart from the lack of attention to spillovers between goals, the crisis has shown a lack of preparedness for the pandemic even in the most direct respects.

Evidence for this appears globally and in almost all countries. Few of the entities nominally responsible had paid sufficient attention to global disease surveillance and pandemic response capabilities (Ross, Crowe and Tyndall, 2015). Regardless of one's views on the adequacy of the response from specific actors, such as the WHO, it seems likely that their funding fell far short of requisite levels to properly fulfil disease surveillance and response responsibilities. National-level preparedness had not adequately addressed the possibility of a pandemic, even where partially anticipated, as reflected, for instance, in the preparation of national plans for influenza and other diseases recommended by WHO. Even those countries with the most extensive national strategic reserves for contingencies had inadequate supplies of many essential health commodities, such as personal protective equipment – needs that disaster planning might reasonably have anticipated.[11] Institutional mechanisms for sharing and analysing information, funding research and development of vaccines and medicines, and otherwise rapidly developing a joint international response had to be improvised after the pandemic declaration because of insufficient prior attention. Such frameworks and practices remain severely inadequate even now, as discussed later. The failure to consider economic and social consequences in addition to health when designing the crisis response was an even greater institutional dereliction.

Even if it seems of no benefit in ordinary times, preparedness is a cost worth undertaking. Precaution by its very nature does not allow for precision. It requires anticipating possibilities that can be only roughly known, even in the optimistic case that the unknowns are known unknowns. Preparedness entails investing in insurance against the worst outcomes. Such investment has no immediate return and must be undertaken without full knowledge of what measures will be necessary and how adequate they will prove. In the stocktaking that has followed the pandemic, some discuss preparedness in terms of a trade-off between short-run, or apparent, 'efficiency' versus 'resilience' (Golgeci et al., 2020). Whereas recent decades of outsourcing and offshoring (globalization) prior to the pandemic had seen much emphasis on increasing efficiency by, for example, streamlining supply chains, using just-in-time inventory and other methods, the pandemic has shown that efficiency narrowly conceived may come at the cost of fragility. Where countries wholly lacked their own production infrastructure, it proved difficult to fill the supply gaps that emerged as a result of the crisis. Robust systems, such as supply chains, require adequate provision for resisting or recovering from shocks, which in turn demands investment in strategic stockpiles, excess capacity and intentional redundancy of production systems. Adverse shocks can diminish the sustainability of a system, providing a further reason to invest in resilience. For instance, the economic consequences of the pandemic may well lead to unsustainable debt loads for many countries and businesses (United Nations, 2020).

The comparatively strong performance of East Asian countries in the aftermath of COVID-19, as measured by lower per capita mortality, underlines that preparedness entails not merely governmental or institutional capabilities, but also those of the population, which may in turn depend on prior experiences and societal investment in building understanding and acceptance of public health requirements. One conjecture, for instance, attributes the comparatively strong response of the East Asian countries to COVID-19 to prior experiences with severe acute respiratory syndrome (SARS), avian influenza (bird flu) and other pandemics, as well as previously established public health practices that enjoy widespread public compliance, such as social distancing and mask wearing, and institutional capabilities, particularly testing and contact tracing (Khor and Heymann, 2020).

LESSON 3: PROTECT IN ADVANCE WITH STANDING SAFETY NETS

Countries with social safety net institutions and infrastructure that could expand automatically to cushion the adverse social and economic effects of pandemic policy response, such as lost income and unemployment, did better in limiting those harms. In most such cases, the institutions and infrastructure was established under different circumstances, but had the capacity to respond quickly and elastically to increases in need for social and economic protection; they were able to scale up rapidly at low incremental costs.[12] The case for standing social safety nets and protection measures rests not only on the need to support individuals who fall between the cracks in normal times, but on sustaining society as a whole, or sizeable sections of it, when the cracks become a yawning gulf in a time of crisis.

Because the design of such standing social institutions and infrastructure does not necessarily target pandemic preparedness or preparedness for emergencies as such (even if it has the effect of providing protection in such circumstances), we should distinguish this lesson from the preceding one on anticipation of crises. Standing safety nets and other relevant response infrastructure serve as a form of preparedness, but a special kind: They exist in ordinary times and play a function then too, but become especially important in the context of a crisis that increases the need for them.

The contrast between societies that possess strong standing social infrastructure to meet growing needs in a crisis and those that do not has appeared most markedly among the developed countries. Some of these, such as Germany, which we discuss later in relation to its Kurzarbeit system[13] of wage subsidies to encourage firms to maintain employment, possessed mechanisms for labour market intervention to sustain employment or diminish the costs of unemployment that many other countries, notably the United Kingdom and the United States, had to invent from scratch in response to the crisis. These latter countries introduced emergency measures, including loans for small businesses in return for refraining from job cuts, temporary extensions or expansions of unemployment insurance, temporary relief from payroll taxes and new temporary provisions for cash supports for individuals and businesses.

Such measures often take time to establish and rely on data collected for other purposes to determine eligibility or to convey benefits, leading to gaps in social protection. Benefit levels are also often determined arbitrarily and prove inadequate. Although 215 economies spent at least US$800 billion on around 1,400 social protection measures in the first three quarters of 2020, many were brief and offered very low amounts:

> Relative to pre-COVID levels, cash transfer benefits nearly doubled, and coverage grew by 240 percent, on average. Yet 'large scale' doesn't mean 'adequate' [...] cash transfer programs lasted 3.3 months on average, with a mere 7 percent of them being extended; 30 percent of programs were one-off payments; and only one-quarter reached more than one-third of the population. In low-income countries, spending per capita amounted to a scant average of $6 per capita. (Gentilini, 2021)

Ad-hoc measures cannot substitute for a standing social protection infrastructure, and the pandemic has highlighted which countries do not have one (Taylor, 2020; Goodman et al., 2020). At the same time, the pandemic has spurred the extension and reconstruction of safety nets now revealed as inadequate, even in countries with relatively formal labour markets and widespread, if limited, social protection coverage (Kelly, 2020). The large informal labour markets in many countries in Asia and elsewhere, especially those without any social protection system, add a further challenge.[14]

Lesson 4: Build and Sustain Trust

The pandemic has underscored that protection and promotion of the public good is a societal as well as a governmental project. The efforts of private citizens and civil society must supplement those of governments to ensure the rapid adoption of desired behaviours. Additionally, success depends on citizens having motivation for taking the right actions and doing so in adequate numbers. Motivation, in turn, depends on public understanding and acceptance of the reasons provided for citizens to act in a particular way. As a consequence, the frequently used metaphor of 'war' for fighting a pandemic may not prove wholly appropriate (Sen, 2020). Of course, even effective mobilization for war depends on consent of the citizenry and on their accepting the arguments for it.

Adherence to prescribed public health measures, such as social distancing, depends on acceptance of a causal account (a presumed relation between acts and consequences) as well as on the motivation to bring about those consequences, whether because of presumed benefits for oneself and one's loved ones or for society at large. This acceptance can, in turn, rest on either prosocial (altruistic) attitudes or on an idea of rationality linked to enlightened self-interest (Reddy, 2020b). Observers have noted that during the pandemic, far from acting as 'rational fools' who pursue a narrowly conceived individual interest at the expense of others, or with indifference to them, many have acted instead in a fashion more concerned with public interest.[15] This willingness in turn suggests a broader idea of rationality than that typically conceived by economists – one expressive of good reasons for one's actions, rather than simply maximizing one's satisfactions according to a given preference ranking.[16]

Cooperation in the game-theoretic sense requires acting in accordance with others so as to produce the best outcome for all including oneself, rather than pursuing a myopic and perhaps self-defeating self-interest, as in the famous Prisoner's Dilemma game. Such cooperation, if it can be upheld, such as by an enforceable compact among agents, will serve the self-interest of all. But the cooperation sought by public health authorities can extend beyond such narrow self-interest, since it can encompass actions motivated by providing benefits for others.

The dependence of public cooperation on shared understanding underscores in turn the importance of past experiences and trust in public authorities. As noted earlier, this may help to explain the relation between prior exposure to the SARS epidemic in East Asia and the region's apparently high levels of citizen compliance with public health messages. More generally, a belief that public authorities speak truthfully and out of regard for the public interest may prove an important determinant of public cooperation. Several observations from the current crisis show that active public scepticism about the validity of public authorities' pronouncements has acted as a major obstacle to public cooperation, leading to active protests against government policies and disobedience of mandates in some countries. But such trust may in turn depend, especially in democratic contexts, on mechanisms for societal review of public health decisions and on the acceptance of legitimate debate about and scrutiny of the assumptions underlying policies.

One of the great questions of our time concerns the role of experts in society. The legitimacy of their role in decisions has increasingly come under question from sections of the public and, indeed, from other experts (Babones, 2018; Easterly, 2014). The COVID-19 pandemic has brought the issue to the forefront, underlining the lack of willingness to defer to experts in many cases, especially where they may be perceived as having made decisions on the basis of non-transparent criteria and selective values (Sandel, 2014). The human development approach's insistence on open and participatory methods of public decision-making has great relevance here, as procedural legitimacy can also aid consequential efficacy. Such public decision-making requires considering diverse values and understandings and weighing them on the basis of accepted collective procedures. Societal decision-making of this kind must be able to draw upon expertise while also keeping it in its appropriate place (Reddy, 1996). How best to combine expertise with democratic values, both in normal times and during an emergency, remains an important unsolved problem. The COVID-19 pandemic has highlighted the difficulty and may spur thinking and innovation about this issue.

LESSON 5: QUESTION SO-CALLED CONSTRAINTS

An important lesson of the pandemic concerns the modifiability of apparent economic or social constraints. For instance, the already severe financial constraints perceived as existing in many countries were incrementally loosened in light of the massive fiscal requirements of responding to the pandemic, such as providing economic stimulus and targeted support to those affected by closures of businesses, loss of employment and other direct and indirect effects. National and international institutions that have previously acted as guardians of economic and financial probity altered their stances as circumstances changed.

In a marked departure from received wisdom, the International Monetary Fund (IMF) and the Organisation for Economic Cooperation and Development (OECD) have both advocated increased fiscal stimulus during the past year. Prominent academic and policy economists have argued that financing fiscal stimulus and public investment via public debt need not prove as undesirable as widely believed in the recent past. This reflects a change of thinking already underway before the pandemic, but which has accelerated in response to it (Blanchard, 2019). This, of course, does not mean overlooking constraints altogether. The appropriate level of fiscal expansion would reflect country-specific factors, such as indebtedness (World Bank, 2021b). Unsurprisingly, given the circumstances and this newly permissive atmosphere, countries have shown considerable willingness to employ fiscal fire power in response to changing needs – although the extent of expansion has varied greatly across countries (IMF, 2021). The differences in the extent of the fiscal response to the crisis may play some role in explaining variations in the extent of GDP contraction across countries. The benefits of fiscal expansion would have been greater if accompanied by more supportive international measures. For instance, the temporary debt-payment moratorium for low-income countries, announced by the Group of 20 and supported by international financial institutions after the onset of the COVID-19 emergency in 2020, does not benefit the majority of countries (World Bank, 2021a). The IMF's newly agreed special drawing rights (SDR) allocation as well as new measures under discussion, such as the development of a global minimum tax on corporate income, may help to address these limitations (Lawder, 2021; Strupczewski, 2021).

Similarly, several factors have alleviated constraints in the health sector over time, including additional hospital beds and equipment, such as ventilators; the development of new medical technologies, such as mRNA vaccines; the training of additional personnel devoted to certain tasks, such as contact tracing; the increased stock of social knowledge about disease transmission; and associated changes in social and personal behaviours. Some of the constraints initially thought most likely to bind, such as supply of ventilators, have proven much less consequential than originally anticipated, in part because of increases in supply (Siddiqui, 2020). In other cases, constraints have appeared in unanticipated areas, such as in scaling-up vaccine production rather than in discovering viable vaccine formulae and in hospital oxygen supplies (Iyer, 2021). Scaling-up may entail diverse requirements. For instance, the freeing of intellectual property rights for COVID-19 health commodities through a World Trade Organization (WTO) Agreement on Trade-Related Aspects of Intellectual Property Rights (TRIPS) waiver on COVID-19 health commodities, as proposed by India and South Africa, might aid in scaling-up vaccine supply in the current situation but will likely need to be accompanied by new production facilities and measures to ensure an adequate supply of physical inputs (Usher 2020; Acharya and Reddy, 2020). A diagnostic approach can help determine which constraints bind and must therefore be relaxed in order to further the policy objectives (Hausmann, Rodrik and Velasco, 2005).

LESSON 6: LEARN TO LEARN

Policies and interventions have the greatest chance of success when they allow for revision over time. This requires the presence of a framework for collecting the data that can inform such revisions. Developing a fruitful learning orientation in policymaking therefore requires forethought. For instance, determining which geographical areas or social groups to focus disease control efforts upon, inferring the probable activities and sites in which transmission takes place, and assessing whether specific policies appear to influence prevalence or transmission – all require collecting detailed information on disease status and on the behaviours and interactions associated with the reported test results. As obvious as this seems, we have no evidence of such systematic data collection throughout the crisis, let alone collection in a format comparable and shareable across jurisdictions.

Developing a data-collection framework that can support decision-making requires identifying the relevant kinds of data and their likely application. Policymakers have not invested adequately in data for decision-making in the current crisis. For example, stark confusion has remained about basic facts such as the rate of infection in the population, as opposed to formal cases or the proportion of the infected among those tested, due to the lack of adequate random or quasi-random testing protocols. In the absence of such information, decision-making has taken place without adequate information and beliefs have persisted without validation or correction by data. Holding fast to specific models with fixed parameters can be costly. An example is the slow pace of resuming in-person schooling in many countries, despite evidence of both the cost of disruptions to schooling and of the limited role of schools in virus transmission. Adaptive policymaking can benefit from flexibility in the choice of models, data gathering to update parameters and data sharing to better understand the sources of observed variation.[17] Previous experiences from prior pandemics have informed some of the inferences (or guesses) about policies that might prove effective, but this knowledge has remained underutilized. For instance, previous experiences with SARS in 2003 and influenza A (H1N1 or swine flu) in 2009 showed the possibility of opening schools with social distancing, shortened and staggered school times, movement of teachers instead of students between classrooms, and other measures, but these prior experiences did not become widely known, even though they underpinned the strategies of jurisdictions that successfully avoided school closures altogether, notably in Taiwan (Province of China) (Viner et al., 2020). Some rapid learning has taken place during the current crisis as scientific knowledge has evolved, such as on the settings that favour transmission or the efficacy of various epidemiological and economic measures, leading to policy adjustments, including greater freedom in relation to outdoor recreation and gatherings. Many more lessons, both from experience elsewhere in the current crisis and from prior experience, could have informed policy actions – but did not.

We noted earlier that the German Kurzarbeit system has influenced policies adopted by other countries, such as the United Kingdom and Spain, to prevent crisis-induced joblessness and business closures. Similarly, the apparent early efficacy of the generalized lockdown applied in Wuhan and later in all of China may have informed decisions by policymakers elsewhere. They were also influenced by the almost singular attention given to this particular measure in quantitative modelling.[18] On the other hand, many lessons from successful East Asian experiences appear to have been neglected (Valli, 2020). Some common-sense measures were very slowly adopted or not at all. For instance, the lack of adequate sick-leave provisions in certain countries has continued as an institutional factor propelling disease transmission in workplaces, such as in Australia,[19] Canada[20] and the United States.[21] Difficulties that some jurisdictions experienced did not influence preparations and policies elsewhere; for example, oxygen shortages in Brazil in late 2020 did not act as a warning to others who later experienced shortages, such as India in April and May 2021 (BBC, 2021; NPR, 2021). On the whole, it appears that institutions and governments require much more 'learning to learn' so as to develop an effective response to the pandemic (Sabel and Reddy, 2007).

LESSON 7: COOPERATE BETTER, MORE, EARLY AND OFTEN

The crisis has demonstrated inadequacy of existing mechanisms of international cooperation. They have failed in the early identification and containment of the disease, in subsequent gathering, sharing and analysis of data and knowledge, in coordination of policies and responses, and so on. One illustration is the failure to develop a vaccine as a common project among nations, recognizing its nature as a global public good, substituting instead a widely decried – because both inefficient and inequitable – 'vaccine nationalism' that prioritizes domestic vaccine access at the expense of the rest of the world (Karp, 2020; Reddy and Acharya, 2020; Acharya and Reddy, 2021).

Whether regional or global, what international cooperation has taken place has mostly appeared too little and too late. Successful international cooperation aggregates efforts to bring about greater benefits for all, as the economic theory of public goods underlines (Samuelson, 1954). But it also benefits from a qualitative dimension: sharing diverse but different capacities. Consider, for example, the collaboration between Oxford-AstraZeneca, developers of one of the current leading vaccines for COVID-19, and the Serum Institute of India, which possesses the largest vaccine-making capacity in the world, or the collaboration between BioNTech of Germany and its leading mRNA research and development capability with Pfizer of the United States with its sizable manufacturing capability (SII, 2021; Pfizer Inc., 2020). These collaborations drew upon the distinct strengths of firms in different countries. International cooperation between governments should similarly both pool efforts and allocate tasks efficiently to take advantage of varying capabilities. But such cooperation does not take place in a vacuum. It benefits from prior mapping of capabilities, experience in collaboration, and established relationships, protocols and institutions of cooperation. Cooperation is more likely to succeed when it is based on prior experience. In other words, effective crisis cooperation requires learning to exercise the muscles of cooperation outside of crises, too.

The lack of a global mechanism for modifying the treatment of intellectual property rights during a global pandemic also highlights the failure of international cooperation. While the WHO recognizes a pandemic as a formal concept, and the WTO recognizes national health emergencies as circumstances in which governments may undertake compulsory licensing and other 'flexibilities', no bridge exists to link the two (WTO, n.d.a). The proposal to suspend intellectual property rights relating to vital health commodities during the pandemic, advanced in 2020 by South Africa and India, arose to fill this vacuum (Usher, 2020). The WTO could easily have evaluated arguments for such a suspension in a potential pandemic and arriving at some general principles, even if specific conditions for application remained undefined. Not only was this not done prior to the pandemic, but there was no move to do this until late in the crisis, resulting in immense health, social and economic costs.

The United Nations (UN) could have had a larger role in responding to the pandemic. The WHO, WTO and other specialized organizations were not well-positioned to grasp the complementarities between areas of their respective competence. In the aftermath of the global financial crisis of 2007–2008, the 2009 Stiglitz Commission recommended creating a Global Economic Coordination Council "established at a level equivalent with the UN General Assembly and the Security Council [... whose] mandate would be to assess developments and provide leadership in addressing economic issues that require global action while taking into account social and ecological factors" (Stiglitz et al., 2010). This recommendation offered a direct response to gaps in the surveillance and response capacities of the international economic governance system that the crisis had revealed: It has never been implemented. Although the United Nations undertook some steps, such as to strengthen the UN Development System (Reddy, 2018), these fall short of those needed to provide early warning of, and responses to, threats of a global nature. The pandemic of 2020 calls for a similar systemic, and systematic, reappraisal. One can hope that the shock experienced by all may at least help to bring about the required coalescence among member states. It remains far too early to see all the lessons of the pandemic for development policy, but it is not too early to identify some ways of seeing policymaking that would have made a difference and that can do so in the future. This chapter has outlined seven such ways of seeing; they include thinking about acting strategically in terms of acting specifically, anticipating and preparing for possible spillovers, protecting populations from the possible impacts of a crisis in advance, regarding trust as a vital resource, viewing constraints as revisable, learning to learn and cooperating early, more, and often.

Appendix 13A.1   Regression of Per Capita GDP Growth on COVID-19 Outcomes

Table 13A.1   Regression of per capita GDP growth on cumulative COVID-19 cases by region

	Africa	America	Eastern Med	Europe	Southeast Asia	Western Pacific	World
	Dependent variable:						
	growth of per capita GDP in 2020						
Cumulative cases per million	-2.70e-06**	-1.39e-07	-6.14e-07	-5.33e-07**	-8.64e-06*	-3.30e-06	-5.38e-07*
	(9.67e-07)	(7.04e-07)	(2.01e-06)	(1.87e-07)	(3.58e-06)	(4.23e-06)	(2.45e-07)
Constant	-0.044***	-0.093***	-0.101*	-0.041***	0.022	-0.048***	-0.059***
	(0.006)	(0.019)	(0.052)	(0.008)	(0.034)	(0.011)	(0.007)
Observations	46	36	19	50	10	25	186
R^2	0.151	0.001	0.005	0.145	0.241	0.026	0.026
Adjusted R^2	0.132	-0.028	-0.053	0.127	0.349	-0.017	0.020
Residual Std. Error	0.034 (df = 44)	0.081 (df = 34)	0.149 (df = 17)	0.029 (df = 48)	0.087 (df = 8)	0.049 (df = 23)	0.072 (df = 184)
F Statistic	7.823*** (df = 1; 44)	0.039 (df = 1; 34)	0.093 (df = 1; 17)	8.130*** (df = 1; 48)	5.829** (df = 1; 8)	0.610 (df = 1; 23)	4.827** (df = 1; 184)

Sources: IMF (2020); WHO (2021).

Note: $*p < 0.10$, $**p < 0.05$, $***p < 0.01$. Growth rates expressed as decimals (i.e., 1 per cent = 0.01). WHO source data downloaded circa 15 January 2021.

Table 13A.2 Regression of per capita GDP growth on cumulative COVID-19 deaths by region

	Dependent variable:						
	growth of per capita GDP in 2020						
	Africa	America	Eastern Med	Europe	Southeast Asia	Western Pacific	World
Cumulative deaths per million	-8.382e-05	-9.623e-07	-0.0001	-2.561e-05**	-0.001	-0.0004	-2.275e-05
	(4.853e-05)	(3.336e-05)	(0.0002)	(8.394e-06)	(0.001)	(0.0005)	(1.228e-05)
Constant	-0.048***	-0.095***	-0.090	-0.043***	0.037	-0.048***	-0.061***
	(0.006)	(0.020)	(0.054)	(0.007)	(0.048)	(0.011)	(0.007)
Observations	46	36	19	50	10	25	186
R^2	0.063	0.00002	0.018	0.162	0.276	0.022	0.018
Adjusted R^2	0.042	-0.029	-0.040	0.145	0.185	-0.021	0.013
Residual Std. Error	0.035 (df = 44)	0.081 (df = 34)	0.148 (df = 17)	0.029 (df = 48)	0.098 (df = 8)	0.049 (df = 23)	0.072 (df = 184)
F Statistic	2.983* (df = 1; 44)	0.001 (df = 1; 34)	0.314 (df = 1; 17)	9.309*** (df = 1; 48)	3.047 (df = 1; 8)	0.515 (df = 1; 23)	3.429* (df = 1; 184)

Sources: IMF (2020); WHO (2021).

Note: *p < 0.10, **p < 0.05, ***p < 0.01. Growth rates expressed as decimals (i.e., 1 per cent = 0.01). WHO source data downloaded circa 15 January 2021.

Acknowledgements

I would like to thank Balazs Horvath, Suzan Nolan, Swarnim Waglé, and Leila Whittemore for their helpful comments. I also thank Xingxing Yang for his invaluable research assistance.

Notes

1. In this chapter, 'Asia-Pacific' is equivalent to the World Health Organization's 'South East Asia' and 'Western Pacific'. All regions in Figure 13.3 and Figure 13.4 are as defined by the World Health Organization (WHO, n.d.a).
2. The analysis in this chapter is based on the worldwide COVID-19 situation as of April 2021.
3. This point has also been forcefully made by Zakaria (2020).
4. See Summers et al. (2020).
5. See Elegant (2020).
6. See Pasley (2020).
7. See McGregor (2021).
8. See Mao (2021).
9. See WHO (n.d.b).
10. For a sharp critique of India's initial response in this dimension and others, see Ray and Subramanian (2020).
11. On the case of otherwise generally well-prepared Switzerland, see Robinet-Borgomano (2020).
12. For a discussion of this feature of standing safety nets, see Reddy (2006).
13. Kurzarbeit is a social insurance programme whereby "companies hit by a downturn can send their workers home, or radically reduce their hours, and the state will replace a large part of their lost income" (*Financial Times*, n.d.).
14. India's National Rural Employment Guarantee scheme, although well suited to reaching informal workers, appears to have been underfunded in the aftermath of COVID-19, especially as a result of the return of migrant workers to their places of origin, and could therefore have benefitted from further expansion (*Deccan Herald*, 2020).
15. The early models of Ferguson et al. (2020) assumed adherence to social distancing and other public health mandates nonpharmaceutical interventions (NPIs) by a much smaller proportion of the population than has been reported to be complying with them. Whereas the models assumed one-half or two-thirds compliance for many interventions for the United States and United Kingdom, actual compliance has been more than 90 per cent "all or most of the time" (Kantor and Kantor 2020).
16. See the foundational article 'Rational Fools' by Amartya Sen (1977) and his subsequent contributions on this theme in Sen (1993).
17. On the importance of adaptive policymaking and the recognition of fundamental uncertainty in the pandemic, see Collier (2020).
18. In particular, from the widely cited Imperial College group (Ferguson et al., 2020).
19. See Kayarma, Burgess and Fitzgerald (2020).
20. See Sim (2021).
21. See Ackers (2021).

REFERENCES

Acharya, A. and Reddy, S. G. 2021. 'Hoarding Is Undermining a Key Effort to Vaccinate the Global Poor'. *Barrons*, 29 January. barrons.com/articles/hoarding-is-undermining-a-key-effort-to-vaccinate-the-global-poor-51611882933.

Akers, W. 2020. 'How Lack of Sick Leave in U.S. Can Make Outbreaks like Coronavirus Worse'. *Healthline*, 16 February. healthline.com/health-news/coronavirus-outbreak-puts-spotlight-on-lack-of-paid-sick-leave-in-the-u-s.

Babones, S. 2018. *The New Authoritarianism: Trump, Populism, and the Tyranny of Experts*. Cambridge, UK: Polity.

Berger, J. P. 1972. *Ways of Seeing*. London: Penguin Books. ways-of-seeing.com.

British Broadcasting Corporation (BBC). 2021. 'Covid-19: Brazil Hospitals "Run Out of Oxygen" for Virus Patients'. 15 February. bbc.com/news/world-latin-america-55670318.

Blanchard, O. 2019. 'Public Debt and Low Interest Rates'. *American Economic Review* 109(4), 1197–1229. aeaweb.org/articles/pdf/doi/10.1257/aer.109.4.1197.

Bulfone, T.C., Malekinejad, M., Rutherford, G.W. and Razani, N. 2021. 'Outdoor Transmission of SARS-CoV-2 and Other Respiratory Viruses: A Systematic Review'. *Journal of Infectious Diseases* 223(4), 550–561. doi.org/10.1093/infdis/jiaa742.

Collier, P. 2020. 'The Problem of Modelling: Public Policy and the Coronavirus'. *Times Literary Supplement*, 24 April. the-tls.co.uk/articles/problem-modelling-public-policy-coronavirus-paul-collier.

Dayaram, K., Burgess, J. and Fitzgerald, S. 2020. 'Workplace Transmissions: A Predictable Result of the Class Divide in Worker Rights'. *The Conversation*, 16 August. theconversation.com/workplace-transmissions-a-predictable-result-of-the-class-divide-in-worker-rights-143896.

Deccan Herald. 2020. 'Covid-19 Cripples World's Biggest Job Programme MGNREGA in India'. 11 September. deccanherald.com/national/covid-19-cripples-worlds-biggest-job-programme-mgnrega-in-india-885751.html.

Easterly, W. 2014. *The Tyranny of Experts: Economists, Dictators, and the Forgotten Rights of the Poor*. New York: Basic Books.

Elegant, N. X. 2021. 'These Asian Countries Have Masterfully Limited COVID Outbreaks. Here's How They Did It'. *Fortune*, 28 December. fortune.com/2020/12/28/asia-covid-success-stories-lessons-learned/.

Ferguson, N., Ferguson, N. M., Laydon, D., Nedjati-Gilani, G., Imai, N., Ainslie, K., Baguelin, M., Bhatia, S., Boonyasiri, A., Cucunubá, Z., Cuomo-Dannenburg, G., Dighe, A., Dorigatti, I., Fu, H., Gaythorpe, K., Green, W., Hamlet, A., Hinsley, W., Okell, L. C., van Elsland, S., Thompson, H., Verity, R., Volz, E., Wang, H., Wang, Y., Walker, P. G.T., Walters, C., Winskill, P., Whittaker, C., Donnelly, C. A., Riley, S., Ghani and A. C. 2020. 'Report 9 – Impact of Non-pharmaceutical Interventions (NPIs) to Reduce COVID-19 Mortality and Healthcare Demand'. Imperial College MRC Centre for Global Infectious Disease Analysis, London. imperial.ac.uk/mrc-global-infectious-disease-analysis/covid-19/report-9-impact-of-npis-on-covid-19/.

Financial Times. No date. '*Kurzarbeit*: A German Export Most of Europe Wants to Buy'. ft.com/content/927794b2-6b70-11ea-89df-41bea055720b.

Gentilini, U. 2021. 'A Game Changer for Social Protection? Six Reflections on COVID-19 and the Future of Cash Transfers'. The World Bank Group, Washington, DC. blogs. worldbank.org/developmenttalk/game-changer-social-protection-six-reflections-covid-19-and-future-cash-transfers.

Golgeci, I., Yildiz, H. E. and Andersson, U. 2020. 'The Rising Tensions between Efficiency and Resilience in Global Value Chains in the Post-COVID-19 World'. *Transnational Corporations* 27(2), 127–141. un-ilibrary.org/content/journals/2076099x/27/2/7.

Goodman, P. S., Cohen, P. and Chaundler, R. 2020. 'European Workers Draw Paychecks. American Workers Scrounge for Food'. *New York Times*, 3 July. nytimes. com/2020/07/03/business/economy/europe-us-jobless-coronavirus.html.

Hausmann, R., Rodrik, D. and Velasco, A. 2005. *Growth Diagnostics*. Cambridge, MA: Harvard University Press.

International Monetary Fund (IMF). 2020. 'World Economic Outlook, October 2020: A Long and Difficult Ascent'.International Monetary Fund, Washington, DC. imf.org/en/Publications/WEO/weo-database/2020/October.

———. 2021. 'Fiscal Monitor Database of Country Fiscal Measures in Response to the COVID-19 Pandemic'. International Monetary Fund, Washington, DC. imf.org/en/Topics/imf-and-covid19/Fiscal-Policies-Database-in-Response-to-COVID-19.

Iyer, J. K. 2021. 'Gasping for Breath: COVID-19 Has Exposed the World's Medical Oxygen Crisis'. *Fortune*, 15 February. fortune.com/2021/02/15/covid-19-medical-oxygen-shortage-crisis/.

Johns Hopkins Coronavirus Resource Center. 2021a. 'See the Latest Data in Your Region, 8 March 2020 to January 2021'. Johns Hopkins University and Medicine, Baltimore. coronavirus.jhu.edu/region.

———. 2021b. 'Cumulative Cases by Days Since 50th Confirmed Case, India Confirmed Cases'. Johns Hopkins University and Medicine, Baltimore. coronavirus.jhu.edu/data/cumulative-cases.

Kantor, B. N. and Kantor, J. 2020. 'Non-pharmaceutical Interventions for Pandemic COVID-19: A Cross-sectional Investigation of US General Public Beliefs, Attitudes, and Actions'. *Frontiers in Medicine* 3(384). ncbi.nlm.nih.gov/pmc/articles/PMC7347901.

Karp, P. 2020. 'Former WHO Board Member Warns World against Coronavirus "Vaccine Nationalism"'. *The Guardian*, 18 May. theguardian.com/world/2020/may/18/former-who-board-member-warns-world-against-coronavirus-vaccine-nationalism.

Kelly, G. 2020. 'Covid Crisis Is a Chance to Adapt and Evolve the UK's Welfare State'. *Financial Times*, 7 December.

Khor, S. K. and Heymann, D. 2020. 'An Asian Pandemic Success Story: What SARS Taught Governments about Fighting Infectious Disease'. *Foreign Affairs*, 21 September. https://www.foreignaffairs.com/articles/united-states/2020-09-21/asian-pandemic-success-story.

Lawder, D. 2021. 'IMF Aims to Distribute SDR Reserves This Summer, Okamoto Says'. Reuters, 12 May. reuters.com/article/us-imf-worldbank-resources-idUSKBN2BZ1Y3.

Mao, F. 2021. 'Covid: Why Australia's "World-Class" Quarantine System Has Seen Breaches'. BBC News, 8 February. bbc.com/news/world-australia-55929180.

McGregor, G. 2021. 'Taiwan Was a COVID-19-Free Haven – Then the Virus Snuck Back In'. *Fortune*, 22 January. fortune.com/2021/01/22/taiwan-covid-19-free-outbreak/.

Nature. 2021. 'Coronavirus Is in the Air – There's Too Much Focus on Surfaces'. 2 February. nature.com/articles/d41586-021-00277-8.

National Public Radio (NPR). 2021. 'Why Is India Running Out of Oxygen?' 5 May. npr.org/sections/goatsandsoda/2021/05/05/989461528/why-is-india-running-out-of-oxygen.

Our World in Data. 2021. 'Cumulative Confirmed COVID-19 Deaths'. Global Change Data Lab, Oxford. ourworldindata.org/grapher/total-covid-deaths-region?time=2020-01-11..latest.

Oxford COVID-19 Government Response Tracker (OxCGRT). 2020. 'Relationship between Number of COVID-19 Cases and Government Response'. Blavatnik School of Government, University of Oxford, Oxford. covidtracker.bsg.ox.ac.uk/stringency-map.

Pasley, J. 2020. 'How Japan, Which Has the World's Oldest Population, Has So Far Managed to Keep Its Nursing Homes Safe during the Pandemic'. *Insider*, 1 December. businessinsider.com/japan-elderly-nursing-homes-safe-during-covid-19-pandemic-2020-9.

Pfizer Inc. 2020. 'Pfizer and BioNTech to Co-develop Potential COVID-19 Vaccine'. *Businesswire*, 17 March. businesswire.com/news/home/20200316005943/en/.

Ramakrishnan, V. 2020. 'Following the Science'. The Royal Society Blog, 18 May. royalsociety.org/blog/2020/05/following-the-science/.

Ray, D. and Subramanian, S. 2020. 'India's Lockdown: An Interim Report'. *Indian Economic Review* 55(2020), 31–79.

Reddy, S. G. 1996. 'Claims to Expert Knowledge and the Subversion of Democracy: The Triumph of Risk over Uncertainty'. *Economy and Society* 25(2), 222–254.

———. 2006. 'Safety Nets for the Poor: A Missing International Dimension?' In G. A. Cornia, ed., *Pro-Poor Macroeconomics: Potential and Limitations*. London: Palgrave Macmillan, 144–165.

———. 2018. 'The UN's Development Function: Time for Renewal'. *Development*, 5 November.

———. 2020a. 'Population Health, Economics and Ethics in the Age of COVID-19'. *BMJ Global Health* 5(7), e003259.

———. 2020b. 'Coronavirus and the Limits of Economics'. *Foreign Policy*, 31 March. foreignpolicy.com/2020/03/31/coronavirus-pandemic-rethinking-economics/.

Reddy, S. G. and Acharya, A. 2020. 'The World Needs a People's Vaccine'. United Nations University World Institute for Development Economics Research, Helsinki. wider.unu.edu/publication/world-needs-people percentE2 percent80 percent99s-vaccine.

Robinet-Borgomano, A. 2020. 'Europe versus Coronavirus: Switzerland and the Principle of Responsibility'. Institute Montaigne, Paris. institutmontaigne.org/en/blog/les-etats-face-au-coronavirus-la-suisse-et-le-principe-responsabilite.

Ross, A. G. P., Crowe, S. M. and Tyndall, M. W. 2015. 'Planning for the Next Global Pandemic'. *International Journal of Infectious Diseases* 38, 89–94. doi.org/10.1016/j.ijid.2015.07.016.

Sabel, C. and Reddy, S. G. 2007. 'Learning to Learn: Undoing the Gordian Knot of Development Today'. *Challenge* 50(5), 73–92.

Samuelson, P. A. 1954. 'The Pure Theory of Public Expenditure'. *Review of Economics and Statistics* 36(4), 387–389. jstor.org/stable/1925895.

Sandel, M. 2014. *The Tyranny of Merit: What's Become of the Common Good?* New York: Farrar, Straus and Giroux.

Scientific Advisory Group for Emergencies (SAGE). 2021. 'Transparency Data: List of Participants of SAGE and Related Sub-groups, Updated 22 February'. Government Office for Science, Crown Publishing, London. gov.uk/government/publications/scientific-advisory-group-for-emergencies-sage-coronavirus-covid-19-response-membership/list-of-participants-of-sage-and-related-sub-groups#scientific-advisory-group-for-emergencies-sage.

Sen, A. 1977. 'Rational Fools: A Critique of the Behavioral Foundations of Economic Theory'. *Philosophy and Public Affairs* 6(4). https://www.jstor.org/stable/2264946

———. 1993. 'Internal Consistency of Choice'. *Econometrica* 61(3), 495–521.

———. 2020. 'Overcoming a Pandemic May Look Like Fighting a War, but the Real Need Is Far from That'. *Indian Express*, 8 April. indianexpress.com/article/opinion/columns/coronavirus-india-lockdown-amartya-sen-economy-migrants-6352132/.

Serum Institute of India (SII). 2021. 'About Us'. Serum Institute of India Pvt. Ltd, Pune. seruminstitute.com.

Siddiqui, F. 2020. 'The U.S. Forced Major Manufacturers to Build Ventilators. Now They're Piling Up Unused in a Strategic Reserve'. *Washington Post*, 18 August. washingtonpost.com/business/2020/08/18/ventilators-coronavirus-stockpile/.

Sim, P. 2021. 'How to Fix the Patchwork System of Paid Sick Leave in Canada'. *Policy Options*, 23 April. policyoptions.irpp.org/magazines/how-to-fix-the-patchwork-system-of-paid-sick-leave-in-canada/.

South China Morning Post (SCMP). No date. 'Not Letting the Facts Ruin a Good Story'. scmp.com/article/970657/not-letting-facts-ruin-good-story.

Statista. 2021a. 'Coronavirus (COVID-19) Deaths Worldwide per One Million Population as of 19 April, by Country'. 22 November. statista.com/statistics/1104709/coronavirus-deaths-worldwide-per-million-inhabitants/.

———. 2021b. 'Proportion of Selected Age Groups of World Population in 2020, by Region, July 2020'. 13 August. statista.com/statistics/265759/world-population-by-age-and-region/.

Stiglitz, J. and United Nations Commission of Financial Experts. 2010. *The Stiglitz Report: Reforming the International Monetary and Financial Systems in the Wake of the Global Crisis*. New York: The New Press. library.fa.ru/files/Stiglitz-Report.pdf.

Strupczewski, J. 2021. 'EU Backs U.S. Call for Global Minimum Corporate Tax, but Rate to Be Decided'. Reuters, 6 April. reuters.com/article/us-usa-treasury-yellen-eu-idUSKBN2BT1YG.

Summers, J., Cheng, H.-Y., Lin, H.-H., Barnard, L. T., Kvalsvig, A., Wilson, N. and Baker, M. G. 2020. 'Potential Lessons from the Taiwan and New Zealand Health Responses to the COVID-19 Pandemic'. *The Lancet* 4(100044). doi.org/10.1016/j.lanwpc.2020.100044.

Taylor, C. 2020. 'European Approach to Pandemic Better for the Economy than US Measures, Nobel Laureate Says'. CNBC, 26 May. cnbc.com/2020/05/26/europe-taking-better-approach-to-pandemic-than-us-nobel-laureate-says.html.

United Nations (UN). 2020. 'World Economic Situation and Prospects: October 2020 Briefing, No. 142'. United Nations, New York. un.org/development/desa/dpad/ publication/world-economic-situation-and-prospects-october-2020-briefing-no-142/.

Usher, A. D. 2020. 'South Africa and India Push for COVID-19 Patents Ban'. *The Lancet*, 5 December. thelancet.com/journals/lancet/article/PIIS0140-6736.20.32581-2/fulltext.

Valli, V. 2020. 'Coronavirus and the Art of not Learning from Other Countries' Experiences'. Turin Centre on Emerging Economies, Turin. osservatorio-economie-emergenti-torino.it/emerging-economies/55-15-may-2020/259-coronavirus-and-the-art-of-not-learning-from-other-countries-experiences.html.

Van Rens, T. and Oswald, A. J. 2020. 'Age-Based Policy in the Context of the Covid-19 Pandemic: How Common are Multi-Generational Households?' Centre for Competitive Advantage in the Global Economy, Warwick. ideas.repec.org/p/cge/wacage/522.html.

Viner, R. M. et al. 2020. 'School Closure and Management Practices during Coronavirus Outbreaks including COVID-19: A Rapid Systematic Review'. *The Lancet* 4(5), 397– 404.

World Bank. 2021a. 'COVID 19: Debt Service Suspension Initiative'. The World Bank Group, Washington, DC. worldbank.org/en/topic/debt/brief/covid-19-debt-service-suspension-initiative.

———. 2021b. *Global Economic Prospects January 2021*. Washington, DC: The World Bank Group. worldbank.org/en/publication/global-economic-prospects.

World Health Organization (WHO). 2021. 'WHO Coronavirus (COVID-19) Dashboard'. World Health Organization, Geneva. covid19.who.int/.

———. No date a. Health Statistics and Information System: Definition of Regional Groupings. Geneva: World Health Organization. who.int/healthinfo/global_burden_disease/definition_regions/en/.

———. No date b. 'National Preparedness Plans'. World Health Organization, Copenhagen. euro.who.int/en/health-topics/communicable-diseases/influenza/pandemic-influenza/pandemic-preparedness/national-preparedness-plans.

World Trade Organization (WTO). No date. 'TRIPS and Public Health'. World Trade Organization, Geneva. wto.org/english/tratop_e/trips_e/pharmpatent_e.htm.

Xu, T. L., Ao, M. Y., Zhou, X. and et al. 2020. 'China's Practice to Prevent and Control COVID-19 in the Context of Large Population Movement'. *Infectious Diseases of Poverty* 9(115). idpjournal.biomedcentral.com/articles/10.1186/s40249-020-00716-0.

Zakaria, F. 2020. *Ten Lessons for a Post-Pandemic World*. New York: W.W. Norton.

Zhu, Y., Bloxham, C. J., Hulme, K. D., Sinclair, J. E., Tong, Z. W. M., Steele, L. E., Noye, E. C., Lu, J., Xia, Y., Chew, K. Y., Pickering, J., Gilks, C., Bowen, A. C. and Short, K. R. 2020. 'A Meta-Analysis on the Role of Children in Severe Acute Respiratory Syndrome Coronavirus 2 in Household Transmission Clusters'. *Clinical Infectious Diseases* 72(12), e1146–e1153. doi.org/10.1093/cid/ciaa1825.

About the Contributors

Avidit Acharya is an associate professor of political science at Stanford University, with affiliations in the Stanford Graduate School of Business and the King Center on Global Development. Acharya's research lies in the fields of political economy and positive political theory. He was previously an assistant professor in the economics and political science departments of the University of Rochester. He earned his doctorate from Princeton University.

Sabina Alkire directs the Oxford Poverty and Human Development Initiative (OPHI) in the Department of International Development at the University of Oxford. Previously, Alkire was Oliver T. Carr Professor of International Affairs and Professor of Economics at George Washington University. She has also worked at Harvard University, the Human Security Commission, and the World Bank. The recipient of several prestigious prizes, including most recently the Queen's Anniversary Prize in 2020 for OPHI, Alkire also holds a doctorate in economics, and master's degrees in development economics and in Christian political ethics, all from the University of Oxford.

Alexandra Fortacz is a research and policy consultant for the Oxford Poverty and Human Development Initiative (OPHI) at the University of Oxford. Fortacz holds a master's degree in international relations from the University of Oxford and a bachelor's degree in political science from the University of Vienna.

Sakiko Fukuda-Parr is a professor of international affairs at The New School. She also serves as the vice chair of the UN Committee on Development Policy. Her co-authored book, *Fulfilling Social and Economic Rights* (with T. Lawson-Remer and S. Randolph), received the Grawemeyer Prize for Ideas to Improve the World Order. Previously, Fukuda-Parr held several positions with the World Bank and the United Nations Development Programme (UNDP), including as lead author and director of the UNDP *Human Development Reports* from 1995 to 2004. She holds a master's in economics from the University of Sussex and a master's in international affairs from the Fletcher School at Tufts University.

Paul Garnett is the founder and chief executive of the Vernonburg Group, a consulting firm in Georgia (US) that works to close the global broadband gap. Garnett previously spent 12 years at Microsoft, primarily extending broadband access to unserved communities in the US and globally. Garnett has also worked for the CTIA-The Wireless Association, US Federal Communications Commission, law firm Swidler Berlin, and Price Waterhouse. Garnett, a member of the District of Columbia Bar, holds a juris doctor, cum laude, from the Catholic University of America Columbus School of Law and a bachelor's degree in political science from Union College.

Khalil Hamdani is a visiting professor at the Graduate Institute of Development Studies of the Lahore School of Economics in Pakistan. He also sits on the board of CUTS International, a Global South consumer-advocacy organization. Hamdani served the United Nations for 29 years; before retiring in 2007, he was the director of the United Nations Conference on Trade and Development Investment Division, where he created the Investment Policy Reviews programme. Hamdani has also authored publications on transnational corporations and globalization. A dual national of Pakistan and Switzerland, he graduated from Johns Hopkins University and holds a doctorate in economics from Georgetown University.

Inge Kaul is a senior fellow at the Hertie School, Berlin, a non-resident fellow at the Center for Global Development, Washington, DC, and an external advisor to various governmental, multilateral and non-profit organizations. She previously served as director of the UNDP Human Development Report Office and the UNDP Office of Development Studies in New York. Kaul is the lead editor and co-author of several publications on the theory and policy practice of global public goods provision, international cooperation financing and global governance. She holds a doctorate from the University of Konstanz.

A. K. Shiva Kumar, a development economist, teaches economics, conducts evaluations, works closely with international agencies, and serves on the governing boards of research and nongovernmental organizations. He has also served as a member of several high-level committees of the Government of India. A regular contributor to global and national human development reports for over three decades, Kumar earned a master's in economics from Bangalore University and a postgraduate diploma in management from the Indian Institute of Management. He also holds a doctorate in political economy and government from Harvard University.

Manuel F. Montes works as a senior advisor for the Society for International Development. Previously, he served as a permanent observer to the United Nations and as a senior advisor at the South Centre. Montes also worked as development strategies chief for the UN Department of Economic and Social Affairs (UNDESA), UNDP regional programme coordinator for the Asia Pacific Trade and Investment Initiative, programme officer at the Ford Foundation, economics studies coordinator at the East–West Centre (Honolulu), and associate professor of economics at the University of The Philippines. Montes has held visiting research fellowships in Tokyo (IDE), Helsinki (UNU/WIDER) and Singapore (ISEAS) and holds a doctorate in economics from Stanford University.

Partha Mukhopadhyay, a senior fellow at the Centre for Policy Research and an Honorary Fellow of the Institute for Chinese Studies, both in New Delhi, also serves on the Scientific Advisory Council of LIRNEasia, in Colombo. Previously, he was part of the founding team of the Infrastructure Development Finance Company (IDFC) and worked for the Export Import Bank of India and the World Bank in Washington, DC. Widely published, Mukhopadhyay has taught at several higher-learning institutions in Asia and has served on a number of Indian government committees. The recipient of numerous fellowships, Mukhopadhyay holds a doctorate in economics from New York University and master's degrees in arts and in philosophy the Delhi School of Economics.

José Gabriel Palma is an emeritus scholar at the Faculty of Economics at the University of Cambridge, and professor at the Faculty of Administration and Economics at the University of Santiago, Chile (USACH). His research focuses on the political economy of development in Latin America and Asia, economic and social inequality, the impact of financializaton on developing countries, and other development issues. He holds doctoral degrees in economics from Oxford University and in political science from the University of Sussex.

Arnico Panday is a senior research fellow at the Institute for Integrated Development Studies (IIDS) and also the chief executive of Ullens Education Foundation, both in Nepal. Previously, he was the Regional Programme Manager of the International Centre for Integrated Mountain Development (ICIMOD)'s Atmosphere Programme while serving on the Steering Committee of the Climate and Clean Air Coalition (CCAC). Panday has also served on the faculty at the University of Virginia's Department of Environmental Sciences. Panday holds a bachelor's degree in environmental science and public policy from Harvard University, a masters in land resources from the University of Wisconsin-Madison, and a doctorate in atmospheric science from Massachusetts Institute of Technology (MIT).

Jonathan Pincus works as a senior economist for the United States Development Programme (UNDP) in Hanoi, Viet Nam, focusing on Southeast Asia. He has held teaching positions in Europe, North America, and Asia, and has worked with various development agencies on issues ranging from agricultural development to macroeconomic policy. He holds a doctoral degree in economics from the University of Cambridge.

Sanjay G. Reddy is an associate professor of economics at The New School for Social Research in New York. Reddy has served as a member of the Independent High-level Team of Advisers to the Economic and Social Council of the United Nations, among other advisory roles. Reddy holds a doctorate in economics from Harvard University.

John E. Roemer is the Elizabeth S. and A. Varick Stout Professor of Political Science and Economics at Yale University. He has authored several works on questions at the intersection of political economy, political philosophy and economic theory, including most recently *How We Cooperate: A Theory of Kantian Optimization* (2019). A past president of the Society for Social Choice & Welfare, Roemer is a fellow of the Econometric Society, the American Academy of Arts and Sciences, a corresponding fellow of the British Academy, and holds doctorates honoris causa from the University of Athens, Queen Mary University of London and the Université Catholique de Louvain.

Ben Shepherd is the principal of Developing Trade Consultants, a boutique trade and development consultancy in New York. He has previously held positions at Princeton University and the World Bank. Shepherd holds a doctorate in economics from Sciences Po, Paris, a master's in international economics from the Graduate Institute of International and Development Studies, Geneva, and a master's in international relations from Cambridge University.

Swarnim Waglé is the chief economic advisor at the UNDP Regional Bureau for Asia and the Pacific in New York. Waglé also chairs the Institute for Integrated Development Studies (IIDS), a South Asian think-tank. Previously, he served as a member and vice-chair of the National Planning Commission of Nepal (for three intermittent years between 2014 and 2018) and as a senior economist at the World Bank in Washington, DC, and UNDP in Hanoi, Colombo and New York. Waglé holds a doctorate in economics from Australian National University and a master's in international development from Harvard University.

Kanni Wignaraja is the United Nations assistant secretary-general and director of the UNDP Regional Bureau for Asia and the Pacific. Previously the director of the United Nations Development Operations Coordination Office, Wignaraja has worked for the UN for over 25 years in the United States and the Asia-Pacific and Africa Regions, including as UN Resident Coordinator and UNDP Resident Representative in Zambia. Wignaraja has published articles on human rights, development policy, leadership and sustainability and holds a master's in public administration and development economics from Princeton University and a bachelor's in economics from Bryn Mawr College.

Index